PROPERTY IN CONTEMPORARY CAPITALISM

Paddy Ireland

First published in Great Britain in 2024 by

Bristol University Press
University of Bristol
1–9 Old Park Hill
Bristol
BS2 8BB
UK
t: +44 (0)117 374 6645
e: bup-info@bristol.ac.uk

Details of international sales and distribution partners are available at bristoluniversitypress.co.uk

© Bristol University Press 2024

British Library Cataloguing in Publication Data
A catalogue record for this book is available from the British Library

ISBN 978-1-5292-3578-4 hardcover
ISBN 978-1-5292-3814-3 paperback
ISBN 978-1-5292-3579-1 ePub
ISBN 978-1-5292-3580-7 ePdf

The right of Paddy Ireland to be identified as author of this work has been asserted by him in accordance with the Copyright, Designs and Patents Act 1988.

All rights reserved: no part of this publication may be reproduced, stored in a retrieval system, or transmitted in any form or by any means, electronic, mechanical, photocopying, recording, or otherwise without the prior permission of Bristol University Press.

Every reasonable effort has been made to obtain permission to reproduce copyrighted material. If, however, anyone knows of an oversight, please contact the publisher.

The statements and opinions contained within this publication are solely those of the author and not of the University of Bristol or Bristol University Press. The University of Bristol and Bristol University Press disclaim responsibility for any injury to persons or property resulting from any material published in this publication.

Bristol University Press works to counter discrimination on grounds of gender, race, disability, age and sexuality.

Cover design: Nicky Borowiec
Front cover image: Museum of the Home

To Joanne, Patrick, Rose and Edward

Contents

Acknowledgements		vii
1	**Introduction**	1
2	**From Thing-Ownership to Bundle of Rights to Social Relation**	13
	Property as thing-ownership: the Blackstonian conception	13
	'Heroic reification': creating objects of property	17
	The conceptual limitations of 'property' and 'ownership'	23
	The rise of property as thing-ownership	28
	From bundle of rights to social relation	30
	Vanishing into thin air: property as a 'conceptual mirage'	35
3	**The Dual Nature of Property**	39
	The revolution in property: institutionalising modern property	39
	Private property, individual autonomy and identity	47
	Personal possessions versus productive resources	49
	Capital, capitalist and capitalism	57
	Property-as-capital	62
	The reconceptualisation of the joint stock company share	66
4	**Profiting from the Efforts of Others**	71
	Capital and investment	71
	Profiting from the ownership of productive resources	75
	The rise of 'rentierism'	80
	The new enclosures	83
	Profiting from debt	85
	The distribution of wealth and capital	87
	The gender, racial and inter-generational dimensions of wealth inequality	93
	Ownership of public debt	96
	Rising private wealth, declining public wealth	100
	Speculating on the future	103

5	**Defending the Property Status Quo: Analytical Jurisprudence**	**105**
	The new essentialism: reviving property as thing-ownership	105
	The ubiquity of property institutions	107
	The dangers of abstraction	109
	Dominium in Roman law	119
	The idea of property in law	121
6	**Defending the Property Status Quo: Law and Economics**	**133**
	The modern corporation and the threat to shareholder rights	133
	Social democracy and the socialised corporation	139
	Defending the rentier: the market for corporate control	142
	Contractual theories of the corporation: reprivatising the public company	149
	The fictional corporation rematerialises	155
	The rise of financialised corporate governance	157
	Information cost theories of property	166
	Facilitating the market: functionalism and efficiency	173
	Property rights as 'special'	179
7	**Safeguarding Property-as-Capital**	**185**
	Universalising capitalism	185
	Historicising property: private property and capitalism	186
	Creating property-as-capital	194
	Prioritising the investor interest	199
	The new aristocracy of finance	202
	Containing democracy: the 'new constitutionalism'	205
	Derisking new property	211
	Neoliberal ideology versus neoliberal practice	217
8	**Property and Social Transformation**	**222**
	Property as a historical category	222
	Thing-ownership, bundle of rights or social relation?	224
	The social relational dimensions of property	229
	Bringing capitalism back in	232
	Capitalism's logic of process	234
	The moral logic of capitalism	243
	Changing the logic: gradual transformative change?	251
References		262
Index		289

Acknowledgements

I would like to begin by thanking everyone at Bristol University Press, particularly Helen Davis, Grace Carroll and Alexandra Gregory, for their invaluable help, support and patience. They have been a pleasure to work with and have done much to help me to complete this project. Many thanks also to the Museum of the Home for granting permission to use 'The Arrival of the Jarrow Marchers in London' by Thomas Dugdale on the book cover. The Jarrow March of 1936 was one of a number of hunger marches that took place in the UK from areas of high unemployment and deprivation during the economic depression of the 1920s and 1930s.

I owe many academic debts. I have been very fortunate to have spent the great majority of my academic career working in two tremendous law schools. For over 30 years I was a member of the University of Kent Law School, first as a student and then as a member of staff. It was a fantastic place to learn and to work. Kent was at the forefront of the critical legal studies movement and the intellectual life of the school was wonderfully open-minded and vibrant. Although at times rather fraught as colleagues with different ideas about law and the study of law battled it out, it was incredibly intellectually stimulating and never boring. I owe an enormous debt of gratitude to many of my erstwhile colleagues there, with particular mention to Ian Grigg-Spall, Wade Mansell and Alan Thomson. If not as much was published as it should have been by Kent's scholars, it was because things were never quite finished. There was always a bit more research to do, a few more things to read, a few more things to find out. This is an unfinished book. I moved to my present home, the University of Bristol, eleven years ago and have been privileged to work in another great law school, benefiting again from an intellectually invigorating environment and great colleagues. I have been very lucky. My biggest debt of all, however, is owed to my wife, Joanne Conaghan. Joanne's brilliance, love and support is my bedrock.

1

Introduction

Every Spring since 1989, *The Sunday Times* has published a list of the 1,000 wealthiest people or families resident in the UK. It mirrors the American business magazine *Forbes*' annual ranking of the world's billionaires, first compiled in 1987. Both rank people by their net wealth. Wealth in this context is usually defined as property in the form of 'marketable assets', meaning non-financial assets such as real estate, land, houses and tangible productive resources, and financial assets such as shares and bonds. Net wealth is calculated by totting up the value of this property, minus any debts or liabilities.[1] Wealth does not include consumer durables such as cars, TVs and electronic goods. All wealth is property, but not all property is wealth. It is possible for someone to be fairly well-endowed with property in the form of consumer durables without possessing much, if anything, in the way of wealth.

The lists are most obviously striking for the way they highlight the extraordinary wealth of the richest members of society. But they also highlight the often dramatic and rapid shifts, upwards and downwards, in the net wealth of these elites: annual rises or falls of billions of pounds are commonplace. In the 2020 list, for example, published in May and reflecting the early effects of the COVID-19 pandemic, £29 billion had been wiped off the wealth of the top 1,000 in the previous 12 months, with some suffering losses as high as £6 billion.[2] On the other hand, between March and June 2020, the wealth of US billionaires was estimated to have increased by $565 billion, with Jeff Bezos leading the way, his wealth increasing by $36.2 billion

---

[1] See Gabriel Zucman, 'Global Wealth Inequality', 11 *Annual Review of Economics*, pp. 109–38 (2019), pp. 112–13.

[2] https://www.thetimes.co.uk/article/rich-list-2020-profiles-1-20-featuring-roman-abramovich-and-jim-ratcliffe-50m6h3xdf; https://en.wikipedia.org/wiki/Sunday_Times_Rich_List_2020.

during that period.³ By 2021, the *Sunday Times* was reporting increases in the wealth of nearly all of its top 20, in some cases by over £7 billion; and in 2022 it recorded huge increases in the wealth of its top two, the Hinduja brothers (whose wealth grew in value by over £11 billion) and Sir James Dyson (whose wealth grew by nearly £7 billion). At the same time, the 2022 list recorded wealth falls of between £1 billion and £3 billion for a number of the top 20.⁴ This raises some obvious questions. What is it about the nature of wealth and the types of property considered to be wealth that generates these huge and rapid fluctuations in value? And what do these fluctuations tell us about the nature of property in contemporary capitalism? These are among the questions addressed by this book.

Scholarly work on, and debates about, the nature of property have a long history. In recent times, within the field of law much of this work has been undertaken by scholars operating from within the analytical jurisprudential tradition and, more recently, law-and-economics. This work has tended to be primarily directed at trying to establish universal 'truths' about property and to identify its alleged transhistorical and transcultural 'essence'.⁵ As a result, it has tended to be highly abstract in nature. This book argues that the analytical value of this search for universal truths about property is limited because property or 'property institutions' only exist in specific empirical forms and are always part of 'exceedingly complex network[s] of structural relations'.⁶ Property institutions are key constitutive elements of socio-economic systems and cannot be understood in abstraction from, and

---

3   Matt Egan, 'US billionaires have become $565 richer during the pandemic', CNN *Business*, 4/6/2020. See also Matt Egan, 'US billionaires have grown $1.1 trillion richer during the pandemic', CNN *Business*, 26/1/2021.
4   https://www.thetimes.co.uk/article/the-sunday-times-rich-list-2021-revealed-b3fcwc vx5; https://en.wikipedia.org/wiki/Sunday_Times_Rich_List_2021; https://news.sky.com/story/sunday-times-rich-list-2022-uk-has-a-record-number-of-billionaires-12617 181; https://en.wikipedia.org/wiki/Sunday_Times_Rich_List_2022.
5   On the idea of 'essence', see Joanne Conaghan, 'The Essence of Rape', 39 *Oxford Journal of Legal Studies*, pp. 151–82 (2019). A substantial body of work on property has also been produced by 'progressive' property theorists, particularly in the US. This work is not one of the main focal points of this book for reasons that are explained later.
6   A Irving Hallowell, 'The Nature and Function of Property as a Social Institution', 1 *Journal of Legal and Political Sociology*, pp. 115–39 (1943), p. 121. The concept of 'property institutions' is deployed by some writers as a more capacious alternative to 'property' in order to emphasise the existence of (and to encompass) arrangements for the allocation of rights over resources in societies without state and law in our sense: see, for example, J W Harris, *Property and Justice*, Oxford: Clarendon Press (1996). Use of the term 'property institution', Robert Ellickson suggests, might also help us to avoid exaggerating the role of private property in the overall system of resource management even in a capitalist society: Robert Ellickson, 'Two Cheers for the Bundle-of-Sticks Metaphor, Three Cheers for Merrill and Smith', 8 *Econ Journal Watch*, pp. 215–22 (2011), pp. 219–20.

without reference to, the specific systems of which they are part.⁷ Indeed, it argues, despite its claims to universality, much contemporary property theory is, in fact, rooted in, and derived from, the historically and culturally specific property institutions of modern capitalism.⁸ As a result, it tends, in different ways, to naturalise not only specifically *private* property, including private property in productive resources, but capitalism. In doing this, it not only risks distorting our understanding of property institutions significantly different from our own, creating a sense of false similarity, but risks narrowing the perceived range of institutional possibility, a serious shortcoming at a time when there is plentiful evidence that our property system is failing. We are facing what some have called a 'polycrisis'⁹: persistent declines in the rate of economic growth in the mature capitalist world, leading to economic stagnation and reductions in living standards; rising indebtedness; growing international conflict and tension; recurring economic crises, which in an increasingly interconnected global economy spread quickly and widely; increasing inequality, and particularly wealth inequality (between generations as well as between classes, genders and ethnic groups); declining social mobility; growing social dislocation and polarisation; an accelerating drift from democracy towards plutocracy; and, of course, environmental degradation and a growing climate crisis. The book suggests that the growing concentration of property ownership in the hands of a small number of extremely powerful individuals and corporate enterprises stands in the way of attempts at significant reform.

The book further argues that, even in terms of understanding property in modern capitalist societies – the societies from whose property institutions it tends to draw – contemporary property theory falls short. It fails fully to grasp the nature of much modern property, not least the nature of the property considered to be wealth, a category that overlaps substantially with property

---

[7] On this and the limits to analytical jurisprudential approaches to law, see Nicola Lacey, 'Jurisprudence, History, and the Institutional Quality of Law', 101 *Virginia Law Review*, pp. 919–45 (2015). Analytical jurisprudence, Lacey suggests, 'has no use for a careful analysis of either its own or law's genealogy', p. 920. See also Michael Lobban, 'Legal Theory and Legal History: prospects for dialogue', in M Del Mar and M Lobban (eds), *Legal Theory and Legal History*, London: Bloomsbury, pp. 3–21 (2014).

[8] The idea of distinctive production systems seems to have first emerged with the 'staged' versions of history constructed by Scottish Enlightenment thinkers, whereby societies are said to have passed through four distinctive stages of development (hunting, pastoral, agricultural, commercial). Marx developed the concept of *Produktionsweise* (ways of producing) or 'mode of production' to describe these different systems.

[9] 'Polycrisis' refers to the simultaneous occurrence of a range of serious, inter-connected problems across different spheres of society. The term has recently been popularised by Adam Tooze: see Tooze, 'Welcome to the World of the Polycrisis', *Financial Times*, 28/10/2022.

that is used (or that is capable of being used) as capital – what I refer to as property-as-capital, a concept that broadly corresponds with what the legal scholar, Bernard Rudden, referred to as 'things as wealth' or 'investments'.[10] Indeed, in terms of understanding property in contemporary capitalism, the so-called 'new essentialist' theories of property as thing-ownership that have emerged in recent decades represent a retrograde step, projecting misleading and ideological accounts of the nature of modern property and of how capitalism and our property system works.

Against this backdrop, the book explores the nature of property in contemporary capitalism, particularly property as wealth and capital, and seeks to provide an approach to the study of property and property institutions that will help us better to understand their nature at any given time and place. It advocates an empirically grounded, historical approach to their study, arguing that only such an approach has the capacity to reveal the 'complex network[s] of structural relations' of which they are always part; to demonstrate their contingent and often highly contested nature; and to make clear the ways in which property rights are sources of power, particularly when they relate to productive resources and the fruits of productive activity. It follows that modern property cannot be fully understood through purely legal, analytical jurisprudential, or, indeed, law-and-economic analyses. Other disciplinary resources have to be deployed. In this respect, it endorses Nicola Lacey's claim that a 'full understanding of legal concepts and, by extension, legal rules, principles and doctrines, can only be attained by supplementing philosophical analysis with a study of social institutions and contexts in which those concepts, rules and arrangements are embedded'.[11] To develop a fuller understanding of property in contemporary capitalism, therefore, it is necessary to make use of the work of scholars from a wide range of different disciplines and to draw on insights drawn from the social sciences, anthropology and history. The approach to the study of property advocated by the book is, therefore, inter-disciplinary and eclectic. Despite being rooted in the belief that our property system is in need of urgent and fundamental reform, the book is more descriptive

---

[10] Bernard Rudden, 'Things as Thing and Things as Wealth', 14 *Oxford Journal of Legal Studies*, pp. 81–97 (1994); see also F H Lawson and Bernard Rudden, *Law of Property*, Oxford: Oxford University Press (3rd ed., 2002), p. 169.

[11] Lacey, 'Jurisprudence, History, and the Institutional Quality of Law', pp 947–8. See also Lobban, 'Legal Theory and Legal History'. In this respect, the book might be seen as asserting, amongst other things, the important role to be played in legal theorising of the 'descriptive sociology' that H L A Hart referred to (and seemed to commend) in *The Concept of Law*, Oxford: Oxford University Press (1961), but that his theoretical framework effectively ruled out.

than normative in intent, though it does conclude with some suggestions about the trajectory reform should take.

The book opens (Chapter 2) with a brief exploration of the three general conceptions of property that have been vying for supremacy over the last century or so: property as thing-ownership; property as a bundle of rights; and property as a social relation. The first corresponds with the everyday common-sense understanding of property as 'things' or thing-ownership. The classic statement of this conception was provided by the eighteenth-century jurist, William Blackstone, when he defined property as the 'sole and despotic dominion which one man claims and exercises over the external things of the world, in total exclusion of the right of any other individual in the universe'.[12] The second conception, mindful of the existence of *intangible* forms of property and of state constraints on the rights of owners, relieves property from any necessary connection to tangible objects and absolute ownership, and conceptualises it as a bundle of rights. The third conception builds on this and, using the work of the legal theorist Wesley Hohfeld, conceptualises property as a social relation, as a relation between people, rather than as, or in addition to, a relation between people and things. While these different conceptualisations of property are not mutually exclusive, they tend to generate different understandings of, and approaches to, the study of property and society more generally.

The work of historians and anthropologists has made it clear that the concepts of 'property' and 'ownership' as we understand them, where they refer to something resembling absolute and exclusive *private* property, are not only historically and culturally specific but relatively modern phenomena. The book argues that their emergence represented an attempt to both capture conceptually and shape perceptions of the changing empirical realities and material practices of an emerging capitalism. In similar vein, the emergence of the bundle of rights and social relational conceptions were, in large part, attempts to capture conceptually, and to shape understandings of, the shifting empirical realities of a changing capitalism. Likewise, the more recent revival of thing-ownership conceptions of property. One of the objectives of the book is, therefore, to try to show, in general terms, the material pre-conditions and foundations for the coming into being and rise of these different conceptions of property, using the famous Blackstonian definition of property as a jumping-off point.

---

[12] William Blackstone, *Commentaries on the Laws of England*, Oxford: Oxford University Press (general ed Wilfrid Prest), 2016 [1765–9], Book II (ed Simon Stern), p. 1. Blackstone took the concept of dominion or dominium, usually interpreted to mean absolute ownership, from Roman law. See C Reinold Noyes, *The Institution of Property*, New York: Longmans (1936).

For many years, the Blackstonian thing-ownership view of property was dominant but during the later nineteenth century – in response to the growing volume and importance of intangible financial and intellectual property and the gradual growth in government regulation – an alternative 'de-physicalised', non-absolute conception of property as a bundle of rights began to emerge.[13] Given further impetus by Hohfeld's work, an academic consensus gradually crystalised around this view and the related view that property is a social relation between people, not (or not merely) a relation between people and things.[14] For much of the twentieth century, in legal academic circles if not in everyday common sense, the bundle of rights conception of property was dominant. Indeed, some went even further, arguing that, unmoored from tangible things and full and despotic dominion, property as a separate legal category was a 'conceptual mirage'[15] that had 'disintegrated' altogether.[16] Despite this, by the late twentieth century a 'standard conceptual apparatus' combining Hohfeld's analysis of juridical relations with Tony Honoré's analysis of ownership, seemed to have been established.[17] In recent decades, however, following the collapse of eastern European communism, the decline of social democracy and vigorous neoliberal promotion of privatisation (the taking into private ownership of previously publicly-owned productive resources), the debates about property and the nature of property have been reignited. Within property scholarship, neo-Blackstonian, 'new essentialist' conceptions of property have emerged and tried to re-establish a thing-ownership view of property rooted in exclusion.[18] This has been manifested in a marked increase in the number

---

[13] On 'dephysicalisation', see Kenneth Vandevelde, 'The New Property of the Nineteenth Century: the development of the modern concept of property', 29 *Buffalo Law Review*, pp. 325–67 (1980); Nicole Graham, *Lawscape: property, environment, law*, Abingdon: Routledge-Glasshouse (2011); Nicole Graham, 'Dephysicalised Property and Shadow Lands', in Robyn Bartel and Jennifer Carter (eds), *Handbook on Space, Place and Law*, Cheltenham: Edward Elgar, pp. 281–91 (2021).

[14] Some property theorists adopt the bundle of rights conception while still linking it to things. Stephen Munzer's version of the bundle theory, for example, sees property as bundle of rights/sticks (a set of normative relations) with respect to things: see Munzer, 'Property and Disagreement', in J Penner and H Smith (eds), *Philosophical Foundations of Property Law*, Oxford: Oxford University Press, pp. 289–319 (2013).

[15] Kevin Gray, 'Property in Thin Air', 50 *Cambridge Law Journal*, pp. 252–307 (1991), p. 305.

[16] Thomas C Grey, 'The Disintegration of Property', 22 *Nomos*, pp. 69–85 (1980).

[17] Lawrence Becker, 'Too Much Property', 21 *Philosophy & Public Affairs*, pp. 196–206 (1992), p. 197. At around the same time, Alan Ryan was writing about the displacement of property and property rights from its central place in political theory: Alan Ryan, *Property and Political Theory*, Oxford: Basil Blackwell (1984).

[18] See C M Hann, 'Introduction: the embeddedness of property', in C M Hann (ed.), *Property Relations: renewing the anthropological tradition*, Cambridge: Cambridge University Press, pp. 1–40 (1998). In discussing 'contemporary propertization', Hann has observed

of references in law journal articles to Blackstone's 'sole and despotic dominion' since the 1990s.[19] As Carol Rose says, notwithstanding criticisms of it, as 'a trope, a rhetorical figure describing an extreme or ideal type rather than reality', Blackstone's 'exclusivity axiom' – the idea of property as absolute dominion over 'things' – remains 'powerfully suggestive ... [and] still molds our thinking about property'.[20] It has, as Joseph Singer says, 'enduring cultural power'.[21]

The book moves on (Chapter 3) to look at the difference between property considered to be 'wealth' and property that is not, examining what has been called the 'dual nature' of property.[22] It explores the idea that property has 'a dual function', governing both the use of things and the allocation of items of social wealth, and that 'it is in this duality of function that its controversiality principally resides'.[23] Property's dual nature finds expression not only in the wealth/not-wealth distinction but in the distinction drawn by some theorists between property in personal possessions and property in productive resources. As the work of historians and anthropologists shows, this is a distinction that has often been drawn in empirical reality. In this context, the concepts of capital and property-as-capital are explored using the work of political economists like Adam Smith, Thorstein Veblen and

---

elsewhere that the 'long history of anthropological engagement with property issues rather fizzled out in the post-colonial decades ... precisely the years in which scholars in other disciplines, notably economics, were laying the foundations for a dogmatic revival of the standard liberal model': Chris Hann, 'The State of the Art: a new double movement? Anthropological perspectives on property in the age of neoliberalism', 5 *Socio-Economic Review*, pp. 287–318 (2007), p. 293. The collapse of communism also played a role, being widely interpreted as evidence that there is no really economically viable alternative to regimes based on absolute private property. It generated a 'privatization frenzy': see Franz von Benda-Beckmann, Keebet von Benda-Beckmann and Melanie Wiber, 'The Properties of Property', in von Benda-Beckmann et al (eds), *Changing Properties of Property*, New York: Berghahn Books, pp. 1–39 (2006), p. 5. It further entrenched dichotomised thinking and the idea that the policy choice was between a system based on privately owned property (capitalism) and one based on publicly/state owned property (socialism/communism). See also Jonchul Kim, 'Propertization: the process by which financial corporate power has risen and collapsed', 1 *Review of Capital as Power*, pp. 58–82 (2018).

[19] See David Schorr, 'How Blackstone Became a Blackstonian', 10(1) *Theoretical Inquiries in Law*, pp. 103–26 (2009).

[20] Carol Rose, 'Canons of Property Talk, or, Blackstone's Anxiety', 108 *Yale Law Journal*, pp. 601–32 (1998), pp. 603–4.

[21] Joseph William Singer, 'Property and Social Relations: from title to entitlement', in G E van Maanan and A J van der Walt (eds), *Property Law on the Threshold of the 21st Century*, Antwerp: Maklu, pp. 69–90 (1996), p. 76.

[22] Enrico Rossi, 'Reconsidering the Dual Nature of Property Rights: personal property and capital in the law and economics of property rights' (2020), https://eprints.lse.ac.uk/105840/1/Rossi_Dual_Nature_of_Property_Rights_2020.pdf

[23] Harris, *Property and Justice*, p. 4.

Karl Marx, and lawyers like Rudden. Capital, it is suggested, is property that has been 'invested' with a view to generating a financial return. It is further argued (in Chapter 4) that a second key characteristic of property-as-capital is its irredeemably social relational nature. This was neatly captured by the US Supreme Court in *Securities and Exchange Commission v Howey* when it held that the test of whether a particular transaction qualifies as an 'investment' and thus as a security for the purposes of federal securities law is whether it involves 'an investment of money in a common enterprise with *profits to come solely from the efforts of others*'.[24] Property-as-capital is thus property 'invested' with a view to making money (or more money) from the efforts of others. The chapter moves on to examine some of the different ways owners of property-as-capital (and wealth) are able profit from the efforts of others, with a particular focus on the ownership of productive resources, including intangible intellectual property, and the ownership of intangible revenue rights like shares and bonds. It concludes by looking at the current distribution of wealth and capital, and its growing concentration in the hands of a small minority, and at the social relational dimensions of these phenomena.

The book then returns (Chapters 5 and 6) to contemporary property theory and the 'new essentialist' revival of thing-ownership-centred conceptions of property, focusing on the work of scholars working from within the analytical jurisprudential tradition, like James Penner (Chapter 5), and from within law-and-economics, like Thomas Merrill and Henry Smith (Chapter 6). It argues that one of the common features of these theories is their highly abstract nature and lack of interest in the empirical realities of property and the way in which the property system actually operates. They purport to identify universal truths about property, abstracting not only from time and place but from specific resources. Thus, little or no distinction is made between tangible and intangible property, or between personal possessions and productive resources. Although they are not without insight, highly abstract theorisations of this sort are of limited analytical value because property and property institutions only exist in specific empirical forms and can only fully be understood as such. In depicting property as a relationship between individual persons and individual things, the new essentialism also downplays the social relational and power dimensions of property. Moreover, buried within its theoretical abstractions are highly contentious, misleading and deeply ideological accounts both of how property operates in contemporary capitalism and of contemporary capitalism itself.

---

[24] *Securities and Exchange Commission v W J Howey Co.* 328 US 293 (1946), per Murphy J, delivering the majority opinion, emphasis added.

This highlights another feature of these theories: their conservatism. In the debates about property, abstract philosophical disagreements often mask what are, at root, quite profound political differences about the merits (or otherwise) of the property status quo. New essentialist theories present themselves as concerned, above all else, with conceptual clarity, operating at a high level of abstraction and steering clear of the more nitty-gritty, property-related debates about power, the distribution of wealth, inequality, the environment and so on. However, much new essentialist scholarship serves implicitly – and in some cases, such as the information-cost theory developed by Merrill and Smith, explicitly – to defend the property status quo. In this context, it is argued, particularly important are the problems thrown up by the rise of the public corporation and corporate economy, and the increasingly social nature of production. Chapter 6 explores the way, by the early twentieth century, commentators as diverse as Veblen, Keynes, Tawney, and Berle and Means were arguing that corporate shareholders had come to resemble creditors more than 'owners', and suggesting that corporations should be regarded and treated as social or quasi-social institutions rather than purely private enterprises. They all questioned whether corporations should be run in the exclusive interest of shareholders and whether shareholders should have exclusive corporate control rights. By the 1950s and 1960s, many were arguing that shareholder rights should be pared down. Chapter 6 moves on to look at how, in response to this threat to shareholder primacy, new empirically implausible and contorted contractual theories of the corporation were constructed. Drawing on the growing reconcentration of shareholdings in financial institutions, these theories, developed mainly by law-and-economics scholars, sought to defend shareholder rights and the property status quo by, in effect, conceptually reprivatising the public corporation. Against the backdrop of increased shareholder power, the chapter also explores the rise of highly financialised modes of corporate governance and the impact on them of the recent growth of large asset management firms.

Chapter 7 looks in more detail at the political (and policy) implications of the growing power exercised by the elites in whom ownership of wealth is so heavily concentrated. Ownership of intangible financial property lies at the heart of power in contemporary capitalism and is central to the wealth of the new financial aristocracy that sit atop the rich lists. It argues that the growing power of these groups has been manifested in the ruthless prioritisation of investor protection, and particularly financial asset-owner protection, over other policy goals, and in the equally ruthless placing of constraints on democracy. To understand these phenomena, the book argues, we need to remind ourselves that financial property takes the form of rights to *future* revenues whose value is based on expectations about *future* financial returns. As such, it is inherently speculative and can be subject to quite rapid change, hence the sometimes dramatic fluctuations in the wealth of – the value of the property owned by – those at the apex of the wealth pyramid. It also follows from this that preserving and protecting the value of property of this sort entails not only safeguarding tangible objects from physical interference but maintaining the social practices and relations that generate the anticipated *future* income streams. It entails controlling the future and extending sovereignty over that which has yet to happen. In this context, democracy is a threat, because to protect intangible property forms of this sort it is not enough to safeguard against appropriations of physical assets; you have also to safeguard against policy changes that might impact deleteriously on future financial returns. This does much to explain the concerted efforts in recent decades to narrow the scope for meaningful democratic decision making and the perceived range of political possibility. In this context, the rise of two modern phenomena are explored: the 'new constitutionalism' and 'derisking'. Both, it is argued, are, at root, processes aimed at creating new investment outlets for owners of property-as-capital and at giving investments and financial property protection (sometimes quasi-constitutional in nature) by diminishing the risk that future revenue streams might fall short of investor expectations. The result is that for some, the owners of property-as-capital, there have been rights enhancements (in particular greater freedom of movement), bail-outs and stronger laws protecting their investment interests, while for others (the great majority) there have been welfare cuts, austerity and reduced employment rights

The book concludes (Chapter 8) by returning to the different conceptions of property vying for theoretical supremacy within property scholarship. It does not to try to determine which of these different conceptions is 'correct', or to provide an alternative (abstract and universal) conception of property. It tries, rather, to assess the contributions the different conceptions might make to our understanding of property in contemporary capitalism. In this context, it argues that while thing-ownership conceptions of property do much to help us to understand the nature of certain types of property, such as tangible personal property (what Rudden calls 'things in themselves'), they are conceptually inadequate when it comes to conceptualising and understanding the nature of property-as-capital. They operate at the level of appearances and do little to help us understand the underlying social relationships involved.

The bundle of rights conception of property, it is argued, has the capacity to help overcome some of these deficiencies. While the thing-ownership conception tends to see property as involving just one person ('the owner') and encourages us to take the 'thingness' of property at face value, the bundle of rights conception encourages us to dig beneath the surface. It highlights the politically and legally constituted nature of property rights, their malleability and contingency, and dependence on public power. By focusing on the rights rather than the 'things' dimensions of property, the bundles of rights conception also highlights its social relational and power dimensions. In this respect, Hohfeld's work remains important, highlighting that property rights involve relations between persons as well as relations between persons and 'things'. However, Hohfeldian analyses tend to be undertaken at the individual, *micro* level. To fully grasp the social relational dimensions of property in contemporary capitalism, one needs to move to a more macro level and to explore the relations between different groups and classes. One needs to 'understand property as a social system'.[25] This is particularly true in relation to property-as-capital, property that is 'invested' with the intention of generating a financial return. Many of the income streams that result from such investments have been legally constituted as property; in Katharina Pistor's phrase, they have been 'coded as capital'.[26] It is not, however, possible, as Pistor seems to suggest, to understand property-as-capital without an examination of the social relational dimensions spotlighted by the court in *Howey*.

Why does all this matter? This book closes by suggesting that, to understand our property system and its failings, you have, as Wolfgang Streeck says, to 'bring capitalism back in' and start thinking in terms of dynamic processes rather than static structures. Different sets of property relations and rights structures, particularly those relating to productive resources, it argues, generate different, historically specific economic and social dynamics. It is these dynamics that distinguish capitalism from other social formations or modes of production. These dynamics have been variously described in terms of 'laws of motion' (Marx), 'rules of reproduction' and the different sets of rules with which economic actors have to comply in order to survive (Robert Brenner) and, my own preferred formulation, 'logics of process' (E P Thompson). Different sets of property relations, Thompson argues, generate different 'logics of process', logics that are economic *and* moral in nature, exerting pressure on all aspects of social life. During the specific historical conditions of the post-war decades, the operation of this logic was softened, paving the way for the emergence of a slightly more humane, less unequal, more socially democratic form of capitalism. In recent decades, however, the manifold legal and policy changes associated with neoliberalism, such as financial liberalisation and privatisation, have seen the strict logic of capitalism not only reasserted but intensified and extended. This has driven us not only towards a markedly more unequal world, but also towards a post-truth world of what the conservative German economist Götz Briefs has called 'marginal ethics' (*grenzmoral*), 'the ethics of those least restrained in the

---

[25] Singer, 'Property and Social Relations', p. 78.
[26] Katerina Pistor, *The Code of Capital*, Princeton: Princeton University Press (2019).

competitive struggle by moral inhibitions'. In contemporary capitalism it is those with minimal ethics who have the best chance of competitive success.[27] As it stands, the economic and moral logic of contemporary capitalism no longer 'works' either for the planet or for the great majority of the people populating it: our property system is in need of radical reform.

Although the book concludes with some suggestions about the trajectory of reform and the potential role of law in this process, it is not its purpose to provide a blueprint for property reform. Its goal is, rather, to widen the conversation about property. It is, therefore, written in an enquiring spirit, seeking to signpost some of the paths that need to be explored if we are to develop a fuller and more rounded picture both of the nature of property in contemporary capitalism and of the way our property system works. It is animated by the belief that it is hard to change the world for the better without first understanding it.

---

[27] Quoted in Wolfgang Streeck, 'Taking Capitalism Seriously', 9 *Socio-Economic Review*, pp. 137–67 (2011), p. 145.

2

From Thing-Ownership to Bundle of Rights to Social Relation

Property as thing-ownership: the Blackstonian conception

In everyday common sense, 'property' is usually understood in terms of things and rights to things – in terms of *thing-ownership*. 'Most people, including most specialists in their unprofessional moments', writes Thomas C Grey, 'conceive of property as *things* that are *owned* by *persons*'. 'Ownership' is taken to mean having 'exclusive control of something – to be able to use it as one wishes, to sell it, give it away, leave it idle, or destroy it'.[1] This common-sense idea of property as thing-ownership identifies property with what the eighteenth-century jurist, William Blackstone, famously referred to as the 'sole and despotic dominion which one man claims and exercises over the external things of the world, in total exclusion of the right of any other individual in the universe',[2] and with what Article 544 of the French Civil Code Napoleon of 1804 refers to as 'the right of enjoying and disposing of things in the most absolute manner'.[3] For some, Blackstone's reference to 'the external things of the world' suggests that his conception of property was based on tangible, material things[4] (as we shall shortly see, this is wrong) and his reference to 'sole and despotic dominion' by 'one man' that his conception of property was based on *absolute private* property, on what has since been called 'full liberal' or 'red-blooded' ownership.[5] As

---

[1] Thomas C Grey, 'The Disintegration of Property', 22 *Nomos*, p. 69 (1980).
[2] Blackstone, *Commentaries on the Laws of England*, Book II, p. 1.
[3] *Code civil des Français*, Paris: Imprimerie de la République (1804), Article 544.
[4] Vandevelde describes Blackstone's conception of property as 'physicalist': 'The New Property of the Nineteenth Century', p. 331.
[5] See Tony Honoré, 'Ownership', in A G Guest (ed.), *Oxford Essays in Jurisprudence*, Oxford: Oxford University Press, pp. 107–147 (1961); Harris, *Property and Justice*.

Robert Gordon says, by the time he was writing in the 1760s, the idea of property as individual absolute dominion over 'things' had emerged as 'one of the central tropes of ... public discourse'.[6] A 'proprietarian ideology' in which private property was 'sacralized' was taking hold.[7] Indeed, according to Blackstone, 'so great ... [was] the regard of the law for private property' that it would 'not authorise the least violation of it; no, not even for the general good of the whole community.'[8] There was 'nothing', he explained, 'which so generally strikes the imagination, and engages the affections of mankind as the right of property'.[9] Despite these assertions, however, Blackstone was clearly anxious about private property's status and legitimacy. Having extolled the positive feelings felt towards it, he welcomed the fact that 'very few ... give themselves the trouble to consider the origi[n] and foundation' of private property rights, 'not caring to reflect that (accurately and strictly speaking) there is no foundation in nature or in natural law' for many of them. It would be better, he argued, 'if the mass of mankind ... obey[ed] the laws when made, without scrutinizing too nicely into the reason for making them'.[10] Today, the absolutist tendencies of the common-sense conception of property continue to find expression in the regular use of the term 'property' to refer to 'things' themselves (*my* property, *my* car, *your* house, *her* jacket[11]) and in the idea that we live in a world of property-owning individuals, free to do whatever they like with what they own subject to minimal restrictions.[12]

---

[6] Robert W Gordon, 'Paradoxical Property', in John Brewer and Susan Staves (eds), *Early Modern Conceptions of Property*, London: Routledge, pp. 95–110 (1996), p. 95.

[7] Thomas Piketty, *Capital and Ideology*, Cambridge: Belknap Press (2019), pp. 123, 153–5.

[8] William Blackstone, *Commentaries on the Laws of England*, Oxford: Oxford University Press (general ed Wilfred Prest), 2016 [1765–9], Book I (ed David Lemmings), p. 94.

[9] Blackstone, *Commentaries on the Laws of England*, Book II, p. 1. By 'mankind', Blackstone meant above all else the 'gentlemen of independent estates and fortune' who were his main audience and who he described as 'the most useful as well as considerable body of men in the nation'. One of the reasons they should read his book, he argued, was because 'the understanding of a few leading principles, relating to estates and conveyancing, may form some check and guard upon a gentleman's inferior agents, and preserve him at least from gross and notorious imposition': see Blackstone, *Commentaries on the Laws of England*, Book I, p. 11.

[10] Blackstone, *Commentaries on the Laws of England*, Book II, p. 1.

[11] Personal possessive pronouns are deployed in many non-property contexts: 'my', 'yours' etc. are often used to signify relationships which have nothing to do with 'owning' in the property sense ('she's my teacher'). Similarly, the verb 'to own' is sometimes used to mean 'acknowledge', rather than implying the existence of property or proprietary rights over something: see Harris, *Property and Justice*, p. 9.

[12] Autonomy is the lodestar of the work of some property theorists: see, for example, Hanoch Dagan, *A Liberal Theory of Property*, Cambridge: Cambridge University Press (2021). See also Hanoch Dagan, 'Autonomy and Property', in H Dagan and B C

Blackstone's detailed account of 'the Law of Things' in Book II of the *Commentaries* is, however, curiously at odds with his conception of property in terms of 'sole and despotic dominion' and the 'external things of the world'. Only about a quarter of Book II is devoted to personal property. Blackstone focuses mainly on land, the most important productive resource in the predominantly agrarian society of which he was part and the resource of most interest to his anticipated readership: men of landed property. As Schorr says, notwithstanding the rhetorical flourishes, 'at every turn, on every page, less-than-absolute property rights [in land] are explicated, delimited and qualified', with several hundreds of pages of counter examples to sole and despotic dominion.[13] Blackstone was clearly aware that landed property rights often fell far short of 'sole and despotic dominion' and that his abstract conception only partially reflected the empirical realities of the time. Much land was still commonly owned and there was still much land in which lesser interests were vested in persons other than the fee simple holder.[14] In addition, many members of the labouring classes still had use rights over particular pieces of land – to gather firewood, glean, graze cattle, cut turves and so on. In Blackstone's account of landed property rights in the *Commentaries*, 'the typical *lack* of an owner with sole and despotic dominion over an external thing' is placed 'front and centre'.[15] Some of the potential problems these empirical realities created for Blackstone's conception of property as absolute dominion were overcome, at least rhetorically, by reifying the lesser estates in land (such as co-ownership and partial ownership). The 'deviations between absolute dominion ideology and the unruly pluralism of much lesser rights recognised in legal practice' were, Gordon argues, dealt with 'by reification': 'each lesser form of right [was redefined] as an "estate" or as a "thing" in itself, so that even if one only held the lesser right, one held it absolutely'.[16] They were made to 'look

---

Zipursky (eds), *Research Handbook on Private Law Theory*, Cheltenham: Edward Elgar, pp. 185–202 (2020).

[13] Schorr, 'How Blackstone Became a Blackstonian', pp. 107, 114.

[14] In common law systems, in a historical throwback to English feudal law, people tend to be seen as acquiring a title not to ownership of the land but to an *estate* in land.

[15] Schorr, 'How Blackstone Became a Blackstonian', p. 107. Blackstone himself distinguished four different sorts of commons: pasture/grazing; piscary; turbary; estovers (taking wood). Blackstone also thought there were limits to property and private ownership, attacking the game laws because he did not consider wild birds and animals to be property: William Blackstone, *Commentaries on the Laws of England,* Oxford: Oxford University Press (general ed Wilfrid Prest), 2016 [1765–9], Book IV (ed Ruth Paley). See also Harry T Dickinson, 'Review Article: comments on William Blackstone's Commentaries on the Laws of England', 104 *History*, pp. 710–28 (2019), p. 723.

[16] Gordon, 'Paradoxical Property', pp. 99–100.

like a species of absolute dominion', like 'things' with a real existence.[17] As various people have pointed out, Blackstone also seems to have identified property not with the things themselves but with rights in them.[18] More generally, although he asserted that property is an 'absolute right, inherent in every Englishman ... which consists in the free use, enjoyment and disposal of all his acquisitions, without any control or diminution', he added '*save only by the laws of the land*'.[19]

It was not, however, only the idea of property as 'sole and despotic dominion' that was belied by the positive laws described by Blackstone. So too was the 'physicalist' conception of property which some think was implied in the idea of dominion over 'the external things of the world'. Some argue that this 'physicalist' conception 'mirror[ed] economic reality to a much greater extent than it did before or has since',[20] but by the time Blackstone was writing it was already highly problematic. Law had been replete with incorporeal 'things' since at least medieval times. Any permanent right that was transferable, Pollock and Maitland argued, tended to be 'thought of as a thing ... very much like a piece of land', assimilated to corporeal things and regarded as property. They illustrated this point using Blackstone's coverage of incorporeal hereditaments and other esoterica.[21] Incorporeal hereditaments – such as advowsons, tithes, commons, ways, offices, dignities, corodies and the like – were nonphysical things, some of which could be bought and sold. They were often, but not always, connected to interests in land, though sometimes only very tenuously. Blackstone was, therefore, clearly well aware of the existence of *intangible* property forms with no direct relationship to physical objects. He was also aware that new forms of intangible property without any obvious physical referents were emerging and growing rapidly in importance. Bonds, joint stock company shares, copyrights, and negotiable instruments all figure in the *Commentaries*, though he struggled to fit some of the more modern and emerging intangible forms of property, like joint stock company shares, into his rather old-fashioned framework.[22]

---

[17] Duncan Kennedy, 'The Structure of Blackstone's Commentaries', 28 *Buffalo Law Review*, pp. 209–382 (1979), p. 347.

[18] A point emphasised by, among others, Kennedy, 'The Structure of Blackstone's Commentaries', p. 347, and Jeanne Schroeder, 'Chix, Nix, Bundle-O-Stix: a feminist critique of the disaggregation of property', 93 *Michigan Law Review*, pp. 239–319 (1993).

[19] Blackstone, *Commentaries on the Laws of England*, Book I, pp. 93–4.

[20] Grey, 'The Disintegration of Property', p. 73; see also Vandevelde, 'The New Property of the Nineteenth Century'.

[21] Sir Frederick Pollock and Frederic William Maitland, *The History of English Law Before the Time of Edward I*, Indianapolis: Liberty Fund (2010), taken from 2nd ed., Cambridge University Press (1898), volume 2, pp. 130-156.

[22] See Mary Sokol, 'Bentham and Blackstone on Incorporeal Heriditaments', 15 *Journal of Legal History*, pp. 287–305 (1994).

'Heroic reification': creating objects of property

Pollock and Maitland argued that the treatment of these incorporeal intangibles as things was 'no fiction invented by speculative jurists', for in the 'popular mind these things are things'. The 'lawyer's business' was 'not to make them things but to point out that they are incorporeal'. Indeed, the quality they had in common, according to Pollock and Maitland, was precisely their 'thinglikeness'. They are 'thinglike rights', they argued, 'and their thinglikeness is of their very essence'.[23] There are good reasons for thinking Blackstone would have agreed with much of this. There is clear evidence that he not only took the 'thinglikeness' of intangibles very seriously but regarded them as part of the 'external things of the world'. This is illustrated by his involvement as a practising lawyer and judge in the legal struggles surrounding one of these new property forms, 'literary property' or copyright. These struggles reveal much about Blackstone's view of intangibles and about the ways in which ideas about the nature and scope of property were changing during the eighteenth century.

From the late sixteenth century, the Stationers' Company held a monopoly on the right to copy written works. By the end of the seventeenth century, this monopoly was based on the Licensing Act 1662. In 1694, however, Parliament refused to extend it, at which point authors and stationers combined forces to demand a new system of licensing. The changing nature of the debates surrounding this issue is striking. Increasingly, they were framed not, as they had previously been, in terms of public policy and the importance of balancing the 'continuing production of useful books' with licensing and censorship, but in terms of the property rights of authors.[24] Eventually, in 1710, the Statute of Anne (or Copyright Act) was passed.[25] Under the new law, authors (or their assignees) were granted copy rights for 14 years (21 years for books already in print), at the end of which period, if the author was still alive, the rights were revested for a further 14 years. After that, works would enter the public domain.[26] These rights created for their holders the possibility of deriving an income from writing and book publishing. In the 1730s, when the statutory copyrights began to expire,

---

[23] Pollock and Maitland, *The History of English Law Before the Time of Edward I*, volume 2, p. 130.
[24] See Ronan Deazley, 'The Myth of Copyright at Common Law', 62 *Cambridge Law Journal*, pp. 106–33 (2003), p. 108. John Locke was prominent among those arguing against renewal of the Act.
[25] 8 Ann. c. 21 or 8 Ann. c. 19. It came into force in 1710 and was not replaced until the passing of the Copyright Act in 1842.
[26] Banner describes copyright as an 'ad hoc discretionary monopoly grant': Stuart Banner, *American Property*, Cambridge: Harvard University Press (2011), p. 24.

publishers began to seek extensions. When Parliament refused to oblige, the publishers turned to the courts. Many of the resulting disputes centred on the claim that the rights of authors were neither created by nor dependent on the Statute of Anne but already existed as property rights at common law and, as such, were perpetual.

In the cases that ensued, some argued that, in the absence of a tangible object, copyright lacked the required qualities of 'property'.[27] In *Tonson v Collins* in 1761, for example, counsel for the defendant, Joseph Yates, working from what he called the 'essential conditions' of property, argued that 'all property ... begins and ends with manual possession' and that 'the subject of property'[28] had to be 'something susceptible to possession'. Blackstone represented the plaintiff in the case. Recognising the value of the income streams copyrights created, Blackstone sought to detach 'property' from physical objects, arguing that 'the one essential requisite of every subject of property, [was] that it must be a thing of value' – by which he meant market or exchange value, the 'capacity of being exchanged for other valuable things'. Whatever 'hath a value is the subject of property'.[29] According to Blackstone, in insisting that property had to have as 'its subject [something] substantial, palpable and visible', Yates had failed to grasp the distinction between corporeal and incorporeal rights, and the ability of the latter to form the basis of property.[30] Blackstone, it seems, had a conception of property as any 'thing' – corporeal or incorporeal – with exchange value and regarded these intangibles as part of the 'external things of the world'.[31]

Although the court did not render judgement in *Tonson*,[32] the case proved to be a rehearsal for *Millar v Taylor* in 1769. In Millar, again representing the plaintiff, Blackstone argued for the existence of perpetual common law copyright, as he did in *The Commentaries*. By a majority, the court agreed with him. Two of the judges, Mansfield and Willes, largely avoided abstract discussion of the nature of property, but the third, Aston, adopted a position very similar to Blackstone's in *Tonson*. The physicalist notion of 'property',

---

[27] See Oren Bracha, *Owning Ideas: a history of Anglo-American intellectual property*, JD Thesis, Harvard Law School (2005), p. 203.

[28] We would now use 'object' rather than 'subject': see Andreas Rahmatian, 'The Property Theory of Lord Kames', 2 *International Journal of Law in Context*, pp 177–203 (2006), p. 179.

[29] *Tonson v Collins* (1761) 96 English Reports 180, 185.

[30] *Tonson v Collins* (1761), p. 188.

[31] Bracha, *Owning Ideas: a history of Anglo-American intellectual property*, p. 208. On this basis some argue that Blackstone operated with an early version of the bundle of rights conception of property.

[32] The court discovered that the action had been brought by collusion, with a nominal defendant, and did not, therefore, render judgment: *Tonson v Collins* (1761), p. 191.

he argued, was now 'very inadequate to the object of property at this day'. The 'objects of property' had been much enlarged by discovery, invention and art', and 'the rules attending property must keep pace with its increase and improvement'. What was required for property was 'a distinguishable existence in the thing claimed as property' and 'actual value', interpreted again to mean exchange value: property was 'anything merchandizable and valuable'. Yates, by now on the bench, dissented, restating his physicalist conception of property. Could, he asked, 'any-thing ... be the object of a proprietary right, which is not the object of corporeal substance'? He answered emphatically in the negative, arguing that it was 'a well-known and established maxim, which ... holds as true now as it did 2000 years ago, that nothing can be an object of property, which has not a corporeal existence'. Yates was well aware that many saw intangibles like copyright as 'property', but he argued that, at the end of every incorporeal property right, there was a piece of land or tangible object that was the real, physical object of the right: all property rights required, ultimately, 'a substance to sustain them'. He was also aware that in business practice intangibles were commonly treated as business assets to be bought and sold, but argued that the mere fact that people treated them as if they were 'property' did not render them such in the eyes of the law.[33] Yates insisted that there had to be an objective, physical essence for property and that it was this that distinguished property rights from other rights. The idea that perpetual copyright existed at common law was, however, dismissed by later courts, first by the Scottish Court of Session in *Hinton v Donaldson* in 1773 and then by the House of Lords in *Donaldson v Becket* the following year. In the latter case, Blackstone, by now a Justice of the King's Bench, continued to argue for the existence of perpetual copyright at common law, but the House of Lords, while deeming copyright in published works to be property, rejected perpetual copyright, holding that it was subject to the limits determined by the Statute of Anne.[34]

Copyrights were not the only rights beginning to be recognised as 'property' during this period despite their lack of any direct relation to a

---

[33] *Millar v Taylor* (1769) 98 English Reports 201, at pp. 221, 229, 232, 237. In the *Commentaries*, Blackstone argued that authors had the right to dispose of their work as they pleased and that any attempt to take it from them amounted to an invasion of their right to property: Blackstone, *Commentaries on the Laws of England*, Book II, pp. 274-6.

[34] *Hinton v Donaldson* (1773) 5 Brn 508: see Ronan Deazley, 'Commentary on *Hinton v Donaldson*', in Lionel Bently and Martin Kretschmer (eds), *Primary Sources on Copyright, 1450–1900*, http://www.copyrighthistory.org/. *Donaldson v Becket* (1774) 1 English Reports 837; 98 English Reports 257: see Ronan Deazley, 'Commentary on *Donaldson v Becket*', in Bently and Kretschmer, ibid.

tangible 'thing'.[35] So too were rights arising out of debt. From the sixteenth century, the growth in market exchange led to a growing shortage in the supply of precious metals and coinage, and a rapid growth in the volume of credit. Initially, as Craig Muldrew has shown, much of this credit was highly personal in nature and 'enmeshed in a web of local obligations'.[36] By the eighteenth century, however, the extent and forms of credit had multiplied in the wake of the growth in trade and industry and the so-called 'financial revolution' in government funding.[37] Highly personal credit of the older sort was gradually being supplemented and replaced by 'increasingly abstract, calculated, artificial credit'.[38] Credit was coming to depend on 'the rationally determined future profitability and the accumulated physical or monetary capital of an enterprise'. The result of the increasing abstraction of credit and rise in more distant credit obligations was a significant increase in the volume of *im*personal rights to receive interest payments on debts.[39]

Rights arising out of debt were, of course, not enforceable by taking physical possession of a tangible object, but enforceable only by taking legal action. As such, they were classified in law as choses in action rather than choses in possession. Moreover, because actions of this sort 'necessarily involve[d] a definite plaintiff and a definite defendant', they were seen as 'personal right[s] of one person against another', as rights *in personam* rather than rights *in rem*, as rights of action personal to the parties bound by the obligation.[40] It followed from this that they could not, in principle, be

---

[35] It should be noted that traditional civil law jurists have been more hesitant about affixing the 'property' label to patents and copyrights: see Rudden, 'Things as Thing and Things as Wealth' ('Things'), p. 85.

[36] Craig Muldrew, 'Interpreting the Market: the ethics of credit and community relations in early modern England', 18 *Social History*, pp. 163–83 (1993), p. 181.

[37] P G M Dickson, *The Financial Revolution in England*, London: Macmillan (1967); see also Julian Hoppit, 'Attitudes to Credit in Britain, 1680–1790', 33 *Historical Journal*, pp. 305–22 (1990).

[38] Muldrew, 'Interpreting the Market', p. 181. In England, the rise of abstract credit was exemplified by the creation of the Bank of England and its issuance of paper money. The development of paper money obviated the need for small-scale credit transactions, creating a form of centralised credit. The rise of paper money also gradually changed the main source of trust from individuals (and their personal reputations) to states and central banks. Trust itself thus became more abstract: see Craig Muldrew, *The Economy of Obligation*, London: Macmillan (1998), pp. 4–6.

[39] Muldrew, 'Interpreting the Market', pp. 181–2.

[40] See W S Holdsworth, 'The History of the Treatment of *Choses* in Action by the Common Law', 33 *Harvard Law Review*, pp. 997–1030 (1920), p. 1000. See also Holdsworth, *A History of English Law*, volume 7, London: Methuen (1925), p. 516. 'Over the last few hundred years, as new types of intangible property interests have come into being, common lawyers have tended to shovel them into the general category of "things in action"': Lawson and Rudden, *Law of Property*, p. 30.

assigned.[41] According to Holdsworth, this was the 'main [legal] characteristic' of choses in action.[42] The rights arising out of debt were thus originally seen, to use the terminology of James Penner, as 'personality-rich', as relations between particular people that lacked the 'personality-poor' qualities and 'thingness' of 'property'. Because choses in action are rights arising out of personal dealings, Penner explains, 'it is natural not to think of either of the parties to such special relationships as substitutable by other people'.[43]

By the eighteenth century the category, choses in action, had come to cover instruments as diverse as bills, notes, cheques, government stock and joint stock company shares, all of which were conceptualised as rights personal to the parties bound by the obligation. As such, they were, in principle, non-assignable and incapable of being independent forms of freely alienable property.[44] Indeed, at common law they could not even be stolen. 'Bonds bills and notes, which concern mere choses in action', Blackstone explained, 'were … at the common law held not to be such goods whereof larciny [sic] might be committed; being of no intrinsic value, and not importing any property in possession of the person from whom they are taken'.[45] Legislation was required to take certain classes of choses in action out of this rule.[46] By this time, however, the legal natures of some choses in action was being modified. Patents and copyrights were nearly always deemed assignable, stocks and shares started to be made expressly assignable by charters and Acts of Parliament[47] and, as business practices changed and credit and debt became ever more impersonal, equity in particular began to recognise the validity of the assignment of debts and

---

[41] Holdsworth, 'History of the Treatment of *Choses*', pp. 1003, 1016, 1018: '[T]he assignment of such a right of action by the act of the two parties was unthinkable'. Inevitably, merchants sought to find ways of circumventing the prohibition on assignment, particularly of debts, seeking from as early as the fourteenth century to get round it by appointing attorneys as assignees, a practice that came to be recognised as valid by the common law courts: Holdsworth, 'History of the Treatment of *Choses*', pp. 1019–22.

[42] Holdsworth 'History of the Treatment of *Choses*', p. 1016: so prominent a characteristic was this that 'lawyers were inclined to place any right permanently or temporarily unassignable in the category of choses in action'.

[43] Penner, 'The Bundle of Rights Picture of Property', 43 *UCLA Law Review*, pp. 711–820 (1996), pp. 802, 813.

[44] Holdsworth, *History of English Law*, volume 7, p. 516. The difficulties surrounding the assignment of joint stock company shares at this time was precisely a reflection of their contractual character and of the *in personam* nature of many of the rights and obligations that constituted them: see Paddy Ireland, 'Property and Contract in Contemporary Corporate Theory', 23 *Legal Studies*, pp. 453–509 (2003).

[45] Blackstone, *Commentaries on the Laws of England*, Book IV, p. 234.

[46] Holdsworth, 'History of the Treatment of *Choses*', p. 1028. See, for example, 2 George II, c. 25, dealing with South Sea bonds, bank notes and East India bonds, among other things.

[47] Holdsworth, 'History of the Treatment of *Choses*', p. 1027.

other financial instruments considered at common law to be choses in action.[48] Indeed, for Blackstone, one of the main improvements to English law in the eighteenth century was 'the introduction and establishment of paper-credit, by indorsements upon bills and notes, which have shewn the legal possibility and convenience (which our ancestors so long doubted) of assigning a chose in action'.[49] Although some contractual rights continued to be considered too personal in nature to permit this, very soon the common law, while maintaining in theory that a *chose* in action was unassignable, began to abandon this principle in practice, particularly in the case of debts. The motivation was 'mercantile convenience or necessity'.[50] As a result, over time, as they became assignable, more and more of these rights changed their original character and became 'very much less like merely personal rights of action and very much more like rights of property'.[51] In other words, credit and debt were gradually ceasing to be 'personality-rich' phenomena in which it fundamentally mattered who the parties to the transaction were and becoming 'personality-poor' phenomena in which 'the personalities of the parties to the relationship determine[d] nothing of [their] nature'.[52] These developments saw a significant expansion in the objects of property. 'By far the most considerable species of personal property', wrote Blackstone, was 'that which consists in action merely, and not in possession'.[53] As Robert Gordon says, 'property in contracts, property in hopes and expectations, was becoming the prevalent form of commercial property'.[54] Indeed, for some, the rise of capitalism is inextricably linked to the 'financial revolution' that began at the end of the seventeenth century and, in particular, to 'the development of the law and practice of negotiable paper'.[55]

---

[48] Holdsworth, 'History of the Treatment of *Choses*', p. 1020.

[49] Blackstone, *Commentaries on the Laws of England*, the final chapter of Book IV on the rise, progress and gradual improvement of the laws of England, cited in Kennedy, 'The Structure of Blackstone's Commentaries', p. 348.

[50] Holdsworth, 'History of the Treatment of *Choses*', pp. 1021–2.

[51] Holdsworth, *History of English Law*, volume 7, p. 543. Holdsworth, 'History of the Treatment of *Choses*', p. 1029.

[52] Penner, 'The Bundle of Rights Picture of Property', pp. 802–12.

[53] Blackstone, *Commentaries on the Laws of England*, cited in Kennedy, 'The Structure of Blackstone's Commentaries', p. 348.

[54] Gordon, 'Paradoxical Property', p. 99.

[55] See, for example, Joseph Schumpeter, *History of Economic Analysis*, Oxford: Oxford University Press (1954), p. 78; For Henry Dunning McLeod the discovery that had 'most deeply affected the human race' was the discovery that 'debt is a saleable commodity': *Principles of Economical Philosophy*, London: Longmans, Green Reader & Dyer (2nd ed., 1872), volume 1, p. 481. See also Geoffrey Hodgson, *Conceptualising Capitalism*, Chicago: University of Chicago Press (2015).

It was their growing transferability that distinguished these particular (bundles of) rights from other rights, facilitating their reification and transformation into objects of property. Transferability gave them market value and turned them, in Blackstone's words, into 'usable wealth'.[56] As they became assets with value that could be traded and inherited, they looked less and less like personal obligations and more like corporeal 'things' and, therefore, more like 'property'. As Bernard Rudden points out, the practice of treating them as corporeal was 'facilitated by the fact that their existence [was] normally attested by writing – treasury bonds, share certificates, commercial paper and so on'. It was this that brought them into the physical world.[57] Nevertheless, making these contractual rights 'fit into the picture of the proprietor standing majestically alone upon his "thing"' required 'heroic acts of reification'.[58] It was 'reification in an extreme form'.[59] Not all legal systems fully followed this particular path, however. Even now, in some jurisdictions, like Germany, reification of this sort is, formally at least, rejected, with both the law of property and the right of ownership generally being held to deal only with physical objects.[60]

The conceptual limitations of 'property' and 'ownership'

These vignettes demonstrate the truth of Francis Philbrick's claim that the 'character and content' of 'property', in both the layman's and lawyer's senses, 'has undergone ... vas[t] changes through the centuries'.[61] The work of anthropologists has also made it clear that the objects of (something resembling) 'property' in the modern sense of the word have varied greatly across cultures. From at least as early as the 1920s, they have been writing about the various tradeable incorporeal 'things', like spirits and songs, that have been treated as if they were objects of property in something resembling the modern sense by indigenous societies.[62] Historians have likewise recorded

---

[56] See Sarah Worthington, *Equity*, Oxford: Oxford University Press (2nd ed., 2006), p. 58.
[57] Rudden, 'Things as Thing and Things as Wealth', p. 86.
[58] Gordon, 'Paradoxical Property', pp. 99–100.
[59] Kennedy, 'The Structure of Blackstone's Commentaries', p. 347.
[60] See Sabrina Praduroux, 'Objects of Property Rights: old and new', in M Graziadei and L Smith (eds), *Comparative Property Law*, Cheltenham: Edward Elgar, pp. 51–70 (2017).
[61] Francis Philbrick, 'Changing Conceptions of Property in Law', 86 *University of Pennsylvania Law Review*, pp. 691–732 (1938), pp. 691–2. This claim was recently reiterated by Bertram Turner: 'Property appears ... as a relative term ... What is considered property is subject to constant change ...': Turner, 'The Anthropology of Property', in M Graziadei and L Smith (eds), *Comparative Property Law*, Cheltenham: Edward Elgar, pp. 26–48 (2017). See also Harris, *Property and Justice*: 'English usage of the word "property" itself has changed over the centuries', p. 10.
[62] Turner, 'The Anthropology of Property', p. 41.

the extraordinary and constantly changing range of 'things' considered capable of being objects of 'property'. Rafe Blaufarb, for example, recently produced a detailed account of the range of public administrative, judicial and sovereign powers and offices that could be held as hereditable, vendible possessions in pre-revolutionary, Old Regime France.[63]

Anthropologists and historians have, however, gone even further, noting the historical and cultural specificity not only of the things considered to be property but of the very concepts of 'property' and 'ownership' as we understand them. Etymologists suggest that the word property is an Anglo-French modification of the Old French word *proprete*, which is itself in turn derived from the Latin *proprietatem* (*proprietas*), originally meaning a quality or distinctive trait belonging to an individual or thing. Use of the term 'property' in something resembling the modern sense of the word as 'thing belonging to a person' can be found as early as the fourteenth century, but only begins to appear with any regularity in the sixteenth century when the Latin word *proprietas*, the Law French word *proprete* (or *propertie*), and the English word *property* started to be used by lawyers in disputes involving chattels and moveables.[64] Whereas, however, one can find definitions of the term 'possession' in sixteenth-century texts, there are none of property.[65] The first explicit definition of property seems to have been provided by John Cowell in 1607.[66] Cowell described '*propertie*' as 'signif[ying] the highest right that a man hath or can hath to any thing, which no way dependeth upon another mans courtesie'.[67] By this time, the term was beginning, at least in England, to be 'appli[ed] to land as well as to other things',[68] though according to Aylmer it was still not being used in the modern abstract sense of absolute individual ownership.[69] Regular usage of the terms 'own' (derived from *ounen* and/or *ahnen* meaning to possess or have), 'owner' and

---

[63] Rafe Blaufarb, *The Great Demarcation: the French Revolution and the invention of modern property*, Oxford: Oxford University Press (2016).

[64] G E Aylmer, 'The Meaning and Definition of "Property" in Seventeenth-Century England', 86 *Past and Present*, pp. 87–97 (1980), pp. 90-92. In its alternative meaning of an attribute, characteristic or quality, the word 'property' seems to date back to at least the fourteenth century: *Oxford English Dictionary*.

[65] Aylmer, 'The Meaning and Definition of "Property"', pp. 87–8. See also Pollock and Maitland, , *The History of English Law Before the Time of Edward I*, volume 2, pp. 160; Online Etymology Dictionary, https://www.etymonline.com/word/property.

[66] Aylmer, 'The Meaning and Definition of "Property"', p. 88.

[67] Aylmer, 'The Meaning and Definition of "Property"', p. 89.

[68] David Seipp, 'The Concept of Property in the Early Common Law', 12 *Law and History Review*, pp. 29–91 (1994), pp. 42, 80. Seipp suggests that 'by the early seventeenth century, "property" had been installed, at least in elementary works on the common law, as a fundamental concept applying to land as well as to other things', p. 80.

[69] Aylmer, 'The Meaning and Definition of "Property"', p. 91.

'ownership' is also a relatively recent phenomenon.⁷⁰ 'Own' seems to date from the thirteenth century, 'owner' from the fourteenth – though the legal historian J H Baker observes that the word 'owner' was 'not ... much used by medieval lawyers' – followed in the late sixteenth century by 'ownership'.⁷¹

In similar vein, the French medieval historian, Marc Bloch, notes that 'it was very rare, during the whole of the feudal era, for anyone to speak of *la propriété*'. The word *propriété*, he explains,

> as applied to landed property, would have been almost meaningless ... For nearly all land and a great many human beings were burdened at this time with a multiplicity of obligations differing in their nature, but all apparently of equal importance. None implied that fixed proprietary exclusiveness which belonged to the conception of ownership in Roman law. The word ownership, as applied to landed property, would have been almost meaningless.⁷²

Echoing this, Pollock and Maitland concluded that, in feudal times, it was 'hardly correct to say that Anglo-Saxon customs, or any Germanic customs, deal with ownership at all. What modern lawyers call ownership or property, the dominium of the Roman system, is not recognised ... Possession,

---

⁷⁰ https://www.etymonline.com/word/own.

⁷¹ J H Baker, *An Introduction to English Legal History*, Oxford: Oxford University Press (5th ed., 2019), p. 241; Pollock and Maitland, *The History of English Law Before the Time of Edward I*, volume 2, p. 160; *Online Etymology Dictionary*, https://www.etymonline.com/search?q=online+etymology+own; https://www.etymonline.com/word/ownership. According to Pollock and Maitland, the lexicographer James Murray dated the terms 'own' and 'owner' to the fourteenth century but could find no instance of 'ownership' before 1583, *The History of English Law Before the Time of Edward I*, volume 2, pp. 160–1.

⁷² Marc Bloch, *Feudal Society*, London: Routledge (2014 [1940]), pp. 123–4. *La propriété* is usually translated as 'ownership' in this context. Bloch went on: 'The tenant who – from father to son, as a rule, ploughs the land and gathers in the crop; in his immediate lord, to whom he pays dues, and who, in certain circumstances, can resume possession of the land; the lord of the lord and so on, right up the feudal scale – how many persons are there who can say, each with as much justification as the other, "That is my field!". Even this is an understatement. For the ramifications extended horizontally as well as vertically and account should be taken of the village community, which normally recovered the use of the whole of its agricultural land as soon as it was cleared of crops; of the tenant's family, without whose consent the property could not be alienated; and of the families of successive lords'. There was, Bloch argues, a 'hierarchical complex of bonds between the man and the soil'. The term that was used in relation to land was not ownership but 'seisin', which Bloch characterises as 'possession made venerable by the lapse of time': pp. 123–4. For a slightly different view, see Susan Reynolds, 'Tenure and Property in Medieval England', 88 *Historical Research*, pp. 563–76 (2015).

not ownership is the leading conception'.[73] Indeed, they observe, in the thirteenth century 'the English language ... had not the word *ownership*, nor, it may be, the word *owner*. In a sense therefore the law knew no ownership either of lands or of goods'.[74] They later assert that it is doubtful 'whether there was any right in movable goods that deserved the name of ownership'[75] and that 'the ownership known to that age' was 'different from the ownership that is known to us'.[76] In France, Blaufarb argues, as late as the eighteenth century it was 'misleading to speak of ownership at all' when describing property rights in real estate.[77] Against this backdrop, it is not surprising that, until the late fifteenth and early sixteenth centuries, lawyers 'got along ... without using any single term that had the scope, application, and explanatory power that later lawyers found in the words "property" and "ownership"'.[78] When they did use the term 'property', it tended to be in the context of goods and animals, not land, and it was in this context that usage of the term came closest to Blackstone's idea of sole and despotic dominion to the exclusion of others.[79] Baker concludes that 'ownership is not an immutable legal concept, any more than "property"'[80] and Greer that 'to project ... words [like property], loaded as [it] is with contemporary assumptions and ideals' too far back into history is 'to court conceptual disaster'.[81]

---

[73] Pollock and Maitland, *The History of English Law Before the Time of Edward I*, volume 1, p. 63. Bloch and Pollock and Maitland's assimilation of modern ideas of 'ownership' with the Roman law concept of 'dominion' needs to be treated with caution.

[74] Pollock and Maitland, *The History of English Law Before the Time of Edward I*, volume 2, p. 5 (footnote on Bracton). This does not prevent them from trying very hard to understand early English law using the concept of 'ownership'

[75] Pollock and Maitland, *The History of English Law Before the Time of Edward I*, volume 1, p. 160. Writing of the thirteenth and fourteenth centuries, they assert that 'the ownership of land was a much more intense and completely protected right than was the ownership of a chattel', pointing out that at that time 'the title to chattels was often implicated with the title to land. The ownership of a manor usually involved the lordship over villeins and the right to seize their chattels; and so when two men were litigating about a "manor", the subject of the dispute was not a bare tract of land, but a complex made up of land and of a great part of the agricultural capital that worked the land, men and beasts, ploughs and carts, forks and flails': pp. 156–60.

[76] Pollock and Maitland, *The History of English Law Before the Time of Edward I*, volume 1, p. 163. The difference they focus on is the 'perplexing habit' of justices in 'ascribing the *propretie*' to trespassers and even thieves, and the rules permitting the wrong-doer to pay the value of the thing but to retain the thing itself.

[77] Blaufarb, *The Great Demarcation*, p. 3.

[78] Seipp, 'The Concept of Property in the Early Common Law', p. 31.

[79] Seipp, 'The Concept of Property in the Early Common Law', pp. 33, 77, 87.

[80] Baker, *An Introduction to English Legal History*, p. 241.

[81] Allan Greer, *Property and Dispossession*, Cambridge: Cambridge University Press (2018), pp. 4–5.

Anthropologists, in particular, have also done much to highlight just how incommensurable the property institutions of different societies often are, and the analytical limitations of concepts like 'ownership' and 'owner', and 'property' and 'proprietor'. Transposing them into other contexts and trying to use them to describe the practices and relations of societies and cultures significantly different from our own is often highly problematic.[82] It is questionable, argues Hann, 'whether the understanding [of property] that has emerged in Western intellectual traditions can provide an adequate base for understanding the whole of humanity'.[83] Indeed, some anthropologists explicitly reject use of the concepts of 'property' and 'ownership'[84] as appropriate tools for analysing many non-Western societies, particularly in relation to certain productively important resources such as land.[85] One of their main concerns is that using these concepts – where 'property' usually means 'private property' – tends to encourage us to misleadingly view these societies as though they are less developed variations of our own modern capitalist societies, essentially individualistic and composed of individual owners of individual things. As a result, people who earlier anthropologists 'would not have hesitated to label "proprietors"' have been redescribed in various ways to try to take account of the fact that they are enmeshed in a complex web of reciprocal relations and obligations – 'embedded in a larger social network' so that 'such authority as [they have over certain objects] is exercised on behalf of a group and not for ... personal benefit'.[86] Other anthropologists, like Marilyn Strathern, have further observed that certain cultures simply do not see the world in terms of the Western subject–object dichotomy.[87]

---

[82] See generally, Greer, *Property and Dispossession*, especially pp. 1–5, 52–64.

[83] Chris Hann, 'The State of the Art: a new double movement?', p. 290. Hann points out that 'property' as a concept 'cannot readily be translated even into a closely related language such as German (where *Vermögen* often seems more appropriate than the standard *Eigentum* ...)', p. 290.

[84] See Greer, *Property and Dispossession*, p. 54; and Paul Nadasdy, ' "Property" and Aboriginal Land Claims in the Canadian subarctic: some theoretical considerations', 104(1) *American Anthropologist*, pp. 247–61 (2002), arguing that in some cultures the idea of 'owning' the land is considered 'crazy'.

[85] Hann, 'The State of the Art', p. 287.

[86] Greer, *Property and Dispossession*, pp. 52–3 for examples of alternative terminologies. See also Colin Scott, 'Hunting Territories, Hunting Bosses and Communal Production among Coastal James Bay Cree', 28 *Anthropologica*, pp. 163–73 (1986).

[87] Marilyn Strathern, *Property, Substance and Effect: anthropological essays on persons and things*, London: Athlone (1999).

The rise of property as thing-ownership

Aylmer suggests that Cowell's definition of property as the 'highest right' that someone could have in something that was not dependant on the 'courtesy' of another caught on during the course of the seventeenth century.[88] Indeed, Holdsworth argues on the basis of his analysis of the actions of trover (personal possessions) and ejectment (land) that it was during this period that the modern, abstract conception of ownership as 'an absolute right as against all the world' came into English law.[89] He adds that, in this respect, 'the development of the law as to the ownership of chattels ran parallel with the development of the law as to the ownership of lands'.[90] In other words, a new, modern concept of 'ownership' as an absolute right held by an individual legal person was slowly emerging.[91] There are good reasons for thinking, as Hann suggests, that this development, together with the growing use of the (new) concept of 'property', was 'closely tied to the history of enclosure and the emergence of capitalism'.[92] Enclosure eliminated many use rights in land and fostered the emergence of a more absolute conception of (private) property, applicable to key productive resources as well as to chattels. Together with the growing volume of market exchange, this in turn contributed both to the growing tendency to view the world through a private property prism and to the gradual reconceptualisation of 'property' in terms of 'things' rather than in terms of the rights that people had in and

---

[88] As Aylmer points out, some commentators merged Cowell's definition with comments made by Sir Edward Coke in his *Reports* on a 1593 case about the property in some swans: Aylmer, 'The Meaning and Definition of "Property"', p. 90.

[89] Holdsworth, *History of English Law*, volume 7, p. 62.

[90] Holdsworth, *History of English Law*, volume 7, p. 458.

[91] Holdsworth, *History of English Law*, volume 7, pp. 62, 458. See also Andrew Reeve, 'The Meaning and Definition of Property in Seventeenth-Century England', 89 *Past and Present*, pp. 139–42 (1980).

[92] Hann, 'The State of the Art', p. 287-89. Hann does not suggest that the term be abandoned, however, merely that it be used with caution, endorsing the claim that 'property regimes ... cannot be easily captured in one-dimensional political, economic or legal models': von Benda-Beckmann et al, 'The Properties of Property', p. 2. Hann highlights the fact that, although common-sense, non-legal, lay understandings of property are very similar across the Western world, lawyers' conceptions of property vary. This is reflected in different approaches to land (civil law conceptions based on ideas of 'ownership', as against common law conceptions based on the idea of 'estate') and to the scope of property. He points out that, roughly speaking, in common law systems the concept of 'property' extends to intangibles, in civil law systems the concept tends to be confined to material assets. On this, see James Harris, 'The Elusiveness of Property', 48 *Scandinavian Studies of Law*, pp. 123–31 (2005).

over things.[93] As J W Harris says, it is 'only since about the seventeenth century that the word "property" has been standardly applied to the thing which is the object of an ownership interest'.[94]

At the same time, the emergence of new intangible property forms like copyright served as a reminder that, legally, the term 'property' often referred not to material things but to 'things' made up of transferable (bundles of) rights with potential market value.[95] Indeed, as the cases on literary property show, it was clearly coming to be recognised that the rise and growing importance of intangible property was rendering any conception of property based on physical-thing-ownership problematic. In his lectures on jurisprudence, delivered in the 1820s and 1830s, John Austin explored the different meanings – some 'extensive', others 'more circumscribed' – attached by lawyers to the word 'things'. Austin observed that Blackstone initially confined the term 'to things properly so called', meaning 'permanent external objects', but that, as he proceeded, he incorporated into the term 'the whole class of rights which may be styled obligations: that is to say, rights arising directly from contracts and quasi-contracts, together with the rights to redress which arise from civil injuries'. This seems to confirm the view that Blackstone's 'external things of the world' extended to intangibles. For Austin this 'extension of the term thing' rendered its meaning 'extremely uncertain'.[96] Anna di Robilant and Talha Syed have observed that, towards the end of the century, Frederick Pollock offered a similarly wide and slippery account of 'things' in law: 'some possible matter of rights and duties conceived as a whole and apart from all others, just as, in the world of common experience, whatever can be separately perceived as a thing'. It was an account of things 'so general', they argue, 'as to run precisely the risk that one may now have 'property' in '*anything*'.[97]

---

[93] As noted earlier, Blackstone seems to have regarded property as rights *in* things rather than as rights *to* things.

[94] Harris, *Property and Justice*, p. 10. Many, like Bentham, objected to the use of the term 'property' to refer to things rather than rights over things.

[95] Morris Cohen, 'Property and Sovereignty', 13 *Cornell Law Quarterly*, pp. 8–30 (1927), pp. 11–12.

[96] John Austin, *Lectures on Jurisprudence*, volume 2, London: John Murray (4th ed., ed Robert Campbell, 1873) pp. 802–3. It is worth noting that Austin insisted that slaves were persons not 'things', even though that was how they were 'sometimes styled': volume 1, pp. 162, 168. Austin, a Benthamite, was no fan of Blackstone.

[97] Anna di Robilant and Talha Syed, 'Property's Building Blocks: Hohfeld in Europe and beyond', in S Balganesh, T M Sichelman and H E Smith (eds), *Wesley Hohfeld a Century Later,* Cambridge: Cambridge University Press, pp. 223–57 (2022), pp. 249–50. Their emphasis. Among the 'things' in which we might have property-like rights, Pollock argued, was the 'exclusive right to ferry passengers across a river for hire at a certain place': Frederick Pollock, 'What is a Thing?', 10 *Law Quarterly Review*, pp. 318–22 (1894), p. 319.

For Austin, similar uncertainties surrounded the term 'property'. Even when defined simply as 'every right in and over a thing', he argued, it was still a 'most ambiguous word' with 'various meanings'. In its 'strict sense', property referred to something resembling Blackstone's sole and despotic dominion over 'a determinate thing'. Indeed, it was often 'taken in a loose and vulgar acceptation to denote not the right of property or dominion, but the *subject* of such a right; as when a horse or a piece of land is called my property'.[98] Austin further noted that, as with the word 'thing', Blackstone began with a narrow concept of 'property' linked to tangible, external objects, but gradually extended it to encompass 'whole classes of rights arising directly from contracts and quasi-contracts, which are not rights over things at all, but rights to acts and forbearances to be done and observed by determinate persons'. This wider conception of 'property', Austin suggested, although 'vague, vulgar and unscientific', accorded with common sense. Thus, when we spoke of 'a man of property, meaning a wealthy man, we seem chiefly to contemplate the value of his rights in external things, or of the debts due to him; the most conspicuous portion of his rights'. Austin concluded that it is 'most difficult to get on with [the term "property"] intelligibly and without endless circumlocution'.[99]

From bundle of rights to social relation

During the course of the nineteenth century, the 'physicalist' and absolutist interpretation of Blackstone's conception of property gradually became ever more obviously problematic. By the second half of the century, we find

---

[98] Jeremy Bentham similarly explained that the term 'property' was often used to refer to a 'thing' that was owned (that which one owns), writing that 'in common speech in the phrase *the object of a man's property*, the words *the object of* are commonly left out': Jeremy Bentham: *An Introduction to the Principles of Morals and Legislation*, Oxford: Clarendon Press (1876 [1780], from the revised ed. 1823), p. 230.

[99] Austin, *Lectures on Jurisprudence*, pp. 817–21. The ambiguities of the words 'thing' and 'property' had already been noted by eighteenth-century commentators: see Rahmatian, 'The Property Theory of Lord Kames', p. 180. Others also operated with a much wider conception of 'property'. Thus John Locke famously argued that 'man ... hath by Nature a power ... to preserve his Property, that is, his Life, Liberty and Estate': Locke, *Two Treatises of Government*, Cambridge: Cambridge University Press (1963, ed Peter Laslett). James Maddison, one of the US founding fathers, suggested that 'in its larger and juster meaning, [property] embraces everything to which a man may attach a value and have a right ... In the latter sense, a man has a property in his opinions and the free communication of them ... In a word, as a man is said to have a right to his property, he may equally be said to have a property in his rights': 'Property', *National Gazette*, 29 March 1792, reprinted in Marvin Meyers (ed.), *The Mind of the Founder*, Indianapolis: Bobbs Merrill (1973), p. 244.

gaining ground the belief, already evident in the eighteenth-century cases on literary property, that the concept of property needed to be detached from things and particularly from physical things. Property, some came to argue, is not a 'thing', but a 'bundle of rights' with certain qualities,[100] most notably excludability and transferability.[101] Some suggest that Blackstone himself was a forerunner of this way of thinking about property,[102] but the phrase, 'bundle of rights', seems to have only begun to appear from the mid nineteenth century.[103] In 1873, George Sweet, writing about the vesting of the rights of ownership in land between different persons, argued that 'proprietorship is a bundle of rights and duties'.[104] From around this time the Scottish economist Henry Dunning Macleod also began explicitly to argue that property was a 'bundle of rights' with exchange value and, as such, a category that encompassed joint stock company shares, various forms of transferable debt, literary property (copyright), patents, and 'many other kinds of incorporeal property'.[105] Echoing Blackstone in *Tonson*, Macleod argued that 'exchangeability alone [i]s the single general idea or quality which constitutes a thing as wealth'.[106] Identifying three forms of property – property 'in specified physical substance', property in one's own labour, and rights or property 'wholly severed and separated from any specific corpus, or matter, in possession' – Macleod asserted that 'anything whatever that can be sold of transferred is of one of these three species of property'.[107]

---

[100] For some data on the growth in the use of the phrase 'bundle of rights', see Daniel Klein and John Robinson, 'Property: a bundle of rights? Prologue to the property symposium', 8(3) *Econ Journal Watch*, pp. 193–204 (2011), p. 194.

[101] As Sarah Worthington says, 'one of the important attributes of property is that it is transferable: it is not just wealth; it is *usable* wealth. Without this attribute, however tightly circumscribed, a right is unlikely to be classed as property': Worthington, *Equity*, p. 58 (her emphasis). Transferability is important also because it gives these bundles of rights thing-like qualities, making possible their reification. Other commentators, like Kevin Gray, lay greater emphasis on excludability as property's key characteristic: Gray, 'Property in Thin Air'.

[102] Schorr, 'How Blackstone Became a Blackstonian', p. 108.

[103] See Banner, *American Property*, chapter 3.

[104] George Sweet, 'Impediments to the Transfer of Land', *Papers Read before the Juridical Society, 1858-74*, London: Stevens, pp. 83–4. Sweet's paper was read on 19/3/1873. Some have suggested that Henry Maine introduced the idea of property as a bundle of rights in *Ancient Law*, first published in 1861, when he used the phrase 'a university (or bundle) of rights and duties ... united by the single circumstance of their having belonged at one time to some person'. The context, however, was rather different: wills and testaments and *universitas juris*. See *Ancient Law*, London: Dent (1917 [1861]), p. 105.

[105] Henry Dunning Macleod, *The Theory of Credit*, London: Longmans, Green & Co (1889), volume 1, pp. 33–5.

[106] Macleod, *The Theory of Credit*, p. 153.

[107] Macleod, *The Theory of Credit*, pp. 158–9.

Indeed, in the modern world, 'the greatest amount of property ... which is bought and sold every day to the amount of millions, is nothing but abstract rights'.[108] By the 1890s, John Commons was declaring property to be 'not a single absolute right, but a bundle of rights' and Richard Ely agreeing that 'we must think of private property not as a single right but as a bundle of rights'.[109]

In the US, the rise to dominance of the bundle of rights conception was further advanced in the early decades of the twentieth century by the work of Wesley Newcombe Hohfeld and the Legal Realists.[110] Although the bundle of rights conception antedates the rise of Progressivism and Hohfeld himself did not deploy the bundle metaphor, his contributions not only helped to establish its mid twentieth-century dominance but gave it an added, potentially radical, twist. Hohfeld sought to clarify the nature of legal interests and to dispel the idea that all legal relations could be reduced to 'rights' and 'duties'. Focusing particularly on the distinction between rights *in rem* and rights *in personam*, Hohfeld argued that what we loosely refer to as 'rights' are in fact a number of distinct legal capacities or entitlements, which he broke down into four groups: right, power, privilege and immunity. On this basis he developed a complex typology of jural correlatives in which each legal capacity of a rights-holder was defined by a corresponding non-capacity among non-rights holders. Influenced by the detachment of the concept of property from concrete, tangible objects, he then applied this typology to a range of legal relations, including the rights *in rem* traditionally understood as rights to 'things' (and therefore as property rights), arguing that these too were actually complex bundles of rights, privileges, powers and immunities. Properly conceptualised, Hohfeld insisted, rights *in rem*, what we think of as property rights, were not rights to things, but were, rather, like all rights, rights against persons, any right over a tangible thing entailing a duty owed by someone else to the rights-holder. The negative side of property rights experienced by non-owners had tended, he argued, to be neglected. Rights *in rem* thus established not vertical relationships between people and things, but reciprocal horizontal relationships between people and other people. Conceptually, this had potentially radical implications. It clearly suggested, for example, that the traditional distinction between rights *in rem* and rights *in personam*, in which the former were seen as involving rights to things

---

[108] Macleod, *The Theory of Credit*, p. 480.
[109] John R Commons, *The Distribution of Wealth*, London: Macmillan (1893), p. 92; Richard T Ely, 'Political Economy', in Richard T Ely (ed.), *Political Economy, Political Science and Sociology*, Chicago: University Association pp. 3–39 (1899), cited in Klein and Robinson, 'Property: a bundle of rights?', pp. 196–7.
[110] Richard Epstein, 'Bundle-of-Rights Theory as a Bulwark Against Statist Conceptions of Private Property', 8 *Econ Journal Watch*, pp. 223–35 (2011), p. 225.

and the latter rights over people, had been incorrectly drawn. According to Hohfeld, the distinction between them was not one of subject-matter but one of scope, of the number of persons affected: rights *in rem* were 'multital', rights *in personam* were 'paucital'. It was the extent of the jural relations that they entailed rather than their association with some object of ownership that distinguished rights as *in rem*.[111] Hence the idea that property is 'not an object at all, but rather a legally defined relationship between persons with respect to an object ... [It] is only an effect, a construction, of relationships between people'.[112] The idea of property as a social relation was not, in fact, new. Marx had argued decades before that capital was a social relation not a thing and that 'an isolated individual could no more have property in land and soil than he could speak'.[113] Since then, the idea of property as a social relation has underpinned many anthropological approaches to property.

For the American Legal Realists, Hohfeld established that property was, indeed, a bundle of rights and a social relation, and highlighted the fact that property rights grant people *power* not only over things but over 'other individuals in reference to things'.[114,115] By 1922, Arthur Corbin was writing that 'our concept of property has shifted ... Property has ceased to describe any res, or object of sense, at all and has become merely a bundle of legal relations – rights, powers, relations privileges, immunities'.[116] Not only did the bundle of rights conception seem better able to capture the

---

[111] Wesley Hohfeld, 'Some Fundamental Legal Conceptions as Applied in Judicial Reasoning', 23 *Yale Law Journal*, pp. 16–59 (1913); 'Fundamental Judicial Conceptions as Applied in Judicial Reasoning', 26 *Yale Law Journal*, pp. 710–70 (1917); Barbara Fried, *The Progressive Assault on Laissez-Faire: Robert Lee Hale and the first law and economics movement*, Cambridge: Harvard University Press (1998), pp. 52–3.

[112] Margaret Davies, *Property*, London: Routledge-Cavendish (2007), p. 13. More precisely, property clearly does not *only* describe a relationship between a person and a *tangible* thing. Most of those who defend the idea that 'property relations all involve a juridical relation between a person or group and a "thing"' extend the meaning of 'thing' to include reified intangibles: see, for example, Tony Honoré, 'Property and Ownership: marginal comments', in Timothy Endicott et al (eds), *Properties of Law: essays in honour of Jim Harris*, Oxford: Oxford University Press, pp. 129–37 (2006), p. 131.

[113] Karl Marx, 'Forms which precede capitalist production', in Karl Marx, *Grundrisse*, (Penguin ed. 1973 [1857–8], with a foreword by Martin Nicholas), pp. 471-514 at p. 485. Di Robilant and Syed have since reiterated that 'there is no such thing as property on a desert island with one person': di Robilant and Syed, 'Property's Building Blocks', p. 227.

[114] Cohen, 'Property and Sovereignty', p. 2. '[T]he law of property', he explained, 'exclude[s] others from using the things it assigns to me. If ... somebody else wants to use the food, the house, the land, or the plo[ugh] which the law calls mine, he has to get my consent': p. 12.

[115] Penner notes its dominance in 'The Bundle of Rights Picture of Property', pp. 713–4.

[116] Arthur Corbin, 'Taxation of Seats on the Stock Exchange', 31 *Yale Law Journal*, pp. 429–31 (1922), p. 429. He was clearly drawing on Hohfeld.

nature of the 'things' considered to be property, encompassing intangible as well as tangible property, it was better able to encompass the fact that, in an era characterised by growing state regulation, the rights of property owners were very rarely, if ever, absolute even when tangible things were involved. Owners of private property possessed a bundle of rights rather than absolute rights over their 'things'. The bundle of rights conception also seemed better able to encompass the fragmentation and splintering of ownership rights among different people. Its dominance was confirmed when the American Law Institute's First Restatement of Property, drafted in 1936, described property rights not as rights to things (*in rem*) but as legal relations between persons with respect to things.[117] Although the bundle of rights metaphor did not catch on in civil law jurisdictions, di Robilant argues that in the first half of the twentieth century, in response to the same changing empirical realities, a new conceptualisation of property as a tree with many branches was formulated by French and Italian jurists. This new conception of property, she argues, shared many of the key features of the bundle of rights. The Europeans thus 'had their own realist revolution in property'.[118]

To the discomfort of some and the approval of others, the bundle of rights and social relational conceptions highlighted property's inter-personal, power dimensions. To the extent that people need or desire the things owned by others, the Realists argued, law confers on property owners a sovereign power, 'limited but real', to shape and direct the behaviour of those others. Hence Morris Cohen's claim that '*dominion* over things is also *imperium* over our fellow human beings'[119] and Robert Hale's claim that property is a form of 'private government'.[120] Hale observed that, because they grant a power to exclude backed by the state, all property rights confer coercive power on their holders.[121] All property owners possess what amounts to

---

[117] American Law Institute, *Restatement of the Law of Property* (1936). Again, the influence of Hohfeld is evident.

[118] Anna di Robilant, 'Property: a bundle of sticks or a tree?', 66 *Vanderbilt Law Review*, pp. 869–932 (2013), p. 871. See di Robilant and Syed, 'Property's Building Blocks'.

[119] Cohen, 'Property and Sovereignty', p. 12.

[120] Robert Hale, 'Coercion and Distribution in a Supposedly Non-Coercive State', 38 *Political Science Quarterly*, pp. 470–94 (1923); 'Law-Making by Unofficial Minorities', 20 *Columbia Law Review*, pp. 451–6 (1920). The idea of 'private government' arising out of private property has recently been used by Elizabeth Anderson provocatively to describe what she calls the 'communism' – used in its authoritarian, Stalinist sense – of the workplace: *Private Government: how employers rule our lives (and why we don't talk about it)*, Princeton: Princeton University Press (2017).

[121] As Nitzan and Bichler put it, 'the most important feature of private ownership is not that it enables those who own, but that it disables those who do not ... In this sense private ownership is wholly and only an institution of exclusion, and institutional exclusion is a matter of organized power': Jonathan Nitzan and Shimshon Bichler, *Capital as Power*, New York: Routledge (2009), p. 228.

sovereign powers over others: 'owners are akin to lawmakers in connection with their property'.[122] From this perspective, property is 'a peculiar form of regulation'.[123] As we shall see, the idea of property as a form of private government that grants some people power over other people is especially significant in relation to property rights in and over productive resources. To the further discomfort of some, the bundle of rights conception of property also highlighted the contingent and malleable nature of property rights: the precise content of the bundles of rights constituting property was politically and legally determined. Even private property in something as tangible as land and buildings can take different forms, depending on the specific content of the laws in different jurisdictions on such things as planning and the rights and duties of landlords and tenants (length of lease periods, capacity of landlords to change rents, to expel tenants unilaterally and so on). As Hanoch Dagan puts it, 'the bundle of rights metaphor captures the truism that property is an artifact, a human creation that can be, and has been, modified in accordance with human needs and values'.[124]

Vanishing into thin air: property as a 'conceptual mirage'

The influence of Hohfeld was also evident in Tony Honoré's later, famous elaboration of the different claim-rights, powers, liberties and immunities that constitute 'ownership'. Moreover, Honoré elaborated them in a way that did not depend on a physicalist notion of property.[125] The extension of the concept of 'property' to intangibles has nevertheless continued to be a source of conceptual problems. Indeed, in some jurisdictions, such as Germany, the concept of property continues, formally at least, to be confined to tangible objects capable of physical possession.[126] A conceptual line is drawn between

---

[122] Jean-Philippe Robé, *Property, Power and Politics*, Bristol: Bristol University Press (2020), p. 53.

[123] Michele Graziadei, 'The Structure of Property Ownership and the Common Law/Civil Law Divide', in M Graziadei and L Smith (eds), *Comparative Property Law*, Cheltenham: Edward Elgar, pp. 71–99 (2017), p. 83.

[124] Dagan, 'The Craft of Property', 91 *California Law Review*, pp. 1517–1571 (2003), p. 1532.

[125] Honoré, 'Ownership'. The main metaphorical sticks in the bundle are: claim-rights to possess, use, exclude, control, manage, and receive income; powers to exclude, sell, devise, bequeath, pledge, waive, and abandon; liberties to consume and destroy; immunity from expropriation without compensation; the duty not to use harmfully; and liability for execution to satisfy a court judgement: see Stephen Munzer, 'A Bundle Theorist Holds on to his Collection of Sticks', 8 *Econ Watch Journal*, pp. 265–73 (2011). For a combining of Hohfeld's and Honoré views, see Munzer, *A Theory of Property*, Cambridge: Cambridge University Press (1990), pp. 22–8.

[126] 'In many civilian jurisdictions, the notion of possession demarcates the province of the law of property. What is capable of possession in Germany, in Italy, and in a number of

the idea of owning and the idea of being owed, with the former being part of the law of property and the latter part of the law of obligations. While claims cannot be 'things' for the purpose of German property law, however, contractual claims do enjoy constitutional protection under Article 14 of the German *Grundgesetz* (Constitution) that protects property.[127] Claims are also protected under European Convention on Human Rights (ECHR) law, with the European Court of Human Rights (ECtHR) consistently affirming that a claim may be regarded as a 'possession' within the meaning of Article P1-1 if there is sufficient basis in natural law.[128]

Some have sought to deal with these conceptual problems by deploying Wittgensteinian family-resemblance analyses. Thus, Jeremy Waldron recognises that the 'proliferation of different kinds of property object' has caused jurists to 'despair' of giving precise definitions of property and ownership, but argues that they can be dealt with by 'discussing property in material resources first before grappling with the complexities of incorporeal property'.[129] This approach tends to deal with any conceptual problems by simply taking the 'thingness' of intangibles at face value. For others, however, the problems run deeper. Sarah Worthington argues that by 'acceding to persistent commercial pressure, [equity] has effectively eliminated the divide between property and obligation, or between property rights and personal rights'. This change has been 'supported and reinforced' by the common law and by statute. The result is that, gradually, more and more obligations, or personal rights, have come to be treated as property. Moreover, not only has the 'notion of property ... dramatically expanded', 'rights that continue to be labelled as "personal" are receiving "proprietary" protection'.[130] For

---

other civilian jurisdictions, is a material portion of the natural world, that is a physical thing. What cannot be possessed, namely brought under the physical control of a subject, cannot become the object of a property relationship in these legal systems, and belongs to other fields of the law, such as the law of obligations, or the law relating to intellectual property': see Graziadei, 'The Structure of Property Ownership', p. 91.

[127] Praduroux, 'Objects of Property Rights', pp. 60–1.

[128] Praduroux, 'Objects of Property Rights', pp. 61–2.

[129] Jeremy Waldron, *The Right to Private Property*, Oxford: Clarendon Press (1988). Waldron argues that, whereas the question of how material resources are to be controlled and their use allocated is one that arises in every society, 'the question of rights in relation to incorporeal objects cannot be regarded as primal and universal in the same way', pp. 33–4. Schroeder argues the opposite: intangibles are more fundamental to human personality than tangible property, Schroeder, 'Chix, Nix, Bundle-O-Stix', p. 261.

[130] Sarah Worthington, 'The Disappearing Divide between Property and Obligation' (2007) 42 *Texas International Law Journal*, pp. 917–40 (2007), p. 919. In *National Westminster Bank v Ainsworth*, the House of Lords argued that '[b]efore a right or interest can be admitted into the category of property, or of a right affecting property, it must be definable, identifiable by third parties, capable in its assumption by third parties and have some degree of permanence or stability': [1965] AC 1175, at pp. 1247–8.

Worthington, this growing recognition of certain rights (like those based on debt obligations) as property rights, despite their lack of any direct connection to 'the external things of the world', has undermined the boundaries between property and obligation.

For still others, the effects of the rise and proliferation of these new intangible property forms and property objects in capitalist societies, and the resulting emergence of bundle of rights and social relational conceptions of property have been even more dramatic, going beyond simply undermining the boundaries between property and obligation. Property, they argue, has been revealed to have no 'special, distinct, and essential [legal] characteristics'[131] and this has plunged it into an identity crisis. For Thomas Grey, it has led not only to the erosion of the view of property as (tangible) thing-ownership, but to the 'disintegration of property' as a concept with a stable essence and a meaningful category of legal analysis. This disintegration, Grey suggests, was 'not a result of attacks on capitalism by socialists' but the product of 'a process internal to the development of capitalism itself'.[132] In his view, it is capitalism that, ironically, has sounded the death knell of property as a coherent concept. In similar vein, Kevin Gray has argued that, on close analysis, 'the concept of "property" vanishes into thin air'. It may appear to be an 'objective reality which embodies our intuitions and needs', but in reality it is a 'gross [and] systematic deception', an 'illusion', a 'fraud', a concept 'of curiously limited content', 'a conceptual mirage', which, on closer analysis, 'dissolves into a formless void'. 'Perhaps more accurately than any other legal notion', he concludes, property 'deserve[s] the Benthamite epithet, "rhetorical nonsense – nonsense upon stilts"'. Pierre-Joseph Proudhon therefore 'got it wrong: property is not theft – it is fraud'. It 'does not really exist: it is mere illusion'.[133] While there may be some conceptual basis for these claims, however, in recent decades, coinciding with the rise of neoliberal capitalism and free market ideologies, there has clearly been a renewed emphasis not only on thing-ownership conceptions of property

---

[131] Davies, *Property*, p. 21.
[132] Grey, 'The Disintegration of Property', p. 74.
[133] Gray, 'Property in Thin Air', pp. 252, 305–6. Although he is critical of Kevin Gray's scepticism about property as a concept and equally critical of Thomas Grey's 'disintegrationist' thesis, J W Harris nevertheless suggests that 'all attempts in the history of theorizing about property to provide a univocal explication of the concept of ownership, applicable within all societies and to all resources, have failed ... any general notion of property is notoriously elusive'. Indeed, he goes on to argue that 'deductions from purportedly universal definitions of the word "property" are to be deplored': Harris, *Property and Justice*, pp. 5–6, 12; see also J W Harris, 'Reason or Mumbo Jumbo: the common law's approach to property', 117 *Proceedings of the British Academy*, pp 445–75 (2002), pp. 454–60.

but on the desirability of converting productive resources into individual private property (privatisation) and on the importance of private property and its protection. Indeed, paradoxically, as we shall see, the disaggregation of property inherent in the bundle of rights conception has, arguably, in some ways strengthened the idea of property as thing-ownership.[134]

---

[134] See Margaret Radin, 'The Liberal Conception of Property', 88 *Columbia Law Review*, pp. 1667–96 (1988), pp. 1671–85, arguing that certain Supreme Court justices were tending to find that government interference with any one of the disaggregated rights associated with property might be a taking. This argument has since been promoted by Richard Epstein.

3

The Dual Nature of Property

The revolution in property: institutionalising modern property

As late as the sixteenth century, a large proportion of English farming was still being undertaken by farmers working within a complex system of open fields and common rights. Two centuries later, notwithstanding widespread enclosure, much land was still commonly held and in many parts of the country it was still often the case that no one landowner enjoyed exclusive rights to use particular tracts of land. Rather, many different people possessed rights, recognised in custom and law, to use land for certain purposes. In the context of such 'variable and divided property', landed property was inevitably seen and experienced, at least in part, as a social relation between people concerning a resource.[1] Embedded in the customary practices of a complex and hierarchical social whole, the use rights held by the labouring classes over land were fiercely defended and critical to livelihoods, enabling full or partial self-sufficiency and reducing dependence on wage-labour and market-purchased goods.[2] These use rights were detailed in *The Commentaries*, where Blackstone described, often in painstaking detail, property rights in land that were not only fragmented and divided, but still to a considerable extent bound up in intricate and visible social relations between people occupying different places in a hierarchically organised and inter-connected social whole. The situation was very similar elsewhere. In pre-revolutionary France, for example, 'real estate, such as land and buildings, was rarely owned independently and completely by a single person. Instead, any given piece of real estate had multiple, partial owners who stood in legally enforced relations of superiority and dependence toward one another'.[3]

---

[1] di Robilant and Syed, 'Property's Building Blocks', p. 17.
[2] See Robert Malcolmson, *Life and Labour in England, 1700–80*, London: Hutchinson (1981), pp. 24–5.
[3] Blaufarb, *The Great Demarcation*, p. 1.

As this suggests, during this period the connections between different classes were often openly recognised, as was the connection between the wealth of the rich and the labour of the poor. Labour was seen as the source of the nation's wealth and as the foundation upon which all riches depended. The agricultural commentator Timothy Nourse observed that 'were it not for … poor labourers, the Rich themselves would soon become poor'. In similar vein, a mid eighteenth-century MP candidly stated that it was from the labour of the 'common people' that the wealthy 'derive[d] their riches and splendour'.[4] Indeed, poverty was seen as socially necessary precisely because it forced people to perform 'those vital laborious tasks on which society depended'. 'In any nation where property is – that is to say, where there any rich', argued the writer and magistrate Henry Fielding, there 'must be' poor people.[5] These realities and inequalities were seen as parts of a divinely ordained social order in which different people had been assigned different positions and roles. Important aspects of this worldview found expression in the work of classical political economists like Adam Smith and David Ricardo, both of whom openly recognised the division of society into social classes and operated with a labour theory of value.

For many years, however, one's place in society was seen as carrying social and political obligations as well as bestowing rights and privileges. Correspondingly, property and property rights, particularly in land, were thought to bring with them wider, status-based, social and public responsibilities. In feudal times, for example, landholding was often conditional upon the performance of services and was bound up in a web of reciprocal obligations. The public status of individuals and their control over others was directly related to their estate and formal position in the landholding hierarchy. Property was thus directly bound up with public, political power.[6] Although the social obligations attaching to property were gradually eroded, the formal association of property with public power remained. Until the late nineteenth century suffrage was granted only to men who held a certain amount of property, and at common law a married woman's property passed to her husband on marriage, giving men direct power over their wives and underlining the hierarchical, status-based nature

---

[4] See Malcolmson, *Life and Labour in England, 1700–80*, p. 12.
[5] See Malcolmson, *Life and Labour in England, 1700–80*, p. 13. On the recognition by the wealthy that they were dependent on labour of the poor and the idea that poverty was socially necessary, see pp. 12–17.
[6] For a detailed account of the ways property was bound up with the performance of public functions (and, therefore, of office holding) in pre-revolutionary France, see Blaufarb, *The Great Demarcation*.

of the institution. Unmarried women could own property, but no matter how wealthy, they were not entitled to vote.[7]

The open and visible social relational dimensions of property were also reflected in the economic nature of markets and in the ways they operated and were experienced. Earlier societies had markets, often on a large scale, and in some cases highly developed commercial networks (the Florentine and Dutch republics, for example). But the dependence of economic actors on markets for the basic requirements of life was markedly lower than it is today, where market dependence is a fundamental condition of life for both workers and producers. Direct producers, like peasants, for example, were still typically in possession of their means of subsistence and production (land, tools and so on). In these societies, markets were, to use Ellen Meiksins Wood's terminology, sources of *opportunity* rather than of *imperatives* as they are today.[8] Moreover, as Craig Muldrew points out, their operational principles were different. The perception of them as sites of pure self-interest is, as he observes, a modern cultural phenomenon. Although by the late sixteenth and early seventeenth centuries, 'almost all people were involved in market relations, and in all probability had been for some time', markets were 'not simply or even primarily concerned with self-interest in the Smithian sense' and people 'did not interpret their behaviour in such terms'.[9] Market relations were, rather, 'interpreted in a way which stressed the consequences of actions on others and the community'.[10] The market economy of the eighteenth century was, in the phrase popularised by E P Thompson, a 'moral economy' or, in the language of Karl Polanyi, more socially 'embedded' than it is today.[11]

By this time, however, social relations were gradually but inexorably changing. The eighteenth century was marked by fierce struggles over rights in and over land. Between 1760 and 1780 alone, when Blackstone was writing, Parliament passed over 770 enclosure acts, which turned land

---

[7] Women were not explicitly excluded from voting until the 1832 Reform Act, which specifically defined voters as 'male persons'. There does not seem to be any evidence, however, of women voting before this, although they were often actively involved in election campaigns.

[8] Ellen Meiksins Wood, *The Origin of Capitalism: a longer view*, London: Verso (1999).

[9] Muldrew, 'Interpreting the Market', p. 169. Many have pointed out the tension between Smith's moral theories, which emphasised sympathy for others, and the seeming egoism of his economics. Elizabeth Anderson suggests that 'Smith, no less than Marx, reviled selfishness as a basis for relating to others': Anderson, *Private Government: how employers rule our lives*, p. 5.

[10] Muldrew, 'Interpreting the Market', pp. 168–9, 177.

[11] E P Thompson, 'The Moral Economy of the English Crowd in the 18th Century', in E P Thompson, *Customs in Common*, London: Merlin Press (1991 [1971]), pp. 185–258; Karl Polanyi, *The Great Transformation*, New York: Farrar & Rinehart (1944).

that had previously been either commonly held or subject to multiple rights claims into exclusive *private* property.[12] Often hard-won customary rights to common land or to use land in particular ways (to graze animals, to glean, to gather firewood for cooking and heating, to cut turves, and so on) were extinguished, and activities that had previously been seen as legitimate exercises of rights were criminalised.[13] As more and more land was turned into pure private property, it was increasingly disembedded from social relationships and became less subject to regulation by custom and the community.[14] It became what Polanyi called a 'fictitious commodity' – something treated as a mere marketable commodity even though it had not been produced for the market or, indeed, produced at all.[15] Enclosure also undermined the self-sufficiency of the labouring classes, rendering them ever more market-dependent. They had to sell their labour to 'earn' a living and to secure the money needed to buy the necessities of life.[16] Like land, labour was being commodified and becoming a 'fictitious commodity'. The separation of working people from their means of subsistence and their growing dependence on wage-labour was a crucial part of the process of what Marx called the primitive (or original) accumulation of capital.[17] In increasing their market dependence, the separation of the labouring classes from the means of production fostered a steady growth in the volume of commodity production and market exchange. The coercion of the state was needed to impose the coercion of the market.

Crucially, the change was not merely quantitative, but *qualitative*. Producers too were becoming ever more market-dependent, needing to enter the market to gain access to land, money and labour and to sell their produce. Moreover, growing competition meant that prices were increasingly market-determined and that producers had to keep a constant eye on production costs. Keeping costs down, by cutting wages or by improving labour productivity through organisational or technological

---

[12] Hannibal Travis, 'Pirates of the Information Infrastructure: Blackstonian copyright and the First Amendment', 15 *Berkeley Technology Law Journal*, pp. 777–864 (2000), p. 789.

[13] Martin Daunton distinguishes three types of enclosure: piecemeal enclosure; enclosure by private agreement; and enclosure by Act of Parliament: see Daunton, 'Open Fields and Enclosure: the demise of commonality', in Daunton, *Progress and Poverty: an economic and social history of Britain, 1700–1850*, Oxford: Oxford University Press, pp. 100–2 (1995).

[14] See E P Thompson's account of the Black Act 1723: *Whigs and Hunters*, London: Allen Lane (1975).

[15] Polanyi, *The Great Transformation*.

[16] 'Enclosure could spell disaster for landless families who supplemented their income by gathering fuel, grazing a few sheep or a cow, or feeding pigs or geese ... Enclosure marked the demise of [many] small rural traders and craftsmen, leaving a more polarized society of landless labourers and farmers': Daunton, 'Open Fields and Enclosure', p. 107.

[17] Marx, *Capital*, volume 1, London: Lawrence and Wishart (1954 [1867]), pp. 667–724.

innovations, became an imperative, a pre-requisite of economic survival. It was not enough to merely cover costs; profits were needed to fund investment in the productivity-enhancing innovations that were central to competitive production. As a result, all producers were under constant pressure to increase labour productivity and reduce costs; all were increasingly subject to market imperatives. Indeed, it was the growing strength of these imperatives that drove the British 'agricultural revolution', which began in the mid seventeenth century and saw unprecedented increases in agricultural productivity. As a result, this period saw the gradual emergence not only of a distinctive set of social property relations but also of a new economic dynamic. What distinguished the socio-economic system that was emerging – what is now commonly referred to as 'capitalism' – was not merely the presence of commodity production (this long predated the rise of capitalism), but its volume, prevalence and extension to land, labour and money (à la Polanyi) and the new dynamic that this engendered. Not only was commodity production gradually becoming ever more generalised, so too was the logic of production for profit and the subjection of economic actors to market imperatives over which they had little or no control.[18] These developments provided the material foundations for the emergence and rise to dominance of the modern Blackstonian concept of property as private property and absolute dominion, and the 'full liberal' concept of 'ownership' that accompanied it.

These developments saw market exchange not only grow in volume and importance, but change in nature. Over time, markets, including money markets, became less local and less personal, and more national and more impersonal. With this, 'people's ethical conception of buying and selling' changed. Gradually, the 'older customary ... obligations' associated with the 'moral economy' were eroded and the nature of trust itself changed.[19] In the early modern era of small-scale credit transactions, trust was rooted in the character and reliability of individuals; by the eighteenth century, it was gradually becoming rooted more in the reliability of impersonal central banks and paper money.[20] It was these changes that made Smith's ideas about people entering markets for reasons of 'self-love' and personal profit

---

[18] See Wood, *The Origin of Capitalism*.
[19] Muldrew, 'Interpreting the Market', pp. 163–6, 181–3. In early modern England the shortage of gold and silver currency meant that most buying and selling was done on credit and, therefore, on trust, hence the existence of numerous personal bonds and relations. For this reason, Muldrew suggests that the culture of early modern markets was explicitly 'moral' not only in times of dearth (as described by E P Thompson), but in normal years as well. He adds, though, that even then it was 'a moral economy of individualistic contractual relations': p. 169.
[20] Craig Muldrew, *The Economy of Obligation*, Basingstoke: Macmillan (1998), p. 6.

'seem like a feasible description of marketing'.[21] The idea that rational self-interest was the key (and, in some cases, sole) motivating force underlying 'the market' (a concept that was itself becoming increasingly singular and abstract) gradually emerged as one of the cornerstones of both the new political economy, which itself gradually morphed into simple depoliticised 'economics', and much social, political and legal theory.

It was in the context of enclosure, more impersonal markets, increasingly abstract calculated credit, a declining 'moral economy', and the rise of more self-interested ('rational') behaviour by market participants that Blackstone formulated his idealised conception of property in terms of 'sole and despotic dominion' and 'total exclusion'. This conception would undoubtedly have appealed to his stated audience: propertied gentlemen. Under this conception, property and property rights in 'things' – including in the key productive resource of land – should, ideally, be absolute and private in nature and should carry few, if any, wider social obligations. Ownership was governed by self-interest: owners could basically do whatever they liked with the objects of property they owned, without regard to others or to the wider social whole. The Blackstonian ideal was never fully realised in reality, not least because customary ideas about obligations and appropriate market behaviour persisted, as did less than absolute private property rights in land, notwithstanding the continuing piecemeal elimination of use rights. Indeed, less than absolute property rights continue to persist today, though not so much because of the existence of old-style use rights over land but because of the restrictions placed on property owners, including landowners, by public regulation – planning laws, environmental laws, health and safety regulation and the like. The idealised absolute, self-interest-oriented conception of property as private property nevertheless became, and remains, a powerfully suggestive trope that shapes much thinking about the world.

In some ways, as Duncan Kennedy has suggested, Blackstone's *Commentaries* straddles two different worlds. On the one hand, parts of it – most notably, perhaps, Book I on the Law of Persons – describe an old world of openly hierarchical relationships between people: king and subject; noble and commoner; master and servant; husband and wife. On the other hand, other parts, such as Book II on the Law of Things, describe a world increasingly characterised not by direct social relations between hierarchically organised persons but by much more impersonal relations between persons and things. Aided by the reification of lesser estates and of choses in action, this was a world of autonomous property owners freely exchanging 'things' in the marketplace.[22] This emerging world was less obviously hierarchical and

---

[21] Muldrew, 'Interpreting the Market', pp. 163, 181.
[22] Kennedy, 'The Structure of Blackstone's Commentaries', p. 350.

more formally egalitarian, at least for white men of a certain class. A clear subject–object divide, let alone formal equality, was of course still absent, most obviously in the case of slaves, who were seen as mere chattels. The subject–object divide was also less than clear and formal equality absent in the case of married women, who could not own property independently, their legal personality being regarded as having been incorporated into that of their husbands under the doctrine of coverture. Although coverture did not turn married women into chattels or alienable property, 'the husband–wife relationship displayed many of the incidents of a property relationship in which wives took the part of the object'.[23] Indeed, many groups – foreigners, Jews, Catholics – continued to be subject to significant legal impediments and restrictions, and in the workplace the openly hierarchical master–servant laws were not repealed until 1875. Indeed, many of the hierarchical elements of the employment contract survived well beyond this and remain in place today.[24]

There are, nevertheless, clear signs in *The Commentaries* of the movement towards a world in which property is seen as describing a relationship between a person and a thing and is unencumbered by social obligation; a world in which, at least on the surface, people dominate objects rather than other people. In Blackstone's conception, property was *private* property and described a relationship between a person and a thing, rather than one between people. Property was being relieved of its social relational and directly political dimensions and detached from moral, social and political obligation. This conception of property both reflected and helped to constitute the increasingly liberal, market exchange-based, capitalist society that was emerging – a society composed, at least in theory, of increasingly formally equal, autonomous, separate, property-owning 'possessive individuals'.[25] It described a world characterised by a clear subject–object divide[26] and by individual private property owners with increasingly absolute liberal ownership rights exchanging 'things' in the marketplace and owing one another, in principle, nothing beyond that contractually agreed.[27] In this world, sovereignty within states was to a considerable degree delegated (á la Hale) to owners of private property, and the economic, political and legal

---

[23] Davies, *Property*, p. 55. She points out that children, treated as largely governed by paternal power, were also in certain respects 'regarded as more like property than persons': pp. 55–6.

[24] Alan Fox, *Beyond Contract*, London: Faber & Faber (1974).

[25] C B MacPherson, *The Political Theory of Possessive Individualism*, Oxford: Oxford University Press (1962).

[26] Davies argues that 'it was in parallel with the formal abolition of slavery that the strong narrative of the separation of persons and property arose': *Property*, p. 77.

[27] See Patrick Atiyah, *The Rise & Fall of Freedom of Contract*, Oxford: Oxford University Press (1979).

realms became, in certain crucial respects, increasingly separate. Property was becoming a purely legal institution, formally only incidentally connected to political power.[28] Moreover, it was argued, by facilitating free market exchange, the new (legal) regime of private property operated for the social benefit: private property and Adam Smith's invisible hand of the market were replacing civic virtue and individual moral rectitude and obligation as the guarantors of the public good.[29] Jean-Philippe Robé aptly describes these processes as the 'institutionalization of the modern concept of property'.[30]

This 'revolution in property'[31] was replicated elsewhere, though it was often a long-drawn-out process, 'making it hard to discern precisely when and how it took place'.[32] One place where it happened with unusual rapidity, however, was France, where the change was, formally at least, relatively sudden and abrupt. The French Revolution saw what Blaufarb refers to as a 'Great Demarcation' in which absolute private property was introduced and separated from public power. Under the old pre-revolutionary regime, there was no clear distinction between property institutions and public administrative, judicial and sovereign powers: venal offices (saleable public offices) abounded, as did seigneuries (rights to exercise civil and criminal justice over the inhabitants of a specified area). Real estate was also rarely owned independently and completely by single persons but was, rather, subject to multiple rights claims from what Blaufarb calls 'partial owners', who stood in legally enforced, hierarchical relations of superiority and dependence. All this was changed abruptly by the revolution. The 'Great Demarcation' saw venal offices and seigneuries abolished at a stroke and public power (the state) separated from private power (property).[33] A radical distinction was drawn between 'the political and the social, state and society, sovereignty and ownership, the public and private'.[34] A new conception of

---

[28] Ellen Meiksins Wood, *Democracy Against Capitalism*, Cambridge: Cambridge University Press (1995), pp. 19–48.

[29] A number of writers have sought to describe the rather different conceptions and traditions of property that were vying for supremacy in the eighteenth century, most notably, perhaps, J G A Pocock, whose work seeks to assert the importance of civic republicanism (see his *Virtue, Commerce and History*, Cambridge: Cambridge University Press (1985)) and, more recently, Gregory Alexander, who contends that two competing conceptions of property – one liberal-capitalist, one civic-republican – have long been operative in American law: *Commodity and Propriety: competing visions of property in American legal thought*, Chicago: Chicago University Press (1997).

[30] Jean-Philippe Robé, 'Taming Property', 4(1) *RED*, pp. 162–9 (2022), p. 162.

[31] Blaufarb, *The Great Demarcation*, p. 1.

[32] Paul Babie, 'A Great Exploitation: the true legacy of property – a review essay', 31 *International Journal of the Semiotics of Law*, pp. 977–93 (2018), p. 980.

[33] By the National Constituent Assembly on 4 August 1789.

[34] Blaufarb, *The Great Demarcation*, p. 1.

absolute property was instituted, articulated in Article 544 of the Civil Code of 1804, a conception that implied the existence of a private domain of 'complete mastery, complete self-direction, and complete protection from the whims of others' – a domain in which there was no need to have regard to others in respect of the things you owned.[35] The 'Great Demarcation', with its new concept of property, Blaufarb argues, 'created a distinctly modern way of thinking'.[36]

Blackstone was, then, living through an era in which a property regime characterised by overlapping use-rights in the same piece of land was being replaced by a regime based on ideas of exclusive land ownership; an era in which ideas about property and markets as sites of self-interest were replacing earlier ideas about property rights and market exchange as entangled in complex webs of hierarchically organised social obligation. Social property relations were being forcibly changed, with clear winners and clear losers, and, unsurprisingly, property rights were, as a result, the site of unusually fierce class conflict.[37]

Private property, individual autonomy and identity

Conflicts and struggles over property are, of course, to be expected because of the power that property rights confer on their holders. This power extends far beyond the immediate power property rights confer over specific objects. Those rich in property enjoy a wider range of options in relation to place of residence, education, healthcare, lifestyle, and so on. Property ownership can also, of course, be a major source of political power and influence. As Davies says, 'private property is one important factor in the *actual* distribution of forms of personal, political, economic, social, or legal power'.[38] Much of this power derives from the right of property owners not only to access resources, both tangible and intangible, but to *exclude* others from them and from the benefits of them. Indeed, for

---

[35] Rose, 'Canons of Property Talk', p. 604. There were and still are, of course, restraints on the use of property but, as Thomas Grey says, these restraints on free use tend to be 'conceived as departures from an ideal conception of full ownership': Grey, 'The Disintegration of Property', p. 69. More recently, a number of theorists have argued that owners should explicitly be bound by a 'social obligation norm': see, for example, Gregory Alexander, 'The Social-Obligation Norm in American Property', 94 *Cornell Law Review*, pp. 745–819 (2009). In similar vein, Joseph Singer has suggested that owners should have a duty of 'attentiveness': 'Democratic Estates: Property Law in a Free and Democratic Society', 94 *Cornell Law Review*, pp. 1009–62 (2009), p. 1048.

[36] Blaufarb, *The Great Demarcation*, p. 14.

[37] See, for example, Thompson, 'The Moral Economy of the English Crowd'.

[38] Davies, *Property*, p. 52.

many property theorists, for whom property is synonymous with *private* property, excludability is property's key distinguishing characteristic. In the words of Morris Cohen, 'the essence of private property is always the right to exclude others'.[39] This exclusivity axiom has led many, like Kevin Gray, to conclude that property is 'not a thing but a power-relationship', 'a legally endorsed concentration of power over things and resources', which is 'constituted by the state's endorsement of private claims to regulate the access of strangers to the benefits of particular resources'.[40] It follows that although property rights in contemporary capitalism take the form of *private* rights and appear in certain crucial respects to be separate from state and public power, they are ultimately dependent on the latter. Property is thus a publicly constituted and publicly enforced power relationship: all property rights, including private property rights, have a public law character; they are never truly private. This led Robert Hale to conclude that private property is a form of publicly 'delegated *private* government', functioning as a delegation of power by the state to a monopoly rights-holder.[41] It is by giving their holders power over 'excludable resources' that property rights also give their holders power over other people. Because the law of property excludes others from using the things it assigns to me, if those others want to use the food, the house, the land, or the car that the law calls mine, they have to get my consent.[42]

During the seventeenth, eighteenth and nineteenth centuries, private property rights and the exclusionary power they gave to their holders over tangible things came widely to be seen as creating a protected sphere of personal sovereignty in which individuals could exercise their free will by appropriating and using the things of the external world. It was on this basis that they came to be seen by some as natural rights and by others as the pre-conditions of individual liberty, agency and self-governance. In continental philosophy, the creation of an independent individual domain of individual self-sovereignty came to be regarded as central to individual moral development. Thus, for Kant, possession of private property was necessary for the development of individual free will and an individual's fundamental moral qualities, while for Hegel, whose views on the 'spiritual' role of private property greatly influenced (among others) Marx, it was central to individual self-development and human personhood. These moral arguments for private

---

[39] Cohen, 'Property and Sovereignty', p. 12. While excludability may be central to private property in tangibles and intellectual artefacts, however, as we have seen, transferability and the acquisition of market value seem to be pre-requisites of the 'propertyisation' of intangibles like debt.
[40] Gray, 'Property in Thin Air', pp. 294, 299.
[41] Hale, 'Law Making by Unofficial Minorities', p. 453.
[42] See Cohen, 'Property and Sovereignty', p. 12.

property rights gave them a natural, pre- or a-social character and suggested they were not in need of consequentialist justification.

For contemporary liberal political theorists and philosophers, too, private property rights are central to human autonomy, free will and personhood, and are justifiable on this basis. Thus, Jeremy Waldron, for example, has mounted a defence of private property rights from within the liberal rights tradition, which eschews the need for reliance on utilitarian claims about their economic contributions to growth.[43] Individual autonomy is similarly the lodestar of theorists such as Hanoch Dagan.[44] In recent decades, the importance of property to individual and group identities has also been offered as a justification for private property, animating the work of theorists like Margaret Jane Radin.[45]

Others, like Margaret Davies, argue that in contemporary capitalism private property is central to our ideas of self and that this helps us better understand our historically specific sense of selfhood and personhood 'as bounded, discrete, self-determining units'. We may not '*necessarily* experience ourselves in this way', she says, but it 'arguably does constitute the substratum of meaning about selfhood in the West – [it] is the dominant story we tell about ourselves and others, particularly in major public arenas – legal, economic, and political'. This is epitomised, she argues, in the idea of 'the person as quintessentially an *owner*', further observing that, while this Western conception of the person might seem natural to us, it is, in fact, 'a rather peculiar idea within the world's cultures'.[46] It is also, some feminist writers argue, 'thoroughly gendered'.[47]

Personal possessions versus productive resources

The traditional liberal justifications for private property tend to abstract from particular resources and to treat all 'things', all resources, in the same way, as abstract equivalents. Some theorists, however, draw distinctions between different resources. Radin, for example, distinguishes personal property, which is connected with and constitutive of the owner's 'personhood' and whose protection is central to human flourishing, from property which is fungible and commodifiable, arguing forcefully for stronger legal and

---

[43] Waldron, *The Right to Private Property*.
[44] Hanoch Dagan, *A Liberal Theory of Property*, Cambridge: Cambridge University Press (2021).
[45] Margaret Jane Radin, *Reinterpreting Property*, Chicago: University of Chicago Press (1993).
[46] Davies, *Property*, pp. 29–31. Davies adds that, in the seventeenth century, when these notions of the 'individualistic, property-defined … self' were emerging, these persons were 'almost invariably male, white and at least upper middle class'.
[47] For a brief discussion of this claim, see Davies, *Property*, pp. 44–7.

constitutional protections for the former, what she calls 'property-for-personhood'.[48] Others draw a distinction between private property rights in personal possessions and in productive resources (the 'means of production'), between personal property and capital. Property, Enrico Rossi argues, has a 'dual nature': the same property can be consumed to fulfil an individual personal need or it can be deployed as a means of production for wealth generation.[49] Harris alludes to this when he argues that 'property has a dual function, since it governs both the use of things and the allocation of items of social wealth'.[50] A number of leading thinkers have insisted that a distinction between property in personal possessions and in means of production not only can but must be drawn. John Rawls, for example, widely regarded as one of the twentieth century's preeminent liberal philosophers, saw the right to hold personal property as one of the 'basic' rights needed to create a sense of personal independence and self-respect, but did not include among these 'basic' rights 'the right to own certain kinds of property (e.g., means of production)'. This right was 'not basic'.[51] In similar vein, Dagan sees private property and the 'private authority' that goes with it as central to autonomy and self-determination and to the creation of a realm of non-interference from the state and other persons, but insists that 'no private authority can be claimed that is in excess of what is required for owners' self-determination, and that such authority must be consistent with the self-determination of others'. This leads him to argue that 'private authority attached to ... commercial property types – notably to ownership of means of production – must be carefully circumscribed'.[52] Indeed, it seems clear

---

[48] Radin, 'The Liberal Conception of Property'. See also Radin, 'Property and Personhood', 34 *Stanford Law Review*, pp. 957–1015 (1982). Radin's theories are based less on a liberal notion of negative freedom, which tends to posit an absolute conception of property as sacred to personal autonomy, and more on an affirmative notion of property as contributing to individual well-being.

[49] Rossi, 'Reconsidering the Dual Nature of Property Rights'. See also David Singh Grewal and Jedediah Britton-Purdy, 'Liberalism, Property and the Means of Production', *LPE Blog*, 25/1/2021, https://lpeproject.org/blog/liberalism-property-and-the-means-of-production/. The distinction is not always, of course, clear-cut.

[50] Harris, *Property and Justice*, p. 4. The distinction between property in personal possessions and property in productive resources is arguably also present in the arguments of those who suggest that ownership – particularly of certain sorts of important resources – should be regarded as an 'office' to which affirmative duties should be attached: see Rutger Claassen and Larissa Katz, 'Property: authority without office?', 3 *Journal of Law and Political Economy*, pp. 570–5 (2023).

[51] John Rawls, *Theory of Justice*, Cambridge: Harvard University Press (revised ed. 1999 [1971]), pp. 53–4.

[52] Dagan, 'Autonomy and Property'. This leads Dagan to recognise, like Joseph Singer, that a liberal property regime might need to impinge on the property rights of owners of the means of production in order to recognise the claims of workers.

that many of the reservations that have at different times been expressed about private property are, in fact, concerned not so much with private property in personal possessions but with private property in productive resources. It is in its 'duality of function', Harris argues, that property's 'controversiality resides'.[53]

Robé explains why the distinction between private property in personal possessions and private property in productive resources is so important, particularly in a capitalism in which production has become much less individual and much more interdependent and socialised. As he says, the use of many objects of private property by individuals has limited consequences for others. 'What I do with my toothbrush is really of no importance or interest [to anyone else]'. He goes on to explain, however, that for other objects of property, 'the autonomy of the owner translates into heteronomy for the non-owners'. This is 'particularly the case for productive assets, such as a farm or a factory. The owner will get to determine who can work using the assets, i.e. who gets hired'. The owner 'will set, as a matter of principle, the production process, the rules to follow to use the property and, indirectly, their consequences [for] the workforce, society at large and the natural environment'.[54] As Robé points out, heteronomy of this sort is a particular problem in today's corporate capitalism in which so many key productive assets are controlled by large, powerful multi-national corporations. By granting their corporate holders so much coercive power over others, private property rights in productive resources often serve to undermine rather than to enhance individual autonomy and self-determination. It is worth adding that it is also much harder to see private property in intangible property forms like corporate shares as quite as indispensable to individual autonomy, personhood and dignity as private property in tangible personal possessions.

The drawing of a distinction between property rights in personal possessions and productive resources has long been a feature of empirical reality, as the work of historians and anthropologists has shown.[55] While

---

[53] Harris, *Property and Justice*, p. 4. Singer has pointed out that, in empirical reality, we already have different models of property in different spheres of social life: the family, housing, business, and so on. These models, he argues, 'are not merely glosses on the basic "title" or "full ownership" theory. Many of them depart so far from the basic model of single owner with consolidated rights that use of the basic model is essentially misleading as a conceptual baseline': 'Property and Social Relations: from title to entitlement', p. 79.

[54] Robé, 'Taming Property', p. 164.

[55] According to Chris Hann, for example, 'land has always enjoyed a privileged status in property theorizing ... This status derives straightforwardly from the fact that land has been a major factor of production and of reproduction in most human societies', Hann, 'The State of the Art: A New Double Movement?', p. 293.

early anthropologists like Maine and Morgan tended to depict property as an institution that had evolved from collectivism and communalism to individualism and the private ownership rights characteristic of modern capitalism, later anthropologists soon began painting a more nuanced picture. Many societies, they suggested, had developed rather different sets of 'property institutions' for personal possessions and for key productive resources. In general terms, they suggested that something resembling 'ownership', in our private-property-based sense of the word, was much more common in relation to the former than the latter. Thus, the late Victorian anthropologist Edward Tylor argued that the early rules of property drew a clear distinction between the key productive resource of land and personal possessions. 'Of the land', Tylor wrote, 'all have the use, but no man can be its absolute owner ... there is a distinct idea of common property in land belonging to the clan or tribe'. At the same time, however, 'personal ownership appears, though still under the power of the family', to prevail in relation to 'personal property in movables'.[56] In the early to mid twentieth century, Robert Lowie similarly concluded that some societies are 'communistic' or 'collectivist' 'as regards one type of goods, yet recognise separate ownership with respect to other forms of property', arguing that, generally, 'purely personal titles' were 'more clearly established' in relation to movable property than in relation to land.[57] Despite holding very different views about anthropology, another leading twentieth-century anthropologist, Leslie White, agreed with Lowie on this. When discussing land, White preferred the word 'held' to the word 'own', arguing that the relationship between rights-holding groups in these societies and the pieces of land that 'belonged' to them was 'a right to use, to exploit the land rather than ownership in our sense of the term'. He nevertheless concluded that in primitive societies 'everyone has free access to the resources of nature' and that 'natural resources are [generally] collectively owned, though often privately exploited by some group, almost never by an individual'. 'Personal property', on the other hand, was 'individually owned' and 'subject to individual

---

[56] Edward B Tylor, *Anthropology*, London: Macmillan (1881), pp. 419–20.
[57] Robert Lowie, *Primitive Society*, New York: Boni & Liveright (1920), pp. 206, 210. In 'primitive society', he writes, 'collective ownership, not necessarily by the entire community, by possibly by some other group, is common': p. 233. Elsewhere he argued that in these societies some things are 'jealously guarded from encroachment', but the 'necessities of life' are often 'shared ... in a manner that sometimes amounts to practical communism': Robert Lowie, 'Incorporeal Property in Primitive Society', 37 *Yale Law Journal*, pp. 551–63 (1928), p. 552. Use of the term 'primitive', with its negative connotations and implication of lesser and backward, is now recognised as problematic and is avoided by anthropologists.

ownership'.[58] Contemporary anthropologists continue to recognise the importance of this distinction, though they are even more careful in their use of the term 'ownership' and even more critical of attempts to categorise property regimes in terms of private versus communal, arguing that it is 'misleadingly simplistic' and somewhat Euro-centric.[59] Lawyers are also now exploring these matters.[60] The distinction is also apparent in the way that in some jurisdictions different sorts of property rights are treated differently by reference to their purpose and function. Despite the guarantees seemingly offered to all property rights by the German *Grundgesetz* (Constitution), for example, the German Constitutional Court distinguishes property rights according to the substantive interests they serve. Property rights that serve an owner's status as an autonomous moral agent are distinguished from those whose function is primarily or exclusively economic, protecting only the former as fundamental constitutional interests. 'In German constitutional law', Gregory Alexander explains, 'property is a fundamental right that is accorded the highest degree of protection only in cases in which the affected interest immediately at stake implicates the owner's ability to act as an autonomous moral and political agent'.[61]

Significantly, the arguments in favour of private property rights in productive resources have tended, historically, to rely less on claims about individual autonomy and identity than those put forward in relation to personal possessions. Defenders of private property rights in productive resources have tended to place much greater emphasis on consequentialist claims about the economic benefits they bring. Indeed, in recent decades, the

---

[58] Leslie White, *The Evolution of Culture*, New York: McGraw Hill (1959), pp. 251–5. Although other tribes could be excluded from a piece of land, it could not be bought and sold, and there was 'no such thing as "absentee ownership" in primitive society'; if a group ceased using the land, 'it revert[ed] to the public domain': p. 251. White drew on Lewis Henry Morgan. Writing of the Iroquois in *Houses and House-life of the American Aborigines*, Washington: Government Print Office (1881), Morgan wrote that: 'Individual ownership, with its right to sell and convey [land] in fee simple to any other person, was entirely unknown to them', p. 79. In *Ancient Society*, however, writing of 'property in the upper state of barbarism', Morgan argued that 'personal property, generally, was subject to individual ownership': Calcutta, Bagchi and Co (1982 [1877]), p. 551. Tylor similarly argued that the people of these societies draw 'the same distinction which our lawyers make between real and personal property': *Anthropology*, p. 419.

[59] Chris Hann, 'The Tragedy of the Privates? Post-socialist property relations in anthropological perspective', *Max Planck Institute for Social Anthropology Working Papers*, No 2. See also Hann, 'The State of the Art', p. 292.

[60] See, for example, Graham, *Lawscape: property, environment, law*; Brenna Bhandar, *Colonial Lives of Property: law, land and racial regimes of ownership*, Durham: Duke University Press (2018)

[61] Gregory Alexander, 'Property as a Fundamental Constitutional Right? The German example', 88 *Cornell Law Review*, pp. 733–78 (2003), p. 739.

consequentialist arguments in favour of private property rights in productive resources have been vigorously promoted by law-and-economics scholars and neo-classical economists within the academy and by the supporters of free markets without. Both argue that free markets are the *sine qua non* of growth, development and economic 'efficiency', and that private property is the *sine qua non* of free markets.[62] In the 1990s, a 'Washington consensus' emerged around these ideas and around policies favouring the creation of new private property rights (through the privatisation of productive resources that were previously publicly owned and, in some cases, through open dispossessions and enclosures of one kind or another) and the enhancement of the freedoms, particularly of movement, enjoyed by private property owners. The structural adjustment policies of the International Monetary Fund promoted these processes. Paradoxically, although these policies were, and are, widely associated with *de*regulation, their implementation has often, in fact, coincided with more regulation and the rise of so-called 'regulatory states'.

The argument is that the privatisation of productive resources and strong protection of private property rights are the pre-conditions of economic development because of their facilitation of the operation of the market mechanisms. These mechanisms, it is claimed, create incentives for people to work hard and for producers to innovate and ensure economically 'efficient' resource allocation and management. In property scholarship, these arguments have figured prominently in many of the recent attempts to revitalise thing-ownership conceptions of property focused on the right to exclude.[63] There are similarities between these contemporary consequentialist arguments in favour of private property and those found in Blackstone. Underpinning Blackstone's analysis of the rise of private property is an account of history drawn from Enlightenment thinkers like Hume and Smith in which societies pass through various 'stages', culminating in 'commercial society' (what we now call 'capitalism'). Part of this account of history (which clearly influenced Marx, though he seems to have abandoned it later in life) is a 'staged' account of the development of property institutions. According to Blackstone, God originally made all things 'the general property of all' and, at first, 'these general notions of property' were 'sufficient to answer all the purposes of mankind'. However, as mankind increased in 'number, craft and ambition', new conceptions of property were required and ideas of private property began to emerge, first in relation to 'houses

---

[62] See, for example, Hernando de Soto, *The Mystery of Capital*, London: Black Swan (2001).
[63] For Thomas Merrill and Henry Smith, for example, 'property at its core entails the right to exclude others from some discrete thing': Thomas Merrill and Henry Smith, *Property: principles and policies*, St Paul: Foundation Press (2007), p. v.

and home-stalls' and 'movables of every kind', and later in relation to key productive resources such as land. 'Had not ... a separate property in lands, as well as movables, been vested in some individuals', human progress would have been impeded. 'Necessity', Blackstone concluded, 'begat property'.[64] Economically determinist arguments of this sort underpin much law and economics scholarship, and in the 1980s and 1990s found expression in the idea that 'there is no alternative' to a social order based predominantly on private property and markets, and in the claim, rather less popular now than in the triumphalist 1990s, that capitalism represents 'the end of history'.[65] One of the dangers of historical determinisms of this sort is that the belief that history (or 'efficiency') is on your side can be, and has been, used to justify changes that involve political repression, forced dispossessions and rights reallocations on the grounds that, even if they seem directly and immediately to benefit a few to the detriment of the many, they do so in the service of the longer-term social good.

For Max Weber it was the way in which the struggles around property rights in productive resources were resolved that held the key to what he considered to be English legal exceptionalism. In Weber's typology of development, the establishment of a rational, predictable legal system was one of the keys to economic progress and modernity. And yet England, 'the first country in modern times to have a highly developed capitalist economy', had a markedly 'less rational and less bureaucratic system of justice' than places like Germany. According to Weber, 'the main reason why capitalism in England was able to come to terms so well with this situation [a less rational legal system]' was that 'the manner in which the courts were organised and the trial procedure, right up to modern times, were in fact tantamount to a virtual denial of justice to the economically weak'. The administration of justice was 'dominat[ed] by notables'.[66] The English experience was thus 'a unique historical case, in which an irrational system of laws was controlled by procapitalist functionaries not generally present in other societies'.[67] For Marx, too, the victories of the dominant classes in the struggles surrounding property in land were central to development in England. Enclosure and the loss of use rights in land rendered the labouring classes 'propertyless',

---

[64] Blackstone, *Commentaries on the Laws of England*, Book II, pp. 1–6.
[65] Francis Fukuyama, *The End of History and the Last Man*, New York: Free Press (1992). Economic determinism of this sort has also been a prominent feature of certain versions of Marxism, the difference being, of course, that communism, rather than liberal capitalism, is seen as representing 'the end of history'.
[66] Max Weber, from *Economy and Society*, reprinted in Walter Runciman (ed.), *Max Weber: Selections in Translation*, Cambridge: Cambridge University Press (1978), pp. 352–4.
[67] Joshua Getzler, 'Theories of Property and Economic Development', 26 *Journal of Interdisciplinary History*, pp. 639–69 (1996), p. 646.

compelling them to become wage-labourers. At the same time, market competition between capitalist producers set in motion an economic dynamic that forced them to seek productivity increases.[68]

As this suggests, in Blackstone's day, the (re)conceptualisation of property was not merely an interesting theoretical and philosophical question, but a vitally important, highly political question with major practical consequences. New individualistic conceptions of property drawing on the political economy of 'improvement' were vying with older, less individualistic conceptions rooted in ideas about social hierarchies and customary rights, obligations and practices. As new intellectual property rights were created, and as enclosures turned the key productive resource of land into ever more absolute private property, new rights and sources of power were created and old rights were destroyed. In these circumstances, as Getzler says, the 'naturalist ideology of the sanctity of property was especially appealing to the powerful class of landowners and to the legal functionaries they supported'.[69] It was, however, difficult to sustain the notion of property rights as pre-social, natural rights that existed prior to state and law, for, as they were forcibly changed, their socially constructed, contingent, changing and contested nature was only too evident. This was reflected both in Blackstone's anxieties about the perceived legitimacy of private property and in his reluctance to rest his case for specifically *private* property on natural rights arguments, notwithstanding the tendency of the major English theorists of property like Hobbes and Locke to do so. Despite occasional rhetorical flourishes about the natural feelings of men towards private property, Blackstone recognised that, 'accurately and strictly speaking', there was 'no foundation in nature or in natural law' for many property rights. Private property was 'probably founded in nature', he argued, but many existing 'modifications' of it were 'entirely derived from society' and rooted in positive law.[70]

It was for this reason that Blackstone felt it necessary to 'examine more deeply the rudiments and grounds of these positive constitutions of society'[71] and to offer utilitarian, consequentialist explanations and justifications for the emergence and extension of private property rights, particularly in land. Blackstone urged steady pursuit of 'that wise and orderly maxim, of assigning to every-thing capable of ownership a legal and determinate owner'.[72] In this context, he drew on the work of Locke and others who

---

[68] See Wood, *The Origin of Capitalism*.
[69] Getzler, 'Theories of Property and Economic Development', p. 642.
[70] Blackstone, *Commentaries on the Laws of England*, Book I, pp. 93–4. See also Albert Alschuler, 'Rediscovering Blackstone', 145 *University of Pennsylvania Law Review*, pp. 1–55 (1996), pp. 29–36.
[71] Blackstone, *Commentaries on the Laws of England*, Book II, p. 1.
[72] Blackstone, *Commentaries on the Laws of England*, Book II, p. 9.

suggested that the creation of private property rights facilitated the more intensive and productive exploitation of land as a resource and thus furthered agricultural 'improvement'. What we find in Blackstone, therefore, is a mix of natural rights inspired rhetoric – underpinning implicit claims about the sanctity of, and the need for absolute respect for, private property[73] – and more grounded consequentialist arguments, what one commentator calls a 'charmed convergence of scared rights and utilitarian progress'. He blends natural rights and utilitarian rhetoric into 'a seamless argument for enclosure and against the continued exercise by the peasantry of their rights in the commons'.[74] Ideas of civic humanism are promiscuously intermingled with ideas about property as an absolute individual right and with claims that the legally guaranteed security of private possession, disposition and alienation are 'required for individual happiness, self-government, political stability, and economic improvement'.[75]

Capital, capitalist and capitalism

As we have seen, the way in which property rights in productive resources are conceptualised is especially important because of the power they confer over people as well as things. This is particularly the case in technologically advanced societies in which production has ceased to be an individual affair and has become highly socialised. As Thorstein Veblen explained, as a result of technological advance, a large volume of material equipment and large productive units are often needed for effective and efficient productive activity, placing those with property rights in such equipment at a 'marked advantage' over those without. He further pointed out that, in technologically advanced societies, those with property rights in this productive equipment are also often able to 'corner' use of the accumulated technological knowledge of the society in question, even if or when they do not possess intellectual property rights over it.[76] For Veblen, this common stock of technological knowledge – the collective product of many generations and 'a by-product of the life of the community at large' – is 'far and away the most important and consequential ... of the community's assets and equipment'.[77] Ownership

---

[73] As Cohen observes, for Blackstone 'no public good is greater than the maintenance of private property': Cohen, 'Property and Sovereignty', p. 8.
[74] Travis, 'Pirates of the Information Infrastructure', pp. 784, 798.
[75] Gordon, 'Paradoxical Property', p. 95.
[76] Thorstein Veblen, 'On the Nature of Capital (I)', 22 *Quarterly Journal of Economics*, pp. 517–42 (1908).
[77] Veblen, 'On the Nature of Capital (I)', pp. 518–19. Veblen referred to this common stock of knowledge as 'the intangible assets of the community' and stressed its importance to economic growth and development. On this, see Hodgson's contribution to 'Institutionalism versus Marxism: perspectives for social science – a debate between

of industrial equipment, he argued, enables a small minority to 'engross' this common stock of communal technological knowledge and exert 'pecuniary domination',[78] with significant consequences for the distribution of the social product.[79]

Veblen made these points in the context of a discussion of the nature of 'capital', a concept associated with property rights in, or derived from, the means of production and productive activity. Notwithstanding its treatment by some 'mainstream economists as a general, ahistorical entity',[80] capital is an historical concept whose meaning has, like that of property, changed over time and been much contested.[81] Indeed, in recent decades there has been 'capital creep', as the term has come to be used increasingly promiscuously to refer not only to anything that contributes to production but to a wide range of very different, non-economic phenomena. This is reflected in the emergence of concepts such as 'cultural capital', 'human capital', 'political capital', 'social capital' and so on. As Geoffrey Hodgson says, more or less everything that yields some kind of return or potential return, pecuniary or otherwise, 'seems to be capable of being regarded as a variety of capital', creating the impression that 'all such political, cultural, social and cognitive phenomena can be valued and traded in monetary terms, and invested like financial capital'.[82] The emergence of the idea of 'human capital' is especially significant, for it threatens to turn all inputs into production into 'capital' and to dispense with the category 'labour' and the class relation between capital and labour. Despite its slipperiness, however, a brief exploration of the different meanings that have been attached to the term 'capital' is illuminating, for it casts valuable light on the nature of certain important

---

Geoffrey Hodgson and Alex Callinicos', University of Hertfordshire Working Papers (2001).

[78] Veblen, 'On the Nature of Capital (I)', pp. 524–7. According to Veblen, 'the practice of investment' arose out of the 'engrossing' by a minority of the community's technological knowledge and its control of material equipment: Veblen, 'On the Nature of Capital (II): investment and intangible assets and the pecuniary magnate', 23 *Quarterly Journal of Economics*, pp. 104–36 (1908).

[79] Veblen, 'On the Nature of Capital (II)', p. 115.

[80] Geoffrey Hodgson, 'Frank A Fetter (1863–1949): Capital (1930)', 4 *Journal of Institutional Economics*, pp. 127–37 (2008).

[81] 'The meaning of capital isn't "uniform and stable"': Thorstein Veblen, 'Fisher's Income and Capital', 23 *Political Science Quarterly*, pp. 112–28 (1908), p. 114.

[82] Hodgson, 'Frank A Fetter', pp. 127–30. 'One would have difficulty', he argues, 'in identifying what enduring entity is not some variety of capital. Capital has now acquired the broad meaning of a stock or reserve of anything of social or economic significance'. The impression is given that 'all such political, cultural, social and cognitive phenomena can be valued and traded in monetary terms, and invested like financial capital'.

forms of property in contemporary capitalism: what I shall refer to as property-as-capital.

Of the triad capital, capitalist and capitalism, 'capital' came first. Derived from the Latin *caput*, meaning head or principal, *capitalis* emerged in the twelfth to thirteenth centuries to refer to 'the property, not necessarily only money, that a rich person owned'.[83] According to the economic historian Fernand Braudel, 'capital' came to designate 'funds, stock of merchandise, sum of money or money carrying interest', before gradually coming to refer more specifically to money invested to make more money.[84] In Postlethwayt's *Universal Dictionary of Trade and Commerce,* published in 1751, 'capital' is defined as the 'sum of money which individuals bring to make up the common stock of a partnership', indicating that it had, by this time, come to be conceived as 'the money invested, not as the things themselves in which the money was invested'.[85] It seems clear, then, that from a fairly early date the term 'capital' was generally used to refer to money invested in some way to generate a revenue, such as the sum of money contributed to the stock-in-trade of a firm.[86] 'Capital' was thus a dynamic form of money – money in motion, deployed to expand through 'investment in commerce' and distinguishable from 'simple', inactive, 'sterile' money.[87] This is reflected in the meaning of the later term 'capitalist', whose origins are Dutch and date from the early seventeenth century. The term 'capitalist' came to designate 'a wealthy person, mostly engaged in money-lending or investment activities'.[88] This Dutch neologism spread rapidly abroad, quickly establishing itself in France, where it was adopted by the Physiocrats to refer to 'wealthy individuals who try to increase their capital by either lending money at interest or investing it in productive enterprises'. Indeed, some considered it synonymous with rentier.[89] It is not until the eighteenth century that the term appears in English; before that, essentially the same phenomena are captured by the concept of 'moneyed' or 'monied' men.

---

[83] See Franz Rainer, 'Word Formation and Word History: the case of CAPITALIST and CAPITALISM', in Olivier Bonami et al (eds), *The Lexeme in Descriptive and Theoretical Morphology*, Berlin: Language Science Press, pp. 43–65 (2018), pp. 45–6. See also Henry Sée, *Modern Capitalism: its origin and evolution* (2004 [1928], translated by Homer B. Vanderblue and Georges F. Dorio), p. 11.

[84] Fernand Braudel, *The Wheels of Commerce*, London: Collins (1983 [1979]), pp. 232–3. See also Hodgson, *Conceptualising Capitalism*, chapter 7.

[85] Edwin Cannan, 'Early History of the Term Capital', 35 *Quarterly Journal of Economics*, pp. 469–81 (1921), pp. 475, 478.

[86] See Hodgson, *Conceptualising Capitalism*, pp. 174–6.

[87] Jonathan Levy, 'Capital as Process and the History of Capitalism', 91 *Business History Review*, pp. 483–510 (2017), pp. 488–9.

[88] Rainer, 'Word Formation and Word History', pp. 46–7.

[89] Rainer, 'Word Formation and Word History', pp. 46–7.

'From the 17th century to the 19th century', Rainer writes, 'the dominant meaning of CAPITALIST in all European languages was that of a wealthy person who made his capital "work" by lending it at interest, buying bonds or shares, or investing it in productive activities'.[90] From the mid eighteenth century the term is increasingly used – almost always pejoratively – to refer to people who make money from money, people who 'already own money and are prepared to use it in order to obtain even more'.[91] Capitalists were 'money merchants', the owners of 'pecuniary fortunes', the possessors of government bonds, stocks and shares, liquid money for investing – rentiers, distinguishable from active, productive entrepreneurs. As such, as the eighteenth century progressed, they became the subjects of growing middle-class and radical attacks on parasitism. The rise of industrial capitalism in the later eighteenth and nineteenth centuries, however, provided capitalists with new opportunities to make money from productive activity instead of from debt, and this saw this money-oriented conception of capital come to be supplemented – and, in some cases, replaced – by a more material conception that associated capital with tangible, physical factors of production.[92] Both Smith and Ricardo, for example, tended to see capital as a stock of physical assets or objects and by the early twentieth century it had become 'usual in expositions of economic theory to speak of capital as an array of "productive goods"', by which was generally meant 'industrial equipment'[93] and/or physical factors of production.[94] Capitalist also came to be used by some as a synonym for 'entrepreneur', understood as someone who organises productive activity, though others carefully distinguished the two concepts.[95]

By contrast, the term 'capitalism' was, as Howard Brick observes, 'an etymological latecomer',[96] appearing for the first time in early nineteenth-century France and Germany.[97] At this time, however, capitalism tends to be used to describe making money from money – an activity – rather than an economic system, often with very negative overtones. Rainer recounts a

---

[90] Rainer, 'Word Formation and Word History', p. 49.
[91] Braudel, *The Wheels of Commerce*, p. 238.
[92] See Levy, 'Capital as Process and the History of Capitalism', pp. 489–94; Hodgson, *Conceptualising Capitalism*, pp. 175–8.
[93] Veblen, 'On the Nature of Capital (I)', p. 517.
[94] See Levy, 'Capital as Process and the History of Capitalism', pp. 485–6.
[95] Rainer, 'Word Formation and Word History', pp. 49–50.
[96] Howard Brick, *Transcending Capitalism*, Ithaca: Cornell University Press (2006), p. 23.
[97] It has been claimed that first usage of the term *capitalisme* can be found in 1753, but doubt has been cast on the accuracy of this: see Rainer, 'Word Formation and Word History', p. 52. Pryor attributes the first German usage to Friedrich Julius Heinrich von Soden's *Nazional-Oekonomie* in 1805: Frederick Pryor, *Capitalism Reassessed*, Appendix 2 'Etymology of Capitalism', Cambridge: Cambridge University Press (2006), https://www.swarthmore.edu/SocSci/Economics/fpryor1/Appendices.pdf.

letter addressed to a statesman that talks of the 'new power of capitalism ... which sacrifices the future to the present, and the present to individualism' and describes it as an 'egotistical, cosmopolitan power that grabs everything, does not produce anything and is only tied to itself'.[98] When the term first seems to appear in English – in William Makepeace Thackeray's novel *The Newcomes*, published in 1854 – it is again used to denote money-making activities. Use of term 'capitalism' in something resembling its modern form to denote an *economic system* does not seem to emerge until the mid nineteenth century and the work of early socialist politicians and writers like Louis Blanc (1845) and Pierre-Joseph Proudhon (1851).[99] Interestingly, Marx, with whom the term is closely associated, made little use of it and only did so later in life. Braudel suggests that the word was 'still unknown' to him when he published *Das Kapital* in 1867, though that seems unlikely.[100] Marx did, however, write of 'capitalist production', of the 'capitalist (or bourgeois) mode of production' (*produktionsweise*, or way of producing) and even of the 'capitalist system', and by his later years the term 'capitalism' to denote an economic system was 'join[ing] the left's lexicon' and it was used in this manner by Engels.[101] Outside socialist circles, however, use of the term to denote a historically specific and, by implication, potentially transient economic system – the antonym of socialism – emerged only slowly and was resisted and decried by many, both because of what were perceived as its pejorative connotations and because of its attribution of historical specificity to processes that were thought universal and natural.[102] Thus, 'capitalism' did not figure in the work of the classical economists (like John Stuart Mill) and was thought objectionable by many conventional economists. The 1911 edition of the *Encyclopedia Britannica*, for example, had no entry on it, though

---

[98] Rainer, 'Word Formation and Word History', p. 53.
[99] Rainer, 'Word Formation and Word History', pp. 54–6. Hodgson, 'Frank A Fetter (1863–1949)', p. 252.
[100] Braudel, *The Wheels of Commerce*, p. 237. By 1870, the term *kapitalismus* was being used by the German economist Albert Schaffle. Engels made greater use of the term. See Eve Chiapello, 'Accounting and the Birth of the Notion of Capitalism', 18 *Critical Perspectives on Accounting*, pp. 263–96 (2007), pp. 276–9.
[101] See Chiapello, 'Accounting and the Birth of the Notion of Capitalism', pp. 276–9; Brick, *Transcending Capitalism*, pp. 25–6.
[102] Even within some socialist circles there was some hesitation about the term. The Fabians, for example, used the term 'cautiously', preferring to contrast 'socialism' or 'collectivism' with 'individualism' or 'private ownership', though in the *Fabian Essays* it does figure in the work of Hubert Bland and William Clarke: see Brick, *Transcending Capitalism*, pp. 26–7. Some current commentators seem to be sympathetic to the view that 'capitalism' is a 'socialist term of abuse' and, at best, a term we use 'as a matter of convenience', rather a genuinely analytically useful concept: see Samuel Moyn, 'Thomas Piketty and The Future of Legal Scholarship', 128 *Harvard Law Review*, p. 49 (2014), p. 51.

under the entry on 'capital' it derided 'much of modern socialist theorizing against "capitalism"' for its failure to appreciate the universality of capital and its indispensability to productive progress'.[103] The term 'capitalism' was not even much used by the German historical school of economists, despite their emphasis on the relativity of economic systems and the challenge they mounted to the idea of universal economic laws. When it was eventually popularised in Germany by Sombart and Weber, 'capitalism' was defined primarily in terms of its motivating values or 'ethic'.[104]

Property-as-capital

The idea of capital as a 'dynamic' form of money was central to Marx's idea of the circuits of capital, in which the term capital is used to refer both to a fund of money for investment *and* the concrete means of production bought with it. Marx identified a number of different routes – circuits of capital – whereby capital in its money form could be used to achieve this pecuniary increase, changing form as it did so. Thus, money could be advanced as a loan, with the repayment covering both the original advance and an additional sum (interest) to create the circuit $M–M^1$. Alternatively, money could be used to buy commodities that are then resold for more money – 'buying cheap and selling dear' – to create the circuit $M–C–M^1$.[105] Usurers or money-lending capital ($M–M^1$) and merchant capital ($M–C–M^1$) were, Marx argued, the dominant early forms of capital, existing prior to the emergence of the bourgeois (or capitalist) mode of production. With the rise of industrial *capitalism*, however, a third expanded circuit emerged and came to dominate: the circuit of industrial capital – $M–C–P–C^1–M^1$ – in which money capital was advanced to buy commodities (plant, equipment, materials, labour power) before being set in motion in a production process whose resultant product (C^1) was sold at a profit (M^1). In the circuit of

---

[103] See T Parsons, 'Capitalism in Recent German Literature: Sombart and Weber', 36 *Journal of Political Economy*, pp. 641–61(1928). See also Brick, *Transcending Capitalism*, p. 26. Many on the right object to the use of the term 'capitalism' because of its allegedly pejorative connotations, preferring terms such as 'free enterprise', and, unaware of the negative connotations associated with the word 'capitalist' in the eighteenth and early nineteenth centuries, mistakenly attribute these negative connotations to Marx and the socialists.

[104] It is widely thought that Sombart's work played an important role in legitimating use of the concept. His *Der Moderne Kapitalismus* appeared in 1902. It has never been fully translated into English or French, in part perhaps because of Sombart's anti-Semitic writings and pro-Nazi stance in the 1930s. Sombart distinguished economic systems on the basis of their differing mental attitudes or spirits, their organisational forms and their techniques, giving priority in his analyses to the spirit of capitalism. Weber's *The Protestant Ethic and the Spirit of Capitalism* appeared in 1904–5.

[105] Marx, *Capital*, volume 1, pp. 145–53, chapter 4.

industrial capital, capital changes form during the course of the production process and the circuit takes place in two spheres: the sphere of production and the sphere of circulation.[106] The rise of the capitalist mode of production and the circuit of industrial capital also changed the social framework and forms of much of the M–M^1 circuit; interest-bearing capital became increasingly tied not to usury but to industrial production and to financing the state; in similar fashion, merchant capital became subordinate to industrial capital, taking the form of commercial capital.[107] As Jonathan Levy points out, implicit in these ideas about circuits is a conception that distinguishes property-as-capital (active/dynamic) from property-as-wealth (static). Thus, rather than seeing it as either money or a material factor of production, Levy argues, 'capital is best understood as a particular kind of economic process. Capital is property capitalized – a legal asset assigned a pecuniary value in expectation of its capacity to yield a likely future pecuniary income … Capital is always in process'.[108]

One feature common to these conceptions is the idea that capital is property of some kind (often money) that is used – 'invested' – to produce a revenue, a future pecuniary income.[109] For some, like the Austrian School economist Frank Fetter, although they overlap, capital is therefore 'not to be confused with wealth'[110]: not all objects of property, not all items of wealth, are 'invested' to generate a monetary return. The comparative lawyer Bernard Rudden makes substantially the same point, though using confusingly different terminology. For Rudden, things become wealth precisely when they are invested to generate a financial return. 'We can treat things for themselves, or we can treat them as investments', he argues. Treated for itself, a thing may be

> possessed, used, and disposed of for its own qualities … On the other hand every thing may be treated merely as the clothing (in-*vestment*)

---

[106] In *Capital*, volume 2, London: Lawrence and Wishart (1956 [1893]), Marx identifies different circuits of capital – for money capital, productive capital and commodity capital – which he uses for different analytical purposes: Part I, pp. 25-123.

[107] For Marx, unlike the historically-prior usurers capital, interest-bearing capital proper does not suppose the conditions of capitalist production. This is why 'in the popular imagination interest-bearing capital should be seen as capital par excellence and interest as the defining revenue of capital as such': Derek Sayer, *Marx's Method*, Hassocks, Sussex: Harvester Press (1979), p. 57. For an alternative view of merchant capital, see Jairus Banaji, *A Brief History of Commercial Capitalism*, Haymarket: Chicago (2019).

[108] Levy, 'Capital as Process and the History of Capitalism', pp. 487, 494–5.

[109] Thus Levy defines capital as 'legal property assigned a pecuniary value in expectation of a likely pecuniary income', ibid, p.487.

[110] Frank Fetter, 'Reformulation of the Concepts of Capital and Income in Economics and Accounting', 12 *The Accounting Review*, pp. 3–12 (1937), p. 8.

worn by a certain amount of wealth … in most legal systems things of the same type may be held by some as necessaries and by others as investments.[111]

For Fetter and Rudden, the difference between things in themselves and things as capital (or, in Rudden's terminology, things as wealth or things as investments) is function. As Rudden explains, in some contexts things are simply tangible objects that people consume to meet particular needs. In others, however, they are part of a business, resources that have been invested in a process aimed at making a profit.[112] This takes us back to the 'dual nature' of property and the distinction between property as personal possessions and property-as-capital, a distinction that itself overlaps significantly with the distinction between property that is wealth and property that is not.[113] It is when they are invested to secure pecuniary gain that things in themselves become capital, that they become property-as-capital. Thus, money, for example, only becomes 'capital' when it is 'invested' to generate a financial return – as when it is loaned out for interest, or used to buy pre-existing revenue rights (like corporate shares), or used to buy material means of production with a view to engaging in profitable productive activity.

In the eighteenth century, as capitalist social relations spread and as the credit system expanded and became more impersonal, the opportunities to 'invest' money to make more money increased.[114] With this, revenue rights grew rapidly in number and importance as financial instruments, such as bills of exchange, notes, cheques, government stock and joint stock company shares, proliferated.[115] Initially, as we have seen, these instruments tended to be classified as choses in action, as personal rights enforceable only by action rather than by taking physical possession. As such, they were conceptualised as rights personal to the parties bound by the obligation and considered, in principle, to be non-assignable.[116] Gradually, however, as a result of changes in business practice and the combined efforts of merchants, lawyers, courts

---

[111] Lawson and Rudden, *Law of Property*, p. 169; Rudden, 'Things as Thing and Things as Wealth', p. 83.
[112] Lawson and Rudden, *Law of Property*, p. 169.
[113] Rossi, 'Reconsidering the Dual Nature of Property Rights'.
[114] As early as 1710, Jonathan Swift was arguing that 'power, which, according to the old Maxim, was used to follow *Land*, is now gone over to *Money*': 13 *The Examiner* (1710, 2 November), quoted in Julian Hoppit, 'Attitudes to Credit in Britain, 1680–1790', 33 *The Historical Journal*, pp. 305–22 (1990), p. 310.
[115] As Miguel Ramirez says, things such as bills of exchange and bank notes were in many ways the derivative financial assets of this period: 'Credit, Indebtedness and Speculation in Marx's Political Economy', 8 *Economic Thought*, pp. 46–62 (2019), p. 48.
[116] Holdsworth, *A History of English Law*, volume 7, pp. 516, 543.

and legislatures, many of these choses in action came to be deemed to be legally assignable and recognised as alienable 'things'. In this way, new objects and forms of property were created (new sorts of intangible revenue rights), facilitating the accumulation of wealth in the form of claims over future productive activity. By the end of the nineteenth century and the beginning of the twentieth century, as Veblen pointed out, the substantial core of all capital had become 'immaterial'.[117] The treatment of these intangibles as corporeal was 'facilitated by the fact that their existence [was] normally attested by writing – treasury bonds, share certificates, commercial paper and so on'. They were 'brought into the physical world and recognised by their papers', either embodied in, or evidenced by, a document.[118] In recent decades, of course, as paper has been by replaced by database entries, 'things' such as shares, bonds and investment securities have been dematerialised.

Against this backdrop, it is perhaps not surprising that Veblen concluded that 'capital' was a fundamentally 'pecuniary' concept that referred to 'investments' of property aimed at securing financial returns; it was, 'invested wealth'.[119] Fetter similarly argued that 'capital is essentially an individual acquisitive, financial, investment ownership concept'. It is 'not co-extensive with wealth as physical objects, but rather with legal rights as claims to uses and incomes. It is or should be a concept relating unequivocally to private property and to the existing price system'.[120] According to Fetter, it 'impl[ied] ownership of a valuable source of income'; it was 'the market value expression of individual claims to incomes'.[121] Echoing this, Bernard Rudden has more recently argued that these 'intangible entitlements' to receive revenues 'usually have no significance beyond pecuniary value ... their primary function is to be treated as investment, as vessels into which wealth is poured and stored'.[122] And in a similar vein, Jonathan Levy has recently argued that 'capital is a legal property assigned a pecuniary value in expectation of a likely future pecuniary income'.[123] Marx labelled these intangible objects of property in the form of revenue rights 'fictitious capital' – property forms whose value is derived from a capitalisation of the revenue streams that are expected to accrue to them in

---

[117] Veblen, 'On the Nature of Capital (I)'.
[118] Rudden, 'Things as Thing and Things as Wealth', p. 86; Lawson and Rudden, *Law of Property*, p. 21.
[119] Veblen, 'On the Nature of Capital (I)'.
[120] Frank Fetter, 'Clark's Reformulation of the Capital Concept', in Fetter, *Capital, Interest and Rent*, Kansas City: Sheed Andrews & McMeel, pp. 119–142 (1977 [1927]), p. 139.
[121] Frank Fetter, 'Capital', in Edwin Seligman and Alvin Johnson (eds), *Encyclopaedia of the Social Sciences*, volume 3, New York: Macmillan, pp. 187–190 (1930), pp. 187, 189–90.
[122] Rudden, 'Things as Thing and Things as Wealth', p. 86.
[123] Levy, 'Capital as Process and the History of Capitalism', p. 487.

the future.[124] They are legal titles to the fruits of future production. Indeed, as Marx observed, with the development of the credit system and interest-bearing capital, capital acquired the ability to 'double itself, and sometimes treble itself',[125] something that has been only too evident in recent decades, with the construction by lawyers of new assets, like derivatives, traded options and other even more exotic financial instruments.

The reconceptualisation of the joint stock company share

The legal reconceptualisation of the joint stock company share provides a good example of the complex legal processes (or 'codings'[126]) through which new property forms of this sort emerged. It is clear that, by the time that Adam Smith was writing, joint stock company shares were seen by many of their holders as revenue rights rather than as shares in physical assets. The 'greater part' of joint stock company shareholders, Smith wrote, 'seldom pretend to understand anything of the business of the company', preferring instead to 'receive contentedly such half-yearly or yearly dividend as the directors think proper to make to them'.[127] Nevertheless, shareholders still tended to be treated in law as akin to (active) partners and joint stock companies to be treated as large partnerships and, as such, as aggregates of individuals. It followed that, for many years, companies, even when they were incorporated, were identified with their members/shareholders and spoken of as 'theys' and conceptualised as aggregates of individuals, rather than spoken of as 'its' and conceptualised as completely separate entities cleansed of people. In similar vein, shares in both incorporated and unincorporated joint stock companies were conceptualised not as they are today as separate pieces of property, but as equitable interests in the company's assets. Shareholders were accordingly regarded as the equitable owners of those assets.[128] This meant, among other things, that if a company owned land, its shares were seen as, in part, interests in real estate. This had significant

---

[124] Karl Marx, *Capital*, volume 3, London: Lawrence and Wishart (1959 [1894]), chapter 25. See also Rudolf Hilferding, *Finance Capital*, London: Routledge & Kegan Paul (1981 [1910]).
[125] Marx, *Capital*, volume 3, chapter 29.
[126] Pistor, *The Code of Capital*.
[127] Adam Smith, *The Wealth of Nations*, Indianapolis: Liberty Classics (eds RH Campbell et al, 1981), volume 2, pp. 740–1. The section on joint stock companies did not appear until the third edition, published in 1784.
[128] Paddy Ireland, 'Capitalism Without the Capitalist: the joint stock company share and the emergence of the modern doctrine of separate corporate personality', 17 *Journal of Legal History*, pp. 41–73 (1996).

consequences for transfers and bequests. Shares were also seen, in part, as shares in the company's contracts and, therefore, as composed, in part, of contractual benefits and burdens. As such, they were categorised as choses in action that could not, in principle, be assigned. As the court in *Duvergier v Fellows* (1828) pointed out, it was legally impossible for assignees to take the place and to assume all the rights and liabilities of assignors, for contractual burdens could not be assigned.[129] Lawyers attempted to find ways around these problems and those surrounding the partnership principle of joint and several unlimited liability, but the only sure way of overcoming them was to obtain corporate status with limited liability and have the instrument of incorporation declare the company's shares personal property and capable of transfer. The enactment of general incorporation laws eventually provided a blanket solution to these problems. Before that, however, the courts had already begun to reconceptualise the nature of joint stock company shares.[130]

The catalyst was the rise of the railways. The dramatic growth in joint stock railway companies from the 1830s saw a significant increase in the number of shares and the rapid development of the share market. This not only rendered shares much more liquid assets, more readily converted into money, but gave them a publicly visible and fluctuating market value of their own quite separate from the value of the company's assets. These developments prompted the courts to reconceptualise the nature of joint stock company shares and to formally recognise the rentier nature of most shareholding. They held that the assets of both incorporated and unincorporated companies, including any real estate they owned, were the property of 'the company' and of 'the company' alone. Shares no longer conferred on shareholders any interest, legal or equitable, in those assets.[131] They were, rather, separate objects of property – *personal* property in the form of intangible, transferable rights to profit. Shares were not, therefore, interests in real estate even if the company owned large tracts of land. Moreover, this was held to be the case even when the company was *un*incorporated and lacked separate corporate personality: the land belonged to 'the company'. In this way, *all* joint stock companies, whether incorporated or not, acquired an existence

---

[129] On the non-assignability of shares in unincorporated joint stock companies, see *Duvergier v Fellows* (1828) 5 Bing 24, per Best CJ; and John George, *A View of the Existing Law Affecting Unincorporated Joint Stock Companies*, London: McDowall (1825), pp. 18–19, 50–1.

[130] Prior to this, lawyers had sought to provide unincorporated companies with some of the benefits enjoyed by incorporated entities (like separate personality and limited liability) using a complicated mixture of various strands of law: partnership law, agency, trust and contract. As Ron Harris has explained, however, they had limited success: *Industrializing English Law*, Cambridge: Cambridge University Press (2000), pp. 137–67.

[131] This was true of both incorporated and unincorporated companies: see Ireland, 'Capitalism Without the Capitalist'.

as property-owning legal entities, quite separate from their (share-owning) shareholders. As such, they came to be referred to not, as they had previously, as 'theys' (their shareholders merged into a single entity) but as 'its' (radically separate entities cleansed of their shareholders). This laid the foundations for the development of the doctrine of separate corporate personality in its modern form.[132]

The perceived nature of shares as free-standing, separate objects of property was reinforced by the legislative introduction of general limited liability and by the development of the practice, aided and abetted by the courts and legislature, of making shares fully paid up.[133] Together, these developments eliminated any residual claims companies had over shareholders and, with the great majority of shareholders now playing no role whatsoever in management, further disconnected shareholders from the companies in which they held shares.[134] They also more or less extinguished the remaining *personam* characteristics of shares, giving them even more fully the character of liability-free, freely assignable rights *in rem* 'only contingently related to any particular person' and separable from any particular individual or owner.[135] Limited liability had become *de facto* no liability. The conditions were set for the emergence of the modern doctrine of separate corporate personality and what Gower calls the 'complete separation' of company and shareholder.[136] Even then, however, the separation was in certain crucial respects still only partial, for while company and shareholders were now *de facto* 'completely separate' for liability purposes (holders of fully paid-up shares had no residual liabilities to the company or its creditors), companies were still identified with their shareholders in that they were now conceptualised as objects of property that were 'owned' by them. It was thought to follow from this that, although companies were now completely separate legal persons, they

---

[132] Ireland, 'Capitalism Without the Capitalist'.

[133] See Paddy Ireland, 'Limited Liability, Shareholder Rights, and the Problem of Corporate Irresponsibility', 34 *Cambridge Journal of Economics*, pp 837–56 (2010).

[134] Even after the introduction of general limited liability, the connection remained as long as residual liabilities were attached to shares.

[135] Penner points out that the underlying *personam* nature of some intangible forms of property, like company shares, sometimes reasserts itself 'when things go awry' and shareholders sometimes 'launch shareholder suits' against their fellow shareholders: Penner, 'The Bundle of Rights Picture of Property', p. 813. Although by the late nineteenth century the likelihood of the *personam* origins of joint stock company shares reasserting themselves was diminishing as shares became fully paid up and residual shareholder liabilities were eliminated, this period also saw the rise of the private company whose shares were not freely transferable and whose underlying *personam* nature was, and still is, sometimes only too evident: see, for example, *Ebrahimi v Westbourne Galleries* [1973] AC 360, *O'Neill v Phillips* [1999] UKHL 24.

[136] L C B Gower, *Principles of Modern Company Law*, London: Stevens (3rd ed., 1969), p. 71.

were also objects of property that should be run in the exclusive interest of their shareholder 'owners'.[137]

In this way, corporate shareholding became the rather curious, hybrid legal phenomenon that it is today. Corporate shareholders have a 'novel status'.[138] On the one hand, they are treated by law as 'insider-owners' with residual proprietary (control and dividend) rights in companies, able to elect and dismiss directors and insist on shareholder primacy. On the other hand, they are simultaneously treated as 'outsiders' who, in certain crucial respects, resemble creditors rather than owners, having transferred ownership of their property to a separate entity (the company/corporation) and become responsibility and liability free.[139] The Janus-faced nature of the corporate share is reflected in the continuing uncertainties surrounding its precise legal nature. Some recognise the problems associated with classifying shares as property 'in the usual sense' but do so because it accords with common sense and practical reality. Thus, L C B Gower gave expression to the view that shares constitute both property and a proprietorial interest in the company. 'It is tempting to equate shares with rights under a contract', he wrote, '[but] a share is something far more than a mere contractual right *in personam*'. While it is doubtful 'whether the rights which a share confers on its holder can be classified as "proprietary" in the usual sense', it is clear that 'the share itself is an object of *dominion*, i.e. of rights *in rem* and not so to regard it would be barren and academic in the extreme'. As he says, for all practical purposes shares are recognised in law, as well as in fact, 'as objects of property which are bought, sold, mortgaged and bequeathed'.[140] Others, on the other hand, continue to question the status of shares as 'property'. Robert Pennington, for example, argued that shares are 'simply bundles of contractual and statutory rights which the shareholder has against the company'. He was aware that this underlines the shareholder's externality to the company and blurs the distinction between shareholders and debenture holders. 'It is tempting', he wrote, 'to deduce from [the contractual nature of the share] that the relationship between [shareholder] and ... company is that of creditor and debtor'. But this, he claims, is 'quite wrong'. He nevertheless showed a marked reluctance to describe the share as 'property'. The contractual rights

---

[137] See Paddy Ireland, 'Corporate Schizophrenia: the institutional origins of corporate social irresponsibility', in Nina Boeger and Charlotte Villiers (eds), *Shaping the Corporate Landscape: towards corporate reform and enterprise diversity*, Oxford: Hart, pp. 13–39 (2017).

[138] Robert Flannigan, 'Shareholder Fiduciary Accountability', *Journal of Business Law*, pp. 1–30 (2014), p. 6.

[139] The hybrid nature of shares and shareholding is discussed at length in Ireland, 'Corporate Schizophrenia'.

[140] Paul Davies, *Gower's Principles of Modern Company Law*, London: Sweet & Maxwell (6th ed., 1997), pp. 300, 400. The words are Gower's and appear in earlier editions of the book.

that make up the share, he argued, are of 'a peculiar nature' in that they are transferable, as a result of which they 'have been called "property"'. He is unable to endorse this view, but considers it 'innocuous enough, provided that it is remembered that they do not comprise any proprietary interest in the company's assets'. 'The most that may be said', he claimed, is that 'shares in a registered company … are a species of intangible movable property which comprise a collection of rights and obligations relating to an interest in a company of an economic and proprietary character, but not constituting a debt'.[141] As we shall see, these seemingly rather arid, academic debates potentially have quite considerable political significance.

---

[141] Robert Pennington, *Company Law*, London: Butterworths (6th ed., 1990), pp. 56–7, 135–6; Robert Pennington, 'Can Shares in Companies be Defined?', 10 *Company Lawyer*, pp. 144–52 (1989). See also Arianna Pretto-Sakmann, *Boundaries of Personal Property: shares and sub-shares*, Oxford: Hart (2005), arguing that 'property' should be more narrowly defined so as to exclude shares. 'When the law of personal property is defined in its strict sense, in contrast with the law of obligations, shares and sub-shares are not property … they lie in the law of obligations': p. 209. Sakmann sees shares as 'stores of wealth'.

4

Profiting from the Efforts of Others

Capital and investment

Capital is more than just property that has been invested to secure a financial gain. It has a second key defining characteristic. This characteristic was captured and highlighted by the US Supreme Court in the case of *Securities and Exchange Commission v W J Howey Co.* in 1946. The question before the court was whether a particular instrument constituted an 'investment contract' for the purposes of federal securities law. The court held that the test was whether it 'involve[d] an investment of money in a common enterprise *with profits to come solely from the efforts of others*'.[1] In reaching this conclusion, the court was confirming the approach of earlier courts that had similarly defined investment as 'the entrusting of money or other capital to another, with the expectation of deriving a profit or income therefrom, to be created through the efforts of others'.[2] The *Howey* test, as it has come to be called, has since been refined a little – the courts have, for example, adopted a more relaxed standard for the derivation of profits by omitting the word 'solely' from the test[3] – but it remains good law.[4] It was reaffirmed by the Supreme Court in *United Housing Foundation v Forman* in 1975[5] and remains central to determining whether a particular financial arrangement constitutes an investment contract and qualifies as a 'security' for the purposes of the Securities Act 1933.[6] The *Howey*

---

[1] *Securities and Exchange Commission v W J Howey Co.* 328 US 293 (1946), per Murphy J, delivering the majority opinion, emphasis added.
[2] *SEC v Bailey*, 41 F.Supp. 647, 650 (S.D. Fla 1941).
[3] *United Housing Foundation Inc. v Forman*, 421 US 837 (1975).
[4] According to Miriam Albert, it has 'arguably ... taken on a quasi-statutory aura': 'The *Howey* Test Turns 64', 2 *William & Mary Business Law Review*, p. 1 (2011), p. 10.
[5] *United Housing Foundation Inc. v Forman*, 421 US 837 (1975).
[6] See Christopher Borsani, 'A "Common" Problem: explaining the need for common ground in the "common enterprise" element of the *Howey* test', 10 *Duquesne Business Law Journal*, pp. 1-17 (2008). The term 'security' is used to cover financial instruments

test is consonant with the US courts' view that 'it is the passive investor for whose benefit the securities laws were enacted'.[7] The *Howey* test for investment is descriptive and factual in nature, though it clearly raises ethical and normative questions.

In its focus on pecuniary returns that come 'from the efforts of others', there are echoes in *Howey* of Veblen's linking of 'investment' with 'absentee ownership' and the extraction of what he called 'unearned incomes'. Veblen observed that more and more property in capitalist societies took the form of claims on revenues produced in large part by the labour and ingenuity of others, hence his assertion that 'the gains of investment are drawn from the aggregate material productivity of the community's industry'.[8] For Veblen, production in modern capitalism had become a fundamentally social process, but one in which much of the resulting 'collective social wealth'[9] was appropriated by a predatory minority, by 'absentee owners' and 'vested interests' not in useful employment.[10] This relatively small, wealthy, parasitical 'leisure class', he argued, gained pecuniary advantage – as well as status, prestige and power – by feeding off the efforts of the 'common man' and the collective technological knowledge of the community, what Veblen called 'the state of the industrial arts'.[11] According to Veblen, they extracted 'unearned incomes' and got 'something for nothing'. This led him to conclude that 'the relation of the leisure (that is propertied nonindustrial) class to the economic process is a pecuniary relation – a relation of acquisition, not of production; of exploitation, not of serviceability'. 'The immediate end of this pecuniary institutional structure ... [was] the greater facility of peaceable and orderly exploitation'.[12]

There are also echoes of both Proudhon and Marx in *Howey*. In 1861, Proudhon defined capitalism as an 'economic and social regime in which

---

that can be traded. In this context, a distinction is often made between equity securities (corporate shares); debt securities (bonds, promissory notes, treasury securities etc.); and derivatives (like options and futures).

[7] *US v Leonard* (2008) 529 F.3d 83 (2d Cir. 2008). See also https://news.law.fordham.edu/jcfl/2020/01/05/when-they-howey-we-all-howey/.

[8] Veblen, 'On the Nature of Capital (II)', p. 106.

[9] On Veblen's theory of collective social wealth, see Philip Anthony O'Hara, 'Thorstein Veblen's Theory of Collective Social Wealth', 7 *History of Economic Ideas*, p. 153 (1999).

[10] Thorstein Veblen, *Absentee Ownership*, New York: Huebsch (1923); Thorstein Velen, *The Vested Interests and the Common Man*, New York, Huebsch (1919).

[11] Thorstein Veblen, *The Theory of the Leisure Class*, New York: Macmillan (1899); Thorstein Veblen, *The Instinct of Workmanship and the State of the Industrial Arts*, New York: Macmillan (1914).

[12] Veblen, *The Theory of the Leisure Class*, pp. 143–4. More generally, Veblen lamented the growing domination of production (industry) by finance (business): *The Theory of Business Enterprise*, New York: Scribner (1904).

capital, the source of income, does not generally belong to those who make it work through their labor'.[13] For Marx too the revenues accruing to capital from 'investment' were ultimately derived from 'the efforts of others': from the 'surplus value' created by unpaid labour.[14] Contrary to appearances and the claims of 'vulgar economics',[15] Marx argued, (property-as-)capital, whether money or means of production, did not have the intrinsic ability to generate financial returns. It only acquired this ability where certain social (and class) relations prevailed. In the final chapter of *Capital* he illustrated this point by recounting Edward Gibbon Wakefield's explanation of the failure of the Swan River colony in Western Australia. Wakefield, an entrepreneur and advocate of settler colonialism, sought to understand why the founder of the abortive colony, Thomas Peel, had not succeeded despite having 'all the elements of success – a fine climate, plenty of good land, plenty of capital and enough labourers'. The explanation, Wakefield said, was 'easy'. Although Peel had taken with him 'a capital of £50,000 and three hundred persons of the labouring class, men, women and children', as soon as the labourers reached the colony 'they were tempted by the superabundance of good land to become land-owners'. Abandoned in this way, Peel was left 'without servants' and 'without servants his capital perished'.[16] Marx argued that Wakefield had 'discovered in the colonies the truth of capitalist production' that 'property in money, means of subsistence, machines, and other means of production, does not yet stamp a man as a capitalist if there be wanting the correlative – the wage worker'. Peel was unable to turn his property into revenue-generating, functioning capital because the labourers he had taken with him, having acquired access to land themselves, had no need or desire to become wage labourers – making it impossible for him to 'profit from the efforts of others'. 'Unhappy Mr Peel', Marx wrote, had

---

[13] Braudel, *The Wheels of Commerce*, p. 237.

[14] The idea in the *Howey* test that the profits captured by 'investments' come from the 'efforts of others' does not require adherence to the labour theory of value of Smith and Ricardo or the law of value of Marx. For Marx, the operation of the law of value, far from being transhistorical, operates only when the capitalist mode of production has conquered all spheres of production: see John Weeks, *Capital and Exploitation*, Princeton: Princeton University Press (1981).

[15] 'Vulgar economics' was the term Marx used to describe the economic theories that rose to dominance after the disintegration of the Ricardian school in the 1830s. These theories rejected the idea that there was an inevitable opposition between wages and profits, arguing instead that the market ensured that the social product was fairly and harmoniously distributed to different 'factors of production'.

[16] Edward Gibbon Wakefield, 'England and America', in M F Lloyd Pritchard (ed.), *Collected Works*, Glasgow: Collins, pp. 313–718 (1968), p. 482. See also Gabriel Piterberg and Lorenzo Veracini, 'Wakefield, Marx and the World Turned Inside Out', 10 *Journal of Global History*, pp. 457–78 (2015).

'provided for everything except the export of English modes of production to Swan River!'.[17] For Marx, this demonstrated that property – whether money, machines or equipment – could only function as capital under certain social conditions and within certain social relations. 'A cotton-spinning jenny is a machine for spinning cotton. It becomes *capital* only in certain relations. Torn from these relationships it is no more capital than gold itself is *money*'.[18] Capital requires wage labour as a correlative. This led him to conclude that 'capital is not a thing, but a social relation between persons, established by the instrumentality of things'.[19] It was 'a definite social relation, belonging to a definite historical formation of society'.[20]

For Marx, (property-as-)capital's seeming ability to generate a pecuniary return in and of itself, independently of 'the efforts of others', was an example of 'fetishism', the process whereby the qualities phenomena acquire only in specific contexts where specific social relations prevail appear instead to inhere in them.[21] Under capitalism, he argued, where social relations are mediated by the market, capital acquires the seemingly innate ability to yield a financial return through 'investment'. In this regard, the 'most fetish-like' form of capital was, for Marx, money- or interest-bearing capital, for as money acquires the universal capacity to yield interest, it seems to have the inherent ability to generate a financial return independently not only of labour and the efforts of others, but independently of production itself. 'It becomes a property of money', Marx argued, 'to generate value and yield interest, much as it is an attribute of pear-trees to bear pears'.[22] While it was

---

[17] Marx, *Capital*, volume 1, London: Lawrence and Wishart (1954 [1867]), p. 717.
[18] Marx, *Wage Labour and Capital*, Moscow: Progress (1974 [1847]), p. 28.
[19] Marx, *Capital*, volume 1, p. 717. Hodgson quips that Marx was 'quipping' when he said this, but this is clearly not the case: Geoffrey Hodgson, 'What is Capital?', 38 *Cambridge Journal of Economics*, pp. 1063-86 (2014), p. 1066.
[20] Marx, *Capital*, volume 3, London: Lawrence and Wishart (1959 [1894]), pp. 814–5.
[21] Marx borrowed the term 'fetishism' from an eighteenth-century essay: Charles de Brosses, *The Cult of Fetish Gods* (1760). He considered capitalism to be permeated by fetishisms: see Dimitri Dimoulis and John Milios, 'Commodity Fetishism vs Capital Fetishism', 12 *Historical Materialism*, pp. 3–42 (2004). In the famous section of *Capital* on commodities, Marx referred to '*Der Fetischcharakter der Ware und sein Geheimnis*' (the fetish-like character of commodities and its secret), which has come to be translated into 'commodity fetishism'. Keston Sutherland suggests that this has encouraged people to elevate this section into a theoretical statement rather than a rather satirical and stylish comment: Sutherland, 'Marx in Jargon', http://worldpicturejournal.com/article/marx-in-jargon/.
[22] Marx, *Capital*, volume 3, p. 392. See also Sayer, *Marx's Method*, pp. 48, 56–60. Many earlier writers alluded to this when they suggested that money – lacking, as Bentham later observed, genitals ('organs for generating any other such piece') – was sterile and barren, and inherently *unproductive*: See Aristotle, *Politics*, I, 8–10; *Nicomachean Ethics*, V, 5. Jeremy Bentham, *Defence of Usury* (1787), in *The Works of Jeremy Bentham*, volume

indeed true that, from the perspective of the individual capitalist, capital seems to be able to make more money independently of its productive employment, this was not true for capital as a whole ('total social capital').[23] As the court in *Howey* recognised, the ability to generate a financial return is not a quality inherent in money but is dependent on 'the efforts of others'.

Profiting from the ownership of productive resources

There are many different ways – a range of different processes through which – owners of property-as-capital can profit from the efforts of others. Most obviously, they can do it through the possession of private property rights in and over productive resources. These are major sources of power and, more specifically, of appropriative power. Owners of productive resources, armed with their state-backed right to exclude, can decide how those resources will be used, where they will be used, who will be granted access to them, on what conditions and so on. In contemporary capitalism, of course, many of these resources, tangible and intangible, are now owned by corporations or, more accurately, by large multi-national enterprises composed of groups of inter-connected corporations. Many other firms lie within their sphere of influence and control by virtue of the power these enterprises are able to wield over the smaller firms in their supply chains. It is because of the power derived from private property rights in productive resources that the philosopher Elizabeth Anderson describes contemporary American workplaces as hierarchical 'communist dictatorships' – in the totalitarian, Stalinist sense of the word – composed of dictators (chief executives), superiors (managers) and subordinates (workers). 'The economic system of the modern workplace', she writes, 'is communist, because the government – that is, the establishment – owns all the assets, and the top of the establishment hierarchy designs the production plan, which subordinates execute … Most workers in the United States are governed by communist dictatorships in their work lives'.[24] As both she and Robé point out, the architects of the liberal order of property did not envisage this. They imagined an economic regime characterised by free and equal, self-governing, individual property owners

---

3, New York: Russell & Russell (1962), p. 16. See also Judith Schenck Koffler, 'Capital in Hell: Dante's lessons on usury', 32 *Rutgers Law Review*, pp. 609–60 (1979).

[23] The fetish suggests that if everyone accumulated enough money capital yielding interest, they could subsist without working. This underlies the idea that if everyone saved enough and invested, they would have no need to rely on others (and their labour) on retirement: See Paddy Ireland, 'Law and the Neoliberal Vision: financial property, pension privatization and the ownership society', 62 *Northern Ireland Legal Quarterly*, pp. 1–32 (2011).

[24] Anderson, *Private Government*, p. 39.

and by dispersed power, not one in which economic power was concentrated in the hands of large multi-national enterprises. They anticipated 'economic liberalism ... not corporate capitalism', 'a free society of equals through free markets via near-universal self-employment'. 'The ideal of a free market society', Anderson points out, 'used to be a cause of ... egalitarian thinkers and participants in egalitarian social movements, starting with the Levellers in the mid-seventeenth century, continuing through the Enlightenment, the American and French Revolutions and the pre-Marxist radicals of the late eighteenth and early nineteenth centuries'.[25] They did not envisage an empirical reality in which decision-making power over key productive resources has become ever more concentrated in large enterprises with the power 'to regulate the use of things without deliberations' and to create enterprise-based 'private legal orders' and 'private governmental structures' that 'rule the activities of those falling under their jurisdiction'.[26] Whatever the merits of the liberal order of property, and it still has many defenders, 'it has been grossly invalidated by the advent of corporate capitalism.' The latter has fundamentally altered the nature and operation of the power system. So much power over productive resources is now concentrated in these enterprises that 'the whole liberal construction is in total disconnect with the realities of the existing World Power System'.[27]

The power that flows from the possession of private property rights, particularly in productive resources, leads Robé to offer an alternative formulation of the bundle of rights conception of property. Robé is sympathetic to its general thrust, but argues that it risks misrepresenting how property operates in the real world. In reality, he says, the right of the owner to do what he or she likes with their property is the rule: 'As a matter of principle, owners rule', setting the rules to be followed by others when they use their property. This is 'particularly the case for productive assets'. What is limited at any point in time is 'not the set of prerogatives, the bundle of *rights*', but 'the set of limitations to the right of property [and] to the autonomy it entails'. 'The autonomy of the owner' – very often meaning, in contemporary capitalism, the autonomy of the large enterprises that dominate economic life – 'is *the rule*' and the limitations placed on this autonomy by law or other political interventions 'are *the exceptions*'. Robé concludes that 'property *is a right as a matter of principle with "bundles of limits"*', bundles of exceptions'. Property is a default rule, installing the owner as the person who, in principle, decides how resources should be used.[28] In

---

[25] Robé, 'Taming Property', p. 166; Robé, 'Taming Property', chapter 6; Anderson, *Private Government*, pp. 1, 36.
[26] Robé, 'Taming Property', pp. 164–6.
[27] Robé, 'Taming Property', p. 167.
[28] Robé, 'Taming Property', p. 162 (his emphases).

the corporate context, the ownership of so many key productive resources by large multi-national enterprises is a major source of economic, political and social power. The main financial beneficiaries (apart from highly paid corporate executives) are corporate shareholders and bondholders, the owners of revenue rights that enable them to profit from the efforts of others. As we shall shortly see, ownership of these revenue rights is very heavily concentrated among the very wealthy.

Crucially, of course, private property rights in and over productive resources are a source of significant power not only over the resources themselves but over other people. 'The extent of the power over the life of others which the legal order confers on those called owners', Morris Cohen argued, 'is not fully appreciated by those who think of the law as merely protecting men in their possession'. This is because 'property law does more. It determines what men shall acquire'. Thus, for example, 'protecting the property rights of a landlord means giving him the right to collect rent, protecting the property of a railroad or a public service corporation means giving it the right to make certain charges'. Thus, 'the ownership of land and machinery, with the rights of drawing rent, interest, etc. determines the future distribution of the goods that will come into being – determines what share of such goods various individuals shall acquire'.[29] The power granted over others by ownership of key resources – and over the future social product – is particularly significant when ownership of those resources is highly concentrated. Historically, one of the reasons land enclosures were so economically and socially significant was that, by turning more and more land into absolute private property and concentrating ownership, they denied labouring people access to a key productive resource and to the means of subsistence. Increasingly, they were compelled to pay for access to land by renting or to sell their labour for a wage on terms and conditions dictated largely by resource owners. Either way, they became subject to the imperatives of the market. In contemporary capitalism, as Robé says, the concentration of the ownership of productive resources in large enterprises is a major producer of heteronomy for individuals, society, the state system, and the natural environment.[30] It is the relationships of power and dependence that result from so many people being 'propertyless' – in the sense of not owning means of production – that enable the owners of key productive resources to appropriate part of the product of their labour. 'Exclude[d] … from exploiting those resources for their own benefit', wrote Leslie White, 'the non-owning class or classes … can live only by working the resources of the owners, in the course of which the owners receive a portion of the

---

[29] Cohen, 'Property and Sovereignty', p. 13.
[30] Robé, 'Taming Property', pp. 164–6.

product … one class owns but does not work; another class works but does not own'.[31] The ownership concentration of so many key productive resources in private hands is also a problem for society as a whole, for the owners of these resources will only mobilise them for productive activity – or allow them to be mobilised by others – when it is profitable for them to do so. For states, creating a favourable 'climate for investment' has become an imperative.

Against this backdrop it is worth briefly considering John Locke's celebrated theory of property. Locke argued that God had given the world to 'men in common', but quickly defused the potential radicalism of this view by arguing that God had not given the Earth to men in common for them to waste but had given it to the 'industrious and rational' for the sake of 'improvement'.[32] For this reason Locke favoured the elimination of the use rights over land possessed by the labouring classes in favour of exclusive private property. Use rights over land were inconvenient restrictions on landowners that stood in the way of 'improvement'. For Locke, improvement justified not only enclosure at home but the appropriation of land by colonial settlers abroad without the consent of indigenous peoples who very often defined their relationship to the land quite differently.[33] Unused or unimproved common land was 'waste' and those who removed it from the commons and took it into private ownership to improve it had given something to humanity, not taken something away.[34] Understandably, this justification of enclosure and colonial appropriation appealed greatly both to landowners and colonial settlers. Locke famously further argued, using the idea of 'self-propriety', that 'Every Man has a *Property* in his own person' and in anything with which he has 'mixed his labour'. As his use of 'man' in this context suggests, Locke's self-owners were men and, indeed, men of a certain class and colour; they were not women, servants, agricultural labourers or slaves. For Locke, private property was, therefore, the just reward for labour. Significantly, he added that 'masters' had property rights in the things with which their 'servants' had 'mixed' their labour. In master–servant relationships, therefore, which for Locke encompassed what we would now call employment relations, some created wealth for others by working for them.[35]

---

[31] White, *The Evolution of Culture*, p. 252.
[32] John Locke, *Two Treatises of Government*, II, paras 25–51 (1689). For an account of how Locke's theory tried to plot a path between Leveller radicalism and Tory absolutism, see Ellen Meiksins Wood, *The Ellen Meiksins Wood Reader*, London: Brill (ed Larry Patriquin, 2012) pp. 172–8.
[33] At the time he was writing, there were quite fierce debates about colonialism and the appropriation of land. Locke held various offices linked to colonial administration.
[34] Locke, *Two Treatises of Government*, paras 25–51.
[35] Slavery, of course, was the most extreme example of this. Locke, who owned stock in slave trading companies, justified slavery on the grounds that a man who lost his liberty by

The exploitation of wage-labour is just one of the ways in which the owners of property-as-capital are able to benefit 'from the efforts of others'. Even when resource owners do not directly exploit wage-labour, they can levy charges in return for granting access to the resources they own. Intellectual property rights, for example, have become a key source of corporate income and dividends. Intellectual property rights (IPRs) holders, with their temporary monopoly rights over ideas, knowledge and other cultural artefacts, are often able to charge inflated prices for the commodities produced using their intellectual property (IP): the charges levied by pharmaceutical companies for drugs is probably the best-known example here.[36] Alternatively, they can charge licence fees for the use of the IP. In other situations, IP enables its owners to collect royalties. In these different ways, they are able secure in money form part of 'the efforts of others' and turn their IPRs into saleable rights to future revenue streams. Owners of land and buildings can do likewise by charging rents. 'I do not directly serve my landlord if I wish to live in the city with a roof over my head', Morris Cohen explained, 'but I must work for others to pay him rent'. The money needed for rent payments and for purchasing other things 'must for the vast majority be acquired by hard labor and ... service to those to whom the law has accorded dominion over the things necessary for subsistence'.[37] As has been well documented, recent decades in the UK have seen the rapid growth of the private rented sector and buy-to-lets.[38] More generally, and more recently, there has been a growing effort to turn residential housing into a safe asset class for institutional investors seeking secure investment outlets offering good yields. Ownership of residential housing by institutional landlords – from private equity firms like Blackstone, the world's largest institutional landlord, to real estate firms like Vonovia – has grown across Europe. This development has been actively encouraged by states and by European legislation aimed at facilitating the creation of housing as an asset class and at derisking it as an investment (more on this later).[39] The result is that more and more people are giving up part of the product of their labour to private landlords.

---

conquest in a lawful war may be spared his life in exchange for permanent servitude: see Ellen Meiksins Wood and Neal Wood, *A Trumpet of Sedition*, London: Pluto (1997), p. 125.

[36] https://www.theguardian.com/business/2021/jul/15/uk-drug-companies-fined-260m-overcharging-nhs.

[37] Cohen, 'Property and Sovereignty', p. 12.

[38] https://sevencapital.com/property-news/the-incredible-growth-of-the-private-rented-sector/.

[39] See Daniela Gabor and Sebastian Kohl, *My Home is an Asset Class*, Greens/EFA (January 2022), https://www.greens-efa.eu/en/article/document/my-home-is-an-asset-class. As Gabor and Kohl document, while these developments have done little to increase housing

The rise of 'rentierism'

Turning key productive resources into private property is, of course, far from being a purely historical phenomenon. Land enclosures continue to take place around the world, from straightforward uncompensated fencing of land to so-called 'land grabs' involving large-scale land acquisitions by corporations, states and individuals. Although most associated perhaps with the less-developed world, in Britain one of the biggest privatisations of recent decades has been the privatisation of public land. Brett Christophers calculates that, since the advent of Margaret Thatcher's government, an eye-watering two million hectares of public land, meaning land held by local and central government, has been privatised – around 10 per cent of the entire British land mass.[40] This important dimension of privatisation has gone largely unnoticed.

More publicly prominent has been the privatisation of more and more previously state-owned public utilities. Since the 1980s privatisation has become a worldwide phenomenon. In the UK, after modest beginnings that saw the partial privatisation of large public sector companies like British Aerospace and Cable & Wireless, the 1980s saw a wave of privatisations: Jaguar, British Telecom, British Gas, British Steel, British Petroleum, Rolls Royce, British Airways. This was followed by the privatisation of major public utilities like water, electricity and rail. New Labour continued the privatisation agenda in a modified form with its private finance initiative (PFI), which morphed into the idea of public–private partnerships. All these different forms of privatisation and part-privatisation have opened up new opportunities for corporations to acquire key productive assets and for investors to 'profit from the efforts of others' through ownership of rights to future revenues. This has generated what Brett Christophers has referred to as 'infrastructure rentierism', a form of monopoly capitalism that is about 'service delivery' or, 'more exactly, about the infrastructure of service delivery and control of that infrastructure'. 'In all cases of infrastructure rentierism', he argues, 'the infrastructure is indispensable to the delivery of the service, and the controller is compensated accordingly'.[41] State subsidies are also common in these spheres.

The private ownership and control of knowledge and data – the enclosure of ideas, knowledge and innovations to create monopolies in the form of

---

supply, they have inflated house prices and created major housing affordability issues across Europe's cities, and exacerbated over-crowding and increased the burden of housing costs.

[40] Brett Christophers, *The New Enclosure: the appropriation of public land in neoliberal Britain*, London: Verso (2018). The sell-offs have been greatest under Tory and Tory-led administrations, but they did not stop under New Labour.

[41] Brett Christophers, *Rentier Capitalism*, London: Verso (2020), pp. 281, 284.

IP – has also become an increasingly important source of pecuniary returns in contemporary global capitalism.[42] Recent decades have seen the creation of numerous new objects of IP,[43] a development that has highlighted the ability of states to not only transfer ownership of existing resources from public to private bodies, but create entirely new property, and, through this, to empower some by excluding others. Intangible IP has become a major source of financial returns, particularly in the pharmaceutical and digital industries. The main instigators of this expansion of IPRs have, of course, been multinationals who, often in the face of fierce opposition, have aggressively sought to extend ownership to more and more products of the mind – ideas, inventions, artistic creations, data sets and knowledge, including, in the case of biopiracy, the traditional knowledge of other cultures. More recently, they have targeted parts of nature: micro-organisms, gene sequences and the like.[44] By allowing the patenting of some living organisms, law has made it possible for genetically modified plants and animals to be privately owned, thereby commodifying parts of life itself. Once again, the goal is to redraw the boundaries between private property and the public domain and to create artificial monopolies in non-rival goods that are not depleted by use.[45] As Kevin Gray has pointed out, this highlights that the limits to property are 'not [fixed] by the "thinglikeness" of particular resources but by the physical, legal and moral criteria of excludability'.[46] Aided by states and international agencies, corporations have gradually developed a formidable legal arsenal to protect their IPRs.

By turning these things into IP, corporations can, of course, exclude others from them and not only use them productively themselves but use them to extract revenues in return for permissions to use. Indeed, the growing importance of IP and other forms of rent-generating assets to money-making, and the distinctiveness of the pecuniary returns they generate from those derived from the kind of productive activities (and surplus value extraction) traditionally associated with capitalism, has led some to argue that we have

---

[42] See Cecilia Rikap, *Capitalism, Power and Innovation*, London: Routledge (2021).
[43] See Pistor, *The Code of Capital*, chapter 5.
[44] In 2013, in *Association for Molecular Pathology v Myriad Genetics Inc.*, 569 US 576, the US Supreme Court had to decide whether unaltered human genes could be patented. On rather narrow and qualified grounds, the court answered that they could not. In essence, the US Supreme Court has deemed that the isolation of unaltered DNA sequences is not patentable, but altering DNA into forms that do not exactly occur in nature is. The US Patent Office has been quite liberally granting patents to gene sequences for some years: see Pistor, *The Code of Capital*, pp. 110–13.
[45] From a free market perspective, of course, this is somewhat paradoxical: IPRs create monopolies in non-rival goods whose utility is not diminished by sharing. Rather than fostering free markets, they enhance market power.
[46] Gray, 'Property in Thin Air', p. 299.

moved towards a new form of what Christophers has called 'rentier capitalism' in which rent – 'the payment to an economic actor (the rentier) who receives that rent ... *purely by virtue of controlling something valuable*' under conditions of limited or no competition – has become the dominant mode of money-making.[47] The 'something', Christophers explains, 'whatever it happens to be, is referred to as an 'asset' that is valuable 'precisely because of the fact that control over it endows the owner with the capacity to generate future income'. Rentier assets are 'as varied as rentiers themselves', he argues: some, like real estate, telecommunications infrastructure and digital platforms, have a physical existence; others, like IPRs, do not.[48]

The suggestion is that rentierism has ceased to be the residual, marginal phenomenon that it was in Marx's, or even Keynes', day and has moved closer to the centre of the stage. 'Rentier capitalism' is characterised by incomes derived from the extraction rather than the creation of value, from predation rather than innovation. It is 'pervaded by a proprietorial rather than an entrepreneurial ethos' and, it is argued, has a built-in tendency towards stagnation because rentiers are inclined to sit on and sweat their income-generating assets rather than innovate.[49] Indeed, some see in these developments the emergence of a new economic regime. The argument is that the emergence of an increasingly digitalised economy and the rise of intangibles is fostering not only a new regime based on rent extraction and predation but one with feudal or neo-feudal characteristics. Thus, for Yanis Varoufakis the growing power possessed by the owners of IP – and, in particular, the privatisation of the internet – has seen the replacement of capitalism by a new 'technofeudal' economic system in which rent charging, rather than material production, has become the main way of profiting from the efforts of others.[50] Cedric Durand has made not dissimilar arguments[51] and Robert Brenner has also suggested that certain features of contemporary capitalism bear some resemblance to its feudal predecessor.[52] Others, however,

---

[47] Christophers, *The New Enclosure*, pp. xvi, xxvi.
[48] Christophers, *The New Enclosure*, pp. xvi–xvii, xxvi–xxvii.
[49] Christophers, *The New Enclosure*, pp. xx–xxxvi. Evgeny Morozov has pointed out, however, that many of the tech giants invest heavily in research and development: Morozov, 'Critique of Techno-Feudal Reason', *New Left Review*, pp. 133–4 (January–April 2022).
[50] Yanis Varoufakis, *Technofeudalism: what killed capitalism*, London: Bodley Head (2022). See also Mariana Mazzucato, 'Preventing Digital Feudalism', *Project Syndicate*, 2/10/19, https://www.project-syndicate.org/commentary/platform-economy-digital-feudalism.
[51] Cedric Durand, *Techno-féodalisme*, Paris: Zones (2020).
[52] Brenner, 'From Capitalism to Feudalism? Predation, decline and the transformation of US politics', lecture delivered at University of Massachusetts, 27/4/21, https://www.youtube.com/watch?v=ZMDF3Hk9B1o. Some of the arguments that have been made seem to be founded in a conception of capitalism rooted in industrial production, in which context it is worth recalling that the term 'capital' originally emerged to describe money

take a different view. They see recent developments as marking a move not towards something other than capitalism but towards the apotheosis of capitalism, towards capitalism par excellence. What has emerged, Maurizio Lazzarato suggests, is, in fact, a truer representation of capital and capitalism. Harking back to the pre-Smithian monetary conception of 'capital' that prevailed from around the fourteenth century – capital as money, the principal of a debt or the money invested in a business – Lazzarato argues that we need to detach the idea of 'capital' from any necessary connection to physical things and any direct link to production and to industrial production in particular. The 'concept of capital becomes a reality not with industrial capital but with finance capital'. His argument is that, until the 1960s, production and profit was the dominant way capital secured a pecuniary return, but in the late 1970s and early 1980s there was 'a decisive strategic shift' that saw seeking pecuniary returns from productive activity subordinated to 'the hegemony of financial rent and taxation'. For Lazzarato, it is capital in these financial forms that 'constitutes the form most appropriate to the concept of "capital"' because it is 'radically indifferent' to the source of its pecuniary returns.[53] This view of the nature of capital broadly accords with that of Hodgson, for whom capital is, in essence, money.[54]

The new enclosures

Because of the analogies with earlier land enclosures, some have dubbed some of these developments a 'second enclosure movement' in which private property rights have been extended not only to public utilities but into the intangible commons, into 'the world of the public domain, the world of expression and invention'. These new enclosures have introduced private property rights 'over subject matter – such as unoriginal compilations of facts, ideas about doing business, or gene sequences – that were previously [thought] to be outside the property system' because they were considered to be either uncommodifiable or part of the commons.[55] Among other things, these developments have rendered more and more key resources much less readily subject to collective community regulation. Thirty years

---

or a stock of goods used to make more money. For a critical discussion of this 'feudalist' turn, see Morozov, 'Critique of Techno-Feudal Reason'.

[53] Maurizio Lazzarato, *Governing by Debt*, Cambridge: MIT Press (2015), pp. 29–30, 141.

[54] 'Capital is money or the realizable value money-value of owned and collaterizable property': Hodgson, 'Conceptualising Capitalism: a summary', 20 *Competition and Change*, pp. 37–52 (2016), pp. 45–6.

[55] James Boyle, 'Enclosing the Genome: what the squabbles over genetic patents could teach us', in Herman Tavani (ed.), *Ethics, Computing and Genomics*, Sudbury: Jones & Bartlett, pp. 255–78 (2005).

ago, Kevin Gray argued that 'the role of property is not simply to guarantee the private ownership of certain goods, but also to stop others more powerful than ourselves from propertising all the goods of life and thereby precluding general access'. This, he suggested, was 'the greatest challenge and the greatest danger confronting the law of property in the twenty-first century'.[56] It is a challenge that has not been met. These new enclosures have seen the range of resources over which private property rights are claimed and from which profits are extracted venture into new territory. It is unsurprising, therefore, that they have had significant distributional consequences. As Charles Reich observed in the early 1990s, the creation of 'new property' has been deployed 'more and more openly as a way for one group to enrich itself at the expense of others … [it] is a powerful way to redistribute wealth, often upward'.[57]

The arguments made in support of these extensions of private property rights echo those made in both Locke's and Blackstone's time. It is claimed that the conversion of resources into private property and the extension of the reach of market mechanisms, coupled with strong protection for property rights and minimal state interference in the operation of markets, fosters economic development and growth by ensuring the efficient allocation of resources.[58] As many, most notably perhaps Ha-Joon Chang, have pointed out, however, this path to development, promoted by international financial institutions such as the International Monetary Fund and the World Bank, is not the path that was followed by major developed countries such as the US and the UK. On the contrary, as Chang points out, they used interventionist and protectionist policies to get rich before 'kicking away the ladder' to try to prevent others from following in their footsteps.[59] A lack of respect for IPRs, especially those of foreigners, also seems to have aided development.[60] It is, of course, argued that well-protected IPRs create incentives for investment in the innovatory research and development which

---

[56] Gray, 'Property in Thin Air', p. 305.
[57] Charles Reich, 'The New Property after 25 Years', 24 *University of San Francisco Law Review*, pp. 223–72 (1989–90), p. 224.
[58] Some fervent law-and-economics scholars even seemed to suggest that we should consider creating markets in babies for adoption: Elizabeth Landes and Richard Posner, 'The Economics of the Baby Shortage', 7 *Journal of Legal Studies*, pp. 323–48 (1976). Posner, worrying that the original article had been used to show the excesses to which law-and-economics scholars would go with their mechanistic analyses, later sought to show that it had been misinterpreted: Posner, 'The Regulation of the Market in Adoptions', 67 *Boston University Law Review*, pp. 59–72 (1987).
[59] Ha-Joon Chang, *Kicking Away the Ladder*, London: Anthem (2003).
[60] See Chang's comments about his youth in South Korea: *Bad Samaritans*, New York: Random House (2007), p. 11; Chang, ibid, pp. 84–5.

is central to the discovery of new socially beneficial technologies.[61] While there is no doubt that constructing property rights structures that create appropriate incentives is important, it is a mistake to assume that all creative behaviour is motivated by highly individualised, profit-driven, rational self-interest. Indeed, there is considerable evidence that, in many contexts, the commodification of knowledge through patents serves to inhibit rather than encourage investment and innovation.[62] Moreover, as many have noted, while innovation does sometimes depend on bold individual entrepreneurship and private investment, much key innovatory scientific research is publicly funded and takes place in institutions like universities. Knowledge generated by publicly-funded research and open-source collaborations is transformed into privately owned intangible assets; the commons is, in effect, privatised and then harvested.[63] With pharmaceuticals, for example, the biggest risks, particularly in the earliest and financially riskiest stages of drug development, are often taken by the state not by the private sector.[64] It is difficult to escape the conclusion that the extension of IPRs is often the product not so much of legitimate attempts to maintain much-needed incentives but of the political power of vested corporate interests.

Profiting from debt

Many other revenue rights are based not on ownership of productive resources but on debt. Debt comes in many different shapes and sizes. Sometimes, it is based on 'unfree' labour relations, such as debt bondage, and involves people providing labour services to pay off debts that in many cases are unlikely ever fully to be repaid. Forced labour of various kinds is also the defining characteristic of indentured servitude and peonage and other forms of so-called 'modern slavery'. More often, however, debt simply involves the payment of interest by one person

---

[61] It has also been argued that turning resources into private property prevents the over-use of resources associated with the so-called 'tragedy of the commons', though this has been challenged by Elinor Ostrom and others and, in any case, such arguments have no application to IP, which is not diminished by use.

[62] See, for example, Ugo Pagano, 'The Crisis of Intellectual Monopoly Capitalism', 38 *Cambridge Journal of Economics*, pp. 1409–29 (2014).

[63] See Rikap, *Capitalism, Power and Innovation*.

[64] See, for example, Mariana Mazzucato, *The Entrepreneurial State*, New York: Anthem (2013); See also Pistor, *The Code of Capital*, pp. 108–15. Pistor points out that the breakthrough underlying the discovery of the breast cancer gene that Myriad Genetics were seeking to patent in a case that came to the US Supreme Court was 'made possible by a major collaborative scientific undertaking, the International Breast Cancer Linkage Consortium, in which hundreds of scientists, supported mostly by government grants, had participated': p. 112.

or entity to another person or entity. It is for this reason that, despite the reification of property forms based on debt, their underlying social relational nature is often closer to the surface. As Tobias Arbogast says, 'every debt, including public debt, constitutes an asset for someone else'.[65] Indeed, it was this, together with the unproductive nature of money, that underlay the long-standing hostility to usury. As we have seen, it was also the nature of debt as involving a personal relationship between two specific persons or entities that underlay the initial legal reluctance to allow debts to be assigned.

The precise nature of the social relations underlying different sorts of debt varies considerably. Debts can be owed by corporations and businesses, by states, or by private individuals and households, and contextual analyses are needed to uncover their specific social content. As Rudden put it, to understand different types of debt you need to explore the 'correlative creditors'.[66] In recent decades, for example, public debt – the debts owed by states – has risen rapidly in the wake of the financial crash of 2008, the COVID-19 pandemic and, more recently, the energy crisis. The interest payments on public debt are drawn from taxation and therefore ultimately involve money transfers from taxpayers to lenders. Household debt comes in many different forms: mortgage debt, consumer and credit card debt, student loan debt and so on, and usually involves a pre-emption of future income from individual labour. In some extreme pay-day loan cases, it resembles old-fashioned usury. By contrast, the interest paid on business and corporate debt is usually drawn directly from productive activities and surpluses, and commonly involves non-financial corporations rendering payments to financial firms standing outside the immediate production process. Fostering debt creation or opportunities for debt creation also fosters opportunities for the creation of new forms of income-yielding financial property. In recent decades the debt landscape has been further complicated by the huge effort that has gone into monetary innovations that turn every debt into a tradeable asset and credit innovations that seek to turn every asset into a basis for new credit. Securitisation has rendered more and more debt assets liquid and fungible and tradeable on secondary markets, and created new, often exotic, forms of debt-based property. These

---

[65] Tobias Arbogast, 'Who Are These Bond Vigilantes Anyway? The Political Economy of Sovereign Debt Ownership in the Eurozone', *MpIfG Discussion Paper*, 20/2 (2020), p. 1.
[66] Rudden, 'Things as Thing and Things as Wealth', p. 86. Lazzarato has gone as far as to argue that the creditor–debtor relation has become more important than the capital–labour relation, and that this has marginalised the working class, Lazzarato, *Governing by Debt*, p. 12.

financial innovations are not the products of chance discovery; they have been systematically pursued.[67]

The distribution of wealth and capital

Although intangible property forms were growing in number and importance, in Blackstone's day land was still the main kind of wealth held by those at the top of the property pyramid.[68] This remains the case today for many middle-class people for whom residential property is their main source of wealth.[69] However, just as not all property is wealth, so not all wealth is capital. As Levy says, wealth is a more static concept than that of capital, implicit in which is some kind of active 'economic process' through which a pecuniary return is generated.[70] Middle-class residential property is usually used as a home rather than as capital to generate a regular income stream, though it does often have considerable long-term investment value in that it has become a significant source of financial gain as a result of asset-price inflation in the real estate sector. By contrast, although the high net-worth individuals that top the *Sunday Times* rich list invest in tangible assets like real estate, gold and even artwork, much of their wealth takes the form of ownership of property-as-capital, particularly property in the form of revenue rights. Some hoped that as more and more people invested in private pensions to provide them with income streams in retirement, ownership of financial property of this sort would spread and become more 'democratised'. However, over the last couple of decades the research of economists like Thomas Piketty, Gabriel Zucman, Emmanuel Saez and Anthony Atkinson into the distribution of income and wealth has unequivocally shown not only that wealth inequalities are more pronounced than income inequalities, but that, in recent decades, wealth, and particularly financial wealth, has become ever more heavily concentrated among those at the top of the

---

[67] See Michael R Krätke, 'The Political Economy of (Public and Private) Debt', Workshop on Debt, University of Lancaster, https://www.lancaster.ac.uk/cperc/docs/2012-07%20CPERC%20DebtWorkshop%20Kraetke.pdf.

[68] Thomas Piketty, *Capital in Twenty-First Century*, Cambridge: Belknap Press (2014), chapter 3.

[69] Adkins at al suggest that, because of the dramatic growth in residential property prices, models of inequality, traditionally centred on employment-based categories like occupational status and wages, need to be revised, pointing out that the capital gains from home ownership often greatly outstrip what it is possible for middle-class earners to save from wages: see Lisa Adkins, Melinda Cooper and Martijn Konings, 'Class in the 21st Century: asset inflation and the new logic of inequality', 53 *Environment and Planning A: Economy and Space*, pp. 548–72 (2021).

[70] Levy, 'Capital as Process and the History of Capitalism', pp. 487–8.

wealth pyramid.[71] This is especially the case with the ownership of financial property. The wealthy are rich in revenue rights that entitle them to claim, in money form, part of the product of the future labour and efforts of others.

The UN's System of National Accounts defines wealth as 'marketable assets': meaning the value of non-financial property (real estate, land, houses, tangible productive resources) and financial property (shares, bonds and the like), minus any debts or liabilities. It does not include consumer durables like cars, TVs and other electronic goods.[72] For a variety of reasons, wealth inequalities are considered more economically and socially significant than income inequalities. Firstly, whereas income can vary from year to year depending on one's employment situation, wealth is more lasting and can be handed down from generation to generation, providing its holders with a degree of security and insulation from the personal economic shocks and crises that arise out of life events such as unemployment, sickness and old age.[73] The cushioning value of wealth was only too apparent during the COVID-19 pandemic. Wealth also brings education, health and employment advantages, and is a source of social prestige and political and economic power and influence: individual politicians, political parties and think tanks can be funded and media outlets owned and/or influenced. Finally, of course, wealth in the form of capital is a source of investment income from rents, dividends, interest payments, licence fees, royalties and the like, as well as a source of potential capital gains. In short, wealth begets wealth. Indeed, according to Piketty, it is primarily because, in the advanced market-based economies of the West, the rate of return on capital has in the long term generally been significantly higher than the rate of economic growth that inequality has increased.[74] For Piketty, the distribution of wealth is closely related to the distribution of income from capital. Crucially, in recent years, as economies have faltered and income from employment has stagnated, both economic and wage growth have been outstripped by the growth in asset values. This has been reflected in the falling labour share

---

[71] See Piketty, *Capital in Twenty-First Century*; Paddy Ireland, 'The Corporation and the New Aristocracy of Finance', in Robe, Lyon-Caen and Vernac (eds), *Multinationals and the Constitutionalization of the World-Power System*, London: Routledge, pp. 53–105 (2016), pp. 85–7.

[72] See Gabriel Zucman, 'Global Wealth Inequality', 11 *Annual Review of Economics*, pp. 109–38 (2019), pp. 112–13.

[73] On the importance of inheritance to wealth inequality, see Anthony B Atkinson, 'Wealth and Inheritance in Britain from 1896 to the Present', 16 *Journal of Economic Inequality*, pp. 137–69 (2018); Sandra Black et al, 'Poor Little Rich Kids? The Role of Nature versus Nurture in Wealth and Other Economic Outcomes and Behaviors', *NBER Working Paper No 21409* (2015, revised 2019).

[74] Piketty, *Capital in Twenty-First Century*, chapter 10. For Piketty, wealth is synonymous with capital.

of gross domestic product (GDP). There is now abundant data suggesting that, since the 1980s, there has been a secular downward trend in the labour share of GDP in the great majority of 'advanced' countries.[75] It is estimated that in the UK the decline has been between 4 and 6 per cent. The fall has been even more acute in the US, standing at over 10 per cent.[76] The result has been that wealth-ownership, and particularly ownership of capital, has grown in importance relative to employment income and status as a determinant of one's economic well-being, life-chances and position in the class structure. Some now argue that we are seeing the re-emergence of 'asset' or 'wealth economies' that resemble those of the late nineteenth and early twentieth centuries.[77]

Income and wealth inequality are complex, multifaceted phenomena that are not easy to measure. Calculating wealth inequality is especially challenging. Over the last 20 or so years, however, new techniques that combine different data sources have been developed by researchers to try to capture wealth inequalities both within countries and between them.[78] As a result, we now have a reasonably clear picture of the general distribution of wealth and the trajectory of inequality. In his *Capital in the Twenty-First Century*, published in 2013, the French economist Thomas Piketty sought to track the trajectory of wealth inequality in a number of Western countries over the last century or so. The data told a very similar story across countries. Wealth inequality was exceptionally high in the nineteenth and early twentieth centuries, fell from around 1914 through to the 1960s, before starting to rise again in the 1970s, without reaching quite the levels of the earlier period. Piketty estimated that the concentration of wealth ownership among both the top 10 per cent and the top 1 per cent of the population had risen significantly since the 1970s and 1980s both in the US and Europe. In the US, by 2010 the share of the top 10 per cent had risen from just over 60 per cent to about 72 per cent, and the share of the top 1 per cent from just under 30 per cent to just under 35 per cent. During the same period in the UK the wealth share of the top 10 per cent rose from just over 60 per cent to 70 per cent, and the share of the top 1 per cent from just over

---

[75] ILO and OECD, *The Labour Share in G20 Economies*, G20 Employment Working Group (2015), https://www.oecd.org/g20/topics/employment-and-social-policy/The-Labour-Share-in-G20-Economies.pdf.

[76] David Cabrelli, 'Addressing the Falling Labour Share in the UK and Beyond', 27 *Edinburgh Law Review*, pp. 1–33 (2023).

[77] Adkins et al, 'Class in the 21st Century'.

[78] For discussions of the methodological issues, see Zucman, 'Global Wealth Inequality', pp. 109–38; Facundo Alvaredo, Anthony B Atkinson and Salvatore Morelli, 'The Challenge of Measuring UK Wealth Inequality in the 2000s', *LSE International Inequalities Institute*, Working Paper 4, December 2015.

20 per cent to just under 30 per cent. In France, the share of the top 10 per cent went from 60 per cent to 63 per cent and the share of the top 1 per cent from 21 per cent to 25 per cent.[79] Edward Wolff painted a broadly similar picture in his analysis of the US Federal Reserve's triennial Survey of Consumer Finances (SCF), arguing that the wealth share of the top 1 per cent in the US rose sharply in the 1980s, levelled out during the 1990s, fell sharply around the turn of the century, then steadily rose: by 2010 the top 1 per cent accounted for 35.4 per cent of total wealth.[80]

More recent research by Gabriel Zucman has confirmed that wealth inequality in the US has 'increased dramatically' since the 1980s, with the top 1 per cent wealth share rising from 25–30 per cent in the 1980s to around 40 per cent in 2016. Since the 1980s, the share of the top 0.1 per cent has risen to nearly 20 per cent. The picture in Europe and China is broadly similar. Wealth inequality seems to have increased less rapidly in France and the UK than in the US, China and Russia, though this seems to be mainly because of rapidly rising housing and real estate prices, which boosted the wealth share of the middle class, 'most of [whose] wealth is invested in housing, while upper groups mostly own financial assets'.[81] However, while rising house prices increase the wealth share of the middle class, they also 'exacerbat[e] inequality between the poor (the bottom 50%) and the middle class (the next 40%)'.[82] At the global level, Zucman reports, wealth is 'highly concentrated', with the top 10 per cent owning more than 70 per cent of total wealth in China, Europe and the US combined; the bottom 50 per cent own less than 2 per cent of total wealth.[83] Indeed, Zucman reckons that the use of offshore tax havens to avoid and evade tax means that recent studies probably underestimate the level of and rise in wealth inequality. Leaks from offshore financial institutions, such as the Panama Papers, suggest that offshore wealth is even more heavily concentrated among the very rich than some studies suggest.[84]

---

[79] Piketty, *Capital in Twenty-First Century*, chapter 10.

[80] Edward N Wolff, 'The Asset Price Meltdown and the Wealth of the Middle Class', 4 *NBER, The Digest* (April 2013). Wolff's top 1 per cent have a net worth of $46.6 million or more; the next 9 per cent have a net worth of between about $900k and $6.6 million.

[81] Zucman, 'Global Wealth Inequality', pp. 109, 111–12, 129–33. Alvaredo et al, while cautioning that the available data is incomplete, conclude that 'wealth distribution [in the UK] is ... highly concentrated' and that 'the share of the top 1 per cent is between a fifth and a quarter of total personal wealth' Zucman, 'Global Wealth Inequality'.

[82] Zucman, 'Global Wealth Inequality', pp. 125–6. Alvaredo et al argue that there is 'some support for the view that wealth inequality increased in the UK over the first decade of the present century', but stress that the evidence on the UK distribution of wealth is far from complete: Zucman, 'Global Wealth Inequality'.

[83] Zucman, 'Global Wealth Inequality', pp. 126–7.

[84] Zucman, 'Global Wealth Inequality', pp. 109, 111–12, 129–33.

The most recent work on global wealth inequality, found in the World Inequality Lab's *World Inequality Report 2022*[85] suggests that the inequalities *between* nations have declined since the end of the Cold War, mainly because of the rapid rise of living standards in China, but that inequality *within* most nations has 'increased significantly'[86] and become even more pronounced as a result of the COVID-19 pandemic: 'The poorest half of the global population barely owns any wealth at all, possessing just 2% of the total. By contrast, the richest 10% of the global population owns around 76% of all wealth'.[87] The annual *Credit Suisse Global Wealth Reports* paint a similar picture: the wealth gap between rich and poor widened during COVID-19, boosted by rising asset prices. Those with financial assets plus property less debt of over $129k are in the top 10 per cent of global wealth holders; those with over $1 million are in the global top 1 per cent.[88] The 2023 report, produced now by UBS, shows that in 2022 the global wealth share of the top 1 per cent fell slightly to 44.5 per cent as a result of a fall in global financial wealth. At the other end of the pyramid, the bottom 52.5 per cent of the world's population held just 1.2 per cent of global net wealth.[89]

Crucially, as Piketty observes, the main source of middle-class wealth is housing, but what he calls 'true wealth … always consists primarily of financial and business assets'. And the higher you venture up the wealth scale, the more wealth is held in precisely these kinds of income-earning forms of property. As many researchers have shown, the distribution of financial assets – of property-as-capital in the form of rights to future revenues drawn from the 'efforts of others' – is even more unequal than the distribution of wealth in general.[90] 'Nearly everyone in the top decile owns his or her own home', Piketty writes, 'but the importance of real estate decreases sharply as one moves higher in the wealth hierarchy'. In the 9 per cent group below the top centile, real estate accounts for about half of total wealth and, for some, more than three quarters. By contrast, 'in the top centile … financial and business assets clearly predominate over real estate. In particular, shares

---

[85] World Inequality Lab, *World Inequality Report 2022* (WIR), co-ordinated by Lucas Chancel, Thomas Piketty, Emmanuel Saez and Gabriel Zucman, https://wir2022.wid.world/www-site/uploads/2021/12/WorldInequalityReport2022_Full_Report.pdf.
[86] World Inequality Lab, *World Inequality Report 2022*, p. 11.
[87] World Inequality Lab, *World Inequality Report 2022*, pp. 10, 88.
[88] Credit Suisse Research Institute, *Global Wealth Report 2021*, https://www.credit-suisse.com/about-us/en/reports-research/global-wealth-report.html.
[89] https://www.ubs.com/global/en/family-office-uhnw/reports/global-wealth-report-2023.html.
[90] '[H]ousehold wealth – in particular financial assets – is much more unequally distributed than income': OECD, *In It Together: why less inequality benefits all*, Paris: OECD Publishing (2015), p. 34.

of stock or partnerships constitute the near totality of the largest fortunes'.[91] Moreover, because financial assets tend to yield a higher return than real estate, those at the top of the hierarchy tend to earn a higher return on their wealth, allowing them to purchase still more revenue rights and other capital assets.[92] The dramatically unequal distribution of property-as-capital, and particularly of revenue rights, thus plays an important role in deepening and enhancing inequality.

Others have confirmed that the ownership of financial property – of rights to receive future revenues – is particularly heavily concentrated among those at the top of the wealth pyramid. According to Edward Wolff, in the US in 2010 the share of what he calls 'non-home' wealth of the richest top 1 per cent stood at 42 per cent and the share of the top 20 per cent at over 95 per cent.[93] The richest 1 per cent of households held about 50 per cent of all outstanding stock, financial securities, trust equity, and business equity, and 36 per cent of non-home real estate; the top 10 per cent accounted for 85–90 per cent of stocks, bonds, trusts, business equity and non-home real estate. In relation to stock ownership specifically, the 2010 SCF showed that 'the richest 10% of households accounted for 81% of the total value of these stocks'; it also showed that there had been a fall in the proportion of US households owning corporate stock (directly and indirectly) from its 52 per cent peak in 2001 to 47 per cent. Wolff concluded that, notwithstanding the growth in private pensions, 'in terms of wealth or income, substantial stock holdings have still not penetrated much beyond the reach of the rich and the upper middle class'.[94] The findings of the 2013 survey suggested that these trends had continued, with

---

[91] Piketty, *Capital in Twenty-First Century*, p. 260.

[92] Piketty, *Capital in Twenty-First Century*, chapter 7. Piketty further notes that the very wealthy are able to afford the most skilled financial managers to manage their investment portfolios and it is, therefore, possible that they obtain higher average returns than the less wealthy owners of financial property: Piketty, *Capital in Twenty-First Century*, chapter 6.

[93] Wolff, 'The Asset Price Meltdown'. The concentration of financial property ownership among the very wealthy contributes to income inequality, as a substantial proportion of their income does not come directly from 'work'. According to Domhoff, only 19 per cent of the income reported by the 13,480 individuals or households making over $10 million came from wages and salaries: G William Domhoff, 'Wealth, Income and Power', https://whorulesamerica.ucsc.edu/power/wealth.html. Piketty confirms that 'a very substantial and growing inequality of capital income since 1980 accounts for a about one-third of the increase of income inequality in the US': Piketty, *Capital in Twenty-First Century*, p. 300.

[94] Wolff, 'The Asset Price Meltdown' p. 144. Wolff's analysis also suggests that the concentration of ownership of 'financial securities' is even greater than the concentration of stock ownership, with the wealthiest 1 per cent accounting for 64 per cent. The holdings of most of these stock-owning households are modest: only 22 per cent owned stocks worth $25,000 or more.

a further decline in the proportion of households owning stock directly and indirectly.[95] More recently, Saez and Zucman used the capital income reported on individual tax returns in the US to assess (property-as-)capital inequality, concluding that 'capital inequality has risen enormously over the last decades', with the share of taxable capital income of the top 0.1 per cent, excluding capital gains, increasing from 10 per cent in the 1960s and 1970s to 33 per cent in 2012. The concentration of what they call 'pure capital income' – meaning the share of the returns accruing to pure rentier investments – has also 'increased significantly', with 'the share of dividends earned by the top 0.1% dividend-income earners [rising] from 35% in 1962 to 50% in 2012'. The rise in 'capital income concentration' is, they conclude, 'a real economic phenomenon'.[96]

The gender, racial and inter-generational dimensions of wealth inequality

The data on the overall distribution of wealth does not, however, tell the whole story, for wealth inequality is a complex, multifaceted phenomenon with gender, racial/ethnic and inter-generational, as well as class, dimensions. The significance of these other dimensions has grown as the economic and social significance of wealth-ownership has grown.[97] In the gender context, extensive research has been undertaken on the gender gap in wages and incomes, but much less undertaken on the gender wealth gap. This is partly because it is not easy to measure. Data on the ownership of wealth and its various components is usually collected at the household, rather than the individual, level. However, in keeping with perceptions of its growing importance, there is now a growing body of research that provides us with a picture of the scale of gender wealth inequalities. The Global Gender Wealth Equity Report produced by WTW for the World Economic Forum, for example, has developed what it calls a wealth equity index to estimate the ratio of female to male accumulated wealth at the point of retirement. The 2022 report found that, on average, female wealth stood at 0.74 on retirement across the 39 countries examined and at 0.77 in Europe. With

---

[95] Jesse Bricker et al, 'Changes in US Family Finances from 2010 to 2013: evidence from the Survey of Consumer Finances', 100 *Federal Reserve Bulletin* (September 2014).

[96] Emmanual Saez and Gabriel Zucman, 'Wealth Inequality in the United States Since 1913: evidence from capitalized income data', 131 *Quarterly Journal of Economics*, pp. 519–78 (2016), at pp. 529–31. 'Capital income' covers, among other things, dividends, interest and rents.

[97] Nicolas Frémeaux and Marion Leturcq, 'Inequalities and the Individualization of Wealth', 184 *Journal of Public Economics*, pp. 1–18 (2020).

a ratio of 0.71, the UK scored second worse.[98] A recent study by Kukk, Meriküll and Rõõm similarly found that there is a significant mean gender wealth gap in 21 of the 22 European countries studied, ranging from 13 per cent in Croatia and Hungary to 42 per cent in Luxembourg. On average, men have 24 per cent more wealth than women.[99] Their work indicates that the gap varies between countries, between household types (single versus couple-headed households) and between positions on the wealth distribution. The gaps tend to be negatively correlated to home ownership but positively correlated to financial property ownership. Because real estate tends to be the most equally distributed asset class, and because homes are often jointly owned, home ownership tends to reduce gender wealth differences. On the other hand, men tend to own significantly more property-as-capital in the form of financial assets like shares and bonds than women. This is a major source of wealth inequalities and explains why the gender wealth gap is often quite small at the lower end of the wealth distribution but widens, often significantly, at the upper end. It is also noteworthy that Kukk et al found no correlation between the gender gaps in wealth and wages, but a positive correlation between wealth gaps and hours worked. This highlights the significance of the gendered division of labour. Despite the progress made by women in relation to access to education and employment, and despite the inroads made into pay inequalities,[100] men are still better paid and continue to be more likely to enter better-paid professions. Even more significant in this context, however, is the fact that men's work is nearly always paid work, unlike that of women, who still carry out the majority of unpaid work in the home. The result is that men are able to accumulate greater wealth, particularly in the form of private pensions. The gender wealth gap is, therefore, linked to the gendered division of work.[101] There

---

[98] https://www.wtwco.com/en-au/insights/2022/11/2022-global-gender-wealth-equity-report. The report feeds into the WEF's annual Global Gender Gap Reports. WTW refers to Willis, Towers, Watson, a multi-national insurance and risk management company.

[99] Merike Kukk, Jaanika Meriküll and Tairi Rõõm, 'The Gender Wealth Gap in Europe', 69 *Review of Income and Wealth*, pp. 289–317 (2023). The exception is Lithuania. The UK was not included in their study. See also Meriküll, Kukk and Rõõm, 'What Explains the Gender Gap in Wealth?', 19 *Review of Economics of the Household*, pp. 501–47 (2021). Their findings broadly confirmed the results of other studies.

[100] Gender is a major dimension of socio-economic inequality, as reflected in the many movements for equal pay. The first estimates of the gender inequality in global earnings has recently been provided by the *World Inequality Report 2022*, chapter 5. There is much less reliable data on the gender dimensions of wealth inequality. On the wealth effects of residential racial segregation, see Lisa Adkins, 'How Wealth Inequalities are Made: an interview with Céline Bessière and Sibylle Gollac', 38 *Australian Feminist Studies* (2023), pp. 1–16 (2023), p. 12.

[101] See Céline Bessière and Sibylle Gollac, *The Gender of Capital: how families perpetuate wealth inequality*, Cambridge: Harvard University Press, (2023); see also Adkins, ibid.

is also evidence that it is growing. It has been estimated that in France the gender wealth gap has widened from 9 per cent in 1998 to 16 per cent in 2015.[102] Céline Bessière and Sibylle Gollac refer to this as 'the gender of capital'.

There is also evidence of a significant racial or ethnicity wealth gap, though the data here is limited. The Wealth and Assets Survey conducted by the Office for National Statistics (ONS) in the UK examined household wealth by ethnicity and found that the median total wealth for all households 2018–20 was £302k, ranging from £32k and £36k for Black African-headed and Bangladeshi-headed households to £332k and £350k for White British and Indian-headed households. Indian, White British and Chinese-headed households had the greatest median real estate wealth (£123–165k); the median real estate wealth of Bangladeshi, Black African and Black Caribbean was zero. Median private pension wealth varies from £85k (White British) to £57k (Indian) to £5k (Pakistani), to virtually nothing (Bangladeshi). Median net financial wealth is very small across the board.[103] Overall, real estate is the most significant wealth component. Interestingly, research in France suggests that residential segregation has seen homes owned by White households appreciate in value faster than those owned by Black households.[104] In the US, there are significant race-based wealth disparities, the 2019 Survey of Consumer finance showing that the median wealth of African-Americans was just 12.8 per cent that of non-Hispanic Caucasians.[105]

It seems clear that developments in the residential property market have also significantly sharpened inter-generational inequalities. For many of the middle classes, home ownership and the benefits of asset-price inflation have been the most likely route to (at least some) wealth acquisition. Indeed, it remains the case that borrowing one's way into home ownership is the most plausible route to some degree of economic security. However, while the 'baby boomer' generations may have been able to buy property through wages alone, residential property inflation and wage stagnation have rendered first-time buyers today more and more dependent on financial help from their parents. Most of them need to be able to draw on the 'Bank of Mum and Dad' to be able to provide the deposit required to get a mortgage on a residential property – a mortgage which will see them give up part of the product of their labour in interest payments to a financial institution of some

---

[102] Frémeaux, 'Inequalities and the Individualization of Wealth'.
[103] https://www.ons.gov.uk/peoplepopulationandcommunity/personalandhouseholdfinances/incomeandwealth/adhocs/14436householdwealthbyethnicitygreatbritainapril2018tomarch2020.
[104] See Adkins, 'How Wealth Inequalities are Made', p. 12.
[105] https://www.ubs.com/global/en/family-office-uhnw/reports/global-wealth-report-2023.html, p. 17.

kind.[106] The alternative is to rent and to give up part of the product of their labour to a landlord. Wage stagnation and rising housing costs (whether mortgages or rents) are also making it ever harder for the younger generations to accumulate pension savings. They have also increased the importance of inheritance. It has become increasingly hard for people to accumulate wealth from savings, with the result that inherited wealth has come to make up a growing proportion of the total wealth of individuals. Research suggests that the inheritance share of private wealth, which stood at around 70–80 per cent in Europe in 1910 but fell to 30–40 per cent between 1914 and 1945, was back to 50–60 per cent by 2010 and still rising.[107]

Ownership of public debt

Further empirical detail has been added to our understanding of the distribution of revenue rights by research into the ownership of public debt. Previously, in the absence of detailed empirical evidence, there was considerable uncertainty and disagreement about the class redistributive effects of public debt and about whether ownership was concentrated in relatively few hands (in a 'bondholding class'[108]) or was widely spread. In the nineteenth century the tax system did little if anything to redistribute downwards from the wealthy and public debt served as an upward mode of redistribution, shifting resources from the ordinary tax-paying citizen to the interest-receiving financial elite.[109] Gradually, however, social spending rose and the tax system became more progressive, making it more difficult to identify the class redistributive effects of public debt and the ultimate beneficiaries of state borrowing, spending and interest payments. Was ownership of public debt still concentrated in a relatively small bondholding class or had it become, as some argued, much more widely spread through intermediaries like pension funds?[110] The work of people like Sandy Hager has sought to penetrate the veil of financial intermediation in the US to

---

[106] See Laurence Troy et al, 'Pathways to Home Ownership in an Age of Uncertainty', *Australian Housing and Urban Research Institute* (2023).

[107] Facundo Alvaredo, Bertrand Garbini and Thomas Piketty, 'On the Share of Inheritance in Aggregate Wealth', 84 *Economica*, pp. 239–60 (2017).

[108] A term first coined by Henry Carter Adams: *Public Debts: a study in the science of finance*, New York: Appleton (1887).

[109] Sandy Brian Hager, *Public Debt, Ownership and Power*, PhD, Toronto: York University (2013).

[110] Wolfgang Streeck observed in 2014 that no one seems to know who the holders of public debt are, though 'we know the names of a few large funds that specialize in the government bond market, like Calpers and PIMCO (Public Investment Management Company)': *Buying Time*, London: Verso (2014), p. 82.

work out who benefits, directly and indirectly, from the interest payments received by financial institutions on government bonds.[111]

Hager's work shows that a significant proportion of the debt interest payments paid by the US state finds its way to the wealthiest in society. Using the 2010 SCF, Hager shows that the level of concentration of US government bond ownership is very high and that in the last three decades 'there has been a massive concentration in the distribution of federal interest towards the top one percent'.[112] During this period, ownership of federal bonds, and thus receipt of interest payments from the state, has become concentrated in the hands of three groups: foreign investors, whose holdings have mushroomed in the last half century, rising from less than 5 per cent in the 1960s to around 50 per cent today; corporations, whose share has fallen from about 40 per cent to 30 per cent; and households, whose share has fallen from about 30 per cent to about 15 per cent.[113] Ownership of the falling volume of debt held directly by households is very heavily concentrated among the very wealthy: the top 1 per cent of households own nearly 69 per cent of the household share.[114] The latter are also the main indirect beneficiaries of the public debt held by corporations,[115] which is concentrated in the large corporations occupying the FIRE sector (finance, insurance and real estate).[116] The dominant corporate owners of the public debt are not, as in the past, 'traditional' intermediaries such as banks, but

---

[111] See Atif Mian, Ludwig Straub and Amir Sufi, 'The Saving Glut of the Rich', *Princeton Economics*, Working Paper 2 (2021), p. 2, https://economics.princeton.edu/working-papers/the-saving-glut-of-the-rich/; Sandy Brian Hager, *Public Debt, Inequality and Power*, Oakland: University of California Press (2016).

[112] Sandy Brian Hager, "What Happened to the Bondholding Class? Public Debt, Power and the Top One Per Cent", 19 *New Political Economy*, pp. 155–82 (2014), p. 173.

[113] Though Hager points out that a substantial proportion of gross US public debt is actually held by the government itself (linked to various government trust fund accounts). From the 1940s until the late 1980s, the intra-governmental share stood at around 10 per cent; it has since grown to just over 30 per cent: see Hager, *Public Debt, Ownership and Power*, pp. 105–6.

[114] See Hager, "What Happened to the Bondholding Class?".

[115] Sandy Brian Hager, 'Corporate Ownership of the Public Debt: mapping the new aristocracy of finance', 13 *Socio-Economic Review*, pp. 505–23 (2015), p. 507. Hager suggests that the ownership share of large corporation has risen from 65 per cent (1957–81) to well over 80 per cent by 2010. According to Cedric Durand, in the US the share of government bonds held by the richest 1 per cent had risen to 40 per cent by this time (2010): Durand, *Fictitious Capital*, London: Verso (2017), p. 89.

[116] The share of the largest corporations grew rapidly after the financial crisis, probably because federal government debt was seen as a safe haven. In this context, institutional investors have replaced traditional banks intermediaries as the dominant owners: see Gillian Tett, 'Elite's grip on US bonds lays bare fiscal divide', *Financial Times*, 15/11/2013, summarising Hager's research.

institutional investors. Some of these institutions, like pension funds, are relatively widely owned and 'broad swathes of the population' have an indirect stake in the public debt they own.[117] However, the share of public debt held by pension funds has fallen sharply, from 14 per cent in the mid-1980s to 6 per cent in 2014, while the share held by mutual funds, characterised by ownership that is much more heavily concentrated among the very wealthy, has risen to around 10 per cent.[118] Hager estimates that, in the wake of the financial crash, the share of US public debt of the wealthiest percentile of the population rose from 38 per cent in 2007 to 56 per cent in 2013. He concludes that there is 'still a powerful bondholding class in the US, one whose power has augmented rapidly over the past three decades'.[119] In essence, rather than taxing the very wealthy, the US government has been borrowing from them. Moreover, as Jerome Roos has pointed out, the shift from decentralised bond ownership by small retail investors and decentralised markets to much more institutionally concentrated bond holdings and much more concentrated international capital markets has greatly increased the structural power of creditors. Creditors can now inflict highly damaging costs on the economies of debtors by withholding credit and attaching conditions to lending. There has been an *'internationalization'* of debtor discipline'.[120] As we shall see (Chapter 6), parallel changes to the institutional framework of corporate shareholding have had similar disciplinary effects.

The picture is much the same in Europe. There too, Arbogast reports, institutional holdings of public debt have become dominant, and the main beneficiaries have once again been those at the top of the wealth pyramid. Interest payments flow from households and states to financial institutions and then on to the very wealthiest. '[T]he holding structure of the public

---

[117] Sandy Brian Hager, 'Public Debt as Corporate Power', *Working Papers on Capital as Power* (2015), p. 3.

[118] The top 10 per cent (in terms of wealth) held only 15 per cent of total pension fund assets in 2010 (up from 8 per cent in 1983), whereas they held 47 per cent of the total assets of mutual funds (up from 40 per cent in 1983): Hager, 'Public Debt as Corporate Power', p. 11. In 2010, only 15 per cent of pension fund assets were owned by the top percentile of US households, as opposed to 47 per cent of mutual fund assets (up from 8 per cent in 1983). According to Durand, in the US the share of government bonds held by the richest 1 per cent had risen to 40 per cent by 2010: Durand, *Techno-féodalisme*, p. 89.

[119] Hager, 'The Rise of the American Bondholding Class', *Roar Magazine* (2016), https://roarmag.org/magazine/sandy-hager-public-debt-bondholding-class/; Hager, 'What Happened to the Bondholding Class?' p. 177. See also Hager, *Public Debt, Ownership and Power*; E Ray Canterbery, *Wall Street Capitalism: the theory of the bondholding class*, Singapore: World Scientific Publishing (2000).

[120] Jerome Roos, *Why Not Default? The Political Economy of Sovereign Debt*, Princeton: Princeton University Press (2019), p. 79 (his emphasis).

debt in Europe disproportionately benefits the wealthy', Arbogast argues, 'because the debt is mostly held by financial institutions whose stakeholders (shareholders; investors; employees) are likely to be wealthy households'. He adds that 'to the marginal extent that households still figure as direct holders of government debt, it is overwhelmingly wealthy households who own the debt'.[121] Public debt now, therefore, entails significant transfers of income from the non-wealthy or less wealthy to the wealthy, with the latter receiving interest payments funded out of the taxes levied on (and efforts of) the general population. In the post-Second World War period, the class redistributive effects of this were partly mitigated by progressive taxation and social spending. However, the evidence suggests that, in recent decades, as tax regimes have become markedly less progressive, rising public debt has served to reinforce and exacerbate income and wealth inequality.

Moreover, these money transfers to those at the top of the wealth pyramid extend beyond public debt to household debt. Research suggests that in the US, since the 1980s, there has been a significant rise in savings by the top 1 per cent of the income and wealth distribution, and dissaving by the government and the rest of the household sector.[122] 'Almost two-thirds of the rise in financial asset accumulation of the top 1%', Mian, Straub and Sufi argue, 'has been a rise in the accumulation of claims on US government and household debt'.[123] Following an examination of net household debt positions across the wealth distribution (household debt held as a financial asset minus household debt owed as a liability), they conclude that 'rich Americans have increasingly financed the borrowing of non-rich Americans'.[124] Between 1982 and 2007, the net household debt position of the bottom 90 per

---

[121] Arbogast, 'Who Are These Bond Vigilantes Anyway?', p. 3. In the 1980s, Margrit Kennedy calculated the interest payments made and interest income received by the ten income deciles of the German population. She found that the bottom eight deciles all paid more interest than they received, the ninth received slightly more than it paid and the tenth (the richest) received about twice as much as it paid out. The bulk of the gains were concentrated in the richest 1 per cent. Interest, she concluded, acts as 'a hidden redistribution mechanism' which 'constantly shuffles' money from poor to rich: Margrit Kennedy, *Interest and Inflation Free Money*, British Columbia: New Society Publishers (revised ed. 1995 [1987]), pp. 9–10.

[122] Mian et al 'The Saving Glut of the Rich', p. 1.

[123] Mian et al, 'The Saving Glut of the Rich', p. 2. They point out that the business equity holdings of rich Americans also represent a substantial claim on debt because non-financial corporations have increased their holdings of money market funds, which are themselves claims on debt. Similarly, Arbogast observes that 'rentier income initially flows not to households but to financial firms as corporate profits of which interest income earned on government debt is one component': Arbogast, 'Who Are These Bond Vigilantes Anyway?', p. 3.

[124] Mian et al, 'The Saving Glut of the Rich', p. 2.

cent fell by 39 per cent, while the net household debt position of the top 1 per cent rose by 12 per cent. In short, there has been 'a dramatic rise in the debt-to-income ratio of households in the bottom 90% of the income distribution'.[125] To summarise, then, what we have seen in recent decades is a sharp rise in the direct and indirect accumulation of financial property by those at the very top of the wealth distribution. The common feature of these revenue rights is that they all involve, directly or indirectly, transfers of part of the product of one person's efforts/labour to another person – in money form.[126] As Morris Cohen observed, 'accumulations of great wealth' are often the product of 'the labor of the many'.[127] This is something Adam Smith also recognised. 'Wherever there is great property', he wrote, 'there is great inequality. For one very rich man there must be at least five hundred poor … the affluence of the few supposes the indigence of the many'. '[S]o far as it instituted for the security of property', he added, 'civil government … is in reality instituted for the defence of the rich against the poor, or of those who have some property against those who have none at all'.[128]

Rising private wealth, declining public wealth

The political significance of this growing concentration of property, including financial property, in the hands of the very wealthy is highlighted by the increasing gap between the net wealth of governments and the net wealth of the private sector. As the authors of the *World Inequality Report 2022* (WIR) observe, 'in recent decades, the weight of private wealth has increased at the expense of public wealth due to deregulation, privatization, and increasing government debt'.[129] In essence, over the last half century or so, the wealthy have become significantly richer, while governments have become significantly poorer. In the 1970s, in most developed countries, public wealth was typically between 40 per cent and 100 per cent of national

---

[125] Mian et al, 'The Saving Glut of the Rich', p. 5. The evidence suggests that since 1980, the bottom 95 per cent have had to borrow more to try to keep their consumption level steady in face of rising income inequality.

[126] On this, see Gary Stevenson, *The Trading Game: a confession*, London: Allen Lane (2024), p.235. A recent study found that firms owned by the top 0.1 per cent of owners enjoyed profitability of $14k per worker employed in 2014. This compared to profitability of $5k per worker of firms owned by individuals in the bottom half of the top decile: Matthew Smith et al, 'Capitalists in the Twenty-First Century', *NBER Working Paper 25442* (June 2019), pp. 18, 48.

[127] Cohen, 'Property and Sovereignty', p. 15. Or as von Benda-Beckmann et al put it, 'command over wealth [is] an important source of political power over people and their labour': 'The Properties of Property', p. 2.

[128] Adam Smith, *Wealth of Nations*, Book V, chapter 1, part II.

[129] *World Inequality Report* (WIR), p. 15.

income. Today, however, in places such as the US and the UK, the share of wealth held by public actors is close to zero or negative, meaning that public assets are worth less than public debt and that the 'totality of wealth is in private hands'. Places such as 'France, Japan and Germany have also experienced significant declines in public wealth, which is now worth just about 10–25% of national incomes according to official estimates'.[130] This trend was exacerbated by the COVID-19 pandemic, during which governments borrowed the equivalent of 10–20 per cent of GDP, essentially from the private sector.[131]

This shift in the distribution of private and public wealth has been politically very significant. As the WIR says, 'today, with either small or negative net public wealth, rich countries' governments are constrained when they want to intervene in the economy, redistribute income and mitigate growing inequality'.[132] The result is that 'growing inequality in ownership of the public debt has gone hand in hand with growing inequality in representation within government policy'.[133] In the post-Second World War period, gradual increases in public expenditures were matched by tax revenues, resulting in falling levels of public indebtedness. However, since the 1970s and the demise of the Bretton Woods system and the liberalisation of finance, the bundles of rights held by owners of financial property have been greatly enhanced. This has greatly increased their bargaining power not only vis-à-vis labour but vis-à-vis states. Wealth, and especially financial wealth, has become much more mobile and, as a result, large corporations and high net-worth individuals have found it much easier to avoid (or evade) taxes. With this and the growth in fiscal competition, states have found it increasingly difficult to raise from taxation the money needed to fund public services and infrastructural investment (let alone fund the emergency bailouts required by the financial crash, the COVID-19 pandemic and the energy crisis). The result is that they now fund a large part of their spending through further borrowing – from those with money to invest – rather than through taxation. As Wolfgang Streeck says, the 'tax state' has become the 'debt state'.[134] The result, he suggests, is that governments now have to satisfy two 'electorates': on the one hand, the *Staatsvolk*, the 'general citizenry', with the right to vote in elections; on the other, the *Marktvolk*, the 'people of the market', the financial institutions representing the rentier class who invest in financial property and cast their votes in financial markets.[135] With

---

[130] WIR, pp. 15, 22–3, 76.
[131] WIR, p. 15.
[132] WIR, p. 76.
[133] Hager, 'Corporate Ownership of the Public Debt', p. 3.
[134] See Hager, *Public Debt, Ownership and Power,* p. 14. Streeck, *Buying Time,* p. 72.
[135] Streeck, *Buying Time,* p. 80.

states financially dependent on the latter, 'finance capital' has emerged as 'a second people – a *Marktvolk* rivalling the *Staatsvolk*', which states have to satisfy for their own survival. Drawing an explicit parallel with corporate governance, Streeck suggests that creditors have risen 'to become a second constituency of the modern state' in a way that is 'strikingly reminiscent of the emergence of activist shareholders in the corporate world under the "shareholder value" doctrine of the 1980s and 1990s'.[136] As Streeck's notion of two electorates suggests, the power of this new financial oligarchy goes well beyond its economic power and ability to shape the distribution of wealth. The growth of huge pockets of wealth has had a profound impact on politics and the political system as the very wealthy increasingly take control of the media and fund the think tanks that often shape policy-making. What we have seen in recent decades, therefore, is the emergence of a 'new aristocracy of finance'[137] – a power bloc comprising those at the top of the wealth and income hierarchy in whom financial property ownership is concentrated, their institutional representatives, the executive class, and a range of financial intermediaries.[138] Prominent among these are what Jeffrey Winters has called the 'agents of wealth defense', a reference to the army of well-paid skilled professionals – lawyers, accountants and the like – employed by the wealthy

---

[136] Streeck, *Buying Time*, pp. 79, 84.

[137] See Hager, 'Corporate Ownership of the Public Debt'; Ireland, 'The Corporation and the New Aristocracy of Finance'. The phrase is taken from Marx who made various references to the existence of an 'aristocracy of finance' that dominated the ownership of government bonds. There was limited social spending at this time (expenditure was directed primarily at wars and interest payments) and a regressive taxation system (the majority of government revenues came from indirect taxes, rather than from taxes on income and property). As a result, public debt had class redistributive effects, seeing transfers of income from tax-paying workers to bondholders. It also, Marx argued, enabled those bondholders to influence government policies. Although he was almost certainly correct, neither Marx nor subsequent commentators who made the same point provided much in the way of empirical evidence of the extent of these effects.

[138] Julie Froud, Sukhdev Johal, Adam Leaver and Karel Williams, *Financialization and Strategy: narrative and numbers*, London: Routledge (2006); Ismael Erturk, Julie Froud, Sukhdev Johal, Adam Leaver and Karel Williams, 'General Introduction', in Erturk et al (eds), *Financialization at Work*, London: Routledge, pp. 1–43 (2008), p. 1. See also Peter Folkman, Julie Froud, Sukhdev Jophal and Karel Williams, 'Working for Themselves? Capital market intermediaries and present day capitalism', 49 *Business History*, pp. 552–72 (2007), pointing out how a diverse bunch of financial intermediaries – corporate advisors and service-providers, securities analysts, hedge fund operators, private equity firms, city lawyers, and the like – have also reaped significant financial benefits from the 'economy of permanent restructuring' that has emerged. These are the groups who have played a key role in generating a finance-oriented corporate culture in which everything is for sale if the price is right.

to protect their assets.[139] Moreover, nowadays, if resource and cash-poor states want to invest in infrastructure or enhance public services, they have to make it attractive to the private financial investors upon whom they are increasingly reliant.

Speculating on the future

The financial element of the property owned by those at the top of the rich lists helps us to understand the often rapid shifts, upwards and downwards, in their wealth. Financial property is property in the form of a right to receive revenues in the *future*. Much of the property of those at the top of the rich lists thus takes the form of rights to draw on revenues that have yet to be produced; they possess multiple claims on the *future* 'efforts of others'.[140] Marx alluded to this when he argued, in *Grundrisse*, that enhancing one's wealth entailed 'stockpiling ... property titles to labour' and that money as capital is 'a claim on future labour'.[141]

It follows that the value of financial property is determined not by the value of particular tangible objects, but by *expectations* about future returns. Assessing its value is, therefore, inherently speculative. As Arjun Appadurai says, investors are 'always and everywhere speculators'.[142] But, as we have seen only too clearly in recent years, expectations about the future can be wrong – either absurdly over-optimistic (as with bubbles) and/or fraudulently manipulated (as with Enron, Carillion and countless others). Ornate techniques for assessing and pricing risk have been developed, but Jens Beckert suggests that these techniques should be understood not as doing 'what they claim to do – that is, to calculate an unknown future', but as 'instruments used to support the credibility of fictional expectations'.[143] The reality is that, based as it is on speculations about the future, the value of financial property can rapidly rise or equally rapidly fall as expectations about the future change. Writing about the eighteenth century, Robert Gordon

---

[139] See Jeffrey A Winters, 'Wealth Defense and the Complicity of Liberal Democracy', LVIII *Nomos*, pp. 158–225 (2017).

[140] Morris Cohen captured this when he argued that when 'a court rules that a gas company is entitled to a return of 6% on its investment, it is not merely protecting property already possessed, it is also determining that a portion of the future social produce shall under certain conditions go to that company. Thus not only medieval landlords but the owners of all revenue-producing property are in fact granted by the law certain powers to tax the future social product': Cohen, 'Property and Sovereignty', p. 13.

[141] Karl Marx, *Grundrisse*, p. 367.

[142] A Appadurai, 'Afterword: the dreamwork of capitalism', 35(3) *Comparative Studies of South Asia, Africa and the Middle East*, pp. 481–5 (2015), p. 482.

[143] J Beckert, *Imagined Futures: fictional expectations and capitalist dynamics*, Cambridge: Harvard University Press (2016), p. 141. See also Gary Stevenson, *The Trading Game*.

observes that the 'intangible and speculative nature of the new contract property deprived it of any fixity or solidity'. Its value was 'dependent on ... economic conditions, on the vagaries of public policy, on the surface tension of speculative bubbles, and on sudden shifts in the business cycle'.[144] This remains true today, and it is especially true of financial property like corporate shares, the returns to which are not fixed in advance. It is fluctuations in the value of the intangible financial assets of those at the top of the wealth pyramid and, in particular, in the value of their corporate shareholdings, that accounts for many of the sometimes dramatic changes in the value of their fortunes.

Alongside the already well-established forms of financial property, there has emerged in recent decades a vast array of new, exotic contract-based financial instruments, such as derivatives, whose precise legal nature and status remains rather opaque. This is one of the areas in which, as Lawson and Rudden put it, law 'seems always to lag behind commerce, so that the new types of asset which are developed and eagerly traded (such as financial derivatives) take on a dynamic of their own before the legal system catches up'.[145] The English courts have recognised the commercial value of these instruments and, in that sense, implicitly recognised that they have, like many other choses in action, some of the key qualities of 'property', not least market value. However, the courts find it hard not to see derivatives, even when there is a genuine hedging element, as, at root, contracts involving speculation for profit. Others have gone further, calling them 'naked bets' akin to gaming contracts.[146] The rapid growth of speculative financial instruments of this sort illustrates Marx's point about the ability of fictitious capital to double and treble itself. Indeed, it has been one of the defining features of contemporary neoliberal capitalism and of what has been called 'financialisation', underpinning, among other things, the changing role of banks and their erosion as old-fashioned credit intermediaries. Banks have become financial engineers, financial entrepreneurs, dealing in all sorts of financial assets. Alongside this, there has been an explosion in specialised forms for financial investment: mutual funds, hedge funds, special purpose vehicles, private equity funds, sovereign debt funds and the like. These are just some of the empirical realities of property in contemporary capitalism with which property scholarship and property theory needs to grapple.

---

[144] Gordon, 'Paradoxical Property', p. 99.
[145] Lawson and Rudden, *Law of Property*, p. 29.
[146] Lynn Stout, 'Uncertainty, Dangerous Optimism and Speculations', 97 *Cornell Law Review*, pp. 1177–212 (2012). One of the things that militates against seeing them as 'property' is the uncertainty about their value.

5

Defending the Property Status Quo: Analytical Jurisprudence

The new essentialism: reviving property as thing-ownership

It is clear not only that the 'things' deemed capable of being objects of property have changed quite markedly over time and vary from place to place, but that the very concepts of 'property' and 'ownership' as we now understand them are peculiarly modern and culturally specific. This has not prevented scholars from searching for a general concept of property that is applicable across time and between cultures and applicable to all resources. During the ascendancy of the bundle of rights conception, however, with its emphasis on contingency, malleability and context, abstract conceptual enquiries of this sort fell out of fashion. Even those working within the analytical jurisprudential tradition largely abandoned the search. In his famous essay on 'Ownership', for example, Tony Honoré adopted an approach that was more functional than analytical and suggested that what the relationships we generally understand as 'property' have in common is not an identifiable, transhistorical and transcultural essence, but a Wittgensteinian 'family resemblance' characterised by the presence of some, but not necessarily all, of certain incidents associated with 'ownership'. In similar vein, Jeremy Waldron argued that property is a 'contested concept' and that the best we could hope to do was to identify particular conceptions of property historically located in a particular culture.[1]

In recent decades, however, amidst an extraordinary outpouring of property scholarship, abstract theorising about property has come back into vogue. Much of this work suggests that property does indeed have a universal, transhistorical and transcultural 'core' or 'essence' centred on

---

[1] Waldron, *The Right to Private Property*.

things and exclusion. There has thus emerged, alongside the renewed interest in conceptual analysis in private law scholarship more generally (the so-called 'New Private Law'), a neo-Blackstonian 'new essentialism' in property scholarship.[2] Much of this work has emanated from scholars working from within analytical jurisprudence and/or law and economics. Among the common characteristics of this work are its tendency to make implicit assumptions about how our property system operates, its highly abstract nature and its tendency implicitly to endorse and/or explicitly to defend and legitimate the private property status quo. In the US, this has prompted self-styled 'progressive' property scholars like Gregory Alexander, Joseph Singer, Laura Underkuffler and Eduardo Peñalver to question both the conceptualisations of property offered by the new essentialists and their suggestion that there is little need for significant change to our property regime. The progressives seek to broaden and enrich property scholarship, much of which in the US has focused primarily on the economic dimensions of property, by highlighting property's relevance to things such as community, solidarity, human flourishing, equality, environmental stewardship, civic responsibility and social relationships more generally.[3] Much of this scholarship advocates enhancing the responsibilities of, and duties owed by, private property owners, with a particular focus on property rights that involve the performance of social functions (such as those in productive resources). On this basis, for example, some argue that ownership of certain resources should be regarded as an 'office'.[4] In 2009, a number of these theorists produced a short 'Statement of Progressive Property', which stresses that property operates as 'both an idea and an institution' and promotes 'plural and incommensurable values'.[5] The work of the progressive property theorists is a welcome antidote to that of the new essentialists, In this chapter, however, I focus on the new essentialism. I do so for two main reasons. Firstly, because of the growing influence of the new essentialism in recent decades, both within the academy and beyond, and its role in legitimating the property status quo; and, secondly, because, as I explain in the concluding chapter of the book, in the context of our existing property

---

[2] Amnon Lehavi, *The Construction of Property*, Cambridge: Cambridge University Press (2013), pp. 46–9. He seems to have first coined the term. See also Katrina Wyman, 'The New Essentialism in Property', 9 *Journal of Legal Analysis*, pp. 183–246 (2017).

[3] The progressive property literature is too voluminous to list. A very useful and succinct summary (and critique) of some of it can be found in Ezra Rosser, 'The Ambition and Transformative Potential of Progressive Property', 101 *California Law Review*, pp. 107–71 (2013).

[4] For a summary of this view, see Claassen and Katz, 'Property: authority without office?'.

[5] Gregory Alexander, Eduardo Peñalver, Joseph William Singer and Laura Underkuffler, 'A Statement of Progressive Property', *Cornell Law Faculty Publications*, Paper 11 (2009).

rights structures I do not believe that attaching social responsibility obligations of some kind to existing property rights, whatever the normative merits of such measures, would be effective in bringing about the kind of change we need. Significant prior reform of property rights structures would, in my view, be needed for such measures to have real impact and these structures should, therefore, be the immediate target of reform efforts.

The ubiquity of property institutions

Many of those who have sought to identify the alleged universal 'essence' of property are well aware of the problems thrown up by its historical and cultural variability. The much-respected work of the legal philosopher and property theorist James Harris is a good example of this. In his book, *Property and Justice*, which appeared in 1996, Harris acknowledges that property is a 'complex' institution and that 'the package of elements it contains varies enormously in time and place and is nowhere static for long'.[6] There is, he says, 'no consensus … about the concept of property'; it is 'so malleable that … there is no agreement about what it is'. Indeed, some even 'deny that there is any such thing'.[7] In similar vein, he argues that 'all attempts … to provide a univocal explanation of the concept of ownership, applicable within all societies and to all resources, have failed'.[8]

Like many property theorists operating within the analytical jurisprudential tradition, Harris tries to deal with this problem by 'abstracting from the dead weight of detail'[9] and developing a very general and capacious concept of 'property' that transcends its history.[10] This approach mirrors that of anthropologists who regard property as a 'human universal' despite its 'relative

---

[6] Harris, *Property and Justice*, p. 3.
[7] Harris, *Property and Justice*, p. vii.
[8] Harris, *Property and Justice*, p. 5.
[9] Harris, *Property and Justice*, vii.
[10] Or, as he puts it elsewhere, by developing 'theoretical constructs which transcend both the popular understanding of property and also the distinct dogmatics of different legal systems': Harris, 'The Elusiveness of Property', p. 129. Nicola Lacey has written eloquently of the detachment of jurisprudential analyses of law from history. It is not, she says, that 'analytical jurists do not think of law as a practical phenomenon, but rather that their enterprise has been to elucidate the deep structure of the concepts that structure the phenomena of law, legal doctrine, and legal argumentation. Their main focus has accordingly been the conceptual elegance and coherence of the relevant ideas … As this form of jurisprudence has become increasingly dominated by sophisticated forms of analytic philosophy, its disciplinary discreteness and closure has become greater, the assumption being that a philosophically adequate conceptualization of law is independent of its history': Lacey, 'Jurisprudence, History, and the Institutional Quality of Law', p. 927. See also, Lobban, 'Legal Theory and Legal History'.

character' and who therefore adopt a very expansive concept of property that can be applied analytically across cultures.[11] Harris himself draws on the work of the anthropologist Irving Hallowell. Hallowell suggested that, despite the 'immense variability' in the specific cultural forms of different human societies, there are 'some basic categorical similarities in human culture the world over', one of which is property.[12] In Harris, this becomes: 'all societies have *property institutions* of one kind or another'; property is 'a ubiquitous human institution'.[13] Harris' concept of 'property institution' is clearly intended to be more commodious than that of 'property', enabling one, for example, to find 'property' or institutional equivalents in societies lacking a state and/or law in the modern sense, societies whose property institutions are or were social rather than legal in nature and that are or were not characterised by generalised private property.[14]

In trying to capture the nature of these universal 'property institutions', Harris again draws on Hallowell.[15] Fearing that attempts to provide more precise definitions of 'property'[16] might be based on 'the provincial data of … one culture', Hallowell argued in favour of 'concepts that lend themselves to structural and functional analysis'.[17] Following this lead, Harris suggests that property and property institutions perform the dual transhistorical and transcultural functions of controlling the use of things and allocating wealth.[18] Others have adopted a similarly functional approach. For Jeremy Waldron, for example, 'the question of how material resources are to be controlled and their use allocated' is universal, 'one that arises in every society'.[19] Echoing this, David Lametti argues that 'the idea of property in its largest sense revolves about the access to or distribution of social wealth

---

[11] See Turner, 'The Anthropology of Property', p. 26; Nadasdy, ' "Property" and Aboriginal Land Claims in the Canadian subarctic', pp. 250–1. Nadasdy points out that one consequence of the anthropological attempt to universalise the concept of property through expansion is that the term 'thing' has been 'exploded' to incorporate songs, magic and rituals.

[12] Harris, *Property and Justice*, pp. 115–16. Hallowell himself draws from Clark Wissler, *Man and Culture*, New York: Thomas Y Crowell Company (1923).

[13] Harris, *Property and Justice*, pp. vii, 8.

[14] 'Property', Harris writes, 'is a social as well as a legal institution': Harris, *Property and Justice*, p. 4.

[15] Although Harris' book engages in anthropological conjectures rather than real anthropology.

[16] Which is often the aim of analytical jurisprudential approaches to property.

[17] Harris, *Property and Justice*, p. 119. Later anthropologists have suggested that property is 'a cover term for how human beings regulate their relations to the things which they value': Hann, 'The State of the Art', p. 290.

[18] Harris, *Property and Justice*, p. 140. These instrumentalities, he suggests, correspond roughly to the ideas of 'property as things' and 'property as wealth', something he seems to have borrowed from Rudden, 'Things as Thing and Things as Wealth'.

[19] Waldron, *The Right to Private Property*, p. 34.

and rules for its control ... property generally is about the use and allocation of resources'[20] and Thomas Merrill argues that 'all human societies' have to have 'strateg[ies] for determining how resources will be used' and that property – by which he means private property – is one such strategy.[21] In similar vein, Marx suggested (following Hegel) that property in general is a universal human phenomenon. In *Grundrisse* he wrote:

> All production is appropriation of nature on the part of an individual within and through a specific form of society. In this sense it is tautologous to say that property (appropriation) is a precondition of production ... there can be no production and hence no society where some form of property does not exist.[22]

Conceptualised in this abstract manner, it is hard to deny that property or property institutions are ubiquitous.

The dangers of abstraction

Abstraction of this sort is, of course, a necessary and integral part of the process through which we develop concepts that help us to grasp empirical reality. The problem is that these assertions about the nature and ubiquity of property/property institutions operate at a very high level of abstraction indeed, and what you can say about property/property institutions at this level of abstraction is limited.[23] Their validity rests precisely on their extreme generality and lack of specific content, and they cast little light on the empirical realities of property at any particular place and point in time. It is for this reason that property theorists have tended to try to give more substance to their abstract concepts of property. In doing this, their goal is not to try to capture the specific attributes of any individual empirical instances of property institutions, but to identify the general attributes, constant through

---

[20] David Lametti, 'The Concept of Property: relations through objects of social wealth', 53 *University of Toronto Law Journal*, pp. 325–78 (2003), p. 334. According to Jeremy Waldron, '[p]roperty is a general term for rules governing access to and control of land and other material resources': see Waldron, 'Property and Ownership', in *Stanford Encyclopedia of Philosophy*, https://plato.stanford.edu/entries/property/
[21] Thomas Merrill, 'The Property Strategy', 160 *University Pennsylvania Law Review*, pp. 2061–95 (2012), p. 2062, where Merrill argues that 'all organised societies use the property strategy to one degree or another'.
[22] Marx, *Grundrisse* pp. 87–8. The German words used by Marx were *Eigentum* (property), *Aneignung* (appropriation), and *Forms des Eigentums* (forms of property).
[23] See Nadasdy, ' "Property" and Aboriginal Land Claims in the Canadian Subarctic', p. 251. For the French jurist Jean Carbonnier, it is a mistake to study property in general: see Robé, *Property, Power and Politics*, p. 9.

time and space, that capture the universal 'essence' of property. In this way, they try to encompass all property institutions and show that they are all, as Harris puts it, 'branches of a common conceptual tree'.[24] The suggestion is that the specific content of property institutions may vary from place to place and may have changed over time, but the essence or core of property as an institution is constant.[25] In this context, some have drawn a distinction between the abstract *concept* of property, of which private property is just one example, and different *conceptions* of property, meaning particular concrete conceptions of the abstract concept.[26]

It is when property theorists are drawn into trying to put a little more flesh on their general, transhistorical and transcultural concepts of property that the limitations and dangers of abstraction – of trying, in Lobban's words, to 'clarif[y] concepts abstracted from all context' - manifest themselves, for they often end up smuggling in 'standard liberal understandings'[27] of property and the features of the property institutions of the societies of which they are a product and part. In other words, they tend to flesh out their abstract concepts of property using the 'provincial data of one culture', projecting categorical abstractions derived from modern Western market capitalist societies on to all property institutions. In this process, what are often, in fact, very different sorts of property institutions – and very different sorts of societies – are conflated and rendered falsely similar. Indeed, it is precisely because of the risk of universalising a concept of property derived from modern Western institutions that anthropologists are reluctant to endorse a single dominant conception of property.[28]

Despite his best efforts, Harris provides an example of how easy it is to fall into this trap. He suggests that 'any general notion of property is notoriously elusive' and that we should 'eschew' the idea that it might have a ' "true" semantic or conceptual essence'.[29] However, after asserting that

---

[24] Harris, *Property and Justice*, pp. 139–42. Here Harris seems to be deploying something resembling the Wittgenstein idea of 'family resemblance' as an alternative to providing an unvarying list of empirical characteristics that all examples of the phenomenon necessarily have to have in common: see Derek Sayer, *The Violence of Abstraction*, Oxford: Basil Blackwell (1987), p. 54.

[25] Lacey, 'Jurisprudence, History, and the Institutional Quality of Law', p. 926.

[26] Waldron argues that *private property* is a concept of which there are many different conceptions: Waldron, *The Right to Private Property*, pp. 5, 31. Lametti argues that *property* is a concept of which there are many different conceptions, of which private property is one: see Lametti, 'The Concept of Property', p. 333.

[27] Lobban, 'Legal Theory and Legal History', p. 2. Lobban argues that 'we must be cautious of a view which implies that pure analysis can tease out timeless legal categories', observing that many concepts are 'not timeless abstractions but arise in particular historical contexts', pp. 11, 12. See also Hann, 'The State of the Art', p. 294.

[28] Turner, 'The Anthropology of Property', p. 38.

[29] Harris, *Property and Justice*, pp. 6, 142.

property carries out the 'dual functions' of controlling the use of things and allocating social wealth,[30] he abstracts from different resources and tries to be a little more specific about the 'essentials' or 'foundations' of property institutions, identifying them as the 'twin notions' of 'trespassory rules' and 'ownership spectrum'. Trespassory rules refer to social rules, legal or other, that exclude non-owners and oblige them not to use a thing without the consent of the owner ('thou shall not steal'). 'Ownership spectrum', on the other hand, refers to a spectrum of rights or 'ownership interests' ranging from 'full-blooded ownership' (the equivalent of Honoré's 'full liberal ownership') to 'mere property' (possession of a proprietary interest of some kind). For Harris, the concept of ownership is the 'organising idea' behind the 'ubiquitous human institution' that is property and lies at the heart of all property institutions. All 'property talk, lay and legal', he argues, 'deploys ineliminable ownership conceptions'.[31]

For Harris, conceptualising property in terms of these 'indispensable' and 'essential features of those universal institutions known as property institutions' corresponds with our 'intuitive sense of what property is'.[32] Moreover, he argues, conceptions of *private* property are *logically*, though not necessarily *historically*, prior to conceptions of non-private forms of property.[33] Full-blooded ownership by single owners over single resources thus emerges, logically, as the paradigmatic type of property/property institution and as the yardstick against which other property institutions and forms of property should be measured. 'The whole idea of "common property"', Harris tells us, 'is infused with the conceptual possibility of individual property' and only makes sense as a concept if we 'already ha[ve] some notion of what it is for something to be the private property of individuals'. It is only the contrast with full-blooded private ownership that gives coherence to the notions of 'communitarian property' used by historians and anthropologists.[34]

There is an important sense in which Harris is right to say that the concept of (full-blooded) private property is prior to other contemporary conceptions

---

[30] Harris, *Property and Justice*, pp. 4, 13, though he adds that 'nowhere is property the only mechanism for controlling the use of things or the exclusive device for wealth-allocation', and elsewhere seems to confine these functions to '*modern* property institutions': Harris, 'The Elusiveness of Property', p. 128.

[31] Harris, *Property and Justice*, pp. 5, 8–9. 'Ownership', he writes, 'has always been a taken-for-granted organizing idea, but its content varies, historically, according to the social presuppositions taken into the law', Harris, *Property and Justice*, p. 129.

[32] Harris, *Property and Justice*, pp. 5–8, 114.

[33] Harris, *Property and Justice*, pp. 100, 111–18. This claim runs contrary to the belief of most property theorists who see private property as a particular conception of the larger concept of property and see the latter as having historical and analytical priority.

[34] Harris, *Property and Justice*, pp. 115–16.

of property. However, this is because the concept of private property is, in an important sense, *historically* prior to these other conceptions. As we have seen, the modern concepts of 'property' and 'ownership', far from being timeless and universal, are not only historically and culturally specific, but relatively recent. They only come into common usage with the emergence of private property. Thus, the term 'property' in something resembling its modern sense of thing-ownership only begins to appear with any regularity from the sixteenth century, and it is only in the sixteenth and seventeenth centuries that the term 'ownership' emerges and begins to be used to refer to an absolute right to something that is good against all the world. As Holdsworth points out, before this plaintiffs in actions did not have to establish abstract 'ownership' of this sort, merely that they had a better right to possession than the defendant.[35] The concept of property in this new form and the related concept of ownership emerged to try to capture an emerging historical reality: the treatment of more and more resources, and especially the key productive resource of land, as 'belonging' exclusively to specific individuals (often only after much struggle and conflict). Increasingly, these individuals were regarded as legitimately entitled to do whatever they liked with their 'property', including land, without regard to others, subject to diminishing legal and customary constraints. In other words, historically, the concepts of property and ownership as we understand them emerged to describe the growing empirical phenomenon of *private* property, particularly in the key productive resource of land. The concept of property in its modern form was thus not only infused from the outset with the idea of specifically *private* property, but also emerged as shorthand for it. And, as Harris says, it is only 'within a system of private property [that] "ownership" plays an indispensable role as an internal organising idea'.[36]

The material pre-conditions for the emergence of these concepts were provided by the growth in the increasingly impersonal, market-based class relations, commodification, and new kinds of human beings associated with the rise of capitalism. Over time, these market-based social relations and practices, and the ever-strengthening market imperatives to which they subjected economic actors, became not only more entrenched and generalised – extending, as Polanyi pointed out, to land, labour and money – but ever more naturalised.[37] With this, the concepts of property and ownership came to be seen as concepts with universal validity that could

---

[35] Holdsworth, *History of English Law*, volume 7, pp. 62, 458.
[36] Harris, *Property and Justice*, p. 112.
[37] Bob Jessop has recently asked whether knowledge should be added to Polanyi's list of fictitious commodities: see Bob Jessop, 'Knowledge as a Fictitious Commodity: insights and limits of a Polanyian analysis', in A Buğra and K Ağartan (eds), *Reading Karl Polanyi for the 21st century: market economy as a political project,* Basingstoke: Palgrave, pp. 115–134 (2007).

be deployed to understand all societies, including societies that were not characterised by generalised, impersonal market relations and that did not have concepts of property or ownership.

Using concepts derived from our culture in this way is, as the legal philosopher Joseph Raz has pointed out, necessary but also potentially problematic. 'To understand other societies', he argues, 'we must master their concepts, for we will not understand them unless we understand how they perceive themselves'. With the right resources, it is possible to do this, he argues, but only if we 'can relate their practices and customs to our own'. Our understanding of alien cultures will 'remain incomplete until we can relate their concepts to ours'. Although we are, therefore, bound to try to understand other cultures using concepts drawn from our own – concepts that may be absent from theirs – we must, Raz argues, draw these concepts in such a way that they are capable of being applied 'to alien cultures as well as to our own'. They have to be concepts 'whose application is not limited by the boundaries of our culture'.[38] Much property theory represents an attempt to develop an abstract concept of property that can be used in precisely this way, hence the claims that property is ubiquitous and that all societies, while not necessarily having property in our sense of private property, have 'property institutions' of one kind or another, even in the absence of any concept of property.

It is arguable, however, that Harris' concept of property fails sufficiently to escape the boundaries of our culture and that this limits its usefulness in helping us understand the property institutions not only of 'alien cultures' but of earlier versions of our own. As Lametti points out, Harris' analysis of property institutions is 'conditioned' by the considerable 'baggage' that comes with his focus on ownership[39] and his insistence that ownership is 'a pervasive organising idea' that is 'everywhere'.[40] This encourages a methodologically individualist approach to the study of property institutions that starts with, and focuses on, individual legal persons and individual resources, rather than with the social whole and the wider set of social relations and practices of which specific property institutions are always constitutive parts. It encourages an approach that regards property institutions as comprehensible through an analysis of discrete individual ownership interests and that regards individuals as intelligible, in principle, without reference to the social relations in which they participate. Thus, one of Lametti's criticisms of Harris' idea

---

[38] Joseph Raz, *Between Authority and Interpretation*, Oxford: Oxford University Press (2009), pp. 42–46.
[39] Lametti, 'The Concept of Property', p. 359. On the ways in which everyday discourse about property is rife with assumptions and metaphors, see Alain Pottage, 'Instituting Property', 18 *Oxford Journal of Legal Studies*, pp. 331–44 (1998).
[40] Harris, *Property and Justice*, p. 64.

of 'ownership spectrum' is that the idea of full-blooded ownership upon which it is based is conceivable only in a vacuum.[41]

An individualistic approach of this sort undoubtedly helps us, at least in part, to understand the property institutions of market-dominated, capitalist societies in which liberal ideas about free-standing, isolated individuals comprehensible independently of society as a whole have some plausibility. This is hardly surprising as the full-blooded property owners that lie at the heart of Harris' concept of property are in many ways the personification of the social attributes of capitalism. Indeed, we see this when he asserts that 'any attempt to articulate a single conception of ownership ... would be hopeless', but adds that all invocations of ownership are united, by among other things, their authorisation of self-seekingness: 'authorized self-seekingness' is, he says, the 'differentiating characteristic of ownership interests'. It is, Lametti argues, '*the* unifying feature at all points along the [ownership] spectrum'.[42] While Harris does not suggest that the pursuit of self-interest is the only thing that motivates those with property interests, it is clear that individual self-interest underpins his concept of property. Muldrew highlights the potential problems with this when he highlights the distorting effects on our understanding of earlier market societies of the idea, associated particularly with Adam Smith (perhaps unfairly), that the dominant motivating force of market activity – and, in some cases, of social activity in general – is self-interest. In early modern England, Muldrew argues, 'almost all people were involved in market relations, and in all probability had been for some time, [but] they were not simply or even primarily concerned with self-interest in the Smithian sense and did not interpret their behaviour in such terms'.[43] As late as the eighteenth century, when Smith was writing, expressions of the ethical attitudes of the earlier period, exemplified by ideas about customary obligations and the 'moral economy', remained common.[44] By this time, however, the nature of markets was changing. They were becoming ever more capitalist in

---

[41] Lametti, 'The Concept of Property', p. 370.
[42] Harris, *Property and Justice*, pp. 5, 75–76, 267; Lametti, 'The Concept of Property', p. 359. As Lametti says, the idea of ownership implies not only that individual owners have the final say over a particular resource, but that, unless specified otherwise, they can do as they like with it.
[43] Muldrew, 'Interpreting the Market', p. 169. Market relations, he argues, 'were, rather, interpreted in a way which stressed the consequences of actions on others and on the community', p. 177.
[44] See Thompson, 'The Moral Economy of the English Crowd'. Muldrew argues that, contrary to the abstract conception of 'the market' derived from the neo-classical economic theories that have come to dominate economic discourse, market exchange takes many different historical forms.

nature: market as opportunity was being replaced by market as imperative and, as economic actors became subject to ever stronger market imperatives, the scope for ethicality was narrowed.[45]

Harris' approach is much less analytically helpful when one is seeking to understand societies markedly different – less individualistic and less market-based – from our own. In many societies individuals simply cannot be understood, even at a superficial level, in isolation, abstracted from the social wholes of which they are part. They can only be understood relationally, by reference to their place in the social whole and their relations to others. Put simply, Harris' approach fails sufficiently to detach his concept of property from its historical origins in private property and the individualism and practices of market-dominated capitalist societies for it to be applied to societies significantly different from our own in ways that do not risk distorting our understanding of them. A conception of property/property institutions that is rooted in universal, abstract notions of ownership and exclusion is much less useful in helping us accurately to capture the empirical realities of property/property institutions in societies with very different social relations, material practices, and conceptions of the individual and society – societies in which something resembling the concepts of '(private) property' and 'ownership', as we understand them, particularly in relation to certain resources, are lacking, missing altogether, or more restricted in scope. It comes to define and shape our understanding of the property institutions, the social relations and practices, and the people of other societies.[46] When all property institutions are viewed through an ownership prism in terms of individual person–thing relationships and authorised self-seekingness, therefore, we risk downplaying the differences between different sets of property institutions and between the societies of which they were/are part. In short, Harris' ownership- and exclusion-centred property universalism tends to lead the property institutions and practices of other societies to be assimilated into our own and to render different sets of property institutions falsely similar.

Vivid examples of the limitations of seeking to universalise individual ownership-centred conceptions of property and the problems of (mis) translation this creates have been provided by the attempts of indigenous peoples to defend their territorial claims in Western courts. They feel bound to recast their relationship to the land and to frame their arguments in terms of Western conceptions of property and ownership, no matter how inappropriate (or distasteful or simply silly) this might seem from within their

---

[45] See Wood, *The Origin of Capitalism*.
[46] See Greer, *Property and Dispossession*, pp. 53, 62–3, arguing that we thereby feed the 'provincialism and collective self-delusions of our own society'.

own cultures.[47] As Eleanor Leacock says, writing of the Cree, although the idea of land ownership makes little or no sense to them, with their lands constantly being encroached upon by White people, it would be 'folly' for them not to argue that they 'own' the land.[48] The result is that members of these societies 'speak differently' about land depending on whether they are addressing members of their own communities or outsiders in what amounts to 'a strategic response to the real challenge of communicating between fundamentally different concepts and languages of space and property entitlement'.[49]

Indeed, the methodological individualism underlying Harris' concept of property limits its value even as a tool for understanding the property institutions of contemporary capitalism. Precisely because his abstract 'essentials' of property institutions/property, while purporting to be devoid of any specific historical content, draw heavily from the private property institutions and social relations of modern capitalism, they inevitably capture some of the empirical realties of property in contemporary capitalism. But the methodological individualism of his approach means that they capture only some of them. When property/property institutions, particularly those relating to productive resources, are viewed through the prism of private (individual or group) ownership of single resources, they tend to be cleansed of the wider social and economic attributes they (and the societies of which they are part) have in empirical reality. When you focus on individual owners (or individual possessors of ownership interests) and individual resources/things, the wider set of social relations of which all specific property institutions are a constitutive part become obscured. You cannot see the wood for the trees. As a result, Harris' approach to the study of property, like (as we shall see) that of the new essentialists in general, tends, even when it is applied to societies in which private property predominates, to conceal as much as it reveals.

---

[47] Nadasdy recounts the story of a young member of the Kluane First Nation trying to explain to his grandmother that he was trying to figure out which land belonged to the Indians and which to the White men. This was, she told him, a crazy thing to do, for no one can own the land; Nadasdy, '"Property" and Aboriginal Land Claims in the Canadian subarctic', p. 247. See also Graham, *Lawscape: property, environment, law*.

[48] Eleanor Leacock, 'The Montagnais-Naskapi of the Labrador Peninsula', in R Bruce Morrison and C Roderick Wilson (eds), *Native Peoples: the Canadian experience*, Toronto: McClelland & Stewart, pp. 140–71 (1986), p. 143.

[49] Greer, *Property and Dispossession*, p. 53. 'When the time comes to defend indigenous lands against white outsiders', he explains, 'it becomes necessary to present a case to officialdom and the courts in the language of territorial sovereignty and private property, even if these do not exactly reflect native land practices'. It made strategic sense, in other words, to exaggerate the degree to which their tenure of land conformed with the dominant culture's idea of private property.

Moreover, in suggesting that private property is logically and ontologically prior to non-private property forms and that ideas about the latter are infused with the 'conceptual possibility' of private property, Harris implies that private property is always present conceptually, even in societies whose property institutions are not based on it. It is suggested that conceptions of private property and 'full-blooded ownership', being ontologically prior to non-private forms of property, underlie all property institutions – and, therefore, because of the latter's ubiquity, are somehow pre-figured in the property institutions of all societies. In this way, the (private) property institutions (the way in which 'things' are controlled and wealth allocated) of a specific historical social formation (capitalism) come to be seen as present, latently, in all societies. Full-blooded private property is implicitly depicted as universal, as present, if not yet visible, in all places where there are property institutions.

From there, it is a short step to the belief that property institutions that are significantly different from our own private property-based institutions are in fact, somehow simply less developed, pre-cursors of our own. Private property is the 'natural' form of property towards which history has always been headed. This is hinted at by Harris. He claims that 'there is no univocal, singular concept of ownership ... applicable to all resources *at all stages of social and legal development*'.[50] The final phrase here is significant, for Harris also describes ownership interests that approach 'full blooded ownership' as being on 'the upper half of the spectrum', while 'mere property' is at the 'lower end', a formulation that seems to suggest that social and legal development moves in the direction of private property and red-blooded' ownership, from a lower to a higher form.[51] Historically, ideas of this sort animated the work of Scottish Enlightenment thinkers like Smith, Hume and Ferguson, who saw societies moving through developmental stages and from lower to higher forms, in Smith's case from the age of hunters, to the age of shepherds, to the age of agriculture, to commercial society – the acme of civilisation.[52] From this perspective, the emergence and rise of full-blooded private property – and, indeed, the rise of capitalism more generally – tends to be seen as little more than the realisation of ever-present tendencies that are somehow inscribed in human nature and the natural self-interest of human beings. As a result, the rise of generalised private property – of private

---

[50] Harris, 'The Elusiveness of Property', p. 129.
[51] Harris, *Property and Justice*, pp. 5, 10.
[52] Smith's idea of history moving in stages greatly influenced Marx, though he did not, of course, see 'commercial society' as marking the end of history: see Robert Brenner, 'The Origins of Capitalist Development: a critique of neo-Smithian Marxism', 104 *New Left Review*, pp. 25–92 (July–August 1977).

property in key productive resources as well as in personal possessions – does not really require explanation. Its prior existence explains its coming into being. The constraints on full ownership just needed to be removed. The very thing that needs to be explained is assumed.

At a time when our property system is failing and when there are good reasons for questioning our property institutions, this approach risks not merely naturalising generalised private property but also closing down the perceived range of institutional possibility, particularly in relation to productive resources. It tends to generate an over-simplified view of the possibilities available to us. This was evident in the attempts of pioneer anthropologists, like Lewis Henry Morgan, to locate property institutions on a spectrum based on a simple binary opposition between societies seen as characterised by either (full or absolute) *private* ownership or (full or absolute) *communal* ownership[53] – a tendency that finds contemporary expression in the mistaken idea that the institutional/political/economic choice facing us is a (more or less) binary one between capitalism (full private ownership) and communism/socialism (full state ownership) or a mix of the two (a 'mixed economy').[54] By contrast, the new anthropology of property recognises the relativity and complexity of property institutions and challenges the 'simple oppositions of individual versus collective property, usufruct versus ownership, modern versus postmodern, nature versus culture, even subject versus object'.[55] The attempts to locate all societies and all types of property on a private–communal property spectrum are rejected as 'inadequate, if not meaningless'[56] and care is taken not to impose standard

---

[53] Like other early anthropologists, Morgan thought that societies progressed from savagery, through lower, middle and upper barbarism, to civilisation. Although this process was driven by technological advances, 'it was the distinctive property regimes that most clearly marked off one stage from another' (Greer, *Property and Dispossession*, p. 56). In Morgan's account, history was marked by evolution from collective property and 'primitive communism' to private property and civilisation. For Marx and Engels, Morgan's work showed the human capacity for co-operation, underpinning their argument that co-operation and sharing could be resumed after capital had completed the task of enhancing productivity and wealth. Later anthropologists like Frank Speck and Robert Lowie retaliated, seeking to debunk the myth of primitive communism by finding private property present and well in these earlier societies. More recently, Alan Macfarlane similarly sought to argue that English property has since time immemorial been individualistic: Macfarlane, *The Origins of English Individualism*, Oxford: Blackwell (1978). For a typically cogent critique of this claim, see Ellen Meiksins Wood, *The Pristine Culture of Capitalism*, London: Verso (1991), chapter 8.

[54] See Paddy Ireland and Gaofeng Meng, 'Post-Capitalist Property', 46 *Economy and Society*, pp. 369–97 (2017); Roberto Unger, *The Left Alternative*, London: Verso (2nd ed., 2009).

[55] Greer, *Property and Dispossession*, p. 63.

[56] Greer, *Property and Dispossession*, p. 54.

liberal understandings of property on the 'complex lived practices of other societies'.[57]

Dominium in Roman law

A good example of the tendency to find precursors of our private property-based property institutions from time immemorial is provided by the way in which scholars, particularly since the eighteenth century, have treated the concept of *dominium* (dominion) in Roman Law. It has become commonplace for modern ideas of 'ownership' to be assimilated with the Roman law concept of *dominium* because of its allegedly absolute and individualistic nature. 'A quick glance at Roman law textbooks', di Robilant and Syed observe, 'reveals the ubiquitous presence of the idea that Roman property is absolute and unitary'.[58] Despite the pervasiveness of this idea, however, according to the Italian Roman law scholar Vittorio Scialoja, it is a 'legend' 'concocted by the "Romano-Bourgeois" jurists, the liberal jurists who, in the nineteenth century, sought to construct a modern, individualistic property law for liberal, capitalist European nation states along the lines of Roman dominium'.[59] In reality, Roman property law was much less absolute and individualistic and unitary than these jurists would have us believe. *Dominium* was just one of a number of different sorts of property institution in Roman law. Alongside it, there existed a 'highly sophisticated' and large 'menu of more limited and differently shaped forms of "ownership" that were largely resource-specific' – tailored to the specific characteristics of and interests implicated by different resources. Roman law classified different 'things' (*res*) 'according to their physical characteristics, the economic and social policy interests they involved and the moral and cultural values they implicated', constructing a range of different sets of entitlements (rights bundles) for different resources. This contextualism has 'attracted scant attention', as has the fact that some 'things' were not considered suitable to be the object of private property and market transactions at all, often because of the public interests involved.[60]

Jean Gaudemet agrees. 'It is often said', he observes, 'that Roman property was absolute' and it is undoubtedly true that 'Justinian's Institutes (II, 4, 4) speak of a full power over the thing and the interpreters of Roman law have analyzed the right of property as the right to use the thing, to receive fruits of it, and to dispose of it either by alienating it or even destroying

---

[57] Hann, 'The State of the Art', p. 294.
[58] di Robilant and Syed, 'Property's Building Blocks', p. 236.
[59] di Robilant and Syed, 'Property's Building Blocks', pp. 236–7.
[60] di Robilant and Syed, 'Property's Building Blocks', pp. 237–8.

it'. But although these analyses can invoke the support of certain Roman texts, they are, he argues, 'above all the work of modern interpreters who, from the 16th until the 19th century, wanted to find in Roman law the expression of their individualistic conception of a right of absolute private property'.[61] In support of this view, Shael Herman notes that Jean-Etienne-Marie Portalis, who was charged with drafting that part of the French Civil Code, *De la propriété*, that contains Article 544, commented that 'one could find everywhere and always traces of the individual right to property'. The use of the word 'traces', Herman argues, is significant, indicating that Portalis was aware that his modern, liberal conception of private property was at odds with earlier property institutions. The drafters of the French Civil Code, he suggests, 'ransacked the Roman texts in search of support for the wording of articles on property and contract ... [and] sometimes found in the Roman law texts what they wanted to find, not what was there'.[62] They did this to try to give legitimacy to their (new) conception of property by giving it an ancient legal pedigree. 'The civil law jurists preoccupation with finding the seeds of a modern civil code in an ancient Latin text is akin to English lawyers' search for the roots of constitutionalism in Magna Carta'. In reality, however, 'despite linguistic similarities, [the French Civil Code and classical Roman law] were fundamentally different products of the human spirit', or, one might say, expressions of fundamentally different sets of social relations. As Herman says, French doctrinal writers and code drafters 'rejected many aspects of Roman law' and 'either transformed or tailored [the] key concepts they [had] allegedly borrowed to "fit" the social and political order of post-Revolutionary France'.[63] Michele Graziadei also argues that 'the formula adopted by the codifiers in Article 544 of the [French civil] code to define the right of ownership was not ... taken from the Roman sources themselves'. These sources did 'not offer anything similar to the definition contained in the civil code because the Roman jurists never provided a definition of *dominium*'. In Germany, he argues, 'Roman law learning was mobilized by nineteenth century German scholars to reconstruct an intellectual model that later guided the codifiers in their efforts to lay down an abstract notion of property right', even though the absolute notion of ownership enacted by the codes 'did not match the living law in the countryside'.[64] Di Robilant and Syed conclude that, as part of the revolution in property that accompanied the rise of capitalist social relations, 'jurists, economists and philosophers

---

[61] Gaudemet is quoted by Shael Herman in 'The Uses and Abuses of Roman Law Texts', 29 *American Journal of Comparative Law*, pp. 671–690 (1981), p. 673.
[62] Herman, 'The Uses and Abuses of Roman Law Texts', pp. 674–5.
[63] Herman, 'The Uses and Abuses of Roman Law Texts', p. 672.
[64] Graziadei, 'The Structure of Property Ownership', p. 86.

embarked in the project of crafting "Roman-bourgeois" property, a new concept of unitary and full property for modern, liberal, capitalist European nation states, modelled along the lines of Roman dominium'.[65] Jurists institutionalised a new, modern concept of property as private property, economists forged a new political economy and political theorists proposed 'a new constitutional vision of equal citizenship based on the demarcation between absolute private property and public sovereignty'.[66] In this process, the economic, the political and the legal were prised apart. Seeing modern conceptions of property as present in Roman law, of course, facilitates the universalisation and naturalisation of the historically specific conceptions of (private) property and ownership that characterise contemporary capitalism.

The idea of property in law

New essentialist theories of property took off after the publication of Harris' book in 1996. Despite their varied nature, they share certain common features. Firstly, they conceptualise property, as Harris did, in terms of thing-ownership and exclusion. Secondly, they tend to engage in high-level abstraction. Thirdly, in keeping with the renewed interest in conceptual analysis in private law in general (the so-called New Private Law movement), they tend to show more interest in legal doctrine than they do in the empirical realities of property as it operates in the real world. Finally, they tend in various ways and to varying degrees to naturalise and legitimate the existing property status quo.

The motivations of the new essentialists vary. For some, particularly those working within the analytical jurisprudential tradition, the search for a transhistorical and transcultural 'essence' for property is primarily motivated by conceptual concerns. This is, for example, the case with one of the first and most influential new essentialists, James Penner, whose *The Idea of Property in Law* appeared in 1997.[67] Penner is relentlessly critical of the 'nominalism' of the bundle of rights concept of property, arguing that, with its 'missing thingness', it is 'positively pernicious', denying the legitimate common-sense idea that property is about 'things' and blurring the distinction between property rights and other legal rights.[68] Echoing Kevin Gray, who points out that, far from resolving the conceptual problems thrown up by

---

[65] di Robilant and Syed, 'Property's Building Blocks', p. 241.
[66] di Robilant and Syed, 'Property's Building Blocks', p. 241.
[67] J E Penner, *The Idea of Property in Law*, Oxford: Oxford University Press (1997).
[68] J E Penner, 'Potentiality, Actuality and Stick Theory', 8 *Econ Journal Watch*, pp. 274–8 (2011), p. 275. See also Henry Smith, 'Property Is Not Just a Bundle of Rights', 8 *Econ Journal Watch*, pp. 279–91 (2011). As Lametti says, property theorists are 'keen to avoid the plague of malleability': Lametti, 'The Concept of Property', pp. 375–6.

the 'unattainable quality inherent in the notion of private property', the conceptualisation of property as a bundle of rights amplifies them, Penner argues that the bundle of rights picture of property 'is not really a useful concept of any kind'; it 'doesn't help judges understand what they're doing when they decide cases' or 'effectively characterize any particular sort of legal relation'.[69] He shares Gray's view that it does not tell us what distinguishes property rights from other (bundles of) rights.[70] It is only by giving some role to objects in the definition of property, Penner argues, that it is possible to distinguish property relations from other relations: property needs its *in rem* quality to be a conceptually distinct juridical relation and legal category. Others have followed Penner's lead and also adopted conceptualisations of property centred on or around thing-ownership, although Penner focuses more on the duties of non-owners and the right to exclude, while others focus more on the authority of and control exercised by owners over things. For theorists like Larissa Katz, for example, the distinctive feature of property and ownership is that 'owners are in a special position to set the agenda for a resource'.[71]

Penner seeks to develop a general theory of property that re-establishes the idea that property has a definable essence centred on things and exclusion that is not contingent on any particular socio-economic context. His work has clearly been influenced by Joseph Raz, his DPhil supervisor at Oxford. Raz sought to draw a distinction between the *nature* of law, which, he claimed, is universal, and the *concept* of law, which is parochial. 'It is easy to explain', Raz argued, 'in what sense legal philosophy is universal. Its theses, if true, apply universally, that is they speak of all law, of all legal systems, of those that exist, or that will exist, and even of those that can exist though they never will'.[72] However, 'while the general theory of law is universal, it is also parochial'. What makes it parochial is that 'the concept of law is itself the product of a specific culture'. Indeed, 'there is no one concept of law', for different cultures have different concepts of law. As a result, Raz argued,

---

[69] Penner, 'Potentiality, Actuality and Stick Theory', p. 1.

[70] Gray, 'Property in Thin Air', pp. 252, 259. Gray emphasises the criterion of 'excludability' as 'the core' of 'property', while others stress the transferability of the rights' bundles and their potential market value; still others emphasise both: Worthington, *Equity*, chapter 3. In similar vein, James Penner argues that the 'dominant' bundle of rights paradigm is 'really no explanatory model at all but represents the absence of one. [It] is little more than a slogan': Penner, 'The Bundle of Rights Picture of Property', p. 714.

[71] Larissa Katz, 'Exclusion and Exclusivity in Property Law', 58 *University of Toronto Law Journal*, pp. 275–315 (2008), p. 278. Having started off as exclusionists, Merrill and Smith have shifted position, arguing that the owner's exclusive right to control things is primary and that exclusion is merely a means to this end: see Wyman, 'The New Essentialism in Property', p. 201.

[72] Raz, *Between Authority and Interpretation*, p. 91.

'talk of *the* concept of law really means *our* concept of law', suggesting that his concept of law was merely a reflection of law as it is in modern Western capitalist societies.[73] From this perspective, legal theory is parochial in the sense that it seeks to explain 'an institution designated by a concept that is a local concept, a product of modern western civilisation'. Raz nevertheless insisted that this concept is universal in that 'it applies to law whenever and wherever it can conceivably be'.[74] Thus, he claimed that 'while the concept of law is parochial, ie not all societies have it', philosophical inquiry into law seeks universal truths 'in that it explores the nature of law, wherever it is found'. The concept of law may be parochial, but legal theory is not.[75]

I am not going to consider Raz's attempts to respond to the (obvious) objection that he is committing 'the familiar philosophical error of mistaking one contested and contingent understanding of law as its unifying and universal essence'[76] and that his admission of parochialism fatally undermines the universal claims he makes for his theoretical endeavours. Raz recognised the problems created for his universal claims by his admission of conceptual parochialism and wrestled with them, introducing modifications and qualifications to his analysis, while continuing to cling on to his key claim that, while concepts of law are parochial, the theory of law is universal. Suffice it to say that not everyone was persuaded. Allan Hutchinson, for example, found his changes of position 'not only far from convincing', but thought they did 'serious damage to the cogency and strength of his theoretical claims'.[77] What matters for our purposes is that Penner seems to follow a very similar path, combining universal claims with parochialism. Just as Raz sought to develop a general theory of law that 'elucidate[s] law's essential features', meaning features that are 'possessed by every legal system', and to identify universal truths about the nature of law 'not contingent on existing political, social, economic or cultural conditions, institutions, or practices'[78], Penner seeks to argue that property has certain essential features that can be conceptually captured at a high level of generality. 'There are' he writes, 'high level abstractions about property which we cannot plausibly do without if we are to understand property rights and property law doctrine'.[79] Thus, the

---

[73] Raz, *Between Authority and Interpretation*, p. 32, 95–6.
[74] Raz, *Between Authority and Interpretation*, p. 38.
[75] Raz, *Between Authority and Interpretation*, pp. 32–3.
[76] Allan Hutchinson, 'Razzle Dazzle', 1 *Jurispridence*, pp. 39–61 (2010), p. 46. See also Brian Tamanaha, *A Realistic Theory of Law*, Cambridge: Cambridge University Press (2017), chapter 3.
[77] Hutchinson, 'Razzle Dazzle', p. 46.
[78] Raz, *Between Authority and Interpretation*, p. 92.
[79] J E Penner, 'Property', in A S Gold et al (eds), *The Oxford Handbook of the New Private Law*, Oxford: Oxford University Press, pp. 277–292 (2020), p. 278.

aim of *The Idea of Property in Law*, he tells us, is 'to say something in general about an idea of property' that 'captur[es] the way in which things are dealt with under existing legal systems'. In his closing comments, he expresses the hope that the idea of property he has elaborated will be 'vindicat[ed] … through the examination of the rules and doctrines of the property law in different jurisdictions, cultures, and historical periods', though this, he says, would be 'the subject of a different book which must await another day'.[80] Although he stresses that his is not a work of comparative law, Penner clearly believes that his abstract idea (or concept) of property is operative in all legal systems and, in that sense, transcends time and place.[81] As a result, although one of his aims is to 'understand property rights and property law doctrine', he steers clear of tying his arguments too closely to any specific set of empirically existing property laws or arrangements, aware, perhaps, that the more detailed and empirically richer and grounded his conceptual analysis, the less plausible might be its universal claims.

Building, like Raz, on Hart's ideas about the 'internal' aspects of law and the belief that in trying to capture law's nature we must draw on the self-understandings of participants in the legal system,[82] Penner argues that property is 'what the average citizen, free of the entanglements of legal philosophy, thinks it is: the right to a thing'.[83] Penner's concept of property is thus very much *our* concept of property. On this basis, Penner argues that property rights can be explained using the concepts of exclusion and use, which, he says, 'interact naturally'. He goes on to suggest that in 'legal systems' categories like property, contract and tort are individuated to reflect the fact that they protect discrete interests. Thus, contract protects our interest in making binding agreements, while property protects the interest we have in using things. Exclusion is simply 'the practical means by which that interest is protected'.[84] This interest-based approach leads Penner to conceptualise property as 'the right to determine the use or disposition of a … thing … in so far as that can be achieved or aided by others excluding themselves from it'.[85] He reconciles the idea of property as a right to a thing with the Hohfeldian idea of it as a correlative juridical relation between people by

---

[80] Penner, *The Idea of Property in Law*, p. 230.
[81] Penner, *The Idea of Property in Law*, p. 2.
[82] The influence of Hart's ideas about describing and analysing law from the internal point of view, and focusing on the way law is understood by those whose law it is, is apparent here: Raz, *Between Authority and Interpretation*, p. 93.
[83] Penner, *The Idea of Property in Law*, p. 2.
[84] Penner, *The Idea of Property in Law*, pp. 70–1. This interest-based approach seems to have been borrowed from Joseph Raz, *The Concept of a Legal System*, Oxford: Oxford University Press (1980).
[85] Penner, *The Idea of Property in Law*, p. 152.

arguing that the object of property – the 'thing' – plays a mediating role between the rights of owners and the general duties of non-owners not to interfere with the property of others.

He has since modified his theory of property somewhat, though only in minor ways.[86] In a recent book, he renews his assault on the bundle of rights conception and what he considers the misguided 'Hohfeld–Honoré synthesis', before going on to argue that property has a tripartite structure that reflects the internal logic of property rules. This structure is 'a sort of "bundle" of jural entities'[87] composed of the right to exclude ('the right to immediate, exclusive possession'[88]) and two powers, the powers to license and to transfer title. He dubs the exclusionary element of this structure 'BPrN, the Basic Property Norm – the Property Exclusionary Norm for Tangible Property' and argues that the three parts of his tripartite characterisation of ownership 'naturally go together': 'the tripartite structure of title is not simply some bundling together of disparate jural norms on the basis of fluctuating, historical, policy considerations ... rather they go together because of their very nature'.[89] Moreover, it is 'fairly easy', he writes, 'to come up with a story' about why this is so. This story centres on the importance of human agency and autonomy in 'dealing with the external resources of the world' and 'the power to voluntarily undertake obligations'. 'Ignoring the contractual side', Penner argues, is perhaps the 'worst facet' of treating property as just a bundle of sticks 'that can be handed out by an owner'.[90]

It is significant that Penner's 'Basic Property Norm' is 'the property exclusionary norm for *tangible* property', for applying his ideas to objects of property that have a corporeal material existence from which others can be physically excluded – Penner's paradigmatic form of property – is conceptually relatively unproblematic. However, as we have seen, intangible forms of property have grown in both number and importance in recent centuries and Penner concedes that their lack of materiality is a source of 'a number of sticky issues' and 'thought-provoking problems'.[91] As Penner says, choses in action, 'unlike property in land or chattels, are not rights *in rem*; they are rights *in personam* held against specifiable individuals'. A debt, for example, is 'a purely intangible, abstract legal relation'. It has, therefore, to be asked, 'how they acquire[d] a property-like character, despite the fact they are in essence personal rights'?[92]

---

[86] J E Penner, *Property Rights: A Re-Examination*, Oxford: Oxford University Press (2020).
[87] Penner, 'Property', p. 283.
[88] Penner, *Property Rights*, p. 14.
[89] Penner, *Property Rights*, pp. 15–16, 26, 209.
[90] Penner, *The Idea of Property in Law*, pp. 15–16.
[91] Penner, *The Idea of Property in Law*, pp. 2, 115.
[92] Penner, *The Idea of Property in Law*, pp. 107–8.

Penner's analysis of how some intangibles have acquired a thing-like and 'property-like' character is illuminating. He develops what he calls a 'separability thesis', the thrust of which is that a necessary criterion of treating some 'thing' (like a bundle of *in personam* rights) as property is that it is only contingently ours and could easily be someone else's. In other words, the thing (or rights bundle) is separate from us and can be transferred to someone else. This becomes possible, Penner argues, when they become 'personality-poor' rather than 'personality-rich'. Penner claims that this separability precedes alienability, that the 'thingness' of intangibles pre-exists their transferability: 'It is not because they are alienable that they are things. Rather, it is because they are things that they are alienable'.[93] Historically, however, this is simply not the case, or at least not always so, as the case of the joint stock company share clearly demonstrates. The recognition of shares in joint stock companies as objects of property completely separate from the company's assets was inextricably tied up with the growth of a developed share market and the ever more frequent buying and selling of shares, the legal efficacy of which was sometimes questioned by the courts.[94] *De facto* transfers and *de jure* transferability underpinned the emergence of shares as separate forms of property, as autonomous 'things'.[95]

Intangibles also pose problems for Penner's new tripartite structure, for, as Penner himself says, 'in the case of an intangible there is nothing to exclude anybody from ... when something is inherently intangible ... there can be no crossing of a boundary where no boundary exists'. Rather than seeing this as a conceptual problem, however, Penner argues that this merely means that 'no exclusionary rules are necessary'[96] and that the case of intangible property is, therefore, 'simpler'. With intangible property, he argues, 'all we have is an underlying right' that doesn't relate to a tangible thing at all', rendering intangible property '*inherently "exclusive"*'.[97] This looks a little like what Nicola Lacey has described in another context as a 'peremptory bundling of inconveniently shaped legal phenomena into the conceptual strait jacket of [one's] theories'.[98] The value of intangible intellectual property rights clearly does depend on being able to exclude people from ideas, knowledge,

---

[93] Penner, *The Idea of Property in Law*, p. 130.
[94] *Duvergier v Fellows* (1828) 5 Bing 24, per Best CJ; George, *A View of the Existing Law*.
[95] As for the duty of non-interference in relation to intangibles, Penner writes that 'the criterion of "thinghood" or separability applies to these rights in such a way that they partake of the duty of non-interference in an *indirect* way' (p. 130, emphasis added).
[96] Penner, *Property Rights*, chapter 1, footnote 52.
[97] Penner, *Property Rights*, p. 14 (his emphasis).
[98] Nicola Lacey, 'Analytical Jurisprudence Versus Descriptive Sociology Revisited', 84 *Texas Law Review*, pp. 945–82 (2006), p. 949.

and the like. But with revenue rights, the main issue is not exclusion but maintaining the social conditions and practices that underpin the revenues.

The limitations of, and weaknesses in, Penner's analysis are rooted (somewhat ironically) in its exclusions. He opens *The Idea of Property in Law* by saying that he wants to 'emphasize the fact that property is something which has an existence in the real world', that it is 'a practice, a way of dealing with things in which people actually engage'. He therefore says that he wants to locate property in its practical setting: property 'is a creature of its environment' and his is an 'environmental approach'. For Penner, however, the 'environment' of property is very restricted in scope. Property's 'natural environment', he tells us, is 'the legal system'. His goal, therefore, is to elaborate the concept of property not as an isolated concept, but as 'part of a broader normative system, a legal system', that contains other concepts such as contract, tort, crime. Thus, his book, he says, could have been called 'The Concept of Property in a Legal System'.[99] His ideas about the 'environment', 'context' and 'practice' of property are, therefore, highly attenuated. He operates with what we might call a second 'separability thesis' in which law and legal systems are separated from the wider economic, political and social systems of which they are part. Indeed, Penner believes that his concept of property, although informed by existing property law doctrine (it is 'our' concept of property), can be abstracted from different economic, political and social systems and from the wider set of social institutions and practices of which empirically existing property systems are always part. In other words, property, as he conceptualises it, is universal, or at least universal to all societies with legal systems, even if the specific socio-economic contexts (Indian, British, Chinese, Russian, Nigerian, American, Brazilian, whatever) within which it is found are very different. 'Property', he says, 'goes merrily along in any system in which people have the right to determine the use of things'.[100] In this way, while recognising that some property rules are the products of policy decisions, Penner portrays his concept of property as somehow untainted by and beyond (or above) policy and politics. In the words of Craig Rotherham, Penner 'makes a case for an absolutist conception of property understood as an analytical, and hence apolitical, truth'.[101]

This becomes clear from his stance on the distributional dimensions of property and property rights. 'The distributive justice of who owns what', he argues, 'has nothing to do with property', but has, rather, 'a lot to do with

---

[99] Penner, *The Idea of Property in Law*, pp. 2–4.
[100] Penner, *The Idea of Property in Law*, p. 5.
[101] Craig Rotherham, 'Review of James Penner, The Idea of Property in Law', 61 *Modern Law Review*, pp. 119–21 (1998), p. 121.

the nature of the economy one lives in, whether that economy emphasises command, or gift, or contract (ie markets)'.[102] For Penner, the distribution of wealth is not an effect of property but of different economic systems, 'the different sorts of economy operating in a society'.[103] Indeed, he not only excludes consideration of the distributional dimensions of property from his analysis, he makes it clear that he thinks them uninteresting: 'is anyone not bored by the project of justifying or decrying inequalities of property ownership?'.[104] As Rotherham says, for Penner, 'the only real issues of distributive justice involved in the law of property revolve around the determination of what can be owned. The degree of protection afforded to these objects is somehow understood to follow analytically from the very notion of property, rather than involving inherently controversial allocative decisions'.[105] In this way, Penner rules out the need for empirical analyses of consequences and of the way property operates 'in practice' or for distinctions to be drawn between different sorts of resources or 'things'/objects of property. In other words, Penner believes that property can be conceptualised without paying much attention to, or without much knowledge of, the world outside legal doctrine.

Moreover, although in pursuit of greater universality Penner seeks to detach his concept of property from any particular economic system, it is clearly based, à la Raz, on *our* concept of property – on property as it exists in modern Western capitalist societies.[106] Indeed, it is precisely because of this that Penner's analysis of property is able to cast light on the nature of property in contemporary capitalism. The distinction he draws between 'personality-rich' and 'personality-poor' rights *in personam*, for example, is very helpful in helping us to understand how some choses in action have acquired thing- and property-like qualities. His idea of property reflects a world in which private property has been generalised, extending to productive resources as well as personal possessions; a world in which property appears to be concerned with 'things' and to involve person-thing relations, even when the 'things' concerned lack a material existence; a world in which the intangible revenue rights that are so central to wealth and power have been reified and rendered personality-poor, concealing the social relations underlying them; a world in which impersonal markets and

---

[102] Penner, *The Idea of Property in Law*, pp. 5, 187.
[103] Penner, *The Idea of Property in Law*, p. 187.
[104] Penner, *The Idea of Property in Law*, p. 6.
[105] Rotherham, 'Review of James Penner', p. 120.
[106] Margaret Davies argues that Penner seems to 'lack ... consciousness that there is a political and cultural tradition informing his argument and in particular its underlying assumptions': 'Review of J E Penner, The Idea of Property in Law', 7 *Social and Legal Studies*, pp. 577–80 (1998), p. 578.

market relations are prevalent; a world in which law and the legal system is seen as autonomous from other social spheres.

Raz further argued that 'in working out a theory of law we are explicating our own self-understanding of the nature of society and politics', and this too is the case with Penner.[107] It is possible to discern in his theory of property an account of 'the nature of society and politics' in contemporary capitalism. It is, however, a highly misleading account, one that reflects capitalism's self-image rather than its empirical realities. In this respect, his general theory of property resembles the general law of contract found in traditional texts. The law of contract explicated in legal texts abstracts from empirical reality and presents itself as a set of universally valid rules that follow logically from a small number of self-evident principles that can be abstracted both from particulars and from consequences. It projects a liberal image of the social order as a just order based on individual autonomy, free will, opportunity, and voluntary exchange. The narrative about the 'nature of society and politics' that underlies Penner's concept of property does much the same, conjuring up an image of a private property-based social order rooted in individual autonomy, free choice, and the free exchange of (mainly tangible) 'things'. It is not only a world of tangible things rather than of intangible intellectual and financial property, but also a world of small producers and simple commodity production rather than of hugely powerful multi-national capitalist enterprises. As Elizabeth Anderson says, 'images of free market society that made sense prior to the Industrial Revolution continue to circulate today as ideals, blind to the gross mismatch between the background social assumptions reigning in the seventeenth and eighteenth centuries, and today's institutional realities'.[108] The real world of power imbalances, inequality and (for many) seriously constrained choice is screened out and hidden behind abstract generalities. It is a triumph of form over substance that reflects the self-image of capitalism. Moreover, the contingencies of capitalism are made to look timeless and eternal, the natural and necessary facts of life. As Rotherham observes, Penner's 'prose abounds with naturalistic metaphors': legal material 'will break on pre-existing fracture lines'; property and contract are 'creatures interacting in an environment'; legal categories are a 'natural feature of legal material'; use and exclusion 'interact naturally'; the legal system is property's 'natural environment'.[109] The fact that his concept of property is not outside history

---

[107] Raz, *Between Authority and Interpretation*, p. 97.
[108] Anderson, *Private Government*, p. 6; Alan Thomson, 'The Law of Contract', in Ian Grigg-Spall and Paddy Ireland (eds), *The Critical Lawyers Handbook*, London: Pluto, pp. 69–76 (1992).
[109] As Rotherham points out: 'Review of James Penner', p. 119.

but has a history is largely concealed. Moreover, in failing to get to grips with the historical conditions of the existence of this concept of property, Penner tends to naturalise and universalise it and its material foundations.[110] As Timothy Mitchell says, despite their seeming neutrality, claims about the universality of property are politically significant, for 'the law of property gains its power by appearing as an abstraction ... [by] seem[ing] to stand as a conceptual structure, based not on particular claims or histories but on principles true in every country'.[111]

Indeed, Penner not only naturalises but endorses 'our' concept of property. Thus, the three elements of his tripartite structure of ownership not only 'naturally go together', but are also expressions of 'self-mastery [and] independence from the choices of others', of human agency in relation to 'the external resources of the world', and of the power individuals have voluntarily to undertake obligations.[112] Indeed, at one point, having detached his abstract concept of property from any particular economic system and absolved it of responsibility for any particular set of empirical outcomes, Penner writes that '[t]he legitimacy of property rights per se strikes me as well nigh indisputable, for the practice of property protects a liberty, i.e. exclusively to determine the use of things, that has proved marvellously productive in contributing to the good life of many'.[113] One wonders whether those for whom the power of some (like large multi-national corporations) over the external resources of the world means, in empirical reality, a loss of self-mastery, independence and agency – and for whom the actual practice of property and property rights has brought exploitation, poverty, hardship and, in the case of some indigenous peoples, dispossession and cultural destruction – would agree. As a result of its contextual blinkers, then, Penner's theory of property provides not only an incomplete but a misleading picture both of property in contemporary capitalism and of the social order from which his concept of property is drawn. It conceals as much as it reveals. It should be noted, however, that although in the past Penner has tended to abstract from different resources and different objects of property, in his recent book he begins to grapple with the differences between resources and the possibility

---

[110] See Penner's casual comments about the collapse of feudal property institutions with their suggestion of efficiency-based inevitability and hints that it is evidence of the superiority of Merrill and Smith's property and exclusion strategy over governance (discussed later): Penner, *Property Rights*, pp. 17–18.

[111] Timothy Mitchell, *Rule of Experts: Egypt, techno-politics, modernity*, Berkeley: University of California Press (2002), p. 11.

[112] Penner, *Property Rights*, pp. 15, 158. He suggests that his focus on self-mastery as independence from others rather than on autonomy is more relational and less individualistic: Penner, *Property Rights*, chapter 8.

[113] Penner, *The Idea of Property in Law*, pp. 206–7.

that a single uniform framework should not be applied across all resources. Environmental concerns lead him, as he 'sport[s] his lefty environmental credentials for a moment',[114] to wonder whether land, 'given its particular features, is a very suitable object of ownership' and to assert that he is not 'a general *proponent* of property rights' who 'insist[s] upon instituting them whenever they can frame our interpersonal relations with respect to some thing, land in particular'.[115] He writes:

> Perhaps the greatest injustice in the history of the institution of property rights was that institution's abuse by the powerful to appropriate lands which, while not 'owned' in the strict sense, were certainly occupied and used. Anyone with any sympathy at all for commoners whose lands suffered enclosure, or with the concept of aboriginal or native title, understands this point.[116]

The limitations of Penner's analysis stem from the limitations inherent in his analytical jurisprudential approach and its restricted field of vision. These lead him, as they do Raz, down a rather 'barren path'[117] from which it is possible to cast only limited light on property as it exists in the real world. Penner's restriction of the 'environment' of property to the legal system and legal doctrine prevents him from seeing property, to use in the words used by Nicola Lacey when analysing another piece of legal philosophical analysis,[118] 'as a social practice that takes place within a [wider] context, the specific nature of which requires investigation because it inflects the relevant [legal] concepts'. 'Once the notion of "context" is made broader', she explains, 'the inexorable conclusion is that illumination of legal practices lies not merely within an analysis of doctrinal language; it lies equally within an attempt to locate the analysis within some general account of history and social role

---

[114] Penner, *Property Rights*, p. 204.
[115] Penner, *Property Rights*, p. 201.
[116] Penner, *Property Rights*, p. 196.
[117] This was Edgar Bodenheimer's description of the path taken by H L A Hart in his inaugural address, 'Definition and Theory in Jurisprudence'. While Bodenheimer thought it an improvement on the attempts to provide dictionary-like definitions of fundamental legal concepts in abstraction from the specific contexts in which the defined words were used, he did not think Hart's offering could 'be regarded as great step forward from bare definition', in part because of his approach's unwillingness to encompass 'extra-legal considerations': 'Modern Analytical Jurisprudence and the Limits of its Usefulness', 104 *University of Pennsylvania Law Review*, pp. 1080–6 (1956), p. 1085. A few years later, Hart described (not entirely convincingly) *The Concept of Law* (1961) as descriptive sociology as well as analytical jurisprudence, a comment that has caused considerable subsequent confusion and argument.
[118] H L A Hart and Tony Honoré's *Causation in Law*, Oxford: Oxford University Press (1959).

of the institutions and the power relations within which that usage takes place'.[119] In other words, there are strict limits to how far a highly abstract concept of property of the sort provided by Penner, with its focus on legal doctrine, can help us understand property at any particular time and place. A full understanding of property at any particular time and place – and of the legal rules, principles and doctrines relating to it – can only be acquired by supplementing the kind of conceptual and philosophical analysis Penner offers with an engagement with empirical reality beyond doctrine and with an exploration of the economic and social relations, institutions and practices within which that particular concept and those rules and principles are embedded and of which they are constitutive.[120] Real-world analysis, not least of property's relevance to power relations, is largely missing from Penner's analysis. Strikingly, for example, corporations and the power they possess through their ownership of huge amounts of productively crucial tangible and intangible property, barely figure, excluded by his narrowly drawn lines of enquiry.[121] His concept of property is thus constituted in part by suppression and by exclusion. The result of this unwillingness to broaden one's contextual gaze beyond doctrine towards the socio-economic conditions of existence of our concept of property is a theory that tends, perhaps inadvertently, towards conservatism, in much the same way as, some have argued, did H L A Hart's *Concept of Law*.[122]

---

[119] Lacey, 'Jurisprudence, History, and the Institutional Quality of Law', p. 969.

[120] Lacey, 'Jurisprudence, History, and the Institutional Quality of Law', pp. 947–8. Lacey points out that, in contrast to many analytical philosophers, Wittgenstein operated with a much broader conception of context that included a whole range of things excluded by Penner, not least social institutions and practices, even if, rather than engaging in empirical research to reveal (some of) them, Wittgenstein instead simply adopted a 'defeatist view of the power of philosophy': Lacey, 'Jurisprudence, History, and the Institutional Quality of Law', p. 968.

[121] In his recent work, as noted above, land and 'objects of cultural significance' have become partial exceptions: Penner, *The Idea of Property in Law*, pp. 199, 201.

[122] See B E King, 'The Basic Concept of Professor Hart's Jurisprudence', 21 *Cambridge Law Journal*, pp. 270–303 (1963), p. 277.

6

Defending the Property Status Quo: Law and Economics

The modern corporation and the threat to shareholder rights

While the work of new essentialists like Penner is motivated primarily by conceptual concerns and tends only implicitly to support the property status quo, the work of other new essentialists, working mainly from within the law-and-economics tradition, is much more explicitly motivated by politics and ideology. The primary goal of much of this work is to offer a defence of the property status quo and of private property, irrespective of context or of the resources involved. This is the case with one of the most influential new essentialist theories to have emerged in recent decades, the so-called 'information-cost' theory of property, developed in a stream of articles by Thomas Merrill and Henry Smith. To understand the ideological underpinnings and motivations of this theory, however, we need first to explore the historical and political backdrop to the emergence of, and role played by, the law-and-economics movement in developing new justifications and legitimations for the property status quo, particularly in relation to corporations and shareholder rights – and, therefore, in relation to key productive resources and the fruits of productive activity.[1]

As Robé observes, the eighteenth- and nineteenth-century architects of the modern liberal order of private property were operating in an economic order characterised by individual (predominantly flesh-and-blood) property owners, large numbers of producers and dispersed power, not an economic order dominated by large, powerful corporations and multi-national enterprises. By the end of the nineteenth century, however,

---

[1] I use the terms 'corporation' and 'corporate' as they are used in everyday usage to refer to large publicly-quoted (joint stock) companies.

production had become a much less individual and much more social affair, as various commentators noted. As we have seen, for example, the increasingly social nature of production, and its growing dependence on the collective technological knowledge of communities, was a major theme in Veblen's writings. The increasingly social nature of production was most obviously manifested in its growing concentration in large corporations and in the ever growing division of labour. With the rise of corporate economies, developed capitalist economies gradually came to be characterised as much by oligopoly, monopoly and planning (both by corporations and the state), as by competitive free markets. Moreover, these corporations were increasingly populated not by active shareholder-members but by inactive rentiers. As we have seen, Smith commented on this in *Wealth of Nations*. A century later, Marx similarly noted that in joint stock corporations, the 'actually functioning capitalist' had been transformed into 'a mere manager, administrator of other people's capital', while the owner of capital, the shareholder, had been transformed into 'a mere money capitalist', receiving their returns in the form, if not at the level, of interest. Joint stock corporations had assumed 'the form of social undertakings as distinct from private undertakings', Marx argued, and the capital invested in them was 'directly endowed with the form of social capital … as distinct from private capital'. The rise of the joint stock corporation, he suggested, represented the 'abolition of capital as private property within the framework of capitalist production itself'.[2]

By the end of the century, these increasingly powerful joint stock corporations had been legally reconceptualised as property-owning legal persons 'completely separate' from their shareholders (as 'its'), not as they had previously as their shareholders merged into a single body (as 'theys'). Gradually, the idea emerged of corporations as objects of property 'owned' by their shareholders. This reconceptualisation of the corporation as a fully separate entity (person/thing) cleansed of its shareholders was underpinned by the fact that corporate shareholders had become both responsibility-free (management had been delegated to specialist managers) and liability-free (the rise to dominance of the fully paid-up share had turned limited liability into *de facto* no liability).[3] As various commentators noted, shareholders now resembled creditors as much as owners. In the US, Veblen led the way, arguing that the ownership of productive resources, which had previously entailed the control of tangible material assets and carried various duties and responsibilities, had come to entail mere passive possession of intangible corporate capital. Corporate

---

[2] Marx, *Capital*, volume 3, pp. 436–8.
[3] See Ireland, 'Corporate Schizophrenia'.

shareholders, he argued, had been reduced to the status of 'absentee owners' detached from the process of production, possessors of mere claims 'to unearned or free income'. He likened them to bondholders, arguing that the lines between debt and property, credit and capital, and stock and bond had been blurred.[4] For Veblen, the reduction of shareholders to the *de facto* status of financial investors who resembled creditors rather than owners was one aspect of the growing domination of industry by finance ('business') that was having a negative productive and social impact. In *Drift and Mastery*, published in 1914, the journalist Walter Lippman echoed Veblen, emphasising the increasingly creditor-like nature of corporate shareholding in the era of the professionally managed corporation. The 'one qualification' to be a corporate shareholder, he argued, was 'the possession of some money and the desire for more'. Shares had become 'little more than claims to residual profits' and shareholders 'transient absentee owners' who flitted 'like ... butterflies from industry to industry'. The modern shareholder, Lipmann concluded, was a 'very feeble representative[s] of the institution of private property'.[5]

In the UK, R H Tawney and Harold Laski offered similar critiques of the absentee rentier shareholder. In 1921, in his influential book *The Acquisitive Society*, Tawney launched a fierce attack on what he saw as the inherently pernicious and parasitic nature of intangible financial property forms such as the share. Like Veblen, he argued that the traditional justifications for private property rights were inapplicable to property forms of this sort. Unlike rights to tangible personal possessions, which could be defended as 'indispensable to a life of decency and comfort' and as encouraging industry and individual initiative, the owners of these new intangible revenue rights were 'functionless'. Indeed, in directing productive activity towards 'acquisition' rather than 'service to society', they were positively *dys*functional, dissipating creative energy and 'corrupting the principle of industry'. Shareholders, Tawney argued, should be stripped of their exclusive

---

[4] See Veblen, *Absentee Ownership*; Veblen, *The Theory Business Enterprise*. By the late 1920s, it had become commonplace to remark on the resemblance between shareholders and bondholders and thereby implicitly to question the former's proprietary status vis-à-vis the corporation. 'The average stockholder in the large corporation', wrote Franklin Wood, 'regards himself more as a security holder than as in any sense a responsible managing partner in the corporate enterprise'. As a result, he argued, the legal distinction between bondholders and stockholders was 'fast becoming a distinction unwarranted by the actual situation': Franklin S. Wood, 'The Status of Management Stockholders', 38 *Yale Law Journal*, pp. 57–76 (1928), p. 59. For a similar view, see Jerome Frank, 'Book Review of Berle and Means, *The Modern Corporation and Private Property*', 43 *Yale Law Journal*, pp. 989–1000 (1933), p. 992.

[5] Walter Lippman, *Drift and Mastery*, Madison: University of Wisconsin Press (1985 [1914]), pp. 46–8.

control rights and relegated to the status of 'creditors paid a fixed rate of interest'.⁶ A few years later, Harold Laski echoed these sentiments in his *Grammar of Politics*.⁷

Questions also began to be asked about the role of corporate managers. In 1912, Louis Brandeis wrote of the need to redefine business as a profession that was directed at 'service to the community' and 'pursued largely for others and not merely for one's self'.⁸ Echoing this, Tawney similarly argued that to redirect industry along a more productively rational and socially beneficial path, management should be turned into a 'profession' akin to medicine and law. Seeking to legitimise their growing power, managers themselves got on board with these ideas by claiming that their job was not simply to make money for shareholders but to direct productive activity towards 'service to the community'.⁹

Even more significantly, questions also began to be asked about the nature of the large corporations that were coming to dominate economic

---

6   R H Tawney, *The Acquisitive Society*, London: G Bell (1921). Tawney was a Christian Socialist, Fabian and member of the Labour Party. He taught at the London School of Economics where he was, for many years, a professor of economic history. He crossed paths with Veblen when he visited the US.

7   H Laski, *A Grammar of Politics*, London: Allen & Unwin (1925). Laski devoted lengthy chapters to 'Property' (chapter 5) and 'Economic institutions' (chapter 9). He argued that the rise of the joint stock corporation had seen a massive growth in functionless property and that an 'investing class' not involved in management had emerged, 'freed from the legal obligation to labour' and 'maintained in parasitic idleness' (pp. 175, 185–6). In order to be 'informed by a purpose relevant to the general well-being', corporate management needed to be made into a profession 'informed by a principle of public service'. For this to happen, there needed to be an 'alteration of the character of the owner of wealth into a person to whom a fixed dividend is paid for the use of his wealth' (pp. 201–9). For Laski, this attenuation of the rights of corporate shareholders was quite defensible. The distinction drawn between 'owning and earning' was, he argued, 'morally legitimate'. Property forms granting people rights to receive part of the product of the labour of others lacked 'the moral penumbra which entitle[d] them to respect'. As far as he was concerned, the 'abolition of the rights' of functionless property was necessary to reorient industry towards 'service' and part of 'the necessary path to justice'. Like Tawney, Laski did not deny the right of investors to receive an income on their capital, arguing that the state needed to protect not only the welfare of the producer and consumer but that of 'the investing public'. Capital was not, however, to be regarded as 'the natural residuary legatee of profit' and should receive only a fixed and limited return (pp. 184–5, 208, 477, 483).

8   L Brandeis, 'Business – a profession', *System* (October 1912), later republished in L Brandeis, *Business – a profession,* Boston: Small Maynard (1914).

9   See Henry Metcalf (ed.), *Business Management as a Profession*, Chicago: AW Shaw & Co (1927). Metcalf was an early organisational theorist and professor of economics. The work of Berle, Veblen, Tawney and Laski featured in the 'selected reading list' at the end of the book.

life. With production having become ever more obviously and objectively socialised, was it still appropriate to see them as purely *private* enterprises? Or were they better seen as *social* or *quasi-social* institutions? By the mid-1920s, John Maynard Keynes was arguing that there was an inevitable tendency for 'joint stock institutions', when they had reached a certain age and size, 'to approximate to the status of public corporations rather than that of individualistic private enterprise'. This 'tendency of big enterprise to socialise itself', he argued, surfaced when shareholders became 'almost entirely disassociated from the management', with the result that 'the direct personal interest of the latter in the making of profit becomes quite secondary'. At this point, Keynes suggested, managers became more concerned about the stability and reputation of the institution and shareholders had to satisfy themselves with 'conventionally adequate dividends'.[10]

These views informed the final section of Adolf Berle and Gardiner Means' celebrated *The Modern Corporation and Private Property*, published in late 1932. Having put empirical flesh on what some had long suspected – that corporate ownership was becoming increasingly dispersed and separated from corporate control – Berle and Means argued that the rise of the modern corporation had effected 'an essential alteration in the character of property', raising questions about the nature of the 'great public' corporations and the allocation of rights in them. Corporate shareholders were now the owners of 'passive' rather than of 'active' property, and it was therefore arguable that the 'traditional logic of property' no longer applied to them. They had relinquished so many of the rights and responsibilities traditionally associated with ownership they could no longer properly, or accurately, be called the corporation's owners. They had 'surrendered the right that the corporation should be operated in their sole interest', entitling the 'community ... to demand that the modern corporation serve ... all society'. Various groups should be 'assign[ed] ... a portion of the income stream on the basis of public policy rather than private cupidity'.[11]

In the years following, views of this sort became commonplace. It was increasingly argued that, given the new empirical realities, it was no longer appropriate to view corporations as purely private enterprises to be run only

---

[10] J M Keynes, *The End of Laissez-Faire*, Amherst: Prometheus Books (2004 [1926]).

[11] Adolf Berle and Gardiner Means, *The Modern Corporation and Private Property*, New York: Macmillan (1932) / New York: Harcourt Brace (revised ed. 1967). Berle first began to ponder the implications of the modern corporation for the institution of private property in 'Corporate Devices for Diluting Stock Participations', 31 *Columbia Law Review*, pp. 1239–65 (1931). However, his initial reaction to what he saw as the emerging problems arising out of the erosion of shareholder control and the rise of managerial power was to advocate a strengthening of directors' fiduciary duties to shareholders, a position he pressed in his famous debate with Merrick Dodd.

in the shareholder interest. They were social or quasi-social institutions. As the US corporate lawyer, E Merrick Dodd, pointed out, while it was difficult to square this claim with conceptions of the corporation that closely identified them with their shareholders, it was perfectly defensible if one took seriously the principle of separate corporate personality and viewed the corporation as a real entity. Thus far, separate corporate personality had only been taken *really* seriously in the context of shareholder liability for corporate debts, for which purposes the corporation and shareholders were treated as completely separate. For other purposes, however, corporations were seen not as separate legal persons, but as objects of property to be run in the interest of their shareholder 'owners'. If one really did treat corporations as fully separate legal persons, Dodd suggested, there was no reason they should not operate, through their managerial agents, as good citizens with a sense of social responsibility.[12]

From this, it was a short step to arguing that the directors of these quasi-social institutions should owe duties not only to shareholders but to employees, consumers, creditors and to society as a whole. Writing in 1934 about the new legislative framework for securities regulation, William O Douglas, shortly to become a member and then chair of the Securities and Exchange Commission, and, later, a Supreme Court justice, echoed this. He described the Securities Act as a backward-looking 'nineteenth century piece of legislation' precisely because it was trying to turn the clock back and restore shareholder control. Instead of trying to 'more closely assimilate [the investor] into the enterprise', he argued, we needed to harness the 'instruments of production not only for the ancient purpose of profit but for the more slowly evolving purpose of service in the sense of the public good'.[13]

At around the same time, in his *General Theory of Employment, Interest and Money*, Keynes observed that the rewards accruing to shareholders rewarded 'no genuine sacrifice', and, anticipating an end to the scarcity of capital, cheerfully foresaw the gradual 'euthanasia of the *rentier*'. He also provided a critique of financialisation and financial markets, analysing the tendency of investors, and especially 'professional investors', to seek short-term gain

---

[12] See E Merrick Dodd, 'For Whom Are Corporate Managers Trustees? 45 *Harvard Law Review*, pp. 1145–63 (1932), at pp. 1159–63. Berle responded with 'For Whom Corporate Managers *are* Trustees', 45 *Harvard Law Review*, pp. 1365–72 (1932). Dodd came back again with 'Is the Effective Enforcement of the Fiduciary Duties of Corporate Managers Practicable?', 2 *University of Chicago Law Review*, pp. 194–207 (1935).

[13] W O Douglas, 'Protecting the Investor', 23 *The Yale Review*, pp. 522–33 (1934). A few years later he likened the institutions of high finance to 'termites' 'interested in immediate profit' feeding off industrial enterprises which they saw 'as mere pieces of paper': W O Douglas, *Democracy and Finance*, New Haven: Yale University Press (1940), pp. 6–12.

by outguessing the market rather than long-term gain by focusing on the underlying productive fundamentals of businesses and assessing the 'probable yield of an investment over its whole life'. Echoing Veblen, he argued that the growing power of these investors and of financial markets was causing 'speculation' to dominate 'enterprise', especially in the US. This was not only damaging to investment in productive plant and equipment but a source of serious instability. As there was 'no clear evidence from experience that the investment policy which is socially advantageous coincides with that which is most profitable', Keynes concluded that a 'somewhat comprehensive socialisation of investment' was needed to channel resources away from speculation towards productive activity, and that the state, which was better placed to take a longer view and to take account of the general social interest, should take greater responsibility for 'directly organising investment'.[14] Keynes was, of course, one of the principal architects of the Bretton Woods system that shackled finance in the post-war years.

Social democracy and the socialised corporation

After the Second World War, against the backdrop of Bretton Woods, the New Deal and the emergence of welfare states, and amidst the long post-war boom and the 'Golden Age' of capitalism, it became commonplace for corporate shareholders to be portrayed as investors in revenue rights who, being responsibility- and liability-free, resembled creditors more than 'owners'. In the US, in *The Corporation in Modern Society*, an influential collection of essays published in 1959, Edward Mason argued that the equity holder had 'join[ed] the bond holder as a functionless *rentier*' and that in the corporate context the 'traditional justifications' for private enterprise and private property had 'gone forever'.[15] A number of other influential commentators – among them Abram Chayes, Bayless Manning and Peter Drucker – argued that shareholder voting rights should be pared down or even rescinded.[16] Similarly, in the UK the then doyen of company lawyers,

---

[14] J M Keynes, *The General Theory of Employment, Interest and Money* (1936), chapters 12 and 24, reprinted in E Johnson and D Moggridge (eds), *The Collected Writings of John Maynard Keynes,* volume 7, London: Macmillan (1973 [1936]). See also J H Davies, 'Keynes on the Socialization of Investment', 19 *International Journal of Social Economics*, pp. 150–63 (1992).

[15] Edward Mason, 'Introduction', in Edward Mason (ed.), *The Corporation in Modern Society*, Cambridge: Harvard University Press (1959), reprinted New York: Atheneum, pp. 1–24 (1966), pp. 2–6, 14–15.

[16] See, for example, Abram Chayes, 'The Modern Corporation and the Rule of Law', in Edward Mason (ed.), *The Corporation in Modern Society*, Cambridge: Harvard University Press (1959), reprinted New York: Atheneum, pp. 25–45 (1966); Bayless Manning, 'Review of J.A. Livingston', *The American Stockholder*, 67 *Yale Law Journal*, pp. 1477–96 (1958), pp. 1490–3.

L C B Gower, argued that directors were regularly taking account of non-shareholder interests in their decision making and that this was not only supported by public opinion but perfectly legitimate, even if it was not technically sanctioned by law. He openly questioned the desirability of restoring shareholder control and argued that the 'exclusive emphasis on the profit-making element in corporate activity' now had 'a slightly old-fashioned ring'.[17] It had become 'almost an accepted dogma', on both left and right, he argued, 'that management owes duties to the four parties of industry (labour, capital, management and the community)', even if this sentiment had not yet 'crystallised into law'.[18] Gower incorporated these ideas into successive editions of his seminal *Principles of Modern Company Law*, arguing that writers of 'very different political leanings' now considered company law to be 'unreal' in treating directors as owing duties only to its members, whereas 'in fact its relationships with its workers, the consumers of its products, and the community as a whole, are of equal if not greater importance'.[19] The idea that the primary duty of directors was to make profits for the shareholders was becoming 'increasingly anachronistic'.[20] The nationalised (public) corporation merely 'recognise[d] openly what the public company is coming to recognise tacitly: that an enterprise should be run for and on behalf of the public as a whole and not merely for the benefit of a small section of it represented by the shareholders'.[21] For Gower, the lack of acknowledgement of the position of the worker, in particular, in the corporate structure was 'anachronistic' and a 'failure of company law'.[22]

Widespread belief in ideas of this sort both reflected and contributed to the emergence of the more socially democratic capitalism of the post-war decades. Many believed that, although the logic of capitalism remained in place, it had been moderated and that, alongside these more 'socialised' corporations, there was emerging a softer, more inclusive, less unequal, less rapacious, more humane, and 'acceptable' form of capitalism. During this period, sometimes characterised as *Les Trente Glorieuses*, the distribution of

---

[17] L C B Gower, 'Review of F Emerson and F Latcham, *Shareholder Democracy*', 68 *Harvard Law Review*, pp. 922–8 (1955), p. 927.
[18] L C B Gower, 'Corporate Control: the battle for the Berkeley', 68 *Harvard Law Review*, pp. 1176–93 (1955).
[19] L C B Gower, *Principles of Modern Company Law*, London: Stevens (2nd ed., 1957), p. 56.
[20] Gower, *Principles* (2nd ed., 1957), pp. 475–6.
[21] Gower, *Principles* (2nd ed., 1957), p. 231. He was not alone in expressing such views. Another leading UK company lawyer, Robert Pennington, expressed not dissimilar views: See R R Pennington, 'Terminal Compensation for Employees of Companies in Liquidation', 25 *Modern Law Review*, pp. 715–19 (1962), pp. 718–19.
[22] L C B Gower, *Principles of Modern Company Law*, London: Stevens (4th ed., 1979), pp. 66–7, 578–80.

the social product was often determined not only by market forces but also by complex tripartite negotiations between capital, labour and the state. The forms of negotiation and distribution varied from place to place, as did the outcomes, but, overall, as Piketty and others have documented, income and wealth inequality declined. Underpinning this softening of the logic of capitalism and moderation of corporate behaviour was, of course, the changed balance of class forces and the changed legal, financial and political structures that came with this, not least the financial regime instituted by Bretton Woods.[23]

These ideas about corporations and corporate shareholders clearly posed a threat to the property status quo and particularly to the corporate property rights and intangible revenue rights that had become central to wealth and power. The threat was mitigated, however, by the belief, widespread on the Left, that politically contentious changes to shareholder rights were unnecessary because corporations and capitalism as a whole were being *de facto* socialised within the existing property rights structures, rendering it unnecessary formally to reduce the rights of shareholders or to change their status, let alone expropriate them. In the UK, this view found expression in the work of Labour Party intellectuals like Evan Durbin[24] and Anthony Crosland. In Crosland's view, 'the decline of capitalist control [did] not mean that the profit motive ha[d] disappeared', but it did mean that maximum profit was no longer pursued at all costs. 'Most businessmen' were now 'tinged by ... more social attitudes and motives'.[25] With 'private industry ... at last becoming humanised', capitalism was 'undergoing a metamorphosis into a quite different system'.[26] 'Capitalist features and attitudes no longer predominated', and it was, therefore, 'misleading' to refer to Britain as a capitalist society.[27] A 'post-capitalist society' was emerging.[28] Crucially, for Crosland, this meant, as it had for Keynes, that taking industry into public ownership (nationalisation) or effecting radical changes to corporate rights structures was no longer necessary to socialise corporations and

---

[23] Jeffrey Gordon argues that 'the 1950s were the high-water mark' of both 'managerialism in corporate governance' and 'stakeholder capitalism in the United States': J N Gordon, 'The Rise of Independent Directors in the United States, 1950–2005', 59 *Stanford Law Review*, pp. 1465–568 (2007), p. 1511.

[24] E Durbin, *The Politics of Democratic Socialism*, London: Routledge (1940).

[25] Anthony Crosland, *The Future of Socialism*, London: Jonathan Cape (1956), pp. 17–22. Later in the book, he wrote: 'what is wrong with large public companies to-day ... is not a lack of "public responsibility"': p. 271.

[26] Anthony Crosland, 'The Transition from Capitalism', in David Reisman (ed.), *Democratic Socialism in Britain*, London: Routledge, volume 9, pp. 33–68 (1951), p. 35.

[27] Crosland, *The Future of Socialism*, pp. 23, 34–5.

[28] Crosland, 'The Transition from Capitalism', pp. 37–8.

capitalism: ownership was 'unimportant'.[29] Trying to effect 'major changes in company law' that would diminish or eliminate the residual proprietary rights of shareholders would simply not be worth the effort: large companies were already being 'socialised', changing the law 'would make no difference to the underlying reality'.[30] Others were less sanguine and there remained, on both sides of the Atlantic, a significant and respectable body of opinion arguing for significant changes to shareholder rights, most commonly the placing of restrictions on, or dilution of, their control rights or for the reclassification of shareholders as types of creditor.[31] It was, however, the Crosland view that prevailed. As we shall see, history proved it to be mistaken.

Defending the rentier: the market for corporate control

It was against this backdrop that the law-and-economics movement emerged, providing, among other things, new contractual or 'nexus of contracts' theories of the corporation that offered new instrumental justifications for shareholder primacy, shareholder property rights and the corporate status quo. These theories sought to counter suggestions that corporations should be regarded as social or quasi-social institutions, shareholder rights curtailed, and directors tasked with balancing a range of different interests. Although these contractual theories have come most to be associated with the work of US writers such as Alchian and Demsetz, Jensen and Meckling, and Easterbrook and Fischel, their origins lie in the work of the law-and-economics pioneer Henry Manne.

In the mid 1950s Manne began to express concern about the threat to shareholder rights posed by contemporary thinking on the corporation. In a critique of Berle and Means, he argued that those advocating the socialisation of the corporation were seeking to abandon 'the ideal of the market as a resource allocator' and to institute a very different economic system. The economic sphere – which, in Manne's view, was fundamentally apolitical if regulated by private property and markets – was being politicised.[32] Pointing to the rise of institutional investment, which was reconcentrating previously

---

[29] Crosland, *The Future of Socialism*, p. 251.
[30] Crosland, *The Future of Socialism*, pp. 271–6.
[31] See, for example, George Goyder, *The Responsible Company*, Oxford: Blackwell (1961); K W Wedderburn, *Company Law Reform*, Fabian Tract 363, London: The Fabian Society (1965).
[32] Henry Manne, 'Book Review of Richard Eells, *Corporation Giving in a Free Society*', 24 *University of Chicago Law Review*, pp. 194–202 (1956), p. 198. See also Henry Manne, 'The "Higher Criticism" of the Modern Corporation', 62 *Columbia Law Review*, pp. 399–432 (1962), pp. 399, 402, 414.

dispersed share ownership and re-empowering shareholders, and to the emergence in post-war America of a small group of shareholder activists, Manne argued that, notwithstanding growing industrial concentration, corporations and corporate managers were still subject to strong, beneficial market disciplines. In Manne's account, however, financial as well as product markets were now responsible for disciplining corporate managers, preventing them from straying too far from their traditional, profit-maximising goal.

His argument was that when enough dissatisfied shareholders, especially large institutional shareholders, sold their shares in a public corporation, they depressed its share price, rendering its managers vulnerable to removal and the corporation vulnerable to take-over.[33] In terms of disciplining managers, therefore, the lack of direct shareholder participation in corporate affairs was unproblematic because shareholder 'exit' or potential 'exit' served to ensure managerial good performance and to constrain 'errant managements' who dared deviate from shareholder primacy. This was especially the case, he argued, in an era of growing institutional shareholding.[34] By the mid 1960s, Manne had developed this argument to claim that there now existed an 'active market for corporate control' and that a 'great many mergers [were] probably the result of [its] successful workings'.[35] Accordingly, he was highly critical of any proposals to dilute or remove shareholder rights, not because he believed that they would (or could) be used by shareholders to restore participative democracy to corporations – shareholders were now 'investors' rather than active participants in corporations – but because they were central to the disciplines imposed by the market for corporate control and thus to the 'rational allocation' of capital and managerial services.[36] Manne thus developed justifications for the rights of rentier investors that relied less on

---

[33] Henry Manne, 'Our Two Corporation Systems: law and economics', 53 *Virginia Law Review*, pp. 259–84 (1967), pp. 265–6.

[34] His claim was that the fight for control was one of the key mechanisms whereby the market weeded out the less efficient and less productive. Manne argued that, in order to make management even more responsive to capital markets, the right of corporate managements to retain earnings – and thus to avoid going to the market for additional capital – should be strictly limited. They should, he argued, be required to pay out all income over the amount necessary for working capital.

[35] Henry Manne, 'Mergers and the Market for Corporate Control', 73 *Journal of Political Economy*, pp. 110–20 (1965).

[36] It was because of its alleged contribution to the proper working of this market that Manne defended insider dealing, arguing that it not only tied the interests of corporate managers more closely to those of shareholders, but helped to ensure that the price of a company's securities reflected its performance and the relative efficiency of its management. By trading in a company's shares, knowledgeable insiders were, in effect, constantly 'correcting' the company's share price: Henry Manne, *Insider Trading and the Stock Market*, New York: Free Press (1966).

the moral force of their (problematic) claims as corporate 'owners', and more on the alleged instrumental value of their rights in disciplining managers, ensuring allocative efficiency and increasing aggregate social welfare.

Berle derided Manne's theories, arguing that they were rooted in the past and refused to recognise the crucial *qualitative* changes that had taken place in the nature of the joint stock corporation and corporate shareholding. It was now 'pure fiction' to suggest, as Manne did, that shareholders in the large public corporations 'invested in' corporations/companies in the sense of actually supplying them with capital. This may have been true in the nineteenth century, but it was now a distortion of reality that flattered them. Shareholders were now predominantly passive, rentier purchasers and owners of pre-existing revenue rights. It was the original purchaser of the company's shares who was the 'genuine investor', who provided the company with money. The modern purchaser of corporate shares simply bought the revenue rights attached to shares issued long ago from others who had done likewise.[37] Berle concluded by reiterating the conclusions he had reached 30 years earlier with Gardiner Means: 'traditional theories of property no longer applied to the relation of stockholders in large corporations'. The passive property of shareholders needed 'new philosophical [and] economic bases', but these were not to be found in Manne's theories. In similar fashion, Berle dismissed Manne's account of the operation of the so-called market for corporate control for its lack of connection with empirical reality: it was 'misdescription' and did 'not fit the facts'. Manne's account of the proxy fight was 'wholly imaginary', as was his account of the market for corporate control'.[38]

In fact, Manne, like many economists before and since, seems to have been unclear in his own mind as to the nature of the shareholder's property. On occasions, he identifies it with the corporation's assets, implicitly adopting the old eighteenth/early nineteenth-century, partnership-based conception of the company and its shareholders, which either denied or downplayed the existence of the company as a property-owning legal person separate from its shareholders, even when incorporated. On other occasions, he seems to recognise that shareholders own shares, autonomous objects of property quite separate from the corporation's assets, but without going on to consider the

---

[37] 'When I buy AT&T or General Motors', Berle explained, 'I do not remotely "invest in" either concern'. This claim was mere 'folklore habit', part of an 'unreal' attempt to describe late twentieth-century processes, institutions and relations in traditional nineteenth-century terms: Adolf Berle, 'Modern Functions of the Corporate System', 62 *Columbia Law Review*, pp. 433–49 (1962), p. 446. Confusingly (and confusedly), Manne sometimes identified the shareholders' property with the corporation's assets, sometimes with its shares.

[38] Berle, 'Modern Functions of the Corporate System', pp. 439, 446, 448–9.

potential significance of this. Despite its confusions, misdescriptions, and empirical limitations, however, some soon began to see Manne's theory as mapping a path whereby shareholder rights could be defended, the private nature of corporations reasserted, the virtues of private property in means of production reaffirmed, and corporations brought back within orthodox economic analysis.

For many years, corporations had been treated within neo-classical economics as unproblematic conflict-free, profit-maximising, productive 'black boxes'. Neither growing oligopolisation, nor Coase's famous 1937 article on 'the nature of the firm', with its rather subversive suggestion that in firms the price mechanism was superseded by administrative decision, had dented this view.[39] Indeed, Coase's work had been largely ignored and, in the wake of Berle and Means, theories of the corporation (such as they were) tended to be managerialist and non-market in nature. After Manne, however, this began to change. In what turned out to be a pivotal moment, in 1969 Manne co-ordinated a symposium on securities legislation and economic policy. The contributors included the economists Armen Alchian, Harold Demsetz, Michael Jensen, William Meckling and Oliver Williamson, and lawyers such as Bayless Manning and Wilbur Katz.[40] The contrasting contributions of Williamson and Alchian were particularly instructive. Examining the efficacy of the various markets described by Manne and others, Williamson concluded that, while they operated so as to constrain managerial discretion, they did not entirely eliminate it and that there was still, therefore, 'something to be said' for managerial approaches to the firm. Neo-classical economic theory needed to be 'supplemented' by organisational theory to get 'to grips with' some of the bureaucratic and empirical realities of large organisations.[41] By contrast, Alchian argued that as long as there was no interference with the ability to make profits or the ability freely to capitalise and sell corporate property rights, the operation of the market would ensure efficient organisational forms. 'In reality', he argued,

---

[39] Ronald Coase, 'The Nature of the Firm', 4 *Economica*, pp. 386–405 (1937).

[40] Henry Manne (ed.), *Economic Policy and the Regulation of Corporate Securities: a symposium*, Washington DC: American Enterprise Institute for Public Policy Research (1969).

[41] Oliver Williamson, 'Corporate Control and the Theory of the Firm', in Manne (ed.) *Economic Policy*, pp. 281–336. It was from around this time that the influence of Coase's work and the transaction cost approach to the firm began to grow, becoming an important pillar of the 'new institutional economics' in whose development Williamson played a leading role. Williamson attempts to use transaction cost economics to explain much of social life. As a result, institutions tend to be viewed as webs of individual contracts rather than as social organisms with a life of their own. Although Williamson places administrative co-ordination at the centre of his analysis of the firm, politics and power still largely disappear from view.

'the firm is a surrogate of the marketplace', from which he concluded that the traditional theory of profits, of private property, market, and competition remained operational.[42]

Alchian's contribution was particularly warmly welcomed by Katz. Recanting what he called his 'adolescent' attachment to the work of Veblen, Tawney and Berle and Means, Katz argued that law teachers (but not, thankfully, economists) had been corrupted by the managerialist literature stemming from Berle and Means. He was 'shocked' by suggestions that the legal duty of directors to manage in the interests of shareholders on a profit-maximising basis should be relaxed and that shareholders should not have votes at all, or not be allowed to vote until they had held their shares for longer than a certain period. He observed, disapprovingly, that Manning had called for less theology and that Williamson, with his nods in the direction of empirical reality, had eliminated 'theology' from his paper. In fact, Katz argued, in relation to corporate theory and shareholder rights, there was a need for 'more theology'. He therefore welcomed Alchian's paper: we needed to 'lose our mutual defensiveness with respect to "theological" beliefs'.[43] Williamson responded by saying that, while 'a normative emphasis in economics [was] very useful ... occasionally reality testing is useful also'.[44]

The lack of empirical support for his theology did not go unnoticed. One respondent remarked that Alchian 'very cleverly ... refuses to do empirical work'.[45] Very soon, however, the empirical validity or otherwise of the various claims being made about the operation of the market for corporate control (and stock markets more generally) became secondary to their ideological usefulness. It was from around this time that the long post-war boom came to an end, that capital began to launch a major counter-offensive and that the power of finance and of rentier investors began significantly to grow,[46] precipitating the demise not only of managerialism but of social democracy in general. By the 1980s, the influence of the financial sphere had become greater than at any time since the 1920s. Shareholding was indeed being gradually reconcentrated in ever larger financial institutions and, as a result, shareholder primacy was beginning to be reasserted with a

---

[42] Armen Alchian, 'Corporate Management and Property Rights', in Manne (ed.), *Economic Policy*, pp. 337–60.
[43] Wilbur Katz, 'Discussion', in Manne (ed.), *Economic Policy*, pp. 363–5.
[44] Oliver Williamson, 'Discussion', in Manne (ed.), *Economic Policy*, p. 372.
[45] Peter Steiner, 'Discussion', in Manne (ed.), *Economic Policy*, p. 367.
[46] The gradual reawakening of interest in finance can be tracked back to the 1960s and 1970s. See, for example, David M Kotz, *Bank Control of Large Corporations in the United States*, Berkeley and Los Angeles: University of California Press (1978). Interest in the role of finance also began to reappear in the pages of Paul Sweezy's *Monthly Review* in the early 1970s.

vengeance. With this, both income and wealth inequality began to rise. The corporate world was gradually coming to bear less and less resemblance to that described by Galbraith, Berle and others in the 1950s and 1960s. Takeovers and divestitures, leveraged buy-outs and growing institutional shareholder activism reversed the trend towards behaviour that might be interpreted as non-shareholder-wealth-maximising.[47] The idea of the market for corporate control became ever more celebrated in the popular and academic literature. Frank Easterbrook and Daniel Fischel, for example, US law professors whose work was about to become very influential, confidently asserted that the market for corporate control 'disciplines or replaces managers if they stray too far from the service of shareholders'.[48]

A lot of research has been undertaken to try to determine whether, in empirical reality, the market for corporate control operates in the ways suggested by its supporters. Do takeovers and mergers really operate to weed out inefficient managers and increase aggregate social welfare? The methodological challenges facing researchers are considerable, not least because it is far from clear what exactly one is trying to measure. Should the focus be primarily on share prices before and after takeovers/mergers as indicators of whether value has been added or destroyed? If so, should the focus be on short-term or long-term changes in share value? What about the aggregate welfare effects and the distribution of those effects, good and bad, on employees, suppliers, consumers and communities? It is not possible here to detail the vast quantity of research that has been undertaken on these matters.[49] Suffice it to say that the picture that has emerged is, even from the purely shareholder perspective, mixed. Notwithstanding the strength of

---

[47] The financial economist Michael Jensen, one of the founding fathers of contractual theory, has been at the heart of many of the attempts to deal with the so-called 'agency problem' – the potential divergence of interest between shareholders and managers. Initially, his favoured solution was the extensive use of share options as part of executive pay to realign the interests of managers with those of shareholders: Michael Jensen and William Meckling, 'Theory of the Firm: managerial behaviour, agency costs and ownership structure', 3 *Journal of Financial Economics*, pp. 305–60 (1976). By 1983, however, he was celebrating the market for corporate control as a market in which 'alternative managerial teams compete for the rights to manage corporate resources': Michael Jensen and Richard Ruback, 'The Market for Corporate Control: the scientific evidence', 11 *Journal of Financial Economics*, pp. 5–50 (1983). Pursuing this, he had by the end of the decade become a leading advocate of the leveraged buy-out: see his 'Eclipse of the Public Corporation', 89 *Harvard Business Review*, pp. 61–75 (September–October 1989), suggesting that the leveraged buy-out organisation was about to replace the public corporation.

[48] Frank Easterbrook and Daniel Fischel, 'The Proper Role of a Target's Management in Responding to a Tender Offer', 94 *Harvard Law Review*, pp. 1161–204 (1981).

[49] For an excellent summary of the issues and the empirical evidence, see David Kershaw, *Principles of Takeover Regulation*, Oxford: Oxford University Press (2016), pp. 1–30.

the theoretical claims that were made, early studies of the operation of the market for corporate control suggested that mergers and acquisitions often brought little in the way of efficiency and welfare gains.[50] In the mid 1990s in Britain, for example, Julian Franks and Colin Mayer concluded that the UK market for corporate control did 'not ... function as a disciplinary device for poorly performing companies'.[51] In similar vein, *The Kay Review of UK Equity Markets and Long Term Decision Making*, published in 2012, noted that 'a substantial body of academic evidence' suggested that 'little or no value is added to business by merger activity'. As a result, the authors of the final report 'd[id] not subscribe to the view that "the market for corporate control" can be relied on to ensure that the management of corporations is always placed in the most capable hands. There are too many instances of failed transactions'.[52] Elsewhere, Kay argued that while 'the theory of the market for corporate control claims that takeovers deliver assets to the people who can secure most value for them', 'the reality is that assets go to those with the greatest hubris'.[53] After surveying the evidence, David Kershaw concludes that the evidence suggests that, overall, while takeover activity might deliver improved returns to shareholders in the short term, 'the longer-term picture is far less positive'. Over a three- to five-year period, takeovers are more likely to destroy value.[54] Some have gone even further and argued that, rather than contributing to the disciplining of poorly performing companies, the overall effect of the market for corporate control is to encourage managerial short-termism and to discourage longer-term investment.[55] Research into the impacts of takeovers on other stakeholders (employees, communities, suppliers, consumers) has been less extensive and systematic, though there

---

[50] See, for example, David J. Ravenscraft and F.M. Scherer, 'The Profitability of Mergers', 7 *International Journal of Industrial Organisation*, pp. 101–16 (1989); Richard E. Caves, 'Mergers, Takeovers, and Economic Efficiency: foresight vs hindsight', 7 *International Journal of Industrial Organisation*, 151–74 (1989); Julian Franks and Colin Meyer, 'Hostile Takeovers and the Correction of Managerial Failure', 40 *Journal of Financial Economics*, p. 163–81 (1996).

[51] Franks and Meyer, 'Hostile Takeovers', p. 180.

[52] *The Kay Review of UK Equity Markets and Long Term Decision Making* (Final Report, July 2012), paras 8.4, 8.5, pp. 57–8.

[53] John Kay, 'Forty Years of Taxiing on UK Runways', *Financial Times*, 4/1/2011.

[54] Kershaw, 'Principles of Takeover Regulation', p. 11.

[55] See, for example, William Lazonick, 'Controlling the Market for Corporate Control: the historical significance of managerial capitalism', 1 *Industrial & Corporate Change*, pp. 445–88 (1992). See also the related papers by A P Dickerson, H D Gibson and E Tsakalotos: 'Short Termism and Underinvestment in Financial Systems', 58 *Manchester School*, pp. 351–67 (1995); 'The Impact of Acquisitions on Company Performance', 49 *Oxford Economic Papers*, p. 344 (1997); 'Takeover Risk and Dividend Strategy: a study of UK firms', 46 *Journal of Industrial Economics*, pp. 281–300 (1998).

is considerable evidence that shareholder gains often come at the expense of workers and involve job losses, disregard for the firm-specific investments made by employees and violations of informal promises of job protection.[56]

The importance of the theories about the market for corporate control, however, lay – and still lies – less in their empirical accuracy and validity (or lack thereof) and more in their ideological utility. As David Campbell says, the significance of Manne's 'discovery' of the market for corporate control lay in its suggestion that corporate managers were subject to market disciplines and that it was, therefore, possible to construct a market-based theory of the firm to rival the non-market-based theories spawned by managerialism. Thus, despite the doubts about the way in which stock markets actually operate, the claims made for their contribution to economic efficiency are 'among the least restrained to be found in agency theory'.[57] Whatever the reality, the alleged existence and efficacy of the market for corporate control and the alleged close correlation between corporate managerial efficiency and the market price of the corporation's shares has become one of the theory's bedrocks. Belief in a properly functioning market for corporate control, theoretically at least, 'places [the managerially controlled company] back under the market' and has made it possible to construct new consequentialist justifications for shareholder primacy and for the retention by shareholders of exclusive voting and control rights.[58]

Contractual theories of the corporation: reprivatising the public company

The theories about the market for corporate control paved the way for the development of the new, highly influential, contractual theories of the corporation that began to emerge in the 1970s and 1980s. These too were directed at providing justifications for the corporate (and property) status quo and for the continued private appropriation by shareholders of corporate surpluses, notwithstanding their passive, creditor-like, rentier nature and the increasingly social character of production. Building on the idea that there exists an effective and functioning market for corporate control,

---

[56] See Bryan Burrough and John Helyar, *Barbarians at the Gate*, New York: Harper & Row (1989). Kershaw cites as an example the takeover of the car breakdown company AA by CVC and Permira in 2007, which resulted in 3,400 UK job cuts: Kershaw, 'Principles of Takeover Regulation', p. 13. See also Andrei Shleifer and Lawrence Summers, 'Breach of Trust in Hostile takeovers', in A J Auerbach (ed.), *Corporate Takeovers: causes and consequences*, Chicago: University of Chicago Press, pp. 33–56 (1998).
[57] David Campbell, 'The Role of Monitoring and Morality in Company Law', 7 *Australian Journal of Corporate Law*, pp. 343–65 (1997), p. 362.
[58] Campbell, 'The Role of Monitoring', p. 359.

contractual theories of the corporation sought to deal with the questions being asked about the legitimacy of shareholder primacy and the possession by shareholders of exclusive control rights.[59]

The essential claim made by contractualists is that, however things might appear, corporations and corporate rights structures (including the residual proprietary rights possessed by shareholders) are the products of voluntary, private, market contracting and, as such, are, *a priori*, economically 'efficient'. Corporations are, it is argued, mere nexuses of contracts and fictional rather than real entities, rendering questions about corporate ownership irrelevant. The claim is that corporations are not dependent for their existence on public/state interventions and privileges but are (or could be) the products of private contracting. The legal benefits of incorporation, including limited liability, it is claimed, could have been achieved almost entirely 'privately' through contract with little or no assistance or interventions from the state. All states have done is to short-circuit the process of private contracting by providing the kind of legal framework that private contracting could and would have produced if left to its own devices. This claim is implausible. As has been pointed out, it would 'effectively be impossible ... to create through contract the affirmative asset partitioning which some see as the "core characteristic of a legal entity"'.[60] It is equally 'clear that without legislative intervention, limited liability [defensive asset partitioning] could not have been attained in a satisfactory ... fashion'.[61] However, on the basis of this claim contractual theorists argue that the corporation is, in Jensen and Meckling's words, 'just a legal fiction which serves as a focus for the complex process in which the conflicting objectives of individuals ... are brought in equilibrium within a framework of contractual relationship'.[62] In

---

[59] The idea of the properly functioning market for Campbell, 'The Role of Monitoring', p. 362.

[60] Henry Hansmann and Reinier Kraakman, 'The Essential Role of Organizational Law', 110 *Yale Law Journal*, pp. 387–440 (2000). Affirmative asset partitioning refers to the processes (distinguishable from the 'defensive' partitioning associated with limited liability) whereby the property of firms, whether corporations or partnerships, came to be treated as constituting a separate estate shielded to some degree from the creditors of their members. Its two main elements are priority of claims and liquidation protection. It was responsible for establishing 'firms' as partially separate entities from an early date: see Henry Hansmann, Reinier Kraakman and Richard Squire 'Law and the Rise of the Firm', 119 *Harvard Law Review*, pp. 1333–403 (1996).

[61] L C B Gower, *Principles of Modern Company Law*, London: Sweet & Maxwell (6th ed., 1997), p. 46.

[62] Jensen and Meckling, 'Theory of the Firm', p. 312. See also Daniel Fischel, for whom the corporation is 'a legal fiction that serves as a nexus for a mass of contracts which various individuals have voluntarily entered into for mutual benefit', 'The Corporate Governance Movement' (1982) 35 *Vanderbilt Law Review*, pp. 1259–92 (1982), p. 1273.

this way, corporations are reduced to mere ciphers through which the owners of different factors of production are brought together through contract. Crucially, with the corporation more or less conceptualised out of existence, it is eliminated as an owner of property other than in a purely formal sense. The assets owned by corporations and the shares (rights to revenue) owned by shareholders are elided, conflated under the rubric 'capital'. Following the lead of Manne, contractual theories of the corporation thus tend to depict shareholders as people who give resources (capital) to corporations rather than as rentier purchasers of pre-existing revenue rights.[63] By portraying them in this way, contractualists try subtly to reinvigorate shareholders, to restore them to their former status as real investors in production. The reality – that they and the contemporary stock market count for 'little or nothing as a source of finance' – is studiously ignored.[64]

In effect, then, nexus of contracts theorists try, like Manne, to turn the corporate-theoretical clock back to the early nineteenth century and the days when corporations had far fewer members than their modern counterparts and were conceptualised as large 'public' partnerships composed of their shareholders merged into a single artificial, fictional entity; to the days when corporations were seen, partnership-style, as aggregations of individuals and referred to as 'theys' rather than 'its'; to the days before joint stock corporations with many thousands of shareholders, general limited liability and fully paid-up (no liability) shares; to the days before developed share markets and easily transferable shares; to the days when shareholders were more like 'investors' who gave money to companies rather than mere coupon-clipping rentiers.[65] In other words, contractual theories turn a blind eye to the many qualitative changes that have taken place in the nature of productive activity and in the nature of public corporations and corporate shareholding. They ignore both the effects and significance of the emergence of the share as an object of intangible property in the form of the right to profit quite separate from the assets of the company and the transformation of shareholders into liability- and responsibility-free rentiers. They also ignore the legal constitution of corporations as property-owning legal persons

---

[63] This is implicit in some of the questions these theorists pose. Why is it, muses one contractualist, that shareholders – who 'furnish inputs into the business' – are 'willing turn large sums of money over to other people (managers) on very ill-defined terms?': K Scott, 'Agency Costs and Corporate Governance', in P Newman (ed.), *New Palgrave Dictionary of Economics and the Law*, London: Macmillan, pp. 26–30 (1998), p. 26. The answer, of course, at least so far as shareholders in public companies are concerned, is that they do not. Buying shares puts money in the hands of the seller of the shares, not in the hands of the company.

[64] Doug Henwood, *Wall Street*, London: Verso (1997), p. 292.

[65] See Ireland, 'Capitalism without the Capitalist'.

radically separate from their shareholders, treating them instead as though they are large partnerships, aggregations of individuals whose constitutive relations can be analysed through the old partnership concepts of agency and contract. It is, therefore, no accident that these theorists commonly begin their analyses with newly formed enterprises[66] or with small firms[67] where their characterisation of the shareholders and of the firms themselves in partnership terms bears a much closer resemblance to empirical reality, before moving on, with little or no analytic modification, to large established joint stock corporations where it is wholly anachronistic.[68] As we shall see, a similar technique has been deployed by property theorists operating within a law-and-economics framework.

With the corporation reduced to a legal fiction, nexus of contracts theories reconnect shareholders both to the corporate assets (the 'capital') and to the corporate managers. With no corporate entity of substance to come between them, the relationship between shareholders and managers can once again be characterised, partnership-style, as 'fit[ting] the definition of a pure agency relationship'.[69] Contractual theory thus defines corporate governance as a simple 'agency problem': how do we align the interests of managers (the agents) with those of shareholders (the principals) so that the former pursue the exclusive interests of the latter?

What is the purpose of this contorted and, at times, bizarre theorising? The answer is that conceptualising the corporation in this way is thought to deal with the tricky questions about ownership (and, therefore, about shareholder primacy) raised by the emergence of corporations as fully-fledged asset-owning legal persons completely separate from their share-owning, rentier shareholders. Viewed as a nexus of contracts and, therefore, as 'legal fictions', corporations cease to be 'things' that can be owned. Thus, Eugene Fama writes of the 'irrelevance of the concept of ownership of the firm'. The corporation, he argues, is 'just the set of contracts covering the way inputs are joined to create outputs and the way receipts from outputs are shared among inputs'. While the various factors of production employed in a firm must be owned by someone, he explains, 'ownership of capital should not be confused with ownership of the firm'.[70] In similar vein, Easterbrook

---

[66] See, for example, Frank Easterbrook and Daniel Fischel, *The Economic Structure of Corporate Law*, Cambridge: Harvard University Press (1991), pp. 5–7.

[67] See, for example, Armen Alchian and Harold Demsetz, 'Production, Information Costs and Economic Organization', 62 *American Economic Review*, pp. 777–95 (1972).

[68] See, for example, Brian Cheffins, *Company Law: theory, structure and operation*, Oxford: Clarendon Press (1997), pp. 31–41.

[69] Jensen and Meckling, 'Theory of the Firm, p. 319. See also Eugene Fama, 'Agency Problems and the Theory of the Firm', 88 *Journal of Political Economy*, pp. 288–307 (1980).

[70] Fama, 'Agency Problems and the Theory of the Firm', p. 290.

and Fischel argue that 'shareholders are no more "owners" of the firm than are bondholders, other creditors, and employees (including managers who devote specialised resources to the enterprise)'. The relationship of all these participants with the enterprise and with one another is purely contractual.[71]

In these implausible accounts, an attempt is made to derive both the manifestly hierarchical and authoritarian structure of corporations and the control rights of shareholders entirely from contract and the market without reference to ownership of the corporation or its assets. Shareholders are deemed to be the owners and providers of capital, a factor of production like any other. The reason it is justifiable and socially beneficial for them to be entitled to the corporate surpluses is that they are 'residual claimants' who only receive payment (dividends) after all the other claimants have been paid. Their entitlements cannot, therefore, be specified precisely in advance – they might not get any financial return at all – making it very difficult for them to protect themselves by contract. Shareholders, the argument runs, only accept the risks associated with their residual position in return for the protections provided by the legal rules that grant them voting rights and that compel managers to act in their interests. Moreover, it is argued, as residual claimants, shareholders have the greatest incentive to ensure that management operates in the most efficient and productive manner.[72] Shareholder control rights and shareholder primacy are not only, therefore, the product of (private) market contracting, they are also economically and socially beneficial.

Crucially, once existing corporate structures and arrangements are deemed to be the products of market contracting, they are also deemed, *a priori*, to be economically 'efficient'. The market ensures that corporate arrangements are subject to continual review and that only the most efficient arrangements survive and flourish. Whatever their origins, the fact that existing governance structures have survived market selection is regarded proof of their efficiency. The triumph of the shareholder-oriented joint stock corporation is thus presented as largely economically (and efficiency) determined, a view that led Henry Hansmann and Reinier Kraakman to announce, at the turn of the millennium, 'the end of corporate history'.[73] Driven by global market forces, they argued, corporate law around the world was converging on a broadly uniform, Anglo-American, stock-market-based, shareholder-oriented legal model. Others agree. The 'underlying unity of the corporate form' around

---

[71] Easterbrook and Fischel, 'Voting in Corporate Law', 26 *Journal of Law and Economics*, pp. 395–427 (1983), p. 396.
[72] See, for example, Easterbrook and Fischel, *The Economic Structure of Corporate Law*, pp. 67–9.
[73] Henry Hansmann and Reinier Kraakman, 'The End of History for Corporate Law', 89 *Georgetown Law Journal*, pp. 439–68 (2001).

the world, one group of leading corporate scholars claim, has been 'induced by ... economic exigencies'.⁷⁴ The Anglo-American shareholder-oriented corporation has outcompeted its less shareholder-oriented rivals, generating a growing normative consensus that managers should act exclusively in the interests of shareholders, a development that should be welcomed as it enhances the efficiency of corporate laws and practices.

That contractual or agency theories of the corporation are able to offer neo-classical economists a solution to the problems generated by the ostensibly non-market nature of firms, enabling them to assert the efficiency of existing corporate structures, is due, in significant part, to the peculiar and highly abstract nature of their concept of 'efficiency'. Within orthodox economic theory, no attempt is made to evaluate the importance of the goal of efficiency relative to other competing goals and the efficiency, or otherwise, of different arrangements and resource allocations is assessed not by careful, wide-ranging empirical comparison, but by reference only to the formal nature of the arrangements and processes of which they are a product. Put simply, if the arrangements can be presented as the product of a process of free market exchange, they are deemed, *a priori*, to be 'efficient'. As John Parkinson observed, once it has been presumed that a governance structure is the product of contracting, 'it follows that it must be efficient'.⁷⁵

In these ways, contractual theories of the corporation seek, in effect, to *reprivatise* the public corporation. Shareholder primacy, the retention by shareholders of exclusive control rights and the continued private appropriation of corporate surpluses, are justified and legitimated not on the problematic grounds of shareholder 'ownership' rights but on the consequentialist grounds of 'economic efficiency' and the public good. The control rights and residual income rights of shareholders are a product of market contracting. Moreover, as a result of the possession by shareholders of these rights, not only corporate managers but corporate arrangements are subject to continual market review. These rights *should*, therefore, be vested in shareholders not because (or not only because) they 'own' the companies concerned, but because this is the most efficient arrangement. As Parkinson says, the central purpose of nexus of contracts theorising has been 'to establish that the large publicly owned company ... is efficient'.⁷⁶ Thus, Easterbook and Fischel tell us that the fictional nature of the corporation 'removes from the field' some of the 'interesting questions' that have hitherto

---

[74] Reinier Kraakman et al (eds), *The Anatomy of Corporate Law: a comparative and functional approach*, Oxford: Oxford University Press (2004), p. 1.

[75] John Parkinson, *Corporate Power and Responsibility*, Oxford: Clarendon Press (1993), p. 125.

[76] Parkinson, *Corporate Power and Responsibility*, p. 122.

concerned legal scholars, such as 'what is the goal of the corporation? Is it profit, and for whom? Social welfare more broadly defined?' These questions can be dismissed with a simple 'who cares?'[77] Corporate governance does not involve highly complex questions of productive organisation, social well-being and social justice, but simply a simple agency problem: how do we ensure corporate manager-agents act in the best financial interests of their shareholder-principals?

The fictional corporation rematerialises

Depicting modern corporations as the products of free market contractual exchanges is not, however, easy. On the contrary, the attempt to reduce corporations to nexuses of contracts draws these theorists into all kinds of distortions. They are compelled to discover 'contracts' – many of them 'implicit' and 'incomplete' – in every corporate nook and cranny. With the irritating constraints imposed by empirical reality lifted, it is hardly surprising that there are different accounts of the 'contracts' constituting the corporation. Once one leaves the real world and enters a realm of theoretical fantasy, the possibilities are – within the contractual bounds set, of course – almost endless.[78] As David Campbell says, because the goal is simply 'to bring the company within the theory', 'real' contracts are placed on the same ontological plane as 'unreal' (but theoretically necessary) contracts – contracts that, in empirical reality, simply do not exist.[79] As a result, despite its claims to tough, hard-nosed realism, contractual theory is, in fact, strikingly *un*realistic and empirically *in*accurate.[80] Hence Campbell's conclusion that, although it describes the company as a nexus of contracts, there are, in fact, 'no contracts ... only a nexus of metaphors'. It is not an

---

[77] Easterbrook and Fischel, 'Voting in Corporate Law', pp. 35–6.
[78] Even some sympathetic to stakeholding joined in, trying to fabricate corporate 'contracts' more favourable to employees and other stakeholders: see, for example, Marleen A. O'Connor, 'Restructuring the Corporation's Nexus of Contracts: recognizing a fiduciary duty to displaced workers', 69 *North Carolina Law Review*, pp. 1189–260 (1991).
[79] Campbell, 'The Role of Monitoring', pp. 360–1.
[80] 'Large corporations', explains Alan Wolfe, 'are composed of people who speak many different languages, have never met each other, work in positions defined by different degrees of power and responsibility, and have wildly different motives, loyalties, and talents. Can contracts exist between people who never meet, have nothing in common, and are unavailable to pass judgment on the behaviour of the other parties to the contract? Perhaps they can in a metaphorical sense, in roughly the same way that early social contract theorists understood the body politic to operate. But no one ever claimed that the social contract was an *empirical* description of actual real world events': Alan Wolfe, 'The Modern Corporation: private agent or public actor', 50 *Washington & Lee Law Review*, pp. 1673–96 (1993), p. 1680.

empirically based theory at all, but one 'carried by metaphor and assertion based on that metaphor'. As a result, it is 'not readily open to rational debate'.[81]

Nor is it surprising, given the theory's disconnection from empirical reality, that when nexus of contracts theorists attempt to elaborate the 'contracts' that allegedly constitute the corporation, they run into difficulties. Take, for example, the corporation's relationships with third parties. Many of these are clearly contractual in nature, but the rights possessed by third parties are, of course, held against the corporation, not its shareholders, and necessarily so for shareholders wanting the benefits of freely transferable, no-liability, no-obligation shares. As a result, in this context, contractualists require the 'fictional' corporate entity to spring briefly back to life. Thus, Easterbrook and Fischel begin their book, *The Economic Structure of Corporate Law*, by curtly dismissing the 'personhood' of the corporation as 'a matter of convenience rather than reality',[82] but find themselves forced to resuscitate it a few pages later when defending limited liability, 'perhaps the distinguishing feature … of corporate law'.[83] 'Not so fast', they tell those who suggest that limited liability is 'the antithesis of contract' and 'a privilege bestowed on investors'. It can 'be depicted as anti-contractual only if it is inaccurately described', for 'corporations do not have limited liability; they must pay all of their debts, just as anyone else must'. In other words, limited liability can be treated as anti-contractual only if the 'personhood' of the corporation is not taken sufficiently seriously. If this looks suspiciously like a case of having one's corporate cake on page 12 and eating it on page 40, it does at least demonstrate that, for contractualists, the reality of the 'personhood' of the corporation, or lack of it, is indeed a matter of convenience. It comes as no surprise, therefore, to find that, 50 pages later, when Easterbrook and Fischel turn their attention to other matters and wish to emphasise the congruity of the corporate and shareholder interests, the separate corporate entity – the legal person brought to life to 'pay all of its debts just as anyone else must' – has vanished into thin air once again. When considering the relationship between shareholders and directors, which they wish to characterise in pure agency terms, making the presence of a genuinely separate corporate entity decidedly inconvenient, they look straight through it, unblinkingly telling us that the 'corporate contract makes managers the agents of equity investors' rather than of a separate corporate entity.[84]

---

[81] Campbell, 'The Role of Monitoring', p. 360.
[82] Easterbrook and Fischel, *The Economic Structure of Corporate Law*, p. 12.
[83] Easterbrook and Fischel, *The Economic Structure of Corporate Law*, p. 40.
[84] Easterbrook and Fischel, *The Economic Structure of Corporate Law*, p. 91.

The rise of financialised corporate governance

Although contractual theories of the corporation do not stand up to empirical scrutiny, their ideological influence and significance has been considerable, in part because of developments in the corporate world, the early stages of one of which Manne correctly identified: the reconcentration of shareholders in financial institutions. The process of reconcentration was only in its early stages in the 1960s when Manne began to write about the market for corporate control, but it gathered rapidly in pace in the 1970s and 1980s. Boosted by increased transnational financial flows and by rapidly growing equity markets, the shift away from direct share ownership by households saw institutional investors massively increase the volume of assets they were managing. With this, the threat of shareholder 'exit' (and a falling share price) was greatly enhanced, enabling shareholders, acting through their institutional representatives, to use their residual proprietary (voting) rights to exert much greater pressure on corporations and their managers. The bundles of rights and *de facto* power possessed by shareholders were further increased by legal and other changes – the dismantling of Bretton Woods, the liberalisation of the rules regulating free trade and the free movement of capital, modifications to the rules on takeovers, the emergence of new forms of investor protection – and by the simultaneous erosion of the legal rights and economic power of labour. Financial and trade liberalisation has proved particularly significant for it has helped not only the very wealthy but multi-national firms made up of multiple corporations to vacate specific territories and to move into an extraterritorial space. With this, power has increasingly come to reside not in institutions that can, at least theoretically, be held accountable through politics, democracy and the state, but in multi-national firms and financial institutions that, in the absence of effective transnational regulatory institutions, are to a considerable degree not only beyond the grasp of nation-state-based regulation and accountability but able to externalise risks and costs (such as negative impacts on the environment) on to society. Indeed, pitted against one another for private productive investment, rather than seeking more rigorously to regulate these powerful behemoths, states have been drawn into amending their legal orders to make them as attractive as possible to them, by creating a favourable 'investment climate'. These developments saw the emphatic and overt reassertion of the principle of shareholder primacy that lay at the heart of the changes that took place in corporate governance – and in the character of capitalism more generally – in the 1980s and 1990s. The new mantra was that of 'shareholder value maximisation'. Maximising shareholder value, it was claimed, benefitted us all by promoting 'efficiency' and by increasing aggregate wealth. In the context of this restored and enhanced financial power and the rising inequality that accompanied it, contractual theories of the corporation came into their own as legitimators of the new status quo despite their obvious shortcomings.

The reconcentration of shareholdings in financial institutions, coupled with the increasing mobility of capital, saw the intensification of the market imperatives to which firms and their managers were subjected. They were now not only under product market pressure to produce a competitive product at a competitive price, but under increasing financial market pressure to produce profits that would deliver competitive financial returns. The financial pressure on managers to deliver shareholder value was further intensified by the growing competition between institutions for investment funds and by the growing competition within them between portfolio managers subject to regular market-based performance evaluation. It was intensified still further by the emergence of new kinds of financial institution – hedge funds, private equity firms and the like – more interested in quick capital gains than in steady long-term revenue streams.[85] For more and more managers, the delivery of good short-term shareholder returns and high share prices became an imperative, whatever the consequences for employees, suppliers, communities or the environment. The focus on shareholder value was further encouraged and reinforced by the growing use of the performance-related forms of executive remuneration (such as share options) that the contractualists had recommended as a solution to the 'agency problem'. By aligning the financial interests of managers with those of shareholders, these forms of remuneration made the single-minded pursuit of shareholder value, particularly high share prices, very lucrative for executives. From the 1980s, executive pay began to skyrocket, and the image of the ideal executive was transformed 'from one of a steady, reliable caretaker of the corporation and its many constituencies to that of a swashbuckling, iconoclastic champion of shareholder value' with little interest in the fate of other corporate stakeholders. The ideals of professionalism, established in American business schools in the 1920s to create 'a managerial class that would run America's large corporations in a way that served the broader interests of society', were 'swept away'.[86] The new corporate governance regime was highly financialised, driven by a focus on financial performance. 'Financial engineering' became the order of the day. Share buy-backs, permitted in the US since 1982 by a new Securities and Exchange Commission rule, have perhaps been the most notable example of this because of their obvious prioritisation of short-term financial gains: they have no effect on revenues, profits or 'efficiency' but, by increasing earnings

---

[85] On private equity, see generally Eileen Applebaum and Rosemary Batt, *Private Equity at Work*, New York: Russell Sage (2014). Rakesh Khurana, *From Higher Aims to Hired Hands*, Princeton: Princeton University Press (2007), pp. 4, 291.

[86] Khurana, *From Higher Aims*, pp. 4, 291.

per share, they give an immediate lift to share prices. Previously regarded as a form of market manipulation, they suddenly became commonplace. Between 2004 and 2015, S&P 500 companies spent more than US$4.5 trillion repurchasing their own shares.[87] For a while, the rhetoric and ideology of shareholder value maximisation, which legitimated these practices, was dominant, as were contractual theories of the corporation.

The concentration of share ownership among the (very) wealthy clearly undermines the claim that share ownership has been 'democratised' and that shareholder value maximisation directly benefits us all (or at least most of us). Quite apart from the doubts that many have expressed about whether the pursuit of shareholder value maximisation operates for the long-term benefit of shareholders, most ordinary people have reaped few benefits either from the distribution of a larger proportion of corporate surpluses to shareholders or from rising share prices. On the contrary, although some of the more privileged members of the working class in the developed world – those with some private pension savings – have made some (usually modest) gains in their capacity as owners of modest amounts of financial property, most have lost out in their capacity as workers. Financialised corporate governance and the pursuit of shareholder value has contributed to the destruction of the old compromises and social alliances; to deregulation followed by reregulation in financial interests; to downsizing, job losses, re-engineering and outsourcing; to relentless downward pressure on wages, whose growth in real terms has stagnated and often fallen; to reductions in job security and declining terms and conditions of work[88]; to the dismantling of social protection systems; to higher income and wealth inequality (testaments to the growing share of the social product accruing to the owners of financial property in the form of dividends and interest); to the 'financialisation' of everyday life; to unpredictable currency fluctuations, reckless capital movements, growing financial instability and recurring financial crises.

The last decade or so have seen further changes in corporate governance. The ideology of shareholder value maximisation was discredited somewhat by various turn-of-the-century scandals (Enron etc.) and further discredited by the financial crash of 2008, which many blamed on the short-termism it encouraged. Since then, public concern about climate change and the environment has also steadily grown, with the result that it has come to be argued that corporate executives need to take a longer-term and more

---

[87] Jan Fichtner, 'The Rise of Institutional Investors', in Mader et al (eds), *Routledge International Handbook of Financialization*, London: Routledge, pp. 265–275 (2020).

[88] The serial restructuring that has accompanied the worship of shareholder value has 'elevate[d] breach of implicit stakeholder contract into a guiding principle of management': Froud et al, *Financialization and Strategy*, p. 100.

socially and environmentally sensitive approach to management. Against this backdrop, there has been a shift away from the rhetoric of shareholder value maximization. Ideas about corporate social responsibility, 'stewardship' and, more recently, 'corporate purpose' have emerged (or in some cases re-emerged) and gained traction. Moreover, these ideas have seemingly been embraced by corporations and financial institutions anxious to improve their public images and to stave off increased government regulation. Many of them have willingly allowed themselves to be recast as 'stewards', loftily claiming that they are looking to build sustainable businesses and create value for all stakeholders. In recent years, 'stewardship codes' have proliferated. At the same time, with the reconcentration of shareholdings in institutions reaching new heights, institutional investors have increasingly delegated investment decisions to asset management firms. The asset management sector has grown exponentially in recent decades. This has precipitated further governance changes. In the first decade of the new millennium, greater shareholder activism was widely touted as a vital component of good governance, initially in pursuit of the then desired goal of maximising shareholder value, later in pursuit of the new desired goals of more socially responsible management and greater sensitivity to ESG (environment, social and governance) issues. However, as it became clear to institutional investors that the great majority of higher-fee, actively managed funds did not, in fact, outperform the market, there was a marked shift towards passive, low-fee, index-linked funds. The burgeoning passive fund sector, particularly but not exclusively in the US, has come to be concentrated in the three largest asset management firms (the 'Big Three'), BlackRock, Vanguard and State Street. In 2000 these firms held between them about 6 per cent of the average S&P constituent's shares; by the end of 2017, they held a 'staggering' 21 per cent.[89] They control around 80 per cent of the exchange-traded-funds market.[90]

There is disagreement about the significance of the rise of these asset management firms and index funds both for corporate governance and for capitalism as a whole. Some have expressed optimism, arguing that we are seeing the emergence of a new corporate governance regime and a new form of 'asset manager capitalism', which, potentially at least, is less short-termist, less rapaciously shareholder-oriented and more socially and environmentally sensitive. Some have gone even further, suggesting that these developments potentially mark a shift not only away from the single-minded

---

[89] Matthew Backus et al, 'Common Ownership in America, 1980–2017', 13 *American Economic Journal: Microeconomics*, pp. 273–308 (2021), p. 285.

[90] For example, they control around 80 per cent of the exchange traded funds market: https://www.barrons.com/articles/etfs-are-dominated-by-blackrock-vanguard-and-state-street-the-sec-is-concerned-51554512133.

pursuit of shareholder value but from 'shareholder capitalism' altogether.[91] This optimism is based on the belief that, because of their huge, diversified portfolios, these asset managers are both 'universal' and 'permanent' owners'.[92] 'Universal owners' because they own a slice of everything and, as such, are less interested in the performance of individual corporations than in the performance of the corporate sector and economy as a whole; 'permanent owners' because exit is not really an option for them. The result, it is suggested, is that they are less likely actively to stoke up competition between firms and to put pressure on the managers of individual corporations to maximise short-term profits. Their power is now derived not so much from the threat of exit as from the enormous size and diversity of their shareholdings and the influence this gives them.[93] Moreover, some have argued, whereas institutional fee structures tended previously to involve significant performance-based elements that encouraged shareholder value maximisation, under the new asset manager capitalism the main goal of the institutions is to maximise the volume of assets under their management.[94] If the 'universal', 'permanent' owner-operators of these passive funds exert pressure at all, the argument runs, it is more likely to be in the form of 'voice' and aimed at securing the adoption by managers of longer-term horizons and a patient 'stewardship' approach to governance aimed at the long-term sustainability of the company, the economy and the environment. In the words of Larry Fink, CEO of BlackRock, 'climate risk is investment risk'.[95] The optimists argue, therefore, that the rise of these firms and of index funds is good, or potentially good, for sustainability, the green transition and ESG issues more generally.

---

[91] Jan Fichtner et al, 'The New Permanent Universal Owners', 49 *Economy & Society*, pp. 493–515 (2020). For an earlier expression of similar optimism which draws on the idea of 'universal owners', see Simon Deakin, 'The Coming Transformation of Shareholder Value', 13 *Corporate Governance; An International Review*, pp. 11–18 (2005).

[92] The idea of 'universal owners' was coined by James Hawley and Andrew Williams, 'The Emergence of Universal Owners', 43 *Challenge*, pp. 43–61 (July–August 2000). They were drawing on Bob Monks and Nell Minow, *Corporate Governance*, New Jersey: Wiley (1995). It seems to overlook the fact that ownership of corporate equity is very heavily concentrated at the top of the wealth pyramid.

[93] See Benjamin Braun, 'Exit, Control and Politics: structural power and corporate governance under asset manager capitalism', 50 *Politics and Society*, pp. 630–54 (2022).

[94] Benjamin Braun, 'Asset Manager Capitalism as a Corporate Governance Regime', in Jacob Hacker et al (eds), *The American Political Economy*, New York: Cambridge University Press, pp. 270–94 (2021), p. 273. Braun points out that the rise of asset management has encouraged the growth of index funds and reduced monitoring and engagement, but that the sheer scale of their holdings limits their scope for 'exit' and pushes them in the opposite direction towards the greater use of 'voice' in governance.

[95] Larry Fink's 2021 Letter to CEOs, https://www.blackrock.com/us/individual/2021-larry-fink-ceo-letter.

Is this optimism justified? There is no doubt that the expansion of asset management and the rise of index funds has coincided with a rhetorical shift, and that both the corporate and asset management sectors have seemingly embraced and become keen to emphasise the importance of corporate social responsibility and their 'stewardship' roles. This is exemplified by the annual letters sent by Larry Fink to corporate executives. In his 2021 letter, for example, Fink not only emphasised that climate change poses risks to the owners of capital but argued that a 'tectonic shift' was taking place as investors moved towards 'sustainability-focused companies'. 'No issue', he claimed, 'ranks higher than climate change on our clients' list of priorities'.[96] It is much less clear, however, whether the rise of asset management firms and index funds has significantly changed corporate practices and governance and whether the new 'asset manager capitalism' is significantly different from its shareholder value-oriented predecessor. On the contrary, as evidence begins to emerge of the voting records of these asset management companies, the more pessimistic views of stewardship sceptics seem to be being vindicated. A recent study by Joseph Baines and Sandy Hager looked at the environmental corporate governance performance of the Big Three asset management firms vis-à-vis the publicly listed carbon majors, the small group of fossil fuel, cement and mining companies responsible for the bulk of greenhouse gas emissions. It reveals that the funds of these firms, including their ESG funds, have large stakes in these companies and that between 2014 and 2021 the Big Three supported only 25 per cent of shareholder resolutions aimed at improving the environment. Indeed, they are more than three times more likely to oppose than support them. Moreover, there is little to distinguish the proxy voting records of their ESG funds from their non-ESG funds. By contrast, the Big Three consistently supported management in votes on director elections and executive remuneration, and invariably supported resolutions on dividends and share buy-backs. Baines and Hager conclude that the Big Three are 'little more than stewards of the status quo of shareholder value maximisation'.[97] Another empirical study by Ami Golland and others of over 180,000 AGM votes on ecological sustainability issues across 263 companies from 2010 to 2019 paints a very similar picture. While pension and sovereign wealth funds supported around 45–60 per cent of proposals, asset managers in

---

[96] Fink, 'Letter to CEOs'. Larry Fink's annual letters to CEOs are available on the BlackRock website: https://www.blackrock.com/us/individual/2021-larry-fink-ceo-letter.
[97] Joseph Baines and Sandy Hager, 'From Passive Owners to Planet Savers? Asset Managers, Carbon Majors and the Limits of Sustainable Finance', 27 *Competition and Change*, pp. 449–71 (2023), p. 449.

general supported only about 25 per cent and the average support offered by the 'Big Three' was still lower at 6–20 per cent.[98]

Support for Baines and Hager's conclusion can also be found from within the Big Three. BlackRock's former chief investment officer for sustainable investing, Tariq Fancy, recruited in 2017 when the company was about to dramatically expand its focus on ESG criteria, has bluntly argued that ESG and 'sustainability investing' are 'deadly distractions' from the climate crisis. Having left BlackRock after concluding that their ESG policies were having 'no demonstrable impact', he now argues that most investment strategies 'are short-term and don't care about long-term issues'. 'All the stuff on "stakeholder" capitalism', he says, 'was hollow marketing – it seemed almost intended to dupe the public into believing that we don't need the overdue government regulation that we need immediately to address the climate crisis'. 'Frankly, acting irresponsibly is often profitable'.[99] This pessimistic view seems to be borne out by the 2022 report of BlackRock's 'Investment Stewardship' (BIS) team on their voting record in 2021–2 and by Fink's 2022 annual letter. Both adopt a rather different tone to ESG issues in light of 'the difficult macro-economic backdrop' and make it very clear that financial performance is BlackRock's key priority. The BIS report shows that in 2021–2 BlackRock supported only 24 per cent of US shareholder proposals on environmental and social (E&S) issues voted on at AGMs, down from 43 per cent in 2020–1. Overall, support for E&S shareholder proposals was down from 36 per cent in 2021 to 27 per cent in 2022. For the BIS team, this suggested that 'most investors took a measured, materiality-based approach' to voting. Average shareholder support for environmental-related proposals specifically also fell in the US, from 51 per cent in 2020–1 to 37 per cent in 2021–2; BlackRock supported just 27 per cent of them. The reason for this, the BIS report says, was that they 'did not consider [the proposals] to be consistent with our clients' long-term financial interests'. Others were rejected for trying to 'micromanage' companies and for trying to 'dictate the pace of companies' energy transition plans ... with little regard

---

[98] Ami Golland, Victor Galaz, Gustav Engstrom and Jan Fichtner, 'Proxy Voting for the Earth System: proxy voting for the earth system: institutional shareholder governance of global tipping elements' (2022), https://ssrn.com/abstract=4067103 or https://dx.doi.org/10.2139/ssrn.4067103.

[99] https://www.climateandcapitalmedia.com/tariq-fancy-esg-and-sustainability-investing-are-deadly-distractions-in-the-climate-crisis/#:~:text=ESG%20as%20a%20measurement%20standard,t%20measured%20isn%27t%20managed, 20/8/2021. See also Tariq Fancy, *The Secret Diary of a Sustainable Investor* (August 2021), https://medium.com/@sosofancy/the-secret-diary-of-a-sustainable-investor-part-1-70b6987fa139.

to the disruption caused to their financial performance'.[100] In similar vein, although in his 2022 letter Fink continued to voice support for 'stakeholder capitalism', he was insistent that stakeholder capitalism 'is [simply] capitalism' and, as such, about 'long-term profitability'. Reflecting gloomily on the economic situation, he explained that BlackRock focuses on sustainability 'not because we're environmentalists, but because we are capitalists and fiduciaries to our clients'. Businesses 'cannot be the climate police'.[101] For Baines and Hager, the change in tone represents not so much a U-turn as a consolidation of 'a long-standing position of climate obstructionism'. For the Big Three, 'environmental stewardship has always taken a back seat to shareholder value'.[102]

We should not be surprised by this. It remains the case, as Fancy says, that 'the system works according to incentives and self-interest'.[103] Asset managers still compete with one another for investment funds on performance and cost, and the linking of management fees to the value of assets creates an incentive to maintain and, if possible, push up, share values.[104] It also remains the case that corporate executives, whose tenures in office are relatively short, are incentivised to focus on short-term shareholder value rather than on problems whose main impacts might still be some years away. Despite the lengthening of the investment chain and the emergence of new layers of agency relationship (and new potential conflicts of interest), therefore, generating shareholder value for financial property owners remains the overriding goal and driver. Over the last half century or so, reconcentration has helped financial property owners to use their residual proprietary rights to reshape the corporate landscape towards this goal, both through financial markets and the threat of 'exit' and, more directly, through ownership and control. Today, the power exercised by finance and the owners of financial property has become ubiquitous. With financial liberalisation, capital is able to move around the globe with astonishing rapidity in search of higher rates of return, with the result that the strict logic of capitalism, whose operation was softened during the long post-war boom, has not only been reasserted, but reasserted in a highly financialised form. At the same time, its reach has been extended into ever more spheres of society by privatisation and marketisation.

---

[100] BlackRock, *2022 Voting Spotlight*, BlackRock Investment Stewardship (2022), pp. 5–6, 48, 51, blackrock.com/stewardship. The report looks at BlackRock's proxy voting record, 2021–2.
[101] Larry Fink, 'The Power of Capitalism', https://www.blackrock.com/corporate/investor-relations/larry-fink-ceo-letter.
[102] Baines and Hager, 'From Passive Owners to Planet Saviors', pp. 451–2.
[103] Fancy, 'ESG and sustainability'.
[104] Braun, 'Asset Management Capitalism'.

Unsurprisingly, the main beneficiaries of financialised governance have been the wealthy rentier owners of the great majority of financial property.[105] The declining labour share of GDP, mentioned earlier, has been one manifestation of this. Another has been the weakness of investment relative to profitability and the decline of policies of 'retain and invest' in favour of policies of 'downsize and distribute'.[106] In the UK, for example, there was a marked upward shift in pay-outs from 13–20 per cent in the 1980s to 20–35 per cent in the 1990s and 2000s.[107] Indeed, there is evidence that 'industries with more quasi-indexer institutional ownership' are characterised by 'higher payouts and lower investment' and that 'firms owned by quasi-indexers and located in industries with more concentration and common ownership … return a disproportionate amount of free cash flows to shareholders'.[108] Financial gains for shareholders have come not only in the form of higher dividends but in the form of higher share prices, with stock-market-focused managers engaging in downsizing, outsourcing and offshoring to reduce costs and wages and to increase profits, and in share buy-backs and other forms of financial re-engineering to push up share values. Research suggests that 'the probability of share repurchases is sharply higher for firms that would have just missed the earnings per share forecast in the absence of a repurchase'; and that 'firms that rely more heavily on stock option-based compensation are more likely to repurchase their stock than other firms'.[109] The result has been the emergence not merely of shareholder-oriented but highly financialised, often short-term-oriented forms of corporate governance which, despite the changed rhetoric, show little concern for the long-term productive health of companies, let alone the interests of employees, communities, the environment, or society as a whole. Indeed, on occasions governance has descended into blatant looting and asset-stripping.[110]

It is the residual proprietary rights still attached to shares – that contractual theories of the corporation have sought to protect – that have made possible

---

[105] See the various articles in Gerald Epstein (ed.), *Financialization and The World Economy*, Cheltenham: Edward Elgar (2005): Gerald Epstein, 'Introduction', in G Epstein (ed.), *Financialization and The World Economy*, Cheltenham: Edward Elgar, pp. 3–16 (2005). Gérard Duménil and Dominque Lévy, 'Costs and Benefits of Neoliberalism: a class analysis', pp. 17–45; Gerald Epstein and Arjun Jayadev, 'The Rise of Rentier Incomes in OECD Countries', pp. 46–76.
[106] William Lazonick and Mary O'Sullivan, 'Maximizing Shareholder Value: a new ideology for corporate governance', 29 *Economy and Society*, pp. 13–35 (2000), p. 18.
[107] See Froud et al, *Financialization and Strategy*, pp. 68, 87–8.
[108] Germán Gutiérrez and Thomas Philippon, 'Investmentless Growth', *Brookings Papers on Economic Activity* (Fall 2017), pp. 89, 92–3.
[109] Gutiérrez and Philippon, 'Investmentless Growth', p. 109.
[110] See, for example, the report of the Work and Pensions, and Business, Innovations and Skills Committee on the running of British Home Stores ('Leadership failures and personal greed led to the collapse of BHS').

this resurgence of private appropriative power and the ruthless pursuit of financial gain whatever the negative impacts on other stakeholders and society as a whole. A firm's financial performance may create value for shareholders, despite the fact that the modes of achieving it may have destroyed value when negative externalities are taken into account. Responsibility for dealing with any deleterious consequences (lost jobs, lower wages, damaged communities, growing inequality, environmental degradation, financial meltdowns and the like) has fallen on individuals, communities and states – states whose ability to raise taxes to deal with the fall-out of financialised governance has been undermined by the practices of those very same institutions and corporations. In recent decades, the governance of public corporations around the globe has been radically desocialised, while the costs associated with financialised governance have been socialised. Moreover, this governance shift has not been confined to the US and UK but has spread across the globe to countries (like Germany) where governance has traditionally been thought to be more inclusive.[111] In recent decades, the OECD has sought to normalise and universalise an essentially Anglo-American, stock-market-based, shareholder-oriented model of the corporation through its *Principles of Corporate Governance*.[112]

Information cost theories of property

The influence of law-and-economist is also apparent in some of the new essentialist theories that have emerged in recent decades, most notably the information cost theory of property developed by Thomas Merrill and Henry Smith. Their theory is not concerned with corporations: despite the vast amounts of productive property they own, corporations barely figure in their analyses. Their theory seeks, rather, to provide an account of property in general, centering on thing-ownership and exclusion, and to explain why property takes this essential form and why this is a good thing. It shares many features with the contractual theories of the corporation: it is highly abstract, very selective in its engagement with empirical reality and deploys functional, efficiency-based explanations and arguments. Although dressed up as neutral conceptual enquiry, their work is clearly ideologically driven and aimed at providing a defence of the property status quo – what they sometimes refer to as 'the [private] property system'.[113] It seeks to do

---

[111] See Wolfgang Streeck, *Re-Forming Capitalism*, Oxford: Oxford University Press (2009).

[112] Susanne Soederberg, *The Politics of the New International Financial Architecture*, London: Zed (2004).

[113] See, for example, Henry Smith, 'Property as the Law of Things', 125 *Harvard Law Review*, pp. 1691–726 (2012), p. 1719. As Ezra Rosser says, 'a defensive bias in favour of the status quo can be seen in their efforts to depose the legal realist bundle-of-sticks conception of

this by offering an abstract account, based on information costs, of why a property system of the sort found in contemporary capitalism – a system centred on generalised, private property rights and exclusion with limited government regulation – is economically and socially beneficial and why it should not, therefore, be changed. Their message is that this system of social ordering and co-ordination has 'worked' for a long time. Moreover, it does so as a complete system. Fiddle with it – any part of it – at your peril.

Together and individually, Merrill and Smith have produced numerous articles reiterating and elaborating their information cost theory. They have tweaked their arguments a little as they have gone along and they do not always speak with exactly the same voice, but their core arguments have remained largely unchanged and the differences between them are minor. Their work has been highly influential: Smith is currently lead reporter in the American Law Institute's Fourth Restatement of Property Law and Merrill one of the associate reporters. It is also marked, like Penner's, by unremitting hostility to the bundle of rights conception of property, and it is in this context that the ideological motivations of their work become clear. Merrill and Smith do not deny the descriptive and analytical usefulness and accuracy of the bundle of rights conception of property.[114] Indeed, in one of their early pieces on the *numerus clausus* principle, Merrill and Smith actually talk about 'property rights bundles'[115] and effectively concede that the basic building blocks that the *numerus clausus* principle delineates are bundles of rights. But they argue that the bundle of rights conception of property is descriptively incomplete, failing fully to capture the nature of property and its essential 'thingness'; indeed, they claim, it is not really a theory at all.

It is clear, however, that the main source of their hostility to bundles of rights conceptions of property is political. As for many others, it is the anti-essentialism of the bundle of rights conception that disturbs them. By suggesting that property has no essential thing-based core, they argue, the bundles conception implies that property rights are radically contingent and, worse still, state-determined and state-dependent. Bundles of rights theories portray property rights as socially constructed and eminently changeable, as capable of being (re)shaped in line with changing policy goals.[116] Their fear is

---

property and replace it with a less dynamic, more fixed versions of property': 'Destabilizing Property', 48 *Connecticut Law Review*, pp. 397–472 (2015), p. 411.

[114] See, for example, Smith, 'Property Is not Just a Bundle of Rights', p. 288; Smith, 'Property as the Law of Things', p. 1696.

[115] Thomas Merrill and Henry Smith, 'Optimal Standardization in the Law of Property', 110 *Yale Law Journal*, pp. 1–70 (2000), p. 36.

[116] As Jane Baron says, 'the information theorists' objection to the notion that property rights are contingent is mainly directed towards the suggestion that the state can alter the bundle at will at any time': 'The Contested Commitments of Property', 61 *Hastings Law Journal*, pp. 917–67 (2010), p. 944.

that these beliefs can be used to justify violations of existing property rights in pursuit of conscious programmes of 'enlightened social engineering'.[117] As a result, they are critical of all who advocate the adoption of a bundle of rights conception of property, including, among others, Ronald Coase.[118]

Merrill and Smith blame the rise of the bundle of rights conception on Legal Realism rather than on the historical changes in the nature of property wrought by the development of capitalism and the rise of intangible property forms and growth in government regulation. In their account, the Legal Realists promoted the bundle of rights conception not to try to capture conceptually the empirical realities of property in modern capitalism but to promote for political reasons what the libertarian legal scholar Richard Epstein – described by Merrill as one of his 'guiding lights' – has called a 'statist' view of property aimed at legitimating and facilitating government regulation.[119] For Merrill and Smith, 'the motivation behind the Realist's fascination with the bundle of rights conception was primarily political. They sought to undermine the notion that property is a natural right in order to smooth the way for activist state intervention in regulating and redistributing property'.[120] Their 'hostility to property'[121] was reflected their desire to 'dethron[e] the sanctity of private property and the private ordering it enables in order to enhance levels of collective control and redistribution'[122],

---

[117] Smith, 'Property as the Law of Things', p. 1697; Smith, 'Property Is Not Just a Bundle of Rights', p. 280.

[118] See Thomas Merrill and Henry Smith, 'Making Coasean Property More Coasean', 54 *Journal of Law and Economics*, pp. S77–S104 (2011). 'Somewhat surprisingly', Smith writes, 'law and economics and the New Institutional Economics are equally committed to the bundle picture because of the analytical convenience that it offers': Smith, 'Property Is Not Just a Bundle of Rights', p. 281. There are some, like Richard Epstein, who try to use the bundle conception to try to get greater protection for property rights by arguing that every stick in the bundle should be treated as a separate and distinct property right capable of being 'taken' for the purposes of constitutional protection. In response, some progressives, like Gregory Alexander, have argued that progressives should abandon the bundle metaphor: see Baron, 'The Contested Commitments of Property', p. 943. Both are, however, outliers within their respective camps.

[119] The bundle of rights conception frightens Epstein because 'the people who put the bundle together are public authorities': Richard Epstein, 'Bundle-of-Rights Theory as a Bulwark against Statist Conceptions of Private Property', 8 *Econ Journal Watch*, pp. 223–35 (2011), p. 225. Merrill was Epstein's student at the University of Chicago: Thomas Merrill, 'Possession as a Natural Right', 9 *New York University Journal of Law & Liberty*, pp. 345–74 (2015), p. 345.

[120] Thomas Merrill and Henry Smith, 'What Happened to Property in Law and Economics?', 111 *Yale Law Journal*, pp. 357–98 (2001), p. 365. See also Merrill and Smith, 'Making Coasean Property More Coasean', p. S82: 'The Legal Realists' motivation for advancing the bundle-of-rights picture was political'.

[121] Thomas Merrill, 'The Property Prism', 8 *Econ Watch Journal*, pp. 247–54 (2011), p. 249.

[122] See Ellickson, 'Two Cheers', p. 216.

as later did the Critical Legal Studies movement.[123] More specifically, the argument runs, the bundle of rights conception suited the Legal Realists' progressive political agenda by suggesting that government interventions involve not 'the violating of property, but rather the rearranging or redefining of the bundle', and that private property rights can be curtailed and adapted without falling foul of the constitutional provisions on 'takings'.[124] Unlike their own scholarship, the intellectually dishonest scholarship of the Legal Realists was infected by ideology and politics.

In common with other new essentialist theories of property, Merrill and Smith argue that, contrary to the bundle of rights view, property is 'the law of things'.[125] They offer a conception of property based on thing-ownership and exclusion that, they argue, firmly establishes property as a distinct legal category with a stable core and an identifiable 'essence', one that is, in certain key respects, 'invariant to context'. Indeed, its 'relative indifference to context' is, Smith argues, one of the 'most useful' aspects of their formalist approach.[126] They do not try explicitly to revive the idea that property rights are natural rights or claim that property is somehow rooted in natural law, though Merrill has argued that what he calls the (private) 'property strategy' for determining how resources are used and by whom is rooted in human nature and is universal. There is, he argues, a natural 'possession instinct' and there are hints in his work with Smith that they believe existing private property rights should be regarded as, in principle, inviolable.[127] As it was for Blackstone, rejection of a simple natural rights view of property is necessary because some of the 'things' regarded as property, lacking material existence, are very clearly social and legal constructs. It is simply impossible to deny that at least some property and some property rights are creations of the state. Indeed, an introductory note to the 2017 preliminary draft American Law Institute Restatement explicitly says that 'legal things are often socially constructed'[128] and Merrill has stated that 'the set of things eligible for treatment as property is socially contingent'.[129]

---

[123] Merrill and Smith, 'What Happened to Property', p. 365.

[124] Daniel Klein and John Robinson, 'Property: a bundle of rights? Prologue to the property symposium', 8 *Econ Journal Watch*, pp. 193–204 (2011), p. 195. Hence Merrill and Smith's criticisms of Coase for embracing the bundle of rights conception: Merrill and Smith, 'Making Coasean Property More Coasean'.

[125] See Smith, 'Property as the Law of Things'.

[126] Smith, 'On the Economy of Concepts in Property', 16 *University of Pennsylvania Law Review*, pp. 2097–18 (2012), p. 2105.

[127] Thomas Merrill, 'The Property Strategy', 160 *University of Pennsylvania Law Review*, pp. 2061–95 (2012); Merrill, 'Possession as a Natural Right'.

[128] See Wyman, 'The New Essentialism', p. 198.

[129] Merrill, 'The Property Strategy', p. 2065.

Like many new essentialists, Merrill and Smith tend to treat tangibles, and especially land, as the paradigmatic example of property.[130] Thus, for Smith, 'the 'prototypical example' of 'the exclusion strategy' is 'trespass to land'.[131] They are aware that intangibles pose potential problems for their thing-centred conception of property and that some question whether intangibles can, or should, be understood as 'property'.[132] Indeed, there are moments when Merrill and Smith seem unclear themselves about the property status of intangibles which cannot be physically possessed and consist only of rights bundles. Thus, Smith distinguishes 'regular property', by which he means land and tangible personal property, from 'intellectual' and 'entity' property'.[133] And Merrill writes of the 'vexed status of intellectual property' and wonders 'how far societies can go in extending the protections associated with property to resources that have no tangible dimensions and hence cannot be possessed in any ordinary sense'.[134] He falls back on the fact that 'copyrights, patents, trademarks and trade secrets are all recognised as intangible forms of property'.[135]

Merrill and Smith do not, however, dwell on these complications or spend much time exploring the nature of the 'thinghood' of key intangible property forms. Instead, they adopt a broad and rather unreflective view of the 'things' that can be property. To qualify as a 'thing' and as property, it is only necessary that the 'thing' is treated by law as a 'separate whole' and that it is transferable, interpreted (Penner-like) to mean 'no more than contingently related with any particular person'.[136] No significant distinction is therefore made between property rights in different things. 'Property rules', Smith writes, 'are particularly suited to the protection of things – and, unlike

---

[130] See Katrina Wyman, 'Property as Intangible Property', in P B Miller and J Oberdiek (eds), *Oxford Studies in Private Law Theory*, volume 1, Oxford: Oxford University Press, pp. 81–106 (2020).
[131] Smith, 'Intellectual Property as Property', 116 *Yale Law Journal*, pp 1742–822 (2007), p. 1745.
[132] See, for example, Simon Douglas and Ben McFarlane, 'Defining Property Rights', in Penner and Smith (eds), *Philosophical Foundations of Property Law*, Oxford: Oxford University Press, pp. 219–43 (2013); Pretto-Sakmann, *Boundaries of Personal Property*.
[133] Henry Smith, 'Semicommons in Fluid Resources', 20 *Marquette Intellectual Property Law Review*, pp. 195–212 (2016), p. 212.
[134] Merrill, 'Possession as a Natural Right', pp. 365–6. Merrill attributes the mass violation of IP rights to the intangibility of the object of property; it does not feel like a taking.
[135] Thomas Merrill, 'Property and the Right to Exclude', 77 *Nebraska Law Review*, pp. 730–55 (1998), p. 749.
[136] See Wyman, 'The New Essentialism', p. 198. Penner also emphasises the separability requirement: 'only those "things" in the world that are contingently associated with any particular owner may be objects of property': *The Idea of Property in Law*, p. 111.

some, I include here intangible things'.[137] All property rights are thus put on the same basic footing. In this way, the theory of property developed by Merrill and Smith provides an abstract, decontextualised defence of exclusionary property rights in both tangibles and intangibles, and in both personal possessions and productive resources. Hence, their reference to the 'de-contextualisation of the exclusion strategy'.[138]

Context cannot, however, be completely excluded (so to speak). Just as contractual theorists are compelled to resurrect the fictional corporation to explain limited liability, 'context' has to be brought back in to explain why some intangibles count as 'things' and therefore as 'property'. Thus, 'thinghood', the draft Restatement tells us, is 'partly a function of physical facts and partly a function of context, including economic and social practices and norms and customs'.[139] On this basis, as long as they satisfy both the separateness and impersonality criteria – in other words, as long as people treat them as separate, transferable 'things' – the bundles of rights that constitute such 'things' as intangible intellectual and financial property can be deemed 'property'. The Restatement further explains that having 'value' and being bought and sold are indications of whether bundles of rights are 'things' for property purposes.[140]

Crucially, Merrill and Smith not only insist that property is about 'things', thing-ownership and exclusion, but argue that there are good reasons why this is the case. It is here that description turns into theory and that Merrill and Smith turn from formalism to functionalism. The reason we have a specifically *private* property regime based on a relatively simple *in rem* conception of property as privately owned 'things' from which owners can exclude others is, they argue, that it 'works'. Why and how does it 'work'? A thing- and exclusion-based conception of property, they claim, is advantageous and necessary in a positive transaction cost world. *In rem* private property rights, unencumbered by social obligations, centred on exclusion and good against the world, transmit a simple message to third parties (non-owners) about the rights possessed by private property-owners over the 'things' they own. Conceptualised as things and centred on exclusion, private property, whether owned by individuals or public bodies, 'allo[ws] owners to undertake the choice among uses without having to justify the decision to third parties', while sending a simple message to non-owning duty-holders.[141]

---

[137] Henry Smith, 'Property and Property Rules', 79 *New York University Law Review*, pp. 1719–98 (2004), p. 1754.
[138] Smith, 'Property as the Law of Things', p. 1710.
[139] Restatement (Fourth) of Property (Preliminary Draft No. 3, September 15th), 2017, p. 4. See also Wyman, 'The New Essentialism', p. 198.
[140] Restatement (Fourth) of Property (Preliminary Draft No. 3, September 15th), 2017, p. 5.
[141] Henry Smith, 'Exclusion and Property Rules in the Law of Nuisance', 90 *Virginia Law Review*, pp. 965–1049 (2004), p. 984; Smith, 'Property as the Law of Things', p. 1702.

This simple message takes the form of an easy-to-follow rule – 'keep off', 'don't touch' – and benefits, they tell us, not only owners but non-owners, because it obviates their need to acquire contextual knowledge and process large amounts of information. In this way, they argue, a property regime (such as our own) based on *in rem* private property rights and exclusion, reduces information and transaction costs, facilitates alienation, and in this way helps to deliver low-cost market co-ordination and ordering. The benefits of reducing information costs through this clear and simple signalling and minimisation of complexity explains why our property system is the way it is and makes it easier to justify. It explains the limitation on property forms (the *numerus clausus* principle[142]) and the centrality to property and the property system of the right to exclude. Moreover, 'the information-cost problems solved by property rights carry over into intangible property forms like intellectual property'.[143] It is their *in rem* and exclusionary nature that distinguishes property rights from other rights and establishes property as a distinctive area of law.

Although their theory of property seeks to be as 'invariant to context' as possible, however, Merrill and Smith have to bring 'context' back in (again) to try to 'capture the facts' and explain why we do not have a regime of absolute sole and despotic dominion in which owners have complete authority over the things they own. 'Contextual factors', they argue, have sometimes led the law to place limits on ownership and sometimes to adopt a strategy based not on private property and exclusion but on the alternative strategy of 'governance'.[144] Merrill and Smith explain this by arguing that exclusionary property provides a 'baseline', a default position, but that sometimes – for example, where simple exclusion does not, for some reason, 'work' or where the costs of exclusion exceed the benefits – the 'exclusion strategy' has to be supplemented by governance. Governance 'focuses in on given uses and prescribes proper behavior with respect to the resource. Governance rules are more tailored and context-specific'.[145] It is clear, however, that Merrill and Smith do not favour 'governance', which could involve state regulation of some kind, because of the information and transaction costs involved. Like the bundle of rights conception of property, which encourages the employment of contextual information, governance is something to be avoided. It seems that it should, wherever possible, be

---

[142] This is the idea that the universe of property forms is closed and should remain so because of the potential information costs.

[143] Smith, 'Intellectual Property as Property', p. 1745.

[144] Smith, 'Exclusion versus Governance: two strategies for delineating property rights', 31 *Journal of Legal Studies*, pp. S483–S487 (2002). Smith has argued that equity is also a second feature of property that limits the authority of owners.

[145] Smith, 'Exclusion versus Governance'.

confined to exceptional cases of 'spillovers' or negative externalities, to situations of what economists refer to as 'market failure'.[146]

Merrill and Smith do not consider the considerable historical and anthropological evidence suggesting that people are able to internalise much more complicated and overlapping entitlements that are not based on exclusive and exclusionary private property rights, particularly in important productive resources. Nor do they explore contemporary examples of successful resource management based on neither exclusionary private property nor exclusionary public or state property – hybrid forms where Honoré's incidents of ownership are split between individuals and collective bodies: the Household Responsibility System, which is widely credited with generating the dramatic increases in agricultural productivity in 1980s and 1990s China, is an example here.[147] There is also little in the way of consideration of the work of Elinor Ostrom, whose *Governing the Commons*, published in 1990, offers strong support for the claim that community-based productive resource management is possible: people can co-operate to manage resources through informal norms rather than through private property rights or state administration.[148] Although some of Smith's early work on the 'semicommons' seems to support Ostrom's views, and although he occasionally cites her work, its implications for their information cost theory are not considered.[149]

Facilitating the market: functionalism and efficiency

Lior Strahilevitz has suggested the basic exclusionary right at the core of the information cost theorists' property regime is a 'hermit's property right' based on the idea of the 'solitary, isolated individual'.[150] Merrill and Smith themselves have said that *in rem* property works as a social ordering system and co-ordination device 'among unconnected and anonymous actors'

---

[146] Smith, 'Property Is Not Just a Bundle of Rights', p. 282. Following law-and-economics convention, they seem to think that any redistribution should generally be done through the tax system rather than through changes to such things as the substantive legal rules governing property.

[147] See Ireland and Meng, 'Post-Capitalist Property'.

[148] Ostrom, *Governing the Commons*, Cambridge: Cambridge University Press (1990). Ostrom's work appeals to some on the left because it makes it clear that successful non-private property-based regimes for resource management are possible, and to some on the right because it shows that people can manage resources without formal government interference.

[149] Carol Rose, 'Ostrom and the Lawyers', 5 *International Journal of the Commons*, pp. 28–49 (2011), pp. 32–5.

[150] Lior Strahilevitz, 'Information Asymmetries and the Right to Exclude', 104 *Michigan Law Review*, pp. 1835–97 (2006), p. 1041.

who connect through things.[151] This leads Baron to suggest that, in Merrill and Smith's world, 'individuals ... are not depicted as interacting much' because 'for functional purposes nothing turns on interactions between them'.[152] However, while it is true that Merrill and Smith's world is, indeed, a world of isolated, self-interested, (private) property-owning individuals, the interactions between these individuals are not quite as functionally irrelevant as this suggests.

Merrill and Smith's argument is an abstract functional explanation of, and argument in favour of, the private property status quo ('the property system') in relation to both personal possessions and productive resources. Indeed, Smith has described his account of property as 'functionally motivated formalis[m]'.[153] The functionalism of their approach is reflected in the fact that, having initially emphasised that exclusion lies at the core of property, an approach that tends to focus on the duties of non-owners, Merrill and Smith have more recently come to argue that exclusion is not an end in itself but a means to the socially beneficial end of enabling owners to exercise their property rights and interest in using 'things' without needing to answer to others for the choices they make. Exclusion is, therefore, a 'strategy', which is 'implemented through a variety of [legal] doctrines that work in tandem'.[154] In this respect, Merrill and Smith's views have moved closer to those of theorists like Larissa Katz, for whom the distinctive feature of ownership is that owners are 'the supreme agenda setters' for resources.[155]

Crucially, Merrill and Smith argue that 'many aspects of property are only fully describable at the level of the property system as a whole' and that some of property's 'desirable (and undesirable) effects emerge holistically'.[156] These desirable, holistic effects are described by Merrill and Smith only in very general terms. 'Properties like efficiency, fairness, justice and virtue promotion', Smith argues, 'are emergent properties of the property system', implying that they are properties that manifest themselves only as the result of various components of a (complex) system working together.[157] This has led Merrill and Smith to deploy the metaphors of property as a machine and as architecture, and to describe it as having a 'modular' structure. However, rather than trying to provide empirical evidence that 'the property system'

---

[151] Thomas Merrill and Henry Smith, 'The Morality of Property', 48 *William and Mary Law Review*, pp. 1849–95 (2007), p. 1852.
[152] Barron, 'The Contested Commitments of Property', p. 958.
[153] Smith, quoted in Wyman, 'The New Essentialism', p. 206.
[154] Smith, 'Property as the Law of Things', p. 1713.
[155] Larissa Katz, 'Exclusion and Exclusivity in Property Law', 58 *University of Toronto Law Journal*, pp. 275–315 (2008), p. 278.
[156] Smith, 'Property as the Law of Things', pp. 1698–9.
[157] Smith, 'Property as the Law of Things', p. 1719.

has yielded these 'desirable effects', Merrill and Smith rely mainly on the fact that our 'property system' has survived, seeing this as evidence that it 'works'. In their view, property is 'a machine, one that ... has been running more or less on its own from long ago until now, and one that is best left alone'.[158]

Indeed, they go further, arguing that tinkering with any one bit of the system – taking away or changing one stick in the property rights bundle or introducing more 'governance' – risks the smooth and successful operation of the whole. 'The idea', Smith writes, 'that doctrines are part of an issue-by-issue balancing of values like community, autonomy, efficiency, personhood, labor, and distributive justice is to commit the fallacy of division'. There is, he suggests, some 'capacity for (bounded) change', but it is limited.[159] Indeed, they suggest that the architecture not only of private property but of private law as a whole needs to be maintained, warning against the 'deceptive attractions' of 'mov[ing] in the direction of more governance style contextualised enquiry' that fails to take account of 'delineation costs'. In a swipe at 'progressive' property scholars seeking to assert the social obligations they believe should accompany private property rights, Smith argues that allowing owners to exclude others might 'see[m] nasty and selfish, but whether it is efficient, fair, just, or virtue-promoting is sometimes only assessable in the context of the system as a whole'.[160] The message is, once again, that even modest change carries risks.

Although the abstract nature of Merrill and Smith's theory means that '[t]here is not much texture in their account of the social world',[161] it is nevertheless possible to see in their abstractions a more concrete picture of the social world that informs their theories. Merrill and Smith seem to envisage a world of separate individual owners of predominantly tangible things, including productive resources, hence Smith's claim that the 'desirable features of a system of property ... relate to the interest in use' and his description of the exclusion strategy as 'defin[ing] a chunk of the world – a thing – under the owner's control'.[162] In this world, duties are owed by non-owners to owners, rather than by owners to others, and property owners are, in principle, allowed to use their things however they like, ideally subject to minimal interference. People are expected to be self-seeking and to engage in trade with other separate, self-seeking, property-owning individuals. For Merrill and Smith, one of the key advantages of 'the formalism of the exclusion strategy and modesty in the governance strategy' is that it 'makes

---

[158] Barron, 'The Contested Commitments of Property', p. 965.
[159] Smith, 'Property Is Not Just a Bundle of Rights', pp 287–8.
[160] Smith, 'Property as the Law of Things', pp. 1717–18.
[161] Barron, 'The Contested Commitments of Property', p. 958.
[162] Smith, 'Property as the Law of Things', pp. 1693, 1702. 'Chunks' implies solid pieces of some-thing.

property more *alienable*'.¹⁶³ In other words, it facilitates market exchanges among strangers. Easy alienability is one of the driving forces of their theory. In this sense, it is very much a theory for the times and a theory for particular interests, fitting very well with the interests of capital and with what property has become in today's highly financialised, global capitalism – a capitalism characterised not only by lengthy supply chains and voluminous international trade in tangibles, but by even more voluminous and rapid trade in intangible financial property. As Smith says, 'the need for far-flung and sometimes socially distant persons to respect property rights calls for simplification and standardization'.¹⁶⁴

Merrill and Smith's 'property system' is, then, based on private property and markets and implicit in their claim that this system is 'working well' are a number of standard economic and law-and-economics claims about the benefits of private property and market ordering. In addition to promoting stability, 'autonomy' and 'fairness', a regime based on clear, well-defined private property rights, they argue, promotes efficiency.¹⁶⁵ It does so, firstly, by creating incentives for owners, particularly of productive resources, to use those resources as productively as possible. The owner has the right to exclude the world and therefore, the argument runs, 'assumes the role of gatekeeper and manager of the asset'. This gives them 'a powerful incentive to invest in and develop the asset, because [they] will capture the benefit of these actions as the residual claimant'.¹⁶⁶ This echoes the contractualists' argument that rentier corporate shareholders should retain their control rights on the grounds that, as the 'residual claimants', they have the greatest incentive to invest in and develop assets. For Merrill and Smith, exclusion thus explains 'the dynamic efficiency of [private] property' in promoting investment and innovation. Not only that, by facilitating transferability and interactions in the form of market exchanges, it also, they argue, facilitates 'the allocational efficiency that comes from the free exchange of rights'.¹⁶⁷ There are important senses, therefore, in which information cost theories of property echo the economically determinist, efficiency-based arguments of contractual theories of the corporation. Just as the latter argue that the triumph of the Anglo-American, shareholder-oriented model of the corporation and corporate governance is the product of

---

[163] Smith, 'Property as the Law of Things', p. 1711 (his emphasis).
[164] Smith, 'Property as the Law of Things', p. 1709.
[165] See Rosser, 'Destabilizing Property', p. 409.
[166] Merrill and Smith, 'Making Coasean Property More Coasean', p. S90.
[167] Merrill and Smith, 'Making Coasean Property More Coasean', p. S90. Merrill and Smith advocate breaking down the complexity of these market interactions into components (modules), a process that begins with property, the *sine qua non* of market ordering.

contract-based market selection, so information theory implies that our private property regime, by facilitating alienability and market exchange, has shown, by being around for a long time without much changing, its functional efficiency and superiority.[168]

It is not insignificant that Merrill and Smith focus on the abstract mechanics of the 'property system' rather than on how it operates in empirical reality. Indeed, despite their celebration of how the system 'works' and expressed desire to 'capture' and 'explain' the 'facts',[169] and their emphasis on how the *in rem* property system operates as a whole, Merrill and Smith, like Penner, show little interest in the empirical realities of contemporary capitalism and the system's actual operation. This is reflected in their desire to marginalise 'context', except where it is needed to encompass deviations from a private property-based regime. Just as contractual theorists of the corporation shy away from engagement with the real world, so too do information cost theorists. The claim that the system 'works', for example, is largely inferred from the fact that it has survived. It is not asked for whom it 'works' or how it 'works' for different groups. As things stand, even within the world's richest countries, the 'property system' works well only for a minority. It works very well for the wealthiest (the top 1 per cent or so) and pretty well for the layer below (the top 20 per cent or so), but much less well for the bottom 50 per cent, more and more of whom are experiencing stagnant or falling real wages and declining living standards. For the growing number of very poor, facing a growing everyday struggle for material survival, it is a disaster.

The information cost theory of property nevertheless provides valuable insights into the benefits of private property, particularly in relation to personal possessions, insights that are very useful to those interested in institutional design. As a description, let alone explanation, of property in contemporary capitalism, however, it falls seriously short. Descriptively, the picture of the world conjured up by Merrill and Smith's abstract theorising is simplistic and nostalgic. It harks back to an economically liberal world of small producers and simple commodity production based on private property (mainly in tangibles) and market exchange, a world in which power is dispersed.[170] Multi-national corporations, financial and non-financial, barely figure in their work.[171] Indeed, just as contractual theorists tend

---

[168] See Barron, 'The Contested Commitments of Property', pp. 960–1.
[169] Smith, 'Property as the Law of Things', p. 1695.
[170] It harks back, in other words, to an imagined world of simple commodity production.
[171] Smith briefly mentions Berle and Means' claim that the separation of ownership and control was calling into question the notion of private property but uses it only to assert (very briefly) the virtues of the modular theory: Smith, 'Property as the Law of Things', pp. 1721–2.

to use new firms or small partnerships that bear little relation to today's large, economically dominant corporations as analytical starting points to support their arguments, so information theorists, when they bother to delve into property in productive resources, tend to select their starting points very carefully. Merrill, for example, uses a family farm to support his claim that property has a basic architecture.[172] As Ezra Rosser observes, 'Merrill's stylised family farm is just that, a family farm, not a gigantic agribusiness defined by its corporate form'.[173] They also show little or no interest in the nature of the intangible bundles of rights that have become such important sources of wealth and power in modern capitalism. The social relational and power dimensions of property – property as a tool of domination[174] – which are central to capturing the empirical realities of the modern property system are conspicuous by their absence. Similarly, little interest is shown in the distribution of property rights, in inequality and poverty, in the growing threat of oligarchy, or in the relationship between the propertied (owners) and non-propertied (non-owners). Indeed, Merrill and Smith's approach eschews and discourages the kind of empirical enquiry that might actually help us better to grasp and understand the nature of the property institutions ('system') of contemporary capitalism. It obscures as much as it enlightens.

Merrill and Smith's message is that, however unequal the distribution of property and unjust the property status quo might seem to some – what with slowing economic growth, wage stagnation, falling living standards, rising inequality and poverty, not to mention environmental degradation – the system is 'working'. There is no need for fundamental reform. Indeed, we should hesitate before implementing even modest reforms for fear of upsetting the system as a whole: 'tinkering' is to be discouraged; 'not much needs to change'.[175] As Rosser says, the attempt to 'construct a simplistic model of property ends up reading as an attempt to justify the status quo and to praise the system'. It is not just a theory for the times, but a theory for particular interests. It provides an abstract, partial and slanted account of property as it has become at a particular place and time, presenting it as the product of beneficent economic forces rather than the product in significant part of the power and influence of particular interest groups making particular kinds of justificatory arguments.[176]

---

[172] Merrill, 'The Property Strategy', p. 2071.
[173] Rosser, 'Destabilizing Property', p. 421.
[174] See Eric Freyfolge, 'Private Ownership and Human Flourishing: an exploratory overview', 24 *Stellenbosch Law Review*, pp. 430–54 (2013), p. 448.
[175] Baron, 'The Contested Commitments of Property', p. 921.
[176] Rosser, 'Destabilizing Property', pp. 419–421.

Property rights as 'special'

For those who wish to maintain the property status quo, maintaining a clear distinction between property rights and other rights, and establishing that property is an analytically distinct legal right rooted in thing-ownership, is vitally important, for in our society property rights in general, and *private* property rights in particular, are widely regarded and experienced as somehow 'special', as 'natural' and sacrosanct, as 'keystone rights'. As Singer explains, 'calling something a property right often reflects an intuition that the right in question implicates a strong moral claim to immunity from loss by the voluntary action of both private and public actors and places a heavy burden on those seeking to "regulate" or "limit" the property right'.[177] And yet, as Kevin Gray has observed, discussions about what distinguishes property rights have a 'horrible circularity'. He argues:

> If naively we ask which rights are proprietary we are told that they are those rights which are assignable to and enforceable against third parties. When we then ask which rights these may be, we are told that they comprise, of course, the rights which are traditionally identified as 'proprietary'. 'Property' is 'property' because it is 'property': property status and proprietary consequence confuse each other in a deadening embrace of cause and effect.[178]

The bundle of rights conception, by highlighting the artificial, contingent, malleable, public-dependent nature of property rights, threatens to undermine this 'special' status. New essentialist theories of property, by (re)asserting their special nature, make it easier to sustain the claim that

---

[177] Singer, 'Property and Social Relations', p. 78. Despite this, for some, they are not treated as special enough. In the US, for example, some lament the fact that property rights are not apparently treated as fundamental rights, equal in status to rights under the due process or equal protection clauses of the constitution. Why are they not treated as fundamental rights in the same way as they appear to be under the German Basic Law? However, as Gregory Alexander points out, appearances can be deceptive: the characterisation of German constitutional law as more protective of property than its American counterpart is 'a gross and inaccurate generalisation': Gregory Alexander, 'Property as a Fundamental Constitutional Right? The German Example', 88 *Cornell Law Review*, pp.733–78 (2003), p. 740. Alexander points out that in Germany different degrees of protection are given to different sorts of property rights. In recent decades in the US the courts have taken an increasingly property-protective stance, prompting some to talk of a return to the *Lochner* era: See Molly McUsic, 'The Ghost of Lochner: modern takings doctrine and its impact on economic legislation', 76 *Boston University Law Rev*iew, pp. 605–68 (1996).

[178] Gray, 'Property in Thin Air', p. 293.

property rights are deserving of greater legal protection than other rights.[179] Thus, certain kinds of rights, like human rights, might regularly be declared inalienable and fundamental, but they are frequently 'trumped by private property rights and equally frequently violated.[180] As Penner says, 'the chief rhetorical value of isolating property norms from others lies in the forceful way in which property norms carry weight in a normative system; if no meaningful basis for distinguishing property norms from other norms can be found, then this rhetorical advantage has no warrant'.[181] Thus, although property may 'not [be] all it is cracked up to be' or be a 'conceptual mirage', acquiring 'property' status for rights nevertheless remains politically as well as economically significant. The idea of property still 'exerts a powerful ... moral leverage and the notions of *meum* and *teum* continue to have have 'deep resonance'. As a result, while it may be true that claims based on notions of property 'do not protect rights of any sacrosanct or a priori nature', they add 'with varying degrees of sophistication ... moral legitimacy to the assertion of self-interest in the beneficial control of valued resources'.[182] Property is 'the legitimate cloth of wealth'.[183]

There are various reasons why private property rights are able to command (and demand) special legal protection. Firstly, as we have seen, private property has come to be seen as the political and social basis for individual self-development, self-governance, emancipation and autonomy, and as central to civility, social stability and democracy. Even if it is recognised that private property rights are social and legal constructs, private property as an institution is frequently depicted as rooted in human nature and as the 'natural' expression of personality, individuality, autonomy and liberty. Human beings 'naturally' come to regard some objects as important

---

[179] Carol Rose, 'Property as the Keystone Rights?', 71 *Notre Dame Law Review*, pp. 329–69 (1996); Laura Underkuffler, 'Property: a special right', 71 *Notre Dame Law Review*, pp. 1033–58 (1996).

[180] Anna Chadwick wonders, using Katharina Pistor's language, whether 'these purportedly equal legal rights were never formally equal in the first place because their legal coding is different. Pistor's analysis, like that of Hohfeld, implies that rights created under different legal regimes carry different legal weights, and that many of the purportedly "fundamental" rights created in public law may correspond to a weaker constellation of powers and privileges than those created under private law': 'Capital without Capitalism? Or Capitalism without Determinism?': 30 *Social and Legal Studies*, pp. 302–11 (2021), at pp. 304–5.

[181] James Penner, 'Misled by "Property"', 18 *Canadian Journal of Law and Jurisprudence*, pp. 75–94 (2005), p. 75.

[182] Gray, 'Property in Thin Air', pp. 305–7. Blackstone prefaced his definition of property in terms of 'sole and despotic dominion by saying that "there is nothing which so generally strikes the imagination, and engages the affections of mankind as the right of property"'.

[183] von Benda-Beckmann et al, 'The Properties of Property', p. 2.

extensions of themselves, informing the way they think of themselves as persons.[184] Indeed, people are often defined in significant part by the 'things' they own to the exclusion of others, including, crucially, the state. Private property rights need special protection because of this. They represent a vital bulwark for the individual against the state, against collectives and against the potentially tyrannical majority. Indeed, they are in many ways the very foundation of the public–private distinction.

Of course, these arguments about private property and personality are more easily applied to some 'things', like tangible personal possessions, than others. They have less intuitive traction in relation to intangibles such as bonds and shares. 'Can the principle of personality', asked Cohen, really 'help us to decide to what extent there shall be private rather than public property in railroads, mines, gas-works, and other public necessities?'.[185] This, perhaps, helps to explain why for some in the civil law tradition true property is composed only of rights over tangible objects. It also helps to explain why the ever more frequent state interventions needed to protect and maintain financial property values tend to be justified not so much in terms of property protection and individual personality, autonomy and/or identity but in terms of avoiding financial collapses. This is one manifestation of the rather different, consequentialist arguments that have been deployed in support of private property in productive resources and the fruits of production. In this context, much has been made of private property's contribution to wealth creation and prosperity. In much the same way that Locke argued for private property (and enclosure) on the grounds of 'improvement', in recent decades many have argued in favour of the privatisation of previously publicly-owned productive resources on the grounds that it creates incentives to use resources productively and brings the benefits that come from the alleged ability of the free market's 'invisible hand' to allocate resources 'efficiently'.[186] Indeed, this idea has been vigorously promoted, becoming a central plank of neoliberal policy

---

[184] Thus, for Hegel, property was an important way in which we transformed our abstract personhood into something concrete.

[185] Cohen, 'Property and Sovereignty', p. 18.

[186] Compare, for example, Boudewijn Bouckaert's rationale for private property, which, centring on its contribution to individual autonomy, leads him to argue that property should be confined to tangible objects, with Wolfgang Mincke's consequentialist economic rationale, which favours a much broader definition of property: Boudewijn Bouckaert, 'What is Property?', 13 *Harvard Journal of Law and Public Policy*, pp. 775–816 (1990); Wolfgang Mincke, 'Property: assets or power? Objects or relations as substrata of property rights', in Harris (ed.), *Property Problems from Genes to Pension Funds*, London: Kluwer, pp. 77–88 (1997). Both are discussed in Harris, 'The Elusiveness of Property', pp. 127–9.

agendas and what Piketty calls the 'neo-proprietarian' ideologies of the late twentieth century.[187]

The result of property's perceived special nature is that, while many legal rights are seen as being within the gift of the state and thus capable of being withdrawn without compensation, private property rights tend to be seen as rights that cannot and should not be taken away or infringed without due process and the payment of appropriate compensation.[188] Private property in both personal possessions and productive resources has, in the words of Piketty, been 'sacralized'.[189] Indeed, it is the special nature of property rights that has led many to seek to extend the category of 'property' to rights they would like to protect. In the 1960s, for example, Charles Reich sought to extend the category to welfare entitlements. These had traditionally been regarded as politically determined, as akin to charity and capable of being withdrawn by the state at any time without compensation. Aware of the special procedural and substantive protections that property rights commanded, Reich sought to recharacterise these entitlements as 'new property' and, as such, as 'things' that could not readily be taken away.[190] In the US, however, unlike the politically-determined rights that constitute intellectual property, welfare rights have never been treated as property under the 'takings' clause of the US constitution and, as a result, have never secured substantive protection. By contrast, in Europe, since the 1990s, the ECtHR has occasionally extended the scope of property rights to social security matters. Case law has held that entitlements such as old age pensions are to be regarded as falling within the scope of Article P1–1 on property protection because of their financial nature, relying on Article 14 ECHR on protection from discrimination in the enjoyment of rights to achieve this.[191]

Indeed, despite his worries about the 'statism' of the bundle of rights conception of property, Epstein has at times seen it as a potential basis for providing even more comprehensive protection for private property rights. Never one to hesitate embracing different intellectual positions as and when politically expedient, Epstein has, to this end, sought to revive an older, nineteenth-century use of the bundle of rights conception of property to extend the idea of 'takings' to get the special protections afforded property

---

[187] Piketty, *Capital and Ideology*, p. 417.
[188] In the well-known US case of *Goldberg v Kelly* (397 US 254, 1970), for example, the question was whether it was constitutional to terminate the welfare benefits of those who already had them without (something resembling) an adversarial trial. The majority, adopting a framework derived from Charles Reich's idea of 'new property', in effect constitutionalised a judicial-like procedure for deciding these cases.
[189] Piketty, *Capital and Ideology*, p. 123.
[190] Charles Reich, 'The New Property', 73 *Yale Law Journal*, pp. 733–87 (1964).
[191] See Praduroux, 'Objects of Property Rights', pp. 62–3.

rights to every single stick in every particular property rights bundle.[192] Thus, for Epstein, taking away any of the sticks in the bundle is a 'taking' requiring the payment of compensation. This renders not only physical expropriations but things such as taxes and regulations potential 'takings'.[193] This is particularly significant in the context of intangible financial property where changes in government environmental and labour protection policies can impact on investment returns and property values without the physical appropriation of material things. Under the 'new constitutionalism' (discussed in the next chapter), it is possible to characterise such policies as 'regulatory takings' and violations of investors' property rights. In this respect, however, Epstein is something of an outlier. Generally, defenders of the property status quo find the thing-ownership conception of property much more attractive than the bundle of rights conception with its 'weak sense of the "thingness" of private property'.[194] As we have seen, for most defenders of the property status quo, the bundle of rights conception, with its emphasis on the man-made nature and malleability of property and property rights, is highly problematic.[195]

The thing-ownership conception of property, by emphasising property as a relation between individual people and individual 'things', also downplays and conceals the economic and social relational dimensions of property, particularly property-as-capital. With financial property, for example, the thing-ownership conception tends to conceal the fact that the revenues that accrue to financial property owners ultimately come from 'the efforts of others'. It helps to maintain the illusion that money's seeming ability to make more money – to generate revenues autonomously – is a quality that inheres in it. A social relational approach to property threatens to expose the social relations and practices that are a pre-requisite of financial property's and money's money-making capacity[196] It threatens, in other words, to expose the links between rich and poor, and between wealth and the labour and 'efforts of others'.

The 'fear', then, is that the bundle of rights conception of property has the potential to lay uncomfortably bare not only the socially constructed nature and public dimensions of property, but its social relational and power dimensions. In highlighting the ways in which property rights represent

---

[192] See Epstein, 'Bundle-of-Rights Theory'. On this older use of the bundle-of-rights approach, see Banner, *American Property*, p. 45.
[193] Richard Epstein, *Takings: private property and the power of eminent domain*, Cambridge: Harvard University Press (1985), pp. 57–62.
[194] Michael Heller, 'The Boundaries of Property', 108 *Yale Law Journal*, pp. 1163–223 (1999), p. 1193.
[195] See Klein and Robinson, 'Property: A Bundle of Rights?', pp. 193–4.
[196] See Sayer, *Marx's Method*, pp. 121–2.

political choices made in an arena of conflict, they threaten to undermine the uncritical acceptance of the legitimacy of existing private property rights, particularly in relation to productive resources. By contrast, as Grey points out, the concept of property as thing-ownership serves an 'important ideological function', helping to legitimate a liberal individualist view of human beings and the distributional status quo, as well as capitalist social relations more generally.[197] These political considerations have undoubtedly been key factors behind the rise of the new essentialism and the desire to minimise what Epstein refers to as the 'shadowy collective presence' hovering over property.[198] This is something of a paradox, for this 'collective presence' and the dependence of much contemporary property on, and need for, public support has been only too evident in recent decades. What would have happened to much of the intangible financial property of the wealthy if the state had not stepped in with bailouts in the wake of the financial crash and, more recently, COVID-19? These objections to 'statism' are an example of ideology and politics taking precedence over intellectual and analytical honesty.

---

[197] Grey, 'The Disintegration of Property', p. 73.
[198] Epstein, 'Bundle-of-Rights Theory', p. 226.

7

Safeguarding Property-as-Capital

Universalising capitalism

In naturalising generalised private property – private property in the means of production as well as in personal possessions – much property theory tends also to naturalise capitalism. The emergence of private property and capitalism tends to be portrayed as not only progressive but more or less inevitable. In this respect, it is at one with the inclination – common since the eighteenth century and running through the work of Hume and Smith, as well as through the work of Blackstone and anthropologists like Morgan – to see history as passing through various stages in which communal property is gradually displaced by private property. In these 'staged' (or stadial) versions of history, private property is commonly seen as both the driving force and endpoint of evolution and as a hallmark of civilisation, its emergence marking the transition from an inferior/lower to a superior/higher culture. Drawing on Smith, Marx also adopted a 'staged' account of history, at least until his later works, but he depicted the bourgeois (or capitalist) mode of production as marking not the end of history but merely a staging post on the road to communism.[1] In recent decades, staged accounts of history have become popular once more. In 1992, Francis Fukuyama boldly, but somewhat prematurely, announced the end of history, proclaiming the triumph of liberal democracy and free market capitalism.[2] Shortly after, in similar vein, Hansmann and Kraakman announced the end of history for corporate law.[3]

---

[1] On Marx's adoption in some his work of a staged account of history derived from Smith, see Brenner, 'The Origins of Capitalist Development'.
[2] Francis Fukuyama, *The End of History and the Last Man*, New York: Free Press (1992).
[3] Hansmann and Kraakman, 'The End of History for Corporate Law'.

In these accounts, private property rights are depicted as 'the basic foundation of capitalism and modernity', as emblematic of progress, and as the key engines of economic development and efficiency.[4] The rise of generalised private property and, therefore, of capitalism as an economic system tend implicitly to be portrayed as the 'logical' and natural realisations of ever-present tendencies inscribed in human nature. They are treated as though they are present in some way, even if only in the interstices, in all forms of society and somehow prefigured in earlier social arrangements lower down the ownership (and social order) spectrum. The underlying suggestion is that we have always been heading to where we are now and that earlier societies with non-private-property-based regimes were (or are) mere stepping-stones on a (progressive) journey towards full-blooded private property and capitalism. From this perspective, the history of property institutions is little more than the story of the processes whereby the various political and cultural obstacles to the development of private property and capitalism have been overcome; a story of functional necessity and the gradual lifting of the constraints on free expression by rational, self-seeking, individual economic actors and on the rational development of free-market-based economic activity. In this 'commercialisation model' of economic history, with its roots in Adam Smith and the Enlightenment thinkers of the eighteenth century, the distinctiveness and historical and cultural specificity of private property and capitalism fade from view. The concepts of private property and ownership found in capitalism are detached from their economic and social and historical conditions of existence, and are universalised, as is capitalism as a socio-economic system. The existence of that which needs to be explained is assumed.[5]

Historicising property: private property and capitalism

What, then, were the historical conditions of existence of Blackstone's definition of property in terms of 'sole and despotic dominion' by individuals

---

[4] These ideas became the basis for the so-called 'Washington Consensus', a set of policy prescriptions promoted by the World Bank, the International Monetary Fund and the US Treasury from the 1990s. Among the influential works that posited that the establishment of private property rights was one of the key pre-requisites of modernity and development was Douglass North and Robert Thomas, *The Rise of the Western World*, Cambridge: Cambridge University Press (1973). Allan Greer wryly observes that nineteenth-century anthropologists had once provided a metanarrative of modernity along these lines. 'A hundred year later', he writes, 'a similar schematic history of human progress found a home in economics. Meanwhile anthropology had moved on': Greer, *Property and Dispossession*, pp. 61–2.

[5] See Wood, *The Origin of Capitalism*, chapter 1.

and Smith's 'radical novel interpretation of the market'? As Muldrew says, there must have been 'changes of fundamental importance' taking place for 'Smith's theory to seem like a feasible account of market[s]'.[6] As we have seen, for Muldrew the key changes were, firstly, the growth in and spread of market relations, a product of the growing division of labour and separation of labour from the means of subsistence. And, secondly, the growing impersonality of those market relations, as reflected in the gradual emergence of the abstract idea of 'the market' and in the rise of 'increasingly abstract, calculated, artificial credit' – credit based on 'rationally determined future profitability' rather than 'individual morality'.[7] These changes, Muldrew suggests, saw 'amoral market relations' become more commonplace and eventually saw neo-classical theories about the market come to dominate economic discourse.[8]

For others, however, the answer lies not simply in the growth of relatively impersonal market relations but in the growth of specifically *capitalist* market relations and in the changes that were taking place in the ways in which some 'profit[ed] from the efforts of others'. Robert Brenner and Ellen Meiksins Wood have described this in terms of a gradual change in the modes of surplus extraction, from feudal modes in which surplus extraction depended on what Marx called 'extra-economic' coercion, meaning juridical, political or military force, to capitalist modes based predominantly on 'purely' economic market compulsions. In the feudal social formations that preceded capitalism, this argument runs, peasant producers possessed their means of subsistence (land, tools etc.) and this made it possible for them materially to reproduce themselves independently. Lords took part of the product of their labour forcibly through labour services, feudal rents, taxes and the like. Their power to do this was, however, bound up with the performance of public, juridical, military and administrative duties. 'Profiting from the efforts of others', therefore, quite visibly depended on hierarchies and 'extra-economic' coercion. The economic, political, social and legal were visibly entwined; in Polanyi's terms, production and distribution were 'embedded' in extra-economic social relations. There was

---

[6] Muldrew, 'Interpreting the Market', p. 181.
[7] Muldrew, *The Economy of Obligation*, p. 7; Muldrew, 'Interpreting the Market', pp. 181–2.
[8] Muldrew, 'Interpreting the Market', pp. 166, 182. A similar, market-based account of the move towards private property was provided by the anthropologist Eleanor Leacock in her work on the decline of primitive communism and rise of private property in Innu society. For Leacock, the agent of change was the fur trade and the advent of commodity production: Greer, *Property and Dispossession*, pp. 58–9. More recently, however, it has been suggested that there remain significant communal elements to social relations: see Colin Scott, 'Hunting Territories, Hunting Bosses and Communal Production among Coastal James Bay Cree', 28 *Anthropologica*, pp. 163–73 (1986).

no pretence of formal equality. Rights were linked to status and property was, in Robert Brenner's phrase, 'politically constituted'.[9] In similar vein, in the era of what Marx called the 'primitive' or 'original' accumulation of capital, slavery and direct physical coercion played a key role in surplus extraction and the amassing of wealth.[10]

Gradually, however, they argue, as producers were separated from their means of subsistence by enclosures, surplus extraction began to depend less on openly coercive political and legal mechanisms and more on the purely economic imperatives of 'the market'. Surplus value was increasingly extracted not through open, extra-economic coercion, but, less visibly and less forcibly, through the exchange of labour power for wages – exchanges that eventually, formally at least, involved nominally free and equal, private property-owning (predominantly male) legal subjects.[11] Profiting from the efforts of others was no longer based on status and the rights derived from it but on the more or less absolute ownership by a minority of key productive resources and the market imperatives facing the propertyless majority who now had to sell their labour power in order to buy the means of subsistence. Indeed, the imperatives of the market imposed themselves on producers too: to produce competitively they now had to produce profitably and, in many cases, to realise at least average profits in order to be able to invest in new productivity-enhancing techniques of production.[12] The possession of private property rights in productive resources, rather than the possession of legal/political rights linked to status, thus became the key to appropriating part of the product of the labour of others. Moreover, private property now took on a 'purely economic form', having 'discard[ed] all its former political and social embellishments and associations'.[13] Property had been relieved of any obligation to perform social/public functions and

---

[9] See Robert Brenner, 'Agrarian Class Structure and Economic Development in Pre-Industrial Europe', 70 *Past and Present*, pp. 30–75 (1977), reprinted in T H Aston and C H E Philp (eds), *The Brenner Debate*, Cambridge: Cambridge University Press, pp. 10–63 (1985). The arguments of Brenner, further developed by Wood, are summarised in Wood, *The Origin of Capitalism*.

[10] When slavery was abolished in Britain, many former slave owners invested the compensation they received in financial property, particularly railways shares: See Paddy Ireland, 'Making Sense of Contemporary Capitalism Using Company Law', 33 *Australian Journal of Corporate Law*, pp. 379–401 (2018).

[11] For many years the relationship was conceptualised in the hierarchical terms of master–servant and subordination incorporated into labour 'contracts' through implied terms: see Fox, *Beyond Contract*. Many of these implied terms still form part of the law.

[12] This underpins capitalism's unique drive to increase labour productivity through, in particular, technological advance: see Ellen Meiksins Wood, 'Marxism and the Course of History', 147 *New Left Review*, pp. 95–108 (September–October 1984).

[13] Marx, *Capital*, volume 3, p. 618. Marx was writing here of landed property.

duties and, formally at least, was only incidentally connected to political power. Harris' ownership as unconstrained 'authorised self-seekingness' was emerging. The coercive power of the state was, as it still is, needed to sustain private property, but, in principle, the exercise of overt physically coercive power was no longer needed for some to profit from the efforts of others. Surpluses could be extracted through the compulsions of the market, through 'purely' economic processes. The ability of some to profit from the efforts of others thus ceased to rest directly on juridical and/or political subordination and came to rest instead on contractual relations between 'free', property-owning individuals. This underlay the gradual separation of the economic from the political and the emergence of a seemingly autonomous legal universe, which itself underlay the rise of the analytical jurisprudential tradition.[14] The conception of property as 'sole and despotic dominion' by individuals was thus made possible by the gradual emergence of capitalist social relations but also played an important role in helping to constitute those relations.[15]

This perspective has undoubted analytical value. It helps us to understand, for example, the material basis for the seeming separation of the economic and the political, and the seeming separation of the political from the legal that characterises capitalist societies. With the gradual shift to 'purely economic' modes of extraction, Brenner argues, the state had 'only' to defend existing property rights and person–thing relations to preserve existing class relations, hence the idea that there was a shift from the rule of men to the rule of law, with the state becoming an objective third-party guarantor

---

[14] One of the key features of the analytical jurisprudential tradition is its identification of an independent and autonomous legal universe. The analytical jurisprudential tradition is, however, itself a historical phenomenon corresponding to a particular, historical form (and era) of law: what we might call the era of autonomous law. Indeed, the tradition of analytical jurisprudence in legal education and research played a vital part in the constitution of autonomous law. From this perspective, the rise of more critical and socio-legal approaches to law – of law and the social sciences – is representative of the gradual demise of autonomous law and the emergence of a new form of (markedly less autonomous) law: see Alan Thomson, 'Law and the Social Sciences: the demise of legal autonomy', paper delivered to Critical Approaches to Law Conference, University of Kent (1981). The rise of neoliberalism and the attempt to separate the economic sphere from the political and the legal is, arguably, seeing the reassertion within certain parts of the academy of legal autonomy.

[15] On the constitutive role of law, see Simon Deakin, David Gindis, Geoffrey Hodgson Huang Kainan and Katerina Pistor, 'Legal Institutionalism: capitalism and the constitutive role of law', 45 *Journal of Comparative Economics*, pp. 188–200 (2017), arguing, among other things, that the rise of the modern form of (autonomous) law – law that 'depends upon an institutionalized judiciary or the state' and involves 'some permanent and institutionalized higher adjudication' – 'is indelibly associated with the historical rise of capitalism': p. 191.

and enforcer of individual rights.[16] It also helps us to understand the liberal constitutionalism associated with the separation of spheres exemplified in the American constitution. In capitalist societies, direct exercises of status-based class power have been largely replaced by indirect exercises of power through property ownership and a seemingly neutral set of legal rules and institutions. From this perspective, while the rise of capitalism did not put an end to domination, it did 'recode' it.[17] Crucially, with these developments, the connection between the wealth of the rich and the labour of others, openly recognised as late as the eighteenth century, also became less visible. The wealth of the rich increasingly appeared to be solely the product of their own efforts and/or of the productivity of their property, particularly their money and their financial investments.[18]

It is, however, a perspective that also needs to be handled with care. As we have seen, there are important senses in which *all* modern property is politically and legally constituted; in which the seemingly autonomous 'economic' sphere under capitalism is itself a political and legal construct. Capitalism may appear to be a system in which the economic and the political are separate, and its supporters may present it as such, but, as Ellen Meiksins Wood herself recognised, this separation is always partial and very often entirely artificial. It is orthodox economic theory that seeks to abstract 'the economy' from politics and to cleanse it of its social and political content, and to remove the issues surrounding the power to direct and control productive activity from the political arena and to define them as purely 'economic' in nature.[19] Much property theory does likewise. It is arguable, however, that the artificiality of the separation has become ever more apparent in recent decades as political interventions in the economy have become ever more obviously necessary to keep the system afloat: bailout has followed bailout and states have become ever more involved in creating new, profitable forms of property-as-capital. This has led some, like Robert Brenner, to argue that the separation within capitalism between the economic and the political has been so eroded that there has emerged a new 'political capitalism'. In the face of declining profitability and economic stagnation, this new political capitalism, he argues, is characterised by much more politically dependent forms of

---

[16] Robert Brenner, 'Ellen Meiksins Wood (1942–2016)', https://solidarity-us.org/atc/181/p4598/. See also Alain Supiot, *Homo Juridicus: on the anthropological function of law*, London: Verso (2005).

[17] Tim Di Muzio, 'Towards a Genealogy of the New Constitutionalism', in Stephen Gill and A Claire Cutler (eds), *New Constitutionalism and World Order*, Cambridge: Cambridge University Press, pp. 81–94 (2014), p. 85.

[18] Ellen Meiksins Wood, 'The Separation of the Economic and Political in Capitalism', 127 *New Left Review*, pp. 66–95 (May–June 1981).

[19] Wood, 'The Separation of the Economic and Political', pp. 66–7.

extracting surplus value, by politically engineered upward redistributions and by predation. It is, he suggests, a capitalism with feudal overtones.[20]

Nor is it the case that coercive extra-economic modes of exploitation and appropriation have disappeared or are somehow external to modern capitalism. Along with the separation of producers from the means of production, violence, racism and dispossession were central features of what Marx referred to as the 'primitive' or 'original' accumulation of capital.[21] They remain features of capitalist social formations today.[22] It remains the case, however, that as capitalist social relations spread and as more and more people were separated from the means of production and subsistence, 'purely economic' compulsions increasingly became the basis upon which some profited from the efforts of others. Thus, while there remained much about the property rights regime surrounding land that contravened Blackstone's conceptualisation of property in terms of sole and despotic dominion, as Blackstone himself so richly demonstrated, various developments – the enclosure movement, growing market dependence and commodity production, the changes that were taking place in the ways markets operated, the changes in 'theories of social interaction' and in 'individuals' conceptions of themselves' – were all acting to make this conception of property more feasible.[23] What Blackstone offered was an abstract, ideal expression of the social relations of an ever more capitalist society, but only in part because hierarchical subordinations – of wives by husbands, servants by masters, of different racial and ethnic groups by others and so on – remained. He gave partial expression to the emerging

---

[20] See Robert Brenner, 'Escalating Plunder', 123 *New Left Review*, pp. 5–27 (May–June 2020); Dylan Riley and Robert Brenner, 'Seven Theses on American Politics', 138 *New Left Review*, pp. 5–27 (November–December 2022). Others, reflecting both on the increasingly overt political dimensions of contemporary accumulation and on the seemingly growing disconnection between financial returns and actual productive activity, have gone further and asked whether the new regime that is emerging is more neo- or quasi-feudal than capitalist. For a summary and critique of this view, see Morozov, 'Critique of Techno-Feudal Reason', and Tim Barker, *New Left Review*, pp. 35–51 (March–June 2023).

[21] 'Original expropriation', rather than the more usual 'primitive accumulation', probably better captures the way Marx saw these processes: see Ian Angus, 'The Meaning of "So-called Primitive Accumulation"', 74 *Monthly Review* (April 2023).

[22] In chapter 31 of *Capital*, volume 1, Marx made it clear that the origins of capitalism were rooted in violence and forced transfers: on the debates among Marxists about the nature of primitive accumulation, see Morozov, 'Critique of Techno-Feudal Reason'. See also David Harvey's idea that 'accumulation by dispossession' has become the dominant form of accumulation in contemporary neoliberal capitalism: *The New Imperialism*, Oxford: Oxford University Press (2003).

[23] See Muldrew, *The Economy of Obligation*, pp. 7, 330. Muldrew summarises the changes as involving a 'shift towards the self'.

idea that society was composed of autonomous, naturally self-interested, utility-maximising, private property-owning individuals largely freed of social and community obligations and linked to others only by market exchange and contract;[24] and to the emerging idea that the individual pursuit of self-interest and the invisible hand of the market, rather than individual and civic virtue, were the guardians of the public good.

The seeming separation of the economic, political and legal spheres that is characteristic of capitalism underlies another feature of thing-ownership conceptions of property: their tendency to abstract – in the sense of removing, separating and disembedding – property institutions from the wider socio-economic and institutional contexts and sets of practices of which they are part. This flows from their tendency to see the relationship between individual persons and individual things as the starting point for analyses of property, a tendency that encourages a perception of property/property institutions as self-subsistent, largely legal phenomena existing apart from other social phenomena; as externally and contingently, rather than internally and integrally, related to other social institutions. As Hallowell says, if we really want to understand any specific set of social institutions we need to investigate 'how they work with reference to other institutions and to the society of which they are a part'.[25] In other words, property institutions need to be analysed as parts of an inter-related whole: 'We have to reckon with an exceedingly complex network of structural relations and a wide range of variables, the specific pattern or constellation of which constitutes the structure of property as a social institution in any particular case'.[26] Or, as Margaret Davies puts it, 'property brings into play an entire social order'.[27]

---

[24] As Margaret Davies points out, these 'possessive individuals' were essentially depictions of White middle-class males: Davies, *Property*, p. 43.

[25] Hallowell, 'The Nature and Function of Property', p. 119.

[26] Hallowell, 'The Nature and Function of Property', p. 121.

[27] Davies, *Property*, p. 2. Davies is at pains to point out that property is 'not just about individuals exercising control over external things and, therefore, over others' but is also a cultural phenomenon: pp. 2–3. Much property theory, particularly that based on thing-ownership conceptions of property, tends to treat law and the (relative) autonomy it acquires when generalised commodity production and market-based, capitalist social relations come to dominate as universal rather than as historically specific and contingent phenomena. As noted earlier, the assumed autonomy of law is one of the premises of analytical jurisprudence and representative of its failure to recognise its own historical specificity and conditions of existence. Davies touches on this in a discussion of Austin and Kelsen and the impact of legal positivism on our understandings of law, when she remarks: 'Of most significance is the idea that law has its own distinctive limits, and is separate from – and institutionally superior to – other normative orders'. She goes on to argue that autonomous law is the 'proper domain of pure jurisprudence' and that jurisprudence treats law as an autonomous 'self-identical and self-defining …

Some of the problems that arise when you try to abstract property/property institutions – and law in general – from the wider socio-political-economic and institutional contexts and sets of practices of which they are part are illustrated by the difficulties Pollock and Maitland encounter in their work on English law in the twelfth and thirteenth centuries. They try to understand the property institutions of this period using the modern legal concepts of ownership and property, but are aware that the legal, social, political and economic are inextricably entwined. Thus, it is simply not possible, they observe, to 'draw the hard line that we draw between ownership and rulership, between private right and public power'. Feudalism, they argue, represented the denial of the distinction we now draw between private and public law; 'all that we call public law is merged in private law', with the same word, *dominium*, being used to stand for both ownership and lordship. Moreover,

> the title to chattels was often implicated with the title to land. The ownership of a manor usually involved the lordship over villeins and the right to seize their chattels; and so when two men were litigating about a 'manor', the subject of the dispute was not a bare tract, but a complex made up of land and of great part of the agricultural capital that worked the land, men and beasts, ploughs and carts, forks and flails.[28]

This underlines the fact that you can gain only a very partial and limited understanding of property/property institutions by examining them abstractly, atomistically and as purely legal phenomena. They need, rather, to be seen as part of a complex network of internal relations within which any single element is what it is only by virtue of its relationship to others.[29] Nicola Lacey's claim that law needs to be recognised as 'embedded in a cluster of social practices and relations' is particularly true in relation to property.[30] Engagement with the empirical complexity of property institutions is a necessary part of theorising about it.[31] Property institutions are 'historical and cultural artefact[s]'[32] that only exist in particular empirical and historical forms and are always embedded in particular historically

---

genuinely unified object, exclusive of unstable, disordered and otherwise unreliable social normativity': p. 34.

[28] Pollock and Maitland, *The History of English Law Before the Time of Edward I*, volume 2, pp. 156–7, 250–1.
[29] Sayer, *The Violence of Abstraction*, p. 19.
[30] Lacey, 'Jurisprudence, History, and the Institutional Quality of Law', p. 926.
[31] See Hann, 'The State of the Art', p. 289.
[32] Davies, *Property*, p. 50.

specific contexts and particular sets of social and production practices and relations. As a result, there are significant limits to the ability of purely theoretical, philosophical, or jurisprudential analyses to further our understanding of them. In effect, analyses of this sort risk theoretically pre-empting what are – and can only be – historical questions. Enquiry has to be empirically, historically and contextually grounded: 'In each historical epoch, property has developed differently and under a set of entirely different social relations ... To try to give a definition of property as ... an independent relation, a category apart, an abstract and eternal idea, can be nothing but an illusion of metaphysics or jurisprudence'.[33] Abstract, general, transhistorical categories, like 'property', acquire 'substantive definition from, and only from, the particular historical contexts to which they are applied'.[34]

This suggests that what is needed is an approach to property institutions that focuses more on the real history of property and less on a search for universal definitions and transhistorical essences. As Lacey says, history 'deserves a more central place in jurisprudential thinking', a claim endorsed by Lobban.[35] Rather than leaving analysis of interests and power, and of the wider social and institutional context of property, to other disciplines, such an historical approach would seek to incorporate it into legal scholarship. By exploring the history of the struggles surrounding property and property rights, and the historical and cultural specificities of particular conceptions of property and particular property practices, such an approach to the study of property would inevitably concern itself with the forces that shape the construction and maintenance of property and property rights – and with the complex web of social relationships we summate as 'property' at any given time and place.[36]

Creating property-as-capital

Derek Sayer has given us an idea of the kinds of things this would entail.[37] Commenting on the work of the historian E P Thompson on the eighteenth century, Sayer observes that Thompson noted the ubiquity of law at this time. Rejecting not only the idea that law is superstructural but the whole

---

[33] Marx, *The Poverty of Philosophy*, Moscow: Progress (1955 [1847]), chapter 2, section 4, on 'Property or Ground Rent'.
[34] Sayer, *The Violence of Abstraction*, p. 21.
[35] Lacey, 'Jurisprudence, History, and the Institutional Quality of Law', p. 920. 'A historical sensitivity to how legal concepts have evolved', Lobban writes, 'can ... be of considerable use to the theorist': Lobban, 'Legal Theory and Legal History', p. 14.
[36] Lacey, 'Jurisprudence, History, and the Institutional Quality of Law', p. 931.
[37] Sayer, *The Violence of Abstraction*, chapter 3.

base-superstructure metaphor, Thompson argued that law 'did not keep politely to a "level"', but 'was at *every* bloody level'. It was,

> imbricated within the mode of production and production relations themselves (as property rights, definitions of agrarian practice) and it was simultaneously present in the philosophy of Locke ... it was an arm of politics and politics was one of its arms; it was an academic discipline, subjected to the rigours of its own autonomous logic; it contributed to the definition of the self-identity of both rules and ruled; above all, it afforded an arena for class struggle, within which alternative notions of law were fought out.[38]

Thompson was making a point made by many Marxists that 'relations of production' take the form of particular juridical and political relations and that these are neither secondary reflexes, nor just external supports, but constitutive of these production relations.[39] The constitutive role of law specifically was highlighted by many in the Critical Legal Studies (CLS) movement and has more recently been reasserted by 'legal institutionalists' who emphasise that law contributes to the constitution of social relations and is not, as the base-superstructure metaphor suggests, epiphenomenal; that it is 'not simply an expression of power relations, but is also a constitutive part of the institutionalized power structure, and a major means through which power is exercised'. In other words, 'law itself is power and not merely its instrument'.[40]

Reflecting on Thompson's observations, Sayer concludes that,

> we may not be able to say in any empirically meaningful way what 'property' was in the eighteenth century without talking about game laws, the 'bloody code', the Parliamentary Acts of enclosure, strict settlement and entail, magistrates regulation of hours of work and rates of pay, Combination Acts, the theatrical ritual of the assizes.[41]

He might have added to this list colonialism and slavery, internalised in the US and externalised in Europe. In his recent work, for example,

---

[38] E P Thompson, 'The Poverty of Theory', in E P Thompson, *The Poverty of Theory and Other Essays*, London: Merlin Press (1979 [1978]), p. 288; see also Thompson's comments on the rule of law: *Whigs and Hunters*, pp. 258–69.

[39] Wood, *Democracy Against Capitalism*, p. 27. See also Jairus Banaji, *Theory as History: essays on modes of production and exploitation*, Boston: Brill (2010), p. 15.

[40] Deakin et al, 'Legal Institutionalism', pp. 189, 191. See also Paddy Ireland, 'History, Critical Legal Studies and the Mysterious Disappearance of Capitalism', 65 *Modern Law Review*, pp. 120–40 (2002).

[41] Sayer, *The Violence of Abstraction*, p. 52.

Thomas Piketty has emphasised how the acquisition of family wealth and the rise of wealth inequality in Western societies is inextricably linked to colonial domination and appropriation – to what Marx referred to as primitive accumulation. Property in persons, the exploitation of slave labour, and post-slavery colonialism were all, Piketty argues, important to the formation of family wealth and modern inequality. A significant proportion of 'the large wealth portfolio of European society in the 19th century and early 20th century came from colonial wealth and colonial appropriation'.[42] Confirming this, a project conducted by researchers at UCL, *Legacies of British Slave-Ownership,* has vividly illustrated the links between slavery and the accumulation of family fortunes, and, later, rentier investment in financial property.[43] John Gladstone, the father of William Gladstone, for example, was one of the largest absentee slave owners in the British West Indies; William's elder brother, Robertson, was also a major slave owner. Indeed, William's early political career was funded in significant part by the wealth from his father's plantations and most of his early contributions to parliamentary debates were on slavery.[44] Gladstone accepted that slavery should be abolished, but was determined to ensure that slave owners like his father and brother (rather than the slaves themselves) were well compensated. If the slave owners were not properly compensated, it was argued, all property rights would be vulnerable to costless expropriation.[45] The Slave Compensation Act 1837 saw the government agree to pay compensation of £20 million to the slave owners for the loss of their property, about 40 per cent of the Treasury's annual spending budget and the equivalent of about £16 billion today.[46] The debt incurred to pay the compensation was not fully repaid

---

[42] Christine Pazzanese, 'How Political Ideas Keep Economic Inequality Going', interview with Thomas Piketty, *Harvard Gazette,* 3/3/2020.

[43] https://www.ucl.ac.uk/lbs/.

[44] John Gladstone did not visit his plantations, one of which was the centre of an insurrection in 1823 that was harshly repressed. William Gladstone admitted that he had what he described as 'a deep, though indirect, pecuniary interest' in the issue: see Roland Quinault, 'Gladstone and Slavery', 52 *Historical Journal,* pp. 363–83 (2009), pp. 365, 368.

[45] This argument was disingenuous in the sense that the property was not being expropriated in order to be passed on to someone else (like the state); it was simply going to cease to be property. Piketty says similar arguments were made during the 1843–8 debates on abolition in France. Compensation of half the market price of the slaves was eventually paid and former slaves were forced to enter long-term labour contracts as plantation workers or domestic servants; otherwise they might be arrested for vagrancy: http://piketty.pse.ens.fr/files/PikettyEconHist2020Lecture3.pdf.

[46] 1 & 2 Vict. c. 3. See Catherine Hall, 'Britain's Massive Debt to Slavery', 27/2/2013, https://www.theguardian.com/commentisfree/2013/feb/27/britain-debt-slavery-made-public; see also Sanchez Manning, 'Britain's Colonial Shame', *Independent,* 24/2/2013,

until 2015.[47] Gladstone was closely involved with his father's compensation claim and unsuccessfully opposed the publication of the compensation payments by Parliament, which showed that his father received over £100k (the equivalent of about £83 million today) for his 2,500 slaves.[48] What happened to the compensation paid to the slave owners? The UCL project has 'followed the money', tracing what the former slave owners did with their compensation. It reveals that half the money stayed in Britain and that much of it was invested in financial property, particularly in railway company shares. Thus, John Gladstone became a substantial shareholder in a string of railway companies,[49] as did Robertson.[50]

From this perspective, analyses of the property institutions of contemporary capitalism need to encompass a wide range of phenomena, not least the processes whereby different forms of property, and especially property-as-capital, are legally constituted and the ongoing processes through which they are protected and maintained. In *Wealth of Nations*, Adam Smith, in a part of the book on the expenses incurred by the sovereign, devoted one section to the costs of administering 'justice'. For Smith, this entailed, above all else, protecting property. One of the duties of the sovereign, he argued, was to 'protec[t], as far as possible, every member of society from the injustice or oppression of every other member of it'.[51] Whereas in earlier societies, those with 'superiority of fortune' maintained many men (who 'depended entirely upon [them] for their subsistence') to defend their property, 'in an opulent and civilised society, a man may possess a much greater fortune, and yet not be able to command a dozen of people'. This rendered civil government 'indispensably necessary' to those who were 'interested to support that order of things, which can alone secure them in the possession of their own advantages'. 'Civil government', he concluded, 'so far as it instituted for the security of property, is in reality instituted for the defence of the rich against the poor, or of those who have some property against those who have none

---

https://www.independent.co.uk/news/uk/home-news/britains-colonial-shame-slave-owners-given-huge-payouts-after-abolition-8508358.html.

[47] https://www.gov.uk/government/news/repayment-of-26-billion-historical-debt-to-be-completed-by-government.

[48] Manning, 'Britain's Colonial Shame'. Handwritten notes have established Gladstone's role in calculating the monetary value of his father's slaves. The UCL researchers reckon that between 10–20 per cent of Britain's wealthiest families had links to slavery. Other beneficiaries included the ancestors of George Orwell, David Cameron, Douglas and Quintin Hogg, Graham Greene and the Barings: https://www.ucl.ac.uk/lbs/project/context.

[49] https://www.ucl.ac.uk/lbs/person/view/8961.

[50] https://www.ucl.ac.uk/lbs/person/view/41819.

[51] Smith, *The Wealth of Nations*, p. 708.

at all'.[52] Elsewhere he argued that 'laws and government may be considered in this and every case as a combination of the rich to oppress the poor, and preserve to themselves the inequality of the goods which would otherwise be soon destroyed by the attacks of the poor'.[53]

In Smith's day, of course, property predominantly took the form of tangible things, whereas nowadays some of the most important property forms are intangible. Exploring the processes whereby these contemporary property forms are constituted and maintained means exploring, among other things, the processes whereby some pure bundles of rights are reified and emerge as new objects of property (new 'things'). The complexities involved in these processes is one of the focal points of Katherina Pistor's recent book, *The Code of Capital*. In order for assets to become capital, Pistor argues, they have to be legally 'coded' and given the key attributes of priority, durability, convertibility and universality.[54] She emphasises that the creation of (property-as-)capital is often done 'not in a top-down fashion by statute, nor even by constitutional law' but is 'a complex process ... pregnant with value judgments and power' in which lawyers, usually working on behalf of wealthy clients, often play a key role.[55] Pistor highlights the flexibility and malleability of legal forms and shows how, by creatively using and adapting existing legal concepts (the legal 'code'), lawyers have been able to fashion new commercial practices and new durable forms of property-as-capital, many of which have later been endorsed by legislatures and courts.

There are many examples confirming Pistor's thesis about the role of lawyers in the creation of new property forms and new commercial practices. She describes, among other things, how lawyers have long been involved in constructing devices for businesses and individuals to shield assets, shift losses and avoid liabilities.[56] She also describes how 'private lawyers have pieced together different portions of legal rules that were adopted in different eras' to create an international legal environment highly favourable to investors and capital.[57] Many other examples can be found. Thus, lawyers were instrumental in the constitution of the joint stock company share as an object of property in its own right, separate from the assets of the company and, indeed, in the making of English company law more

---

[52] Smith, *The Wealth of Nations*, volume 2, pp. 711–15.
[53] Smith, *The Wealth of Nations*, volume 2, p. 715. See also Adam Smith, *Lectures on Jurisprudence*, Oxford: Oxford University Press, (1978 [1762–3]); Douglas Irwin, 'Adam Smith's "tolerable administration of justice" and the Wealth of Nations', 67 *Scottish Journal of Political Economy* (2020), pp. 231–47.
[54] Pistor, *The Code of Capital*, p. 13.
[55] Pistor, *The Code of Capital*, p. 28.
[56] Pistor, *The Code of Capital*, pp. 56–64.
[57] Pistor, *The Code of Capital*, p. 154.

generally.[58] In the eighteenth and early nineteenth centuries, when the privileges of corporate status, limited liability and share transferability were not readily available from the state, lawyers made considerable efforts to secure their benefits for clients using the private law instruments of contract, trust and property.[59] Not only did they have some success, some of the techniques they pioneered influenced the legal framework established by the Companies Acts of 1844–62. Later, they played a similarly important role in eliminating the residual liabilities attached to shares, paving the way for the rise of liability- and responsibility-free corporate shareholding.[60] They also successfully fought for companies to be able to own shares in other companies and to be treated as completely separate entities from their shareholders, even when shareholders and the company were more or less synonymous, as with one-man and small private (closely-held) companies and with wholly-owned or near wholly-owned subsidiaries.[61] In doing this, they paved the way for the rise of the modern multi-national enterprise composed of multiple corporations and the avoidance and evasion of liabilities and taxes by both these enterprises and high net-worth individuals. This, in turn, facilitated regulation-dodging and the corporate exploitation of competition between jurisdictions. 'Capital coded in portable law', writes Pistor, 'is footloose; gains can be made and pocketed anywhere and the losses can be left wherever they fall'.[62]

Prioritising the investor interest

Moreover, just as it is not possible to say in any meaningful way what property was in the eighteenth century without talking about things such as the game laws, the 'bloody code' and enclosure, it is not possible to say in any meaningful way what property is in contemporary capitalism without exploring the highly varied and complex mechanisms that have been developed to protect it. Protecting property-as-capital, in particular, is unusually challenging. As we have seen, much of it is intangible in nature, its value deriving not directly from the specific qualities of physical objects but from expectations about its ability to yield future revenues.[63] Protecting

---

[58] See Paddy Ireland, 'Property and Contract in Contemporary Corporate Theory', 23 *Legal Studies*, pp. 453–509 (2003); Ireland, 'Capitalism Without the Capitalist'.
[59] See Harris, *Industrializing English Law*, chapters 6 and 9.
[60] See Ireland, 'Limited Liability'.
[61] See Paddy Ireland, 'The Rise of the Limited Liability Company', 12 *International Journal of the Sociology of Law*, pp. 239–60 (1984).
[62] Pistor, *The Code of Capital*, p. 9.
[63] See Levy, 'Capital as Process', p. 494. Levy argues that capital is 'always in process' (p. 494) and observes that 'capital valuation is always prospective and always occurring under conditions of uncertainty' (p. 487). He points out that the term 'process' appears throughout Marx's writings: p. 494.

it, therefore, involves not only preventing physical appropriations of tangible objects (such as those owned by corporations), but taking steps to ensure that the income streams that give intangible property its value continue to flow into the future.

Thus, protecting intellectual property entails preventing the unlicenced use of non-rival goods not depleted by use: ideas, discoveries, inventions, cultural artefacts and so on. Only if the monopoly rights of the IP owner are secured can they levy fees. Moreover, in today's highly globalised capitalism, this has to be accomplished on a global scale. There needs 'to be a respect for [these property forms] that trumps national law'.[64] As a result, protecting IPRs requires both considerable nation-state and co-ordinated international action. Protecting financial property is similarly challenging, involving taking steps to ensure that the revenue streams that give it value are safeguarded. As Jonathan Levy says, because revenue rights of this sort are 'always prospective', they are 'always occurring under conditions of uncertainty'.[65] They represent claims over the *future* efforts of others, over *future* labour, over wealth that has yet to be produced. In an increasingly globalised capitalism, the revenue streams and the people involved in their generation are (*Howey*'s 'others') often located in distant lands. In the case of corporate shares, the uncertainties are further amplified by the fact that the rate of return is not fixed in advance but varies with profitability. Even if the value of the tangible assets owned by companies remains relatively stable, their share value often fluctuates alarmingly as perceptions of their future earning power change. Indeed, because it is always based on expectations (or speculations) about future returns, the value of financial property is inherently vulnerable to manipulation, fraud and speculation. If you can persuade people that the future returns accruing to a particular piece of financial property are going to be very good, you can push up its market value. Protecting the integrity of financial property, therefore, requires a wide range of legal and other interventions to try to eliminate fraud, deceit, swindling and manipulation to ensure that its market value reflects with reasonable accuracy its future income-generating potential. This is reflected, among other things, in the many and varied sources of the rules protecting investors found in company, security, bankruptcy, takeover and competition laws, as well as in stock exchange regulations and accounting standards.

Property protection provides a useful prism through which to view neoliberalism, for one of the defining characteristics of neoliberal policy making has been the prioritisation of the interests of capital and investors. This has been manifested not only in the drive to create new opportunities

---

[64] Quinn Slobodian, *The Globalists*, Cambridge: Harvard University Press (2018), p. 29.
[65] Levy, 'Capital as Process', p. 487.

for profitable capital investment ('privatisation' in its various forms) but in the prioritisation of protecting the revenue rights of investors over protecting of the interests and welfare of ordinary citizens and the environment.[66] Thus, the financial crash saw governments around the world bail out financial institutions. In the US, banks were saved by taxpayers via the Emergency Economic Stabilization Act of 2008 and the $700 billion Troubled Asset Relief Program (TARP). By contrast, little was done to stop mortgage foreclosures and 'the large scale transformation of what were formerly private homes into rental units, a process that yielded a fortune to a collection of billionaire vulture investors'.[67] In the UK, a £500 billion bank rescue package, composed of loans and lending guarantees from the taxpayer and taxpayer investment in banks, was arranged to try to restore the financial system and investor confidence. While these bail outs were depicted in terms of 'protecting the economy' and keeping markets functioning for the benefit of us all, they were directed above all else at protecting financial property and its owners. While many of the investment bankers primarily responsible for the crash walked away with millions, for the majority the bailouts meant 'austerity' and cuts in public spending on health, education and social welfare. As many have pointed out, the profits from pre-crash financialisation were privately appropriated but the losses it caused were socialised and transferred to the public. 'The response to the crisis in Europe', concludes David Grewal Singh, 'suggested that Brussels now operates as an arm of finance capital and that monetary union is more likely to prove the undertaker of European social democracy than its savior'.[68] Since then, policy has continued to focus more on cutting public expenditures than on creating a more resilient tax system and enhancing revenues by clamping down on avoidance and evasion, let alone on more radical economic reform.

Similarly, COVID-19 saw a giant multi-trillion-dollar bailout of US non-financial corporations paid for by the taxpayer. The pandemic saw the corporate debt market freeze, putting many corporations at serious risk of bankruptcy and leaving owners of corporate debt facing potentially huge losses.[69] To refloat the bond market, the Federal Reserve acquired large quantities of corporate debt regardless of its rating, in effect bailing out financial property owners by socialising credit risk. As Robert Brenner says,

---

[66] This is one of the themes of Streeck's *Buying Time*.
[67] See Brenner, 'Escalating Plunder'.
[68] David Singh Grewal, 'The Laws of Capitalism', Book Review of Thomas Piketty, *Capital in the Twenty First Century*, 128 *Harvard Law Review*, pp. 626–67 (2014).
[69] As a result of being unable to service their current debts because of the income losses caused by COVID-19, and unable to refinance except at cripplingly high interest rates. Much has been written about so-called 'zombie corporations', companies that are earning just enough to service their debts but not enough to pay those debts off.

the Fed's revival of the bond market 'bailed out lenders and protected their assets'. As the market recovered, 'investors avoided huge losses'.[70] The sums allocated for direct cash payments to individuals and families were much more modest. It is hardly surprising, therefore, that both the crash and COVID-19 saw dramatic upward redistributions of wealth. During COVID-19, as output, employment and investment slumped around the world, after an initial dip the stock and bond markets of the major economies hit all-time highs as vast amounts of credit money were injected into economies.[71]

The new aristocracy of finance

The prioritisation of the interests of capital and investors finds expression in much more than just bailouts, however. Protecting financial property entails taking steps to ensure not only that expectations about future revenue streams are not manipulated but that the social relations and practices conducive to the generation of those income streams are maintained. It is this that leads Levy to adapt one of Marx's well-known aphorisms to argue that 'it is not so much the past but the future which weighs on the brains of the living'.[72] The future-dependent nature of financial property renders it vulnerable to anything that might impede the ability of its holders to profit from the future efforts of others, to anything that might disrupt the flow and size of the pecuniary returns that give it value. It is vulnerable to anything that threatens future profitability, future debt servicing and the future distribution of the fruits of production between capital and labour. It is, therefore, vulnerable to everything from changes in the general economic outlook and business climate to changes in policy that raise labour and/or environmental standards or otherwise alter the relative bargaining strength of capital and labour. Property-as-capital is thus vulnerable not only to outright expropriations of physical assets but to changes in government policy that impact on the income streams accruing to intangible property,

---

[70] Brenner, 'Escalating Plunder'. Brenner suggests that the long-term stagnation of the US economy has seen the American ruling class abandon productive investment and turn instead to the upward redistribution of wealth by predatory, political means. This suggests that it is not only the legal coding that 'protects the asset holder from the headwinds of ordinary business cycles and gives his wealth longevity' (Pistor, *The Code of Capital*, p. 6), but the willingness of the state to act to protect asset values. It also casts doubt on Pistor's claim that 'asset holders do not need to capture the state directly, much less win class struggles or revolutions; all they need is the right lawyers on their side who code their assets in law': Pistor, *The Code of Capital*, p. 22.

[71] See Michael Roberts, 'Covid and Fictitious Capital' (January 2021), https://thenextrecession.wordpress.com/2021/01/25/covid-and-fictitious-capital/.

[72] Levy, 'Capital as Process', p. 500.

particularly intangible financial property. This is a particular problem in an era of widespread universal suffrage.

Historically, the private property status quo, particularly in relation to productive resources, has been protected from democracy in three main ways: firstly, by restricting the franchise by attaching minimum property qualifications to the right to vote[73]; secondly, by stopping democracy at the factory gates and keeping it out of the productive sphere; and, thirdly, by providing private property rights with constitutional protections that constrain the state. Although attempts continue to be made to manipulate the franchise, outrightly denying it to adult citizens is now widely seen as illegitimate.[74] Universal suffrage has been normalised and citizenship rights are rarely formally dependent on private property ownership. As a result, protecting the property status quo from democracy has come to rely more on shaping public opinion and narrowing the 'Overton window', the range of policies seen as acceptable or 'sensible', and on developing new legal mechanisms for constraining states. On the other hand, attempts to democratise economic/productive activity have generally been successfully resisted and placing constitutional limitations on state action in relation to property and property rights has long been seen as perfectly legitimate. One of the main goals of the men who drafted the US Federal Constitution, for example, was to protect property, including intangible financial property, from the *demos* and to maintain the domination of master over slave, capitalist over worker, and colonialist over native.[75] Recently, however, with ownership of property-as-capital becoming an increasingly global, transnational affair, concerted efforts have been made to further constrain states by simultaneously subjecting them to greater market pressures and new legal obligations.[76]

---

[73] Women were not explicitly prohibited from voting before 1832. Before this 'the disenfranchisement of women had been by custom rather than by statute … and it is impossible to conclude that women never voted' before this: Neil Johnston, *The History of the Parliamentary Franchise* (2013, Research Paper 13/14), p. 7. The Great Reform Act of 1832 explicitly excluded women from voting by defining voters as 'male persons'. When the franchise was finally extended to women in 1918, the vote was granted to women over 30 who were householders, the wives of householders, occupiers of property with an annual rent of £5, and graduates of British universities.

[74] It now tends to be manifested in attempts to make it harder for (certain) people to actually exercise their right to vote as in some US states and in the UK (voters now have to show photo ID to vote in some elections). Margaret Thatcher's attempt to develop a surrogate (the community charge or 'poll tax') proved politically unpalatable.

[75] See Jennifer Nedelsky, *Private Property and the Limits of American Constitutionalism*, Chicago: University of Chicago Press, 1990; Di Muzio, 'Towards a Genealogy', p. 82.

[76] 'Following in the footsteps of the legal scholar Samuel Moyn, one might remark that it was not by accident that the advent of radical capital mobility coincided with the advent of universal human rights. Both curtailed the sovereignty of nation states': Adam Tooze,

Considerable effort has been made by neoliberals to facilitate the free movement of goods, services, capital and persons across borders. In such a world, they believe, global market forces will operate to put pressure on and to discipline labour, states and democracy. If they are subjected to more intense market pressures, states will be compelled to maintain 'good climates for investment' in which capital can secure acceptable pecuniary returns. In this context, as many have noted, the dismantling of the Bretton Woods system and restoration of capital mobility in the 1980s were key moments, prefacing the emergence of a much more liberal international financial regime. It became increasingly easy for wealthy individuals and corporations freely to move their money around the world and to choose where to locate production, wealth and profits. Tax avoidance and evasion have since become global phenomena. This has driven investment-hungry states into a competitive race to attract capital. These changes have not only significantly strengthened the bargaining position of capital vis-à-vis labour, with major distributional consequences, it has weakened the fiscal foundations of states, narrowing their perceived policy options and diminishing the democratic threat to property-as-capital. As Wolfgang Streeck says, these changes have seen 'tax states' become 'debt states', with the result that governments in contemporary capitalism now have to satisfy two 'electorates': on the one hand, the *Staatsvolk*, the 'general citizenry' with the right to vote in elections; on the other, the *Marktvolk*, the 'people of the market', the owners of financial property and their institutional representatives who cast their votes in financial markets.[77] With states increasingly financially dependent on the latter, 'finance capital' has emerged as a second electorate – 'a second people, a *Marktvolk* rivalling the *Staatsvolk*' – which states have to satisfy for their own survival. Drawing an explicit parallel with corporate governance, Streeck suggests that creditors have risen 'to become a second constituency of the modern state' in a way that is 'strikingly reminiscent of the emergence of activist shareholders in the corporate world under the "shareholder value" doctrine of the 1980s and 1990s'.[78] As Streeck's notion of two electorates suggests, the power of this new financial oligarchy goes well beyond its ability to shape the distribution of wealth. It wields enormous political as well as

---

'Neoliberalism's World Order', Review of Quinn Slobodian's *The Globalists*, *Dissent Magazine* (Summer 2018).

[77] Streeck, *Buying Time*, pp. 79–90. Streeck's residual commitment to European social democracy, which he believes has been undermined by globalisation, has led him to advocate trying to maintain national borders against immigrants as a last line of defence for the welfare state. Streeck's *Marktvolk–Staatsvolk* schema has met with severe disapproval from Adam Tooze: see Tooze's 'Review of Streeck's *Buying Time*' in *London Review of Books*, 5/1/2017 and the subsequent exchange of letters.

[78] Streeck, *Buying Time*, pp. 79, 84.

economic power, exerting huge influence over the media, much of which it owns, and, through that, over the way we think about and understand the world. What we have seen in recent decades is the emergence of a 'new aristocracy of finance' – a power bloc comprising those at the top of the wealth and income hierarchy in whom financial property ownership is concentrated. They are supported by their institutional representatives, by the executive class and by what Jeffrey Winters has called the 'agents of wealth defence', a reference to the army of well-paid skilled professionals (lawyers, accountants, bankers and the like) employed by the wealthy to protect their property and incomes.[79] One might add to this list the politicians and political parties who make the rules and who increasingly benefit from, and depend upon, donations from large corporations and high-net-worth individuals. Quinn Slobodian has described this process in terms of the triumph of the world of *dominium* (property) over the world of *imperium* (government).[80]

Containing democracy: the 'new constitutionalism'

The *Marktvolk*, however, want not only to be able to move their capital freely across borders but to be able to do so without fear of expropriation.[81] Moreover, from their perspective, it is not enough simply to prevent the expropriation by states of tangible productive resources through nationalisations. It is also necessary to deter, and if possible prevent, policy changes – to tax regimes, labour standards, environmental protection regulations and the like – that might negatively impact on the pecuniary returns accruing to and value of their capital, tangible and intangible. It is in response to these needs that there has emerged in recent decades what the political scientist Stephen Gill has called a 'new constitutionalism'.[82]

For Gill, this 'new constitutionalism', far from marking the triumph of liberal democracy as the epithet might suggest, is the political and legal dimension of the class-based project of 'disciplinary neo-liberalism', a project aimed at extending and intensifying market disciplines and at constraining democracy in the interests of capital.[83] Lawyers who have adopted the concept argue that the new constitutionalism seeks to provide international

---

[79] See Folkman et al, 'Working for themselves'; Winters, 'Wealth Defense'.
[80] Slobodian, *The Globalists*, p. 10.
[81] Slobodian, *The Globalists*, p. 29.
[82] See Stephen Gill, 'Globalisation, Market Civilisation and Disciplinary Neoliberalism', 23 *Millennium: Journal of International Studies*, pp. 399–423 (1995).
[83] See Stephen Gill and A Claire Cutler, 'General Introduction' to Gill and Cutler (eds), *New Constitutionalism and World Order*, Cambridge: Cambridge University Press, pp. 1–19 (2014), p. 6; see also Gill, 'New Constitutionalism, Democratisation and Global Political Economy', 10 *Pacifica Review*, pp. 23–38 (1998).

property owners with legal protections against policy changes that might lower financial returns and asset values by immunising them, as far as possible, from the kind of changes in state policy that democracy might bring.[84] By 'imposing, internally and externally, binding constraints on the conduct of fiscal, monetary, trade and investment policies', the new constitutionalism seeks to neutralise democracy by insulating key aspects of economic life from majoritarian politics. In limiting what states can legally do and narrowing the range of political possibility, it seeks to 'provide political anchorage for capital in the long term'.[85]

For lawyers, the rise of this new constitutionalism is exemplified by the emergence of what has come to be called 'international investment law' and investor-state-dispute-settlement (ISDS) treaties aimed at protecting foreign investments. The origins of international investment law, argues Kate Miles, date back to the imperial and colonial eras and the 'oppressive protection of commercial interests'.[86] It was, however, only after decolonisation and the end of direct rule that ISDS treaties, international investment law's main contemporary vehicle, began to proliferate. ISDS treaties were, Gus van Harten argues, 'invented in the 1960s as a substitute for colonial rule' by officials of the former colonial powers and the World Bank.[87] From the 1990s these treaties began to grow rapidly in number and the international investment law regime began to 'secure foreign investments in [the] legally sophisticated ways we associate with the new constitutionalism'.[88] The regime that has emerged is a complex transnational legal framework for the liberalisation of foreign investment and protection of foreign investors. It has been actively promoted and developed by the leading OECD countries on the grounds that the more a country offers protection to foreign investors and improves its 'investment climate', the more it will benefit from the investments that generate growth, a claim the supporting evidence for

---

[84] David Schneiderman, 'Constitutional Approaches to Privatization: an inquiry into the magnitude of neo-liberal constitutionalism', 63 *Law and Contemporary Problems,* pp. 83–109 (2000), p. 106.

[85] Gill, 'Globalisation, Market Civilisation and Disciplinary Neoliberalism', p. 413.

[86] Kate Miles, *The Origins of International Investment Law,* Cambridge: Cambridge University Press (2013), p. 2. A periodisation of the stages in the emergence of contemporary investment law can be found in Muthucumaraswamy Sornarajah, *Resistance and Change in the International Law on Foreign Investment,* Cambridge: Cambridge University Press (2015).

[87] Gus Van Harten, *The Trouble with Foreign Investor Protection,* Oxford: Oxford University Press (2020), p. 2.

[88] David Schneiderman, 'How to Govern Differently: neo-liberalism, new constitutionalism and international investment law', in Stephen Gill and A Claire Cutler (eds), *New Constitutionalism and World Order,* Cambridge: Cambridge University Press, pp. 165–78 (2014), p. 172.

which some question.[89] Composed of a network of legal and quasi-legal agreements, institutionalised standards, as well as domestic constitutional changes of the traditional sort, the regime's central pillars are over 2,000 bilateral investment treaties (BITs), the investment chapters of 'free trade' deals like NAFTA (the North American Free Trade Agreement); and, at the multilateral level, things such as the agreement on Trade-Related Investment Measures (TRIMs) and legal instruments like the agreement on Trade-Related Aspects of Intellectual Property Rights (TRIPs), and other multilateral agreements that authorise ISDS.[90]

The regime discourages a wide range of state activity by enabling investors to claim damages for policies that, even if supported by the local population, adversely impact on the value of their investments. Thus, measures equivalent to expropriation (in whole or in part), measures that favour local nationals over foreigners, and measures that deny investors 'fair and equitable treatment' can all provide grounds for investors to seek damage awards of hundreds of millions of dollars from states. The expanded concept of 'expropriation' is, perhaps, the regime's most noteworthy feature, for it gives investors rights against states not only in cases involving outright takings of tangible property but in cases where states have implemented policies that have (or might have) the effect of reducing the income-generating potential (and therefore the value) of their capital. These are deemed to be 'creeping' or 'regulatory' expropriations.[91]

Moreover, very strong enforcement mechanisms have been constructed to support foreign investors seeking to bring these claims. They are entitled to enforce treaty terms in investment arbitration tribunals that are outside local judicial institutions. Increasingly, therefore, adjudicatory power has been transferred from states to international experts and arbitrators. In this process, states have, in effect, conferred on international organisations powers that, when exercised by states themselves, are usually referred to as 'sovereign powers'.[92] Neoliberals have, in Slobodian's words, sought 'a complete protection of private capital rights', in which supranational judicial

---

[89] See Van Harten, *The Trouble with Foreign Investor Protection*, p. 3.
[90] See David Schneiderman, *Constitutionalizing Economic Globalization*, Cambridge: Cambridge University Press (2008).
[91] See David Schneiderman, 'Investment Rules and the Rule of Law', 8 *Constellations*, pp. 521–37 (2001); David Schneiderman, 'Investment Rules and the New Constitutionalism', 25 *Law & Social Inquiry*, pp. 757–87 (2000). Many of the rules centre on the idea of 'non-discrimination' and the principle that states should not distinguish, for regulatory purposes, between foreign and domestic investors. The principle of non-discrimination rules out such things as rules calling for the use of local goods, labour or services.
[92] See Dan Sarooshi, *International Organizations and their Exercise of Sovereign Powers*, Oxford: Oxford University Press (2005).

bodies like the European Court of Justice and the World Trade Organisation are able to 'override national legislation that might disrupt the legal rights of capital'. It is for this reason that he describes the emergence and rise of institutions like the International Monetary Fund, the World Bank, the European Central Bank, the European Union, and the World Trade Organisation as 'the crowning victory of the neoliberal project'.[93]

The arbitrators adjudicating investor–state disputes have generally adopted investor-friendly interpretations of the treaties that take an expansive view of state obligations and investor entitlements, encouraging the use of ISDS, particularly by large multi-nationals, as a weapon and potential source of compensation. The result has been 'regulatory chill'. States, dependent on the resources ultimately controlled by the very wealthy, are constrained not only by fear of capital flight but by fear of litigation arising out regulatory activities aimed at protecting the environment and public health and welfare that might reduce the value of investments.[94] The international investment regime thus places significant limits on states and their democratic ability to implement policies aimed at the welfare of their citizens.[95] Rule regimes that protect foreign investments are established and then frozen and in some cases rolled back if they do not conform with investor needs: once investors have entered, if states impose further or new conditions that threaten future revenue streams and undermine the value of their property, they risk legal action. The aim, Schneiderman argues, is 'to bind states far into the future, whatever political combinations develop at home to counteract it, by imposing punishing monetary disciplines that make resistance difficult to sustain, if not futile'.[96] Countries have become increasingly locked into a rule of investment law that 'renders foreign investors immune from legislative and administrative action that reduces the returns to, and value of, foreign investments'.[97]

The result, as van Harten says, is that ISDS treaties 'give extraordinary powers and protections to owners of international wealth, mostly huge corporations and ultra-wealthy individuals at the expense of countries and their populations'. Indeed, he argues, they were designed from the outset to

---

[93] Slobodian, *The Globalists*, pp. 12–13, 23.

[94] Examples include the use by tobacco companies like Philip Morris and R J Reynolds of the investment chapter of NAFTA to deter governments from legislating plain packaging of cigarettes on the grounds that it is tantamount to an expropriation of their trademarks and goodwill: see Schneiderman, 'How to Govern Differently', p. 173; Van Harten, *The Trouble with Foreign Investor Protection*, pp. 115–20. See also cases such as *Metalclad Corp. v United Mexican States* (Award 30 August 2000), 40 ILM 36.

[95] See Schneiderman, *Constitutionalizing Economic Globalization*, pp. 1–8, 25–44.

[96] Schneiderman, *Constitutionalizing Economic Globalization*, p. 6.

[97] Schneiderman, 'Rule of Law', p. 522.

do precisely this. ISDS is such 'an extraordinary tool for safeguarding wealth' that 'it is justifiable to call [it] a Bill of Rights for the global rich'.[98] The regime perpetuates and exacerbates global inequality by, in effect, facilitating wealth transfers to the wealthy by helping them, in their guise as foreign investors, to profit from the efforts of others in far-off lands with as little risk as possible, even in the absence of direct colonial rule. Both democracy and the needs of local populations are subordinated to the interests of large corporations and wealthy individuals.

It is the way the treaties create political and legal mechanisms that are difficult to change and mimic certain functions performed by the national constitutional systems found in capital-exporting states that led to the regime being dubbed a 'new constitutionalism'. It amounts, some argue, to an attempt to create an economic constitution for the world, a global system of economic governance that operates to a considerable extent beyond the reach of nation states and democracy.[99] Providing constitutional or quasi-constitutional protection to the financial property and revenue rights of investors – what Slobodian calls, drawing on Hayek, 'xenos rights', the rights of the alien or stranger – was one of the main goals of early neoliberals like Hayek and von Mises.[100] Although the term 'new constitutionalism' has caught on in academic circles, some, like Gus Van Harten, one of the international investment law regime's fiercest and most outspoken critics, disapprove of the invocation of constitutionalism to describe the regime, arguing that it risks 'elevating investment treaties beyond their actual significance'. He points out that states can renegotiate or abrogate the treaties, 'so why tell people that their governments are bound constitutionally when, in fact, they are not?' For him, the regime is 'simply neo-liberal', and demonstrates that 'the neo-liberal project draws on, or seeks to co-opt, constitutionalist traditions'.[101] This resonates with those who argue that neoliberalism should be seen not so much as an economic project but as a project of politics, statecraft and law. For them, neoliberalism is about trying to find 'a legal and institutional fix' for the potentially disruptive effects of democracy on property rights and market disciplines.[102] From this perspective, growing inequality is, in many ways, a measure of the project's success – a reflection of the ability of very wealthy property owners, and especially financial property owners, to secure an ever-larger proportion

---

[98] Van Harten, *The Trouble with Foreign Investor Protection*, pp. 1–4.
[99] Slobodian, *The Globalists*, p. 54, though it still relies to a considerable extent on those nation states for enforcement.
[100] Slobodian, *The Globalists*, p. 123.
[101] Gus Van Harten, 'Investment Rules and the Denial of Change', 60 *University of Toronto Law Journal*, pp. 893–904 (2010), pp. 901–2.
[102] Slobodian, *The Globalists*, pp. 11, 92.

of the social product. The success of neoliberal ideas derives not so much from their intellectual force or truth but from the growing economic and political power of the very wealthy, with their ability to fund think-tanks and research institutes, to influence and control the media and politicians, and to shape understandings of the world.

Indeed, recently, there have also been suggestions that financial property owners might seek quasi-constitutional protection for other forms of financial property. In December 2011, the *Financial Times* reported that a Madrid-based hedge fund, Vega Asset Management, was threatening to take legal action against officials negotiating Greece's debt restructuring if the losses they suffered on their bonds became too great.[103] What had originally been considered 'a ludicrous possibility' was becoming 'all too real'.[104] The following month, the *New York Times* reported that hedge funds were considering bringing an action in the European Court of Human Rights against Greece, whose government was considering passing legislation to force all private bondholders to take losses, while exempting the European Central Bank, for violation of bondholder rights. Their argument was that it amounted to a violation of their property rights and, as such, of their human rights.[105]

This constitutionalisation of rights is seen by some as a positive development — as power-diffusing, as spreading liberal, egalitarian values and the 'rule of law'. Certainly, there is no doubt that the trend towards constitutionalisation has empowered the judiciary. The world, Ran Hirschl has suggested, has 'been seized by a craze for constitutionalization and judicial review', a development that has been welcomed by some academics and activists. Judicial institutions have been transformed into important political actors at both the national level and supranational level (the European Court of Justice, the European Court of Human Rights and so on). There are, however, very good reasons for doubting whether the trend towards constitutionalism, and the rise of what Hirschl calls 'juristocracy', is really driven by a genuine commitment to democracy, social justice or universal rights. As Hirschl says, it is more likely part of a 'broader process whereby political and economic elites, while ... profess[ing] support for democracy, attempt to insulate policy making from the vicissitudes of democratic politics'.[106]

---

[103] *Financial Times*, 'Funds threaten to sue over Greek bond losses', 21/12/2011.

[104] Tyler Durden, 'Greek "voluntary" restructuring on verge of collapse as hedge fund Vega threatens to sue Greece for excessive haircut', *Zero Hedge*, 21/12/2011.

[105] Kandon Thomas Jr, 'Hedge funds may sue Greece if it tries to force losses', *New York Times*, 18/1/2012.

[106] Ran Hirschl, 'The Political Origins of the New Constitutionalism', 11 *Indiana Journal of Global Legal Studies*, pp. 71–108 (2004), pp. 71–3, 105; see also Ran Hirschl, *Towards*

Derisking new property

The rise of international investment law and the new constitutionalism is one aspect of a wider phenomenon that increasingly characterises property protection in contemporary capitalism: that of 'derisking'. 'Derisking' refers to the processes whereby the state facilitates private investment and the creation of new property-as-capital, new 'asset classes' in the language of finance (usually in the form of revenue rights), by reducing the risks attached to them, in particular the risk that the financial returns investors expect to receive might not materialise. To alleviate this risk and to smooth the way for private investment, states take steps to try to ensure, and in some cases guarantee, that revenue streams acceptable to investors will be forthcoming.

The financial economist, Daniela Gabor, has led the way in the analysis of the phenomenon of derisking. She points out that there have been two main drivers for its rise. Firstly, the search for new outlets for profitable investment by global institutional investors and asset managers faced with a savings (or portfolio) glut emanating primarily from the money of the wealthy in the Global North. [107] And, secondly, the growing difficulty states face, in an era of low-tax ideologies and tax avoidance/evasion by large corporations and high net-worth individuals, raising sufficient revenue to fund public services (health, education, welfare, pensions) and infrastructural upgrades and innovations (transport, the green transition) in the traditional manner through public funding. This is a particular problem for states in the less wealthy Global South. With strong encouragement from private finance, national development agencies and international agencies like the International Monetary Fund and the World Bank, governments have been pressed to draw the conclusion, in the words of the OECD, that 'public resources alone cannot deliver the required investments in climate, health, education, infrastructure and ... housing' and that private finance has to be mobilised.[108]

The problem is that 'the market' by itself is often unable to deliver the private investments required because they are considered too risky. It is only by 'derisking' them so they provide more or less guaranteed revenue flows to investors that they can be made 'investible'. In order to mobilise private finance in these spheres, therefore, the state has to provide safety nets for investors that minimise the threats to their financial returns. It is in this

---

Juristocracy: the origins and consequences of the new constitutionalism, Boston: Harvard University Press (2004).
[107] See Daniela Gabor, 'The Wall Street Consensus', 52 *Development and Change*, pp. 429–59 (2021).
[108] OECD, *Blended Finance Guidance*, 29/9/2020, https://www.oecd.org/dac/financing-sustainable-development/blended-finance-principles/.

context that there has in recent years been an explosion of derisking and of public–private partnerships (PPPs) and 'blended finance'. PPPs are long-term contractual arrangements in which the private sector finances, constructs and/or manages public services in return for state subsidies and guarantees. They entail a shifting of risk from the private to the public sector. PPPs create new property, often in the form of rights to future revenues linked to new asset classes, though, as Gabor points out, using Pistor's terminology, it is not easy to 'code' them into capital and to produce derisked securities that meet the risk–reward demands of institutional investors, hence the complexity of PPP contracts.[109] Suitably derisked, however, private investment in services and infrastructure that have traditionally been part of the public sector is attractive to investors, for commodified public services generate regular income streams in the form of user-fees. There is, of course, a potential loss of fee income if the poor cannot afford to pay, but this can be mitigated by welfare payments or some form of universal basic income. Indeed, PPP investments are potentially less risky than purely private sector investments in which the pecuniary returns are entirely dependent on genuine profitability.

Gabor distinguishes two basic types of derisking: regulatory and financial. Regulatory derisking involves removing the impediments to such things as free capital movement and PPPs, and minimising the political risks to profits from nationalisation, higher minimum wages, tighter environmental regulation and so on. This is, of course, one of the defining features of the new constitutionalism. Financial derisking, on the other hand, involves such things as subsidies, tax relief and guarantees about future income streams.[110] At the macro level, it involves 'redirect[ing] fiscal resources or monetary policy interventions to align the risk/return profile of new asset classes with investor preferences'.[111] One of the main risks associated with privatised infrastructure assets, for example, is that the demand from users (and therefore fee revenues) might fall below expectations and threaten the income streams flowing to shares and bonds. An important aspect of derisking is, therefore, 'demand derisking' in which the state guarantees to cover any gaps between the fees paid by essential service users and the fees required to deliver satisfactory returns to private investors. Thus, in sectors like transport, one commonly finds minimum revenue guarantees in which the government bears some (often most) of the downside risks of a PPP project by guaranteeing a minimum level of profitability whenever usage and revenues fall below a certain level, including demand falls caused by extreme

---

[109] Gabor, 'The Wall Street Consensus', p. 439.
[110] Gabor, 'The Wall Street Consensus', pp. 433–4.
[111] Gabor and Kohl, *My Home Is an Asset Class*, p. 13.

climate events.¹¹² Currency derisking that ensures that the profits of private PPP operators can be converted into dollars or euros and repatriated at the agreed exchange rate is also 'ubiquitous in contracts'.¹¹³

Although derisking PPP investments involves the transfer of risk from investors/property owners to taxpayers, it is still attractive to states because the derisking commitments do not count as public debt, appearing off balance-sheet in the form of contingent liabilities. There are significant drawbacks to PPPs, however. They are, in most cases, a significantly more expensive way of financing service and infrastructure provision and the fiscal costs of things such as demand derisking can be considerable: PPPs can easily turn into 'budgetary timebombs'.¹¹⁴ This has been the case with a number of PPP projects to finance infrastructural investment in Africa.¹¹⁵ Indirectly, PPPs also often reduce the public resources available for developmental state investments.

The derisking of new investments by the state is not new. The earlier practices of encouraging the growth of domestic industry through protectionism and industrial policy were, in many ways, early forms of derisking. More recently, it has been a feature of the privatisation of previously publicly owned industries. Rail privatisation in the UK is a good example of this. Whereas in privatised industries, such as water, it is usually possible to generate profits by simply appropriately charging customers,¹¹⁶ the fee income generated by politically sensitive rail fares is often insufficient to guarantee the returns required by investors. Substantial public subsidies are needed to make railway companies profitable and attractive to investors seeking good, reliable returns. In the UK's byzantine privatised railway system, for example, the train operating companies (TOCs) have been in receipt of two forms of direct subsidy – franchise subsidy payments and revenue support. The former are, in effect, grants to ensure the TOCs get commercial returns; the latter are paid by the state when TOC revenue dips

---

¹¹² See, for example, Omid Rouhani et al, 'Revenue-Risk-Sharing Approaches for PPP Provision of Highway Facilities', 6(4) *Case Studies on Transport Policy*, pp. 439–48 (2018); see also Gabor, 'The Wall Street Consensus', pp. 439–43.

¹¹³ Gabor, 'The Wall Street Consensus', p. 448; Ndongo Samba Sylla and Daniela Gabor, 'Planting Budgetary Time-Bombs in Africa', *Groupe d'études géopolitiques*, 23/12/2020, https://geopolitique.eu/en/2020/12/23/planting-budgetary-time-bombs-in-africa-the-macron-doctrine-en-marche/.

¹¹⁴ Gabor, 'The Wall Street Consensus', p. 442.

¹¹⁵ Sylla and Gabor, 'Planting Budgetary Time-Bombs in Africa', 884; Gabor, 'The Wall Street Consensus', pp. 441–3.

¹¹⁶ This is not to say that water companies are not a burden on the public purse. When they were privatised all their debts were written off, but they are now over £60 billion in debt. Much money has been paid out in dividends rather than invested in infrastructure. One result of this, of course, has been rising sewage discharges.

below a certain level. TOCs are also in receipt of indirect public subsidies, for Network Rail, the quasi-public company that runs the rail infrastructure, itself receives very large public subsidies that enable it to charge the TOCs artificially low track access charges. Although they are only profitable because of the direct and indirect subsidies they receive, there are no rules preventing TOCs from distributing those profits to shareholders, which they have on a grand scale.[117] Despite the subsidies, however, some TOC owners, like Virgin, have walked away from their franchises. This is because the premiums paid by the TOCs are backloaded. This has encouraged them to game the system, taking early rewards before abandoning the franchises to avoid later risks. The financial penalties for doing this are modest.[118] Recently, in the wake of COVID-19, emergency agreements were reached that have become the basis of new National Rail contracts under which the companies 'bea[r] no revenue risk and very little cost risk ... and no significant contingent capital risk' under the annual budgets agreed with the state.[119] In the UK's privatised rail system, therefore, what we effectively have are politically-constructed profits based on redistributions from taxpayers to shareholders, which enable the latter, the majority of whom are very wealthy, to profit from the efforts of both rail-users and taxpayers.

The derisking of private investments by the state can now be found in many sectors. In recent years, for example, institutional investment in residential housing has been actively encouraged by many states and by European legislation. These interventions have been aimed at facilitating the creation of housing as a new asset class and at derisking investments in it. In the UK, this has been done, inter alia, by providing income support to rent-paying households to ensure stable investor returns.[120] Elsewhere, in Italy, the National Recovery and Resilience Plan recently provided for the allocation of €960 million for student accommodation to increase the number of places for out-of-town university students. The reform facilitated

---

[117] See Centre for Research on Socio-Cultural Change (CRESC), *The Great Train Robbery: rail privatisation and after*, Manchester: CRESC (2013).

[118] CRESC, *The Great Train Robbery*, p. 50.

[119] FirstGroup, 'FirstGroup Signs New National Rail Contracts for South Western Railway and Transpennine Express', 20/5/2021, https://www.firstgroupplc.com/news-and-media/latest-news/2021/05-20-21.aspx.

[120] See Gabor and Kohl, *My Home Is an Asset Class*. Institutional landlords still account for a relatively small proportion of the market compared to small private landlords, but their share is growing. One reasons why states have encouraged their greater involvement is that they act as a counter-cyclical force when property markets are under pressure and falling. As Gabor and Kohl document, while these developments have done little to increase housing supply, they have inflated house prices and created major housing affordability issues across Europe's cities, exacerbated over-crowding and increased the burden of housing costs.

participation in financing for private investors as part of PPPs. It did this by supporting the 'sustainability of private investment' through concessionary taxation; by allowing the new housing to be used flexibly, meaning that if the accommodation could not be used to house students it could be rented to third parties; by relaxing the minimum requirements for common spaces; and, 'the icing on the cake', by providing that for private investors the Ministry of Universities and Research would cover in advance the 'charges corresponding to the first three years of management of the structures'.[121]

A further UK example is provided by the way private energy companies and the energy market have been regulated. In response to unconscionably high energy tariffs, an energy price cap setting the maximum price energy firms can charge on their default tariffs was introduced by the regulator (Ofgem) in 2019. It was calculated on the basis of the total costs faced by energy retailers plus an allowance for a 1.9 per cent profit on top, though retailers often reaped significantly higher profits than this. In October 2020, in face of soaring energy prices resulting from the war in Ukraine, an energy price guarantee was introduced to limit bills. In return, the government agreed to compensate energy companies for the difference between the retail capped price and the wholesale price to protect (and guarantee) their profits. All this has been paid for from the general Treasury budget. Originally, the government proposed to do this for two years, at an estimated cost of £160–170 billion, but it has since been announced that the scheme will end in March 2024. 'Instead of benefitting households', Gabor argues, 'the cap is designed to benefit companies, redistributing funds away from taxpayers and towards energy companies and their shareholders'.[122] As these examples show, states have in various ways become actively involved in the creating and sustaining of new forms of financial property that meet the demands of institutional investors for new, derisked investment outlets. Indeed, COVID-19 and the growth in public debt the pandemic generated has seen the push for PPPs reinvigorated.[123]

---

[121] Alessandro Bonetti, 'Housing as an Asset Class, Italian Edition', *Italics*, 24/9/2021, https://italics.substack.com/p/housing-asset-class-italy.

[122] Daniela Gabor, 'This economic chaos is a form of class war on the British public', *The Guardian*, 6/10/2022, https://www.theguardian.com/commentisfree/2022/oct/06/economic-chaos-class-war-british-liz-truss.

[123] COVID-19 prompted states to enter *de facto* PPPs by assuming the risks on bank loans and private sector wages. During the COVID-19 pandemic, for example, the regime ensured that remuneration was paid to rights holders and pharmaceutical capital protected when states temporarily overturned patents in order to respond to national emergencies: Article 31 of the TRIPS Agreement sets forth the requirements for the compulsory licensing of patents, including the obligation to pay 'adequate remuneration in the circumstances of each case, taking into account the economic value of the authorization' (Article 31(h), TRIPS Agreement). Article 31(b) of the TRIPS Agreement exempts the compulsory

Derisking has not only extended its reach but emerged as a global phenomenon as PPPs have become central to the financing of both the UN's sustainable development goals (SDGs) and the low-carbon transition. Broadly speaking, there are two ways of realising these goals: through the state and public investment (green new deals) or through private finance and PPPs. The latter are winning out. Global institutional investors and international agencies, Gabor explains, are engaged in 'an elaborate effort to reorganise development interventions around partnerships with global finance', citing as examples the World Bank's *Billions to Trillions* and *Maximising Finance for Development* and the G20's *Infrastructure as an Asset Class*. They seek to portray development as a matter of closing funding gaps through partnerships with global institutional investors.[124] In the words of Jim Yong Kim, the World Bank group president: 'we have to start by asking routinely whether private capital, rather than government funding or donor aid, can finance a project. If the conditions are not right for private investment, we need to work with our partners to de-risk projects, sectors, and entire countries'.[125] The goal is to get states to create investible development projects capable of persuading global investors to orient their trillions towards SDG-related projects. States are, therefore, called upon to 'escort' capital into derisked, investable securities that will yield satisfactory revenue streams. Inevitably, in this new 'development as derisking paradigm', institutional investors, asset managers and corporate executives, as the finance providers, are able to shape the terms on which poor and middle-income countries 'join the global supply of "SDG" securities'.[126] In the context of the green transition specifically, it means that they can express their commitment to the SDGs, while at the same time shaping where investments are made and the pace of decarbonisation – with profitability as their principal goal.[127]

---

licensing of patents for pharmaceutical products from certain requirements of Article 31 of the TRIPS Agreement, but does not exempt from the obligation to pay adequate remuneration: see WTO, *Compulsory Licensing of Pharmaceuticals and TRIPS*, https://www.wto.org/english/tratop_e/trips_e/public_health_faq_e.htm. See also Jessica Sklair and Paul Gilbert, 'Giving as "De-Risking": philanthropy, impact investment and the pandemic response', 4 *Public Anthropologist*, pp. 51–77 (2022). The WTO and others argue that patent protection is good for vaccine access because it promotes innovation. Sklair and Gilbert, however, argue that the evidence suggests that pharmaceutical firms are attempting to derisk their revenue streams by investing less in R&D and more in patent holding.

[124] Gabor, 'The Wall Street Consensus', pp. 430–3.
[125] Quoted in Gabor, 'The Wall Street Consensus', p. 429. Or in the words of John Kerry, US Special Envoy for Climate, we need to 'create the capacity to have bankable deals. That's doable for water, it's doable for electricity, it's doable for transportation': cited in Gabor, 'The Wall Street Consensus at COP27', *Phenomenal World*, 19/11/2022.
[126] Gabor, 'The Wall Street Consensus', p. 453.
[127] See Fancy, 'ESG and Sustainability Investing'.

The result, Gabor argues, has been the rise of the 'de-risking state', of 'a state-mediated project of constructing new development asset classes' – new property in the form of steady, reliable revenue rights – for global institutional investors and their (mainly very wealthy) clients. This leads her to conclude that 'financial globalisation is alive and well', the old Washington Consensus having been replaced by a new, equally neoliberal, 'Wall Street Consensus' in which facilitating the creation of new financial property through derisking has become a central feature of state policy, a new state imperative. Indeed, she argues, these developments are seeing the state itself restructured. It is 'a state-building project' aimed at reducing direct public investments in, and delivery of, services and at handing them over to the private sector. The ambition is 'not simply a Thatcherite privatisation onslaught', but a transformation of the state, aimed at 'reduc[ing] statecraft to de-risking investments for global financiers'. As financial capital colonises the infrastructure of the state, 'industrial policy' comes to amount 'to little more than planning and overseeing PPP projects'. Global finance, she suggests, is putting in place the institutional basis for a 'new regime of de-risking as accumulation', a regime that benefits Northern capital by extending the scope for it to profit from the efforts of others across the globe.[128]

Neoliberal ideology versus neoliberal practice

These developments highlight not only the role of the state in creating and protecting private property in the means and fruits of production but the gulf between the ideology and rhetoric and the practice of neoliberalism. There is a tendency to take neoliberalism's claims about itself at face value and to interpret neoliberal policy-making in terms of facilitating the free movement of goods, services, capital and labour, and of extending the reach of deregulated free markets in order to increase individual freedom and the efficient allocation of resources. Neoliberalism is thus commonly seen as an ideology that, above all else, favours shrinking the state and insulating the economy from political 'interference'. The stated hope is that political and legal changes that extend the reach of private property and free markets will have the effect of 'depoliticising' the economic sphere.[129]

What the rise of intangible property rights (which are self-evidently socially and legally constructed) and phenomena like privatisation and

---

[128] Gabor, 'The Wall Street Consensus', pp. 430–2, 436, 453; Sylla and Gabor, 'Planting Budgetary Time Bombs in Africa'.

[129] In Brenner and Wood's terms, the goal is to create a world in which profits can be made by simply enforcing existing property rights and allowing the 'purely economic' imperatives of the market to operate, a world in which there is little or no need for openly coercive 'political' interventions.

the new enclosures, derisking and recurring state bailouts (financial crash, COVID-19, energy crisis) make clear is the growing dependence of property-as-capital in contemporary capitalism on the state. Increasingly extensive state interventions are needed both to create and to maintain it. These interventions are not exogenous to property in contemporary capitalism, they are integral to it, so much so that it is not possible to say much that is empirically meaningful about property today without recognising and encompassing their indispensability. Significantly, when the enforcement of property rights and the operation of market forces alone prove insufficient to ensure that property-as-capital gets its pecuniary rewards, neoliberals have few qualms about supporting more directly coercive political interventions.[130] These interventions underline the need to take neoliberal mantras about the importance of free markets and the need to minimise state interventions in the economy with a large pinch of salt. While extending the scope of 'free' markets is undoubtedly a key part of neoliberal rhetoric, viewing neoliberalism primarily, let alone only, through this prism conceals as much as it reveals. The modern corporate capitalist economy is only a 'free market economy' in a limited sense. Much of the international trade that is seen as the hallmark of globalisation, for example, actually takes place between the various corporate entities that compose the large multi-national enterprises that dominate the world economy. It is composed of intra-enterprise trade that is co-ordinated and regulated not by markets and freely negotiated contracts but by administrative planning. These enterprises, whose existence as enterprises (rather than as multiple individual corporations) is barely recognised by law, use both markets and the corporate legal form as and when it suits them to reduce labour costs and tax bills to increase profits.

The founders of neoliberalism were, in fact, fully aware that this 'depoliticised' market sphere would have to be politically and legally created and maintained. They did not believe that markets were self-creating or self-regulating and could take care of themselves. Notwithstanding the rhetoric, they knew markets and their component parts, including, crucially, property rights, are not 'natural', pre-regulatory phenomena that are subjected to artificial, external, political 'interference'. 'The realization of the 1930s for the neoliberals', Slobodian writes, 'was that the self-regulating market was a myth'.[131] They knew that markets were as much the products as the subjects of regulation, and that active states played an indispensable role in

---

[130] Von Mises had 'no qualms about using government military power to open and secure overseas markets' or about the use of state power against labour unions: Slobodian, *The Globalists*, p. 33.

[131] Slobodian, *The Globalists*, p. 95. '[S]elf-described neo-liberals did not believe in self-regulating markets': p. 2.

their creation and maintenance. Far from being committed to inactive (or small) states, as is sometimes supposed, therefore, neoliberals generally seek to change the nature of the state rather than abolish it, vigorously supporting some kinds of state activity, while equally vigorously opposing other kinds. They seek the *right kind* of states rather than *no* states. Thus, as we have seen, in recent decades neoliberals have been strongly supportive of interventions by states and international organisations aimed at creating new (derisked) property-as-capital and good climates for investment and profit-making. Hence the multiple reforms aimed at enhancing the rights and power of capital, at diminishing the rights and power of labour and trade unions, and at subjecting workers to more intense disciplinary market pressures. Lawyers have played a key role in these processes, working hard on behalf of capital, not least to fashion legal changes that increase the bargaining power of capital vis-à-vis labour. Recently, for example, they have sought on behalf of capital to reclassify workers as something other than employees, arguing that those whose work generates revenue for platform companies exploiting digital technologies are not employees but independent suppliers of services and, as such, not entitled to legislative employment protections: sick pay, holiday pay, social security payments and the like.[132] Collectively, these reforms have contributed to the major changes in the relative bargaining power of capital and labour that have underpinned the increases in income and wealth inequality.

Despite claims to the contrary, then, the neoliberal era has not been characterised by 'deregulation'. On the contrary, the extension of private property rights and market mechanisms has seen more regulation, not less: more markets have meant more rules and more state regulation of the private sphere. This is reflected in the significant expansion of the scope of purposive or regulatory law, in the enormous growth in the number of regulatory bodies, and in the claim that we have seen the rise of 'regulatory states'.[133] Quite a lot of this regulation is, as Sol Picciotto says, 'the tribute that corporate capitalism has been obliged to pay for continuing to maintain the private forms which allow its domination by a tiny elite, creaming off enormous wealth'.[134] Its growth has been partly obscured by the fact that much of it now takes a privatised or part-privatised form, occupying a legal space between public and private law in which the distinction between

---

[132] See Isabelle Daugareilh, Christophe Degryse and Philippe Pochet, 'The Platform Economy and Social Law: key issues in comparative perspective', *ETUI Research Paper – Working Paper 2019.10* (2019).

[133] For an early discussion of this (1981) in terms of the decline of legal autonomy, see Thomson, 'Law and the Social Sciences'.

[134] Sol Picciotto, 'Regulation: Managing the Antinomies of Economic Vice and Virtue', 26 *Social & Legal Studies*, pp. 676–99 (2017), p. 693.

them is blurred. Much contemporary regulatory law involves 'negotiated self-regulation' by private bodies.[135] In reality, therefore, the commitment of neoliberals to deregulation, market freedoms, competition and non-interventionism is highly selective. Most neoliberals are untroubled by the fact that competition often leads to oligopoly and monopoly and are generally quite happy to support the free association of capital in large corporations, while at the same time frowning upon the free association of workers in trades unions and any growth in the collective power of labour.[136] Similarly, most neoliberals, while railing against nationalisation and state monopolies, support the strengthening of IPRs even though they represent the creation by the state of monopoly privileges. The actual practitioners of neoliberalism have always been prepared to discard neoliberal ideology when the occasion requires.

The deviations of neoliberal practice from neoliberal rhetoric suggest that neoliberalism is better and more accurately viewed not as a free market project but as a class project.[137] Both states and market forces have been deployed selectively and pragmatically by neoliberals to further the interests of capital. From its inception, protecting existing property and creating opportunities for the creation of new property-as-capital to enable investors to profit from the efforts of others was one of the defining characteristics of neoliberalism. Indeed, as Quinn Slobodian has pointed out, its origins lie precisely in the threat some of its founding fathers, like Ludwig von Mises, felt was posed to 'the order of private property' – by, variously, the wartime planning undertaken during the First World War, which made a more collectively directed, planned and egalitarian economy look possible; by the demise of open-door free trade imperialism; and by the rise of universal suffrage.[138] The fears of the self-styled neoliberals were exacerbated by the aftermath of the

---

[135] See Iage Miola and Sol Picciotto, 'On the Sociology of Law in Economic Relations', 31 *Social & Legal Studies*, pp. 139–61 (2022), locating this work within the wider field.

[136] 'Early neoliberalism ... was united in the belief that the state had crucial economic and social functions [to perform, including] ... to police and prevent monopoly', but beliefs like this were 'slowly eroded ... Neoliberalism in the revised Chicago version of Friedman, Director and Stigler ... did not recognise this problem' – at least in the corporate sphere. 'From the Chicago perspective, the more worrying manifestation of monopoly was trade union power': Daniel Stedman Jones, *Masters of the Universe: Hayek, Friedman and the birth of neoliberal politics*, Princeton: Princeton University Press (2012), pp. 7, 335, 342. On Friedman's shifting position on monopoly, see Angus Burgin, *The Great Persuasion*, Cambridge: Harvard University Press (2012), pp. 171–4, 180.

[137] On this and on the divergences between neoliberal ideology and rhetoric and neoliberal practice, see David Harvey, *A Brief History of Neoliberalism*, Oxford: Oxford University Press (2005), pp. 64–86.

[138] Slobodian, *The Globalists*, pp. 28–33. See also Clara Mattei, *The Capital Order*, Chicago: University of Chicago Press (2022).

1929–30 crash, which saw the erection of tariff walls around imperial blocs, a dramatic decline in international trade, the dissolution of the gold standard, and the resurrection of planning in various forms. For people like von Mises, who 'earned his livelihood for much of his adult life as a forthright advocate for the needs of business',[139] these developments placed private property 'at the mercy of national democracy'.[140] Acting as lobbyists for capital, the neoliberals set about trying to build a national and international order in which property rights were secure from nation states and democracy. The threats to property that the neoliberals so feared, and that contemporary neoliberals still fear, may have receded, but they are always there, lurking in the shadows, particularly when economic times are tough.

---

[139] Slobodian, *The Globalists*, p. 31. Somewhat paradoxically, von Mises, the great advocate of free markets, spent many decades living in New York in a rent-controlled apartment.

[140] Tooze, 'Neoliberalism's World Order'.

8

Property and Social Transformation

Property as a historical category

In his inaugural lecture at Oxford, in a foretaste of what was to become *The Concept of Law*, H L A Hart argued that one should try to describe the practice of law before attempting to develop definitions and theories. 'Though theory is to welcomed', he wrote, 'the growth of theory on the back of definition is not'.[1] His stance was not anti-theoretical but advocated empirically informed theorisation. It was in this spirit that Craig Muldrew warned against the tendency to derive assumptions about the operation of actual markets from the economic theories developed in the wake of Adam Smith, arguing that these theories, which see markets as operating in fundamentally the same way in all places and at all times, have limited applicability to actual pre-eighteenth-century market practices. The relationship between economic theory and history 'needs to be reversed'. A 'thickly researched historiography of the complex motivations and practices of agents acting out relationships of economic exchange – together with an understanding of how they themselves interpreted such actions – [sh]ould inform future theory, rather than the other way round'.[2]

The historian E P Thompson made very similar arguments about the relationship between history and theory. The concepts he used in his historical researches, he said, were 'historical concepts, arising from the analysis of diachronic process, of repeated regularities of behaviour over

---

[1] H L A Hart, 'Definition and Theory in Jurisprudence', in Hart, *Essays in Jurisprudence and Philosophy*, Oxford: Clarendon Press, pp. 21–48 (1983 [1953]), p. 25.

[2] Muldrew, 'Interpreting the Market', p. 164. There are echoes here of Oliver Wendell Holmes' suggestion that 'a page of history is worth a volume of logic': *New York Trust Co. v Eisner* (1921) 256 US 345, p. 349.

time', concepts that were 'often resisted, and even wilfully misunderstood by the synchronic disciplines'.³ Thus, for Thompson class was not a static category, measurable in positivist or quantitative terms, but a historical category describing people in relationship over time. This led him to advocate an 'interactionist epistemology' in which knowledge arose from a continual dialogue between 'conceptualisation and empirical observation, hypothesis and experiment'.⁴ Theory arose out of open, empirical enquiry. He agreed with Marx that, like thought in general, it was 'not self-generating' but was 'the product ... of the working-up of observation and conception into concepts'.⁵ For Thompson, history was a structured process and theoretical knowledge – the knowledge of structures – was not a matter of 'static conceptual representation' that belonged to a 'different, empirical sphere of cognition' from history. Rather than being separated and opposed, structure and history needed to be united. Theory needed to be able to accommodate historical categories, concepts appropriate to the investigation of specific empirical processes.⁶ The development of concepts capable of grasping property/property institutions at any given time and place thus requires 'thick research' in which one immerses oneself in the actual property practices of the society under investigation and a continual dialogue between those empirical observations and attempts to conceptualise them.⁷ The 'importance of real history', Thompson explained, is that 'it not only tests theory, it reconstructs [it]'.⁸

Not everyone will welcome such an approach. Just as Blackstone warned against reflecting too deeply into the origins and foundations of property rights or 'scrutin[zing] too nicely into the reason for making them', some today would prefer it if this kind of 'thick research' was not undertaken for fear it might uncover uncomfortable truths. As Quinn Slobodian has

---

[3] E P Thompson, 'History and Anthropology', in E P Thompson, *Making History: writings on history and culture*, New York: New Press, pp. 199–225 (1995), p. 217. For recent support for such a diachronic approach, see Lobban, 'Legal Theory and Legal History', p. 12.

[4] E P Thompson, 'Caudwell', *Socialist Register*, pp. 228–76 (1977), p. 245. See also Wood, *Democracy Against Capitalism*, p. 79.

[5] Marx, *Grundrisse*, p. 101; see also Thompson, 'Poverty of Theory', p. 255.

[6] Wood, *Democracy Against Capitalism*, p. 79; Thompson, 'Poverty of Theory', p. 237.

[7] 'In the end', Thompson wrote, 'the dialectic of social change cannot be fixed in any metaphor that excludes human attributes. We can only describe the social process – as Marx showed in The Eighteenth Brumaire – by writing history. And even so, we shall end with only an account of a *particular* process, and a selective account of this': E P Thompson, 'The Peculiarities of the English', in *The Poverty of Theory and Other Essays*, p. 79.

[8] Interview with E P Thompson, 3 *Radical History Review*, pp. 4–25 (1976), p. 16. Echoing this, Michael Lobban recently argued that history has the ability to 'test the accuracy of theoretical formulations': 'Legal Theory and Legal History', p. 13.

observed, early neoliberals, like von Mises and Hayek, were only too aware of its dangers. Having initially shown considerable interest in empirical data and particularly business cycles, from the 1930s their interest in the empirical details of economic processes receded and their attention shifted to broad and abstract questions about the 'economic constitution'.[9] They sought, Adam Tooze argues, 'to outlaw prying questions about how things actually worked, because it was when you started asking for statistics and assembling spreadsheets that you took the first dangerous step towards politicizing the economy'. He adds that, to the extent that the opponents of neoliberalism themselves operate at this abstract level 'rather than investigating [the concrete] processes of accumulation, production and distribution', they are 'playing the neoliberals at their own game'. Neoliberalism's 'deliberately elevated level of discourse' and 'airy talk of orders and constitutions' obscures the realities of power and 'the engines large and small through which social and economic reality is constantly made and remade'. It is when you immerse yourself in its empirical realities that you 'meet, real, actually existing neoliberalism'.[10] The elevated and airy nature of much property theory – with its attempt to abstract from specific empirical realities in search of a transhistorical and transcultural 'essence' for property or for universal truths about it – may not always be a deliberate attempt to obscure and to depoliticise, but that is often its effect. By contrast, a 'thickly researched' approach to property that explores the empirical realities of property at any given time and place would lead us into situated engagements with the ways in which property and property rights have been constructed and maintained, and encourage us to uncover the real history of the power struggles between capital and labour, landlords and tenants, rich and poor, developed and developing world, colonisers and colonised, corporations and citizens, that surround it.

Thing-ownership, bundle of rights or social relation?

What, then, of the debates about the nature and essence of property? Is property best conceptualised in terms of things and thing-ownership? Or is it better and more accurately conceptualised as a bundle of rights? Or as a social relation? The need for a more empirically grounded approach to the study of property does not mean that these theoretical debates are unimportant. On the contrary, they remain central to developing a proper understanding of property in contemporary capitalism and to people's perceptions of the issues surrounding it. As the work of psychologists researching cognitive

---

[9] Slobodian, *The Globalists*, chapter 2.
[10] Tooze, 'Neoliberalism's World Order'.

framing shows, the way in which issues, problems and choices are presented to people – how they are 'framed' – affects their perceptions of them. Recent research conducted by Jonathan Nash and Stephanie Stern in an experimental setting suggests this is true of issues concerning property rights. How we conceptualise or 'frame' property and property entitlements, they argue, influences the way those entitlements are experienced, affecting their perceived strength and perceptions of the possibility and legitimacy of changing them. Their work, they suggest, provides statistically significant support for the claim that framing property in terms of bundles of rights rather than in terms of thing-ownership (what they call 'discrete asset' framing) 'weakens perceptions of ownership and unlimited control, and decreases resistance to subsequent restrictions'.[11]

The thing-ownership conception portrays property as a fundamentally private and individual affair involving 'special', more or less absolute, rights: 'it's mine and I can do what I like with it'. Others only come into the picture when rights are violated or voluntarily exchanged. As we have seen, it is a conception of property frequently presented as 'natural', as historically omnipresent (if only embryonically), as not circumscribed by time or place and as capable, therefore, of being used as a basis for analysing the property institutions of all societies. As historians and anthropologists have shown, however, attempting to abstract from particular social contexts and from particular, empirically existing property institutions in order to construct a transhistorical and transcultural conception of property is highly problematic, particularly in relation to property in productive resources and the fruits of production. It divorces property institutions from their specific social attributes. It is, of course, difficult for those of us who are products of contemporary capitalist societies to stop seeing all societies through the prism of private property and thing-ownership. To us, property appears to be a relationship between individual legal persons and things; this seems to be its universal essence. No matter how common sensical it might seem to us, however, when this conception of property is taken beyond the historical and cultural boundaries of modern capitalism and is applied to significantly different kinds of societies, it risks distorting rather than furthering our understanding of them. It risks naturalising generalised private property and encourages a perception of the different property institutions of other societies as less sophisticated versions of our own, as mere stepping-stones on the (inevitable) path to where we are today. As Pierre Bourdieu says,

---

[11] Jonathan Nash and Stephanie Stern, 'Property Frames', 87 *Washington University Law Review*, pp. 449–504 (2010), pp. 449–50, 452–3; see also Jonathan Nash, 'Packaging Property: the effect of paradigmatic framing of property rights', 83 *Tulane Law Review*, pp. 691–734 (2009).

'every established order tends to produce ... the naturalization of its own arbitrariness'.[12] In reality, the conception of property as 'sole and despotic dominion' by individuals – and, indeed, the emergence of a seemingly autonomous legal universe – was made possible by the rise of, and helped to constitute, capitalist social orders.

This does not mean that the thing-ownership conception of property does not have an important role to play in helping us understand the property institutions of contemporary capitalism. On the contrary, there are important senses in which these institutions *are* about things and thing-ownership, and need to be understood as such – even if not all the 'things' involved have a physical existence. Not only is this how property is experienced in common sense, conceptualising property in terms of thing-ownership, private property, full liberal ownership and person–thing relations captures important aspects of the empirical realities of property in capitalist societies, the social relations of which take in significant part the form of exchanges of 'things' by property owners. Among other things, it helps us to understand the extraordinary power bestowed on large corporate enterprises by private property rights in productive resources. The huge decision-making power that is now vested in these firms, who in recent decades have increasingly been able to free themselves from effective state oversight and regulation, lies at the heart of Robé's 'world power system'.[13] It also lies at the heart of the revenue rights that are central to the wealth of those at the top of the rich lists. The absolute-thing-ownership conception of property may be an abstract ideal expression of property in contemporary capitalism, and it may bear the stamp of history, but it is indubitably part of the specific social reality that it seeks to depict and has an important role to play in helping us to understand the world around us.[14]

It is equally clear, however, that there are important aspects of the property institutions of contemporary capitalism that the thing-ownership conception of property does *not* enable us adequately to grasp, no matter how closely it seems to accord with experience and common sense. There are certain important senses in which it operates on the surface, focusing on the way the world appears. As we have seen, for example, it tends to take the 'thingness' of intangibles at face value, downplaying the fact that property – and particularly property-as-capital – does not always take the form of rights over 'the external things of the world', let alone absolute rights

---

[12] Pierre Bourdieu, *Outline of a Theory of Practice*, Cambridge: Cambridge University Press (1977), p. 116.
[13] Robé, *Property, Power and Politics*, though Robé does not himself subscribe to the thing-ownership conception of property.
[14] Sayer, *Marx's Method*, pp. 126–7.

over those things, but the form of intangible revenue rights and intangible intellectual property rights that have no direct connection to physical objects. The term 'thing' has been extended to these intangible rights bundles, and understandably so, because, as a result of being bought, sold, licensed and so on, they have acquired thing-like qualities. They *appear* to be and are treated as though they are tangible 'things'. These rights bundles have been reified and their reification seems to give property as a whole a definable, thing-related 'essence' that clearly and decisively distinguishes property rights from other rights, justifying their special status and treatment. Remaining at the level of appearances, however, requires us not to delve too much into the underlying nature of these intangible property forms.

By contrast, the bundle of rights conception of property encourages us to dig beneath the surface and to recognise that many of the most important objects of property in contemporary capitalism are intangible and nothing more than rights bundles, and that even when they directly relate to tangible things, property rights are typically less than absolute. In doing this, it highlights not only the legally constructed, contingent and malleable nature of property but also its political and public dimensions in ways that thing-ownership conceptions tend not to do. As a result, the thing-ownership conception tends to narrow perceptions of what sorts of property institutions – and, indeed, what sorts of social relations and societies – might be possible. By contrast, the bundle of rights conception helps us better to appreciate the full range of institutional possibility, which is why it attracts so much hostility from some quarters.

In focusing on the rights (rather than the things) dimensions of property, the bundle of rights conception also makes more visible the inter-personal, social relational dimensions of property highlighted by Hohfeld and others. To take one example, the power of corporations is usually portrayed as fundamentally impersonal, as power exercised not by 'a someone' but by 'a something'.[15] If we dig beneath the surface, however, and delve into the intangible property rights derived from corporate ownership of productive assets – intangible revenue rights like shares and bonds – and into the sources of the revenues that accrue to them, people (shareholders, bondholders, workers and so on) re-enter the picture. Corporate power begins to look less like power that is exercised by and for a 'disembodied entity', an 'autonomous self-directed economic being', and more like power that is exercised by and for particular individuals and social groups over others.[16]

---

[15] Ted Nace, *Gangs of America*, San Francisco: Berrett-Koehler (2003), p. 3.

[16] Gregory Mark, 'The Personification of the Business Corporation in American Law', 54 *University of Chicago Law Review*, pp. 1441–83 (1987), p. 1445. See also Ireland, 'The Corporation and the New Aristocracy of Finance'.

Because of the aspects of property that they downplay (or ignore), thing-ownership conceptions of property provide only a limited and partial picture of the nature of the property institutions of contemporary capitalism. They are apt to understate property's coercive and power dimensions, tending to conjure up an abstract, idealised picture of social relations in contemporary capitalism as involving voluntary (non-coercive) contractual exchanges of 'things' by free, formally equal, property-owning legal persons. In a much-cited passage in *Capital*, Marx pointed out some of the analytical limitations of such exchange-focused approaches to understanding capitalism. The sphere of exchange, he wrote, appears to be 'the very Eden of the innate rights of man [where] alone rule Freedom, Equality, Property and Bentham'. Freedom, 'because both buyer and seller of a commodity ... contract as free agents, and the agreement they come to is but the form in which they have to look for equivalent'. Property, 'because each disposes only of what is his own'. And Bentham, 'because each looks only to himself. The only force that brings them together and puts them in relation with each other, is the selfishness, the gain and the private interests of each. Each looks to himself only, and no one troubles himself about the rest'. However, Marx argued, when you left the sphere of circulation 'where everything takes place on the surface and in view of all men' and entered 'the hidden abode of production',

> a certain change takes place ... in the physiognomy of our *dramatis personae*. He who was previously the money-owner now strides out in front as a capitalist; the possessor of labour-power follows as his worker. The one smirks self-importantly and is intent on business; the other is timid and holds back, like someone who has brought his own hide to market and now has nothing else to expect but a tanning.[17]

Marx's point was, of course, that to properly understand capitalism, you have to look beyond the sphere of exchange where seemingly formally equal, abstract, individual property owners freely exchange equivalent 'things', and explore the specific nature of the concrete, often highly

---

[17] Marx, *Capital*, volume 1, chapter 6, p. 172. Echoing this, the philosopher Elizabeth Anderson recently suggested that 'the economic system of the modern workplace is communist' in the Stalinist sense of the word, meaning dictatorial and authoritarian. 'I expect this description of communist dictatorships in our midst, pervasively governing our lives, often to a far greater degree of control than the state, would be deeply surprising to most people. Certainly, many US CEOs, who see themselves as libertarian individualists, would be surprised to see themselves depicted as dictators of little communist governments'. Why, she asks, has 'public discourse and political philosophy largely neglect[ed] the pervasiveness of authoritarian governance in our work and off-hours lives?: *Private Government*, pp. 36–40.

unequal, social relations (in this case, of production) lying beneath the surface. Feminists have pointed out that, on the same basis, you also need to explore the social relations and processes of *reproduction* and the role played by the reproductive labour – care giving, child-raising, housework and so on – that is predominantly carried out by women and goes largely uncompensated and unrecognised. Both the bundle of rights and social relations conceptions of property have the potential to facilitate this, not least by highlighting the Hohfeldian insight that property rights involve relations between persons as well as relations between persons and things. By casting light on the social relational and power dimensions of property in ways that the thing-ownership conception does not, they have the capacity to bring the 'correlative … have nots' much more that clearly into the picture.[18]

The social relational dimensions of property

The social relational dimension of property rights highlighted by Hohfeld has tended, however, to be deployed at the individual, micro level, whereas if we really want fully to grasp the social relational dimensions of property, and particularly of property-as-capital, we need to move beyond this to more macro levels. Understanding property institutions requires theorisation of the social totalities of which they are part. If we wish to understand property as an aspect of social inequality and power, particularly at the structural level, we need to explore the relations not only between abstract isolated individuals but between individuals embedded in particular empirically specific sets of social relations, arrangements and practices; between individuals who are members of particular social groups and classes. When one does this, one sees that property resembles class not merely because it is a historical category, but because it is, in certain important respects, a historical category describing groups of people in relationship over time. Property and class are intertwined.

The social relational conception of property is particularly important when we are seeking to understand property-as-capital – property 'invested' with a view to securing a pecuniary return – and the rights it creates over productive resources and the fruits of future productive activity. It is in this context that the conception of property as a social relation is indispensable and that the *Howey* test, with its attribution of the returns on 'investments' to 'the efforts of others', is so revealing. The revenues accruing to property-as-capital do not somehow emanate autonomously from the 'things' themselves (in the way that it is 'an attribute of pear-trees to bear pears'). On the contrary,

---

[18] Chadwick, 'Capital Without Capitalism?', p. 304.

they have their origins in social relations that are often concealed behind the reified property forms themselves.

Indeed, the social-relational nature of property-as-capital suggests that we would benefit analytically from reminding ourselves of the original *in personam* nature of financial property and strive conceptually to make these property forms more personality-rich once more, not necessarily at the individual level (though this may be possible and desirable in some cases) but at the wider social level. Put simply, property in contemporary capitalism can only fully be understood by excavating the specific social relations that underlie its many specific forms. Ultimately, only such a social relational approach to property will encourage exploration of the many different phenomena that need to be encompassed to understand property institutions at any given time and place. What Greer calls 'the infinitely varied spectrum of human property systems' reflects infinitely varied systems of social relations.[19]

From this perspective, the approach to understanding capital recently suggested by Katharina Pistor is problematic. Pistor rightly argues that 'capital is not a thing', that its existence is not confined to one particular historical epoch, and that its 'outward appearance' and the 'social relations that underpin it' have changed over time. Following Levy, she defines capital as 'legal property [that is] assigned a pecuniary value in expectation of likely future pecuniary income'.[20] For Pistor, it is made up of two elements: an asset and a legal code. In her view, with the right legal coding, any asset can be turned into capital. It cannot, she says, be 'pinned down' to class relations and to the 'fraught social relations between labor and its exploiters who own the means of production, which gives them the power to extract surplus from labor'.[21] As argued earlier, it is certainly the case that capital has long been able to profit from the efforts of others through commercial and credit relations as well as through wage relations.[22] However, Pistor's downplaying of the class and the social relational aspects of (property-as-)capital, leads her to the rather odd conclusion that 'legal coding accounts for the value of assets, and thus for the creation of wealth and its distribution'.[23] For Pistor, it seems, 'capital owes its wealth-creating capacity to its legal coding'; capital is

---

[19] Greer, *Property and Dispossession*, p. 54.
[20] Pistor, *The Code of Capital*, pp. 10, 12.
[21] Pistor, *The Code of Capital*, p. 10. Elsewhere in the book Pistor asserts that 'using the analytical lens developed in this book', she later writes, 'it is possible to explain the political economy of capitalism without having to construct class identities': p. 208.
[22] On this, see Ulysse Lojkine, 'Critical Political Economy beyond the Production/Circulation Dichotomy', *LPE Blog*, 17/5/2021, https://lpeproject.org/blog/critical-political-economy-beyond-the-production-circulation-dichotomy/.
[23] Pistor, *The Code of Capital*, p. 19.

'a *legal* quality that helps create and protect wealth'.[24] It seems to me that these claims risk obscuring key characteristics of property-as-capital and might be read as suggesting that money, if properly legal coded, really can make more money quite independently of effort, labour or productive activity.

The downplaying of the social relational nature of property-as-capital also leads Pistor to argue that, 'with a little bit of engineering', human beings can turn themselves into (code themselves as) 'capital'. In support of this claim, she cites the example of a freelancer who 'can capitalize her labor by establishing a corporate entity, contributing her services to it in kind and taking out dividends as the corporation's shareholder in lieu of salary'. The 'only input to this entity is human, but with some legal coding, it has been transformed into capital'.[25] In this situation, however, although one might have some of the trappings and *forms* of capital, the *substance* is missing. The returns on the freelancer's shares – and her notional capital investment – do not derive from the 'efforts of others' but from her own labour. So while it may indeed be a mistake to try to 'pin capital down' only to direct production relations given the pecuniary returns (and appropriations) achieved through such things as commercial and credit relations and ownership of intellectual property, not to mention market speculation, it is impossible fully to understand property-as-capital without an understanding of the social relations, processes and practices underlying the pecuniary returns it receives. As Veblen pointed out, 'the gains of investment in the aggregate are drawn from the aggregate material productivity of the community's industry'.[26] Pistor risks directing our gaze away from the very things we need to be examining if we wish to understand property-as-capital and the dynamics of contemporary capitalism. As Anna Chadwick says, Pistor does not seem to appreciate that 'a particular social world needs to exist' for assets/property to be capable of being capital. 'The ability of any "capital" asset to have a value, or to generate wealth in the future', Chadwick points out, 'depends on the existence of a capitalist economic system predicated on the generalization of commodity production and exchange'. By contrast, Pistor 'at times [creates] the impression ... that it is possible to have capital without capitalism'.[27] Thus, although Pistor's book 'is replete with examples from history, as well as from contemporary financial markets, that highlight the legal experiences of the "have nots" – those on the other side of these newly-minted capital

---

[24] Pistor, *The Code of Capital*, p. 12 (her emphasis).
[25] Pistor, *The Code of Capital*, p. 11.
[26] Veblen, 'On the Nature of Capital (II)', p. 106. Marx argued: 'Political economy confuses on principle two very different kinds of private property, of which one rests on the producers' own labour, the other on the employment of the labour of others': *Capital*, volume 1, chapter 33.
[27] Chadwick, 'Capital Without Capitalism', pp. 307–8.

"coins"' – she 'does not explicitly specify the "correlative" effect of each of the legal powers she identifies'.[28]

There are, then, important senses in which property in contemporary capitalism is simultaneously a thing, a bundle of rights, and a social relation. On the surface, property does, indeed, appear to relate to things and thing-ownership; dig down a little and it emerges, particularly in some contexts, as a bundle of rights; dig deeper still and its social relational aspects come into focus. In a world in which intangibles are so important to wealth and power, there are important aspects of modern property that the thing-ownership conception of property, by itself, simply cannot adequately grasp. Indeed, it can be, and is, sometimes deployed precisely to suppress the coercive, power-related, and social relational dimensions of property. In the context of productive property and property in the fruits of productive activity, it often conceals as much as it reveals.

Bringing capitalism back in

Seeing property as a social relation is also analytically indispensable in the context of property-as-capital because of the way that it steers us away from a static understanding of it as a 'thing' towards a dynamic understanding of it as a process. This in turn directs our attention towards the ways in which the property rights structures of a society – particularly those relating to productive activity – play a key role in shaping a society's economic dynamic. Indeed, it is the dynamic generated by its historically specific property rights structures that distinguishes capitalism from other social forms or modes of production. This dynamic is central to the many problems currently facing us: recurring economic crises that spread rapidly in an increasingly interconnected global economy; economic stagnation in the mature capitalist world, leading to widespread reductions in living standards; increasing inequality; growing social dislocation and polarisation; rising international tension; an accelerating drift from democracy towards plutocracy; and, of course, environmental degradation and a growing climate crisis. In an interview in early 2012 the German political economist, Wolfgang Streeck, reflecting on these problems, painted an unremittingly bleak picture of the state of the world and was unequivocal about the need for radical change. It was a 'tall order' but 'nothing less' than a 'break with possessive individualism, competitive greed [and] hedonistic consumerism ... would do'.[29] A few years earlier, in *Re-Forming Capitalism*, he had explored the changes that had

---

[28] Chadwick, 'Capital Without Capitalism', p. 304.
[29] 'Interview with Wolfgang Streeck', *The Current Moment*, 3/1/2012, https://thecurrentmoment.wordpress.com/2012/01/03/interview-with-wolfgang-streeck/.

taken place in the German post-war model of political economy. Tracing the long-term evolution of five institutional spheres – collective bargaining, the organisation of capital and labour, social and welfare policy, public finance and corporate governance – he documented the withering away of social regulation in the face of growing marketisation and commodification, and the gradual demise of German social democracy. To explain these changes, Streeck argued, it was necessary to 'bring capitalism back in'.[30] Observing that what was happening in Germany mirrored what was happening elsewhere, he argued that capitalist economies everywhere were 'subject to general forces of capitalist development' in the form of 'powerful endogenous pressures' for 'a continuous widening and deepening of market relations'.[31] The changes that had occurred, he concluded, were the products not of democratic processes but of 'the historical reassertion of the logic of capital accumulation' and a self-driven process of commodification of values and marketisation of social transactions. All capitalist societies had become increasingly subject to this logic, even exemplary European-style social market economies such as Germany. The logic had, for a limited period, been contained by democratic politics but in recent decades it had reasserted itself, reducing democracy to 'an empty shell', a formal ritual, not just in the US but in Europe.[32] To understand this generalised development, Streeck argued, you needed to focus 'not so much [on] the differences between national capitalisms at a given point in time as [on] the historical trajectory on which they are together moving as a family'.[33] You had to take their specifically *capitalist* nature seriously.[34] Thus the subject of his book, *Re-Forming Capitalism*, Streeck declared, was '*not institutions but capitalism*'.[35] As capital had released itself from the constraints imposed by post-war social democracy, 'it became more like itself', revealing its 'true nature' or 'essence'. In the neoliberal era, capitalism had become 'progressively more capitalist'.[36]

---

[30] Streeck, *Re-Forming Capitalism*, pp. 230–72. See also Wolfgang Streeck, 'Institutions in History: Bringing Capitalism Back In', *MPIfG Discussion Paper 09/8*, Cologne: Max-Planck-Institut (2009).

[31] Wolfgang Streeck, 'On Re-Forming Capitalism', *The Montreal Review*, March 2012, https://www.themontrealreview.com/2009/Re-Forming-Capitalism-Institutional-Change-in-the-German-Political-Economy.php.

[32] Streeck, *The Current Moment*. Streeck refers to a sign seen in the Indignados camp in 2011 that read (in Spanish): 'How can one speak of democracy if one cannot change the economic system at the ballot box?'.

[33] Streeck, 'On Re-Forming Capitalism'.

[34] Wolfgang Streeck, 'Taking Capitalism Seriously: towards an institutionalist approach to contemporary political economy', 9 *Socio-Economic Review*, pp. 137–67 (2011).

[35] Streeck, *Re-Forming Capitalism*, p. 3 (his emphasis).

[36] Streeck, 'Taking Capitalism Seriously', p. 164.

For Streeck, therefore, the concept of 'capitalism' is much more useful in helping us understand these changes than the 'functionalist construct called "the economy"' because it 'avoids the fallacies of misplaced abstractness' that plagues mainstream economics and rational choice social science and 'prevent[s] them from engaging the world *as it really happens to be*'. 'Speaking of capitalism', he argued, 'has the advantage of conceptualizing the economy as inherently dynamic – as a historical social formation defined by a specific, characteristic dynamism, and as an evolving social reality in real time'.[37] For this reason, Streeck was highly critical of the 'varieties of capitalism' literature, arguing that, to understand the world, we have to focus on the commonalities of capitalism and see it as an internationally variegated system, rather than focus on the differences between different individual capitalisms. We also have to start thinking in terms of dynamic processes rather than static structures.[38]

Capitalism's logic of process

There has been a tendency within radical/critical legal academic circles to question the analytical value and legitimacy of the concept of 'capitalism'. This tendency came to permeate the Critical Legal Studies (CLS) movement of the 1980s and 1990s as it gradually became ever more non- and/or anti-Marxist.[39] Some members made use of the term, but there lingered a feeling that most of them doubted whether anything that might usefully be called 'capitalism' existed in empirical reality.[40] Duncan Kennedy, for example, one of the leading CLSers and proponents of the 'indeterminacy' thesis that animated so much CLS scholarship, used the term but seems increasingly to have come to doubt its analytical value. Commenting sceptically on certain critiques of legal institutions, he describes them as 'presuppos[ing] the existence and current functioning of something called the capitalist mode

---

[37] Streeck, *Re-Forming Capitalism*, p. 230.
[38] Streeck, *Re-Forming Capitalism*, p. 1. See also Wolfgang Streeck, `E Pluribus Unum? Varieties and Commonalities of Capitalism', *MPIfG Discussion Paper 10/12*, Cologne: Max-Planck-Institut (2010). On Streeck's gradual intellectual shift, see Jerome Roos, 'From the Demise of Social Democracy to the End of Capitalism: the intellectual trajectory of Wolfgang Streeck', 27 *Historical Materialism*, pp. 248–88 (2019).
[39] On the complicated relationship between CLS and Marxism, see Akbar Rasulov, 'CLS and Marxism: A History of an Affair', 5 *Transnational Legal Theory*, pp. 622–39 (2014); Rob Hunter, 'Critical Legal Studies and Marx's Critique: a reappraisal', 31 *Yale Journal of Law & the Humanities*, pp. 389–412 (2021); Emilios Christodoulidis and Marco Goldoni, 'Marxism and the political economy of law' in Emilios Christodoulidis, Ruth Dukes and Marco Goldoni (eds), *Research Handbook on Critical Legal Theory*, Cheltenham: Edward Elgar, pp. 95–113 (2019).
[40] See Duncan Kennedy, *A Critique of Adjudication*, Cambridge: Harvard University Press (1997), pp. 280–95.

of production, understood to be a coherent system that is in a meaningful sense "in force"', and later talks of the capitalist mode of production 'in so much as it actually functions in the world'.[41] Indeed, he goes as far as to argue at one point that understandings of law based on 'Marx's notion of the commodity mode of production' are 'the enemy'.[42] The tendency to reject the concept of capitalism is still alive and well, characterising the work of some of those associated with the current Law and Political Economy (LPE) movement. Samuel Moyn, for example, has bluntly asserted that 'there is no such thing as capitalism'.[43] This tendency seems to be driven by an aversion to Marxism, or, more accurately, by an aversion to a particular version of Marxism treated as representative of Marxism *tout court* – Marxism understood as a rather crude, economically and technologically determinist body of thought driven by a unilinear, staged concept of history and rooted in ideas about bases and superstructures and rigid 'laws of motion'.[44] While there is no doubt that huge weight has been attached, by both Marxists and non-Marxists, to some of Marx's problematic shorthand aphorisms, they

---

[41] Duncan Kennedy, 'The Role of Law in Economic Thought: essays on the fetishism of commodities', 34 *American University Law Review*, pp. 939–1001 (1985), p. 998. Elsewhere he wrote that 'our capitalism' was a 'mixed' capitalism with 'no overall system logic': Kennedy, *A Critique of Adjudication*, p. 287. See also Kennedy, 'The Stakes of Law; or Hale and Foucault!', 4 *Legal Studies Forum*, pp. 327–66 (1991).

[42] Kennedy, 'The Role of Law', p. 1001. The final paragraph of the article from which this is drawn is somewhat incoherent, but this seems to be the message. It reads: 'I conclude that a realist/institutionalist understanding of law destablises Marx's notion of the commodity mode of production in much the same way that it destablises the law of value. As I have interpreted it, this understanding of law is the enemy, in our understanding of social and economic life, of false necessity, in the same way that Marx's analysis of commodity fetishism is the enemy of false necessity'. The idea of 'false necessity' presumably comes from Unger; that of the 'commodity mode of production' (rather than 'capitalist') seems to come from the philosopher and Weberian scholar Catherine Colliot-Thélène's afterword to Isaac Ilych Rubin's *A History of Economic Thought*, London: Ink Links, pp. 385–429 (1979), which Kennedy quotes approvingly at length. In it, Colliot-Thélène argues that there was a crucial flaw in the logical structure of Marx's law of value and questions (as have many Marxists, see text below) the 'supposed autonomy of the field of the Economic' as presented in the base-superstructure metaphor: Rubin, ibid, p. 428.

[43] Samuel Moyn, 'Thomas Piketty and the Future of Legal Scholarship', 128 *Harvard Law Review*, pp. 49–55 (2014), p. 55. Elsewhere, Moyn has suggested that Marxists need to consider 'whether to continue believing' that capitalism has 'fundamental systemic imperatives' and has 'a systemic identity': Samuel Moyn, 'Reconstructing Critical Legal Studies', Yale Law School, Public Law Research Paper (4 August 2023), p. 33.

[44] This tendency has not gone unchallenged. For a recent defence of the value of the critical Marxist tradition to critical legal scholarship?', see Talha Syed, 'Did CLS have (much of) any Theory?', *LPE Blog*, 10/10/2023, https://lpeproject.org/blog/did-cls-have-much-of-any-theory/. As Syed says, CLS was marked by a rather debilitating 'flight from explanatory theory'. For a critique of Moyn's view, see Matthew Dimick, 'Is Capitalism a Thing?', *LPE Blog*, 23/10/2023, https://lpeproject.org/blog/is-capitalism-a-thing/.

do not take account of how rarely some of them, like base-superstructure, appear in his work. Nor do they take account of the fact that they often do not accurately capture the theoretical principles with which Marx himself and many others working within the Marxist tradition operate.

Contrary to those who do not think there is any such thing as capitalism, I think that Streeck is right to argue that the concept of capitalism is much more analytically useful than abstract, general concepts like 'the economy' and that it helps us to grasp the historical specificities of the processes and dynamics at work in the modern world.[45] As we have seen, the term 'capitalism' was an etymological latecomer, only coming to be used, in a manner that owed much to Marx, to refer to an historically specific economic system in the late nineteenth and early twentieth centuries. Indeed, Werner Sombart, the first volume of whose magnum opus, *Der modern Kapitalismus*, appeared in 1902, went as far as to attribute 'the discovery' of capitalism to him.[46] In similar vein, E P Thompson argued that one of Marx's major achievements was his identification in history of different 'modes of production' (capitalist and so on) with their own different, historically specific and distinctive dynamics and forms of economic functioning, crediting him with having discovered 'capitalism-as-system'.[47] It was the distinctive economic functioning of the 'bourgeois mode of production' that Marx sought to uncover in his critique of political economy. Although Streeck has tended to look to Polanyi rather than Marx for critical inspiration, it is a conception of capitalism derived largely from Marx – capitalism as an economic system with its own specific dynamic – that he deploys when he asserts the determining power of the 'forces of capitalist development' and the 'logic of capital accumulation'. 'Once you bring history back into social science', he argues, 'you cannot possibly bypass Marx' or overlook key explanatory categories like power, class and

---

[45] Notwithstanding his assertions about the continuing importance of Marx and the Marxian tradition, Streeck would, I suspect, be somewhat surprised to find that he is, according to Moyn, an 'institutionally minded Marxist': Moyn, 'Piketty', p. 53. Moyn seems inclined to regard anyone who utilises the term 'capitalism' – other than as 'a matter of convenience' – to denote an economic system with an historically specific logic of process as 'a Marxist' and therefore locked into an outdated nineteenth-century mindset with an economically determinist, base-superstructure view of the world in which 'necessary laws like those of gravity or thermodynamics apply': ibid, p. 51.

[46] See Chiapello, 'Accounting and the Birth', p. 277.

[47] Thompson, 'Open Letter to Leszek Kolakowski', in *The Poverty of Theory and Other Essays*, p. 143. Jonathan Levy argues that 'an economy in which capitalization has risen to principal economic status may be said to be a capitalist economy ... Capitalism is an appropriate designation when the capital process has become habitual, sufficiently dominating economic life, having appropriated the production and distribution of wealth towards its pecuniary ends': Levy, 'Capital as Process', p. 487.

conflict. Streeck is now 'convinced that present trends in modern societies cannot be even approximately understood without the help of key concepts from the Marxian tradition'.[48]

What, then, did Marx have to say about the dynamics of capitalism? He did, indeed, argue that the capitalist mode of production is characterised by certain 'laws of motion', laws that are the product of capitalism's distinctive set of property relations in which one class, the bourgeoisie or capitalist class, owns the means of production and the other, the proletariat is 'propertyless' in the sense that it lacks property rights in productive resources. These laws, Marx argued, are empirically observable, systematic, and historically specific and are characterised among producers by a compulsive search for surplus value and profit that prompts a relentless hunt for reductions in production costs. These can be achieved by cutting wages and other input costs, by intensifying the labour process, or by increasing the productivity of labour through the introduction of organisational innovations or new technologies. Investing in new technologies, in particular, becomes a pre-requisite of competitive survival. For Marx it was the 'coercive laws of competition' that imposed these imperatives on producers. They didn't 'depend on the good or ill will of the individual capitalist'. 'Free competition', he wrote, 'brings out the inherent laws of capitalist production, in the shape of external coercive laws having power over every individual capitalist'.[49] Producers have to keep trying to lower costs by outsourcing to places where labour costs are lower, by intensifying labour processes, or by introducing productivity-enhancing technological advances. Propertyless workers have to sell their labour (power) for a wage to earn the money needed to buy subsistence goods. Compliance with these market imperatives is a pre-requisite of survival. Capitalist property rights structures thus generate what the social and economic theorist and historian, Robert Brenner, calls their own specific 'rules of reproduction', their own specific sets of rules with which economic actors have to comply in order to self-reproduce. 'Once established', Brenner argues, 'social property systems ... tend to set strict limits and impose certain overall patterns upon the course of economic evolution' by 'restrict[ing] the economic actors to certain limited options, indeed quite specific strategies, in order best to

---

[48] Wolfgang Streeck, 'Social Democracy's Last Rounds', *Jacobin*, 25/2/2016, https://jacobin.com/2016/02/wolfgang-streeck-europe-eurozone-austerity-neoliberalism-social-democracy; Streeck, *Buying Time*, p. xvi.

[49] Marx, *Capital*, volume 1, p. 257. Marx suggested that the 'innermost secret' of any social structure was the specific way in which 'unpaid surplus labour was pumped out of the direct producers': Capital, volume 3, p. 791.

reproduce themselves – that is, to maintain themselves in their established socio-economic conditions'.[50]

In certain important respects, orthodox economic accounts of capitalism echo this. In these accounts, too, capitalism is depicted as an economic system with a specific economic dynamic. This dynamic is depicted not as it is by Marx as based on power and exploitation but as based on consensual contractual exchanges between private property owners that are secured and guaranteed by a neutral state. The self-interested pursuit of unlimited material gain by property owners in free markets, it is argued, generates a dynamic that operates in the wider public interest by ensuring the efficient allocation of resources, maximising aggregate social wealth and encouraging productivity-enhancing technological innovation: private vice yields public benefits. There should be no ceiling on the size of the material gains that market actors might secure as long as they play by the rules: greed is good.[51] It is also natural: the search for unlimited wealth is '*rational, ... natural and normal*, and therefore *to be expected*' because it is consonant with human nature.[52] Unlike many of their opponents, the supporters of capitalism argue, they are free from moral self-deception for they recognize that capitalism accords with, and reflects, human nature and the egoism of *homo economus* and her natural passion and insatiable appetite to consume. Moreover, as any large accumulations of wealth arising out of market processes are the products of voluntary and consensual exchanges, they are *prima facie* legitimate. Orthodox economic accounts thus portray the imperatives generated by free market competition as wholly positive forces and its distributional outcomes as fair and just. From this perspective, the privatisation of previously publicly owned resources and the internationalisation and liberalisation of markets associated with neoliberalism are to be welcomed.

It is often forgotten that Marx endorsed parts of this account, for he too considered the capitalist mode of production to be an economically progressive force – a historically important means of developing the material forces of production[53] – and a civilising force that enhanced freedom and helped the human race to overcome 'universal mediocrity'. It was no coincidence that from around the second half of the eighteenth century and the advent of an identifiably capitalist society GDP per capita began

---

[50] Robert Brenner, 'The Agrarian Roots of Modern Capitalism', 97 *Past and Present*, pp. 16–113 (1982), p. 16, reprinted in T H Aston and C H E Philp (eds), *The Brenner Debate*, Cambridge: Cambridge University Press, pp. 213–327 (1985).

[51] Hence, perhaps, why Peter Mandelson was 'intensely relaxed about people getting filthy rich': see David Wighton, 'Mandelson plans a microchip off the old block', *Financial Times*, 23/10/1998.

[52] Streeck, 'Taking Capitalism Seriously', p. 149 (his emphases).

[53] See, for example, Marx, *Capital*, volume 1, p. 457.

rapidly to rise in Europe. Indeed, Marx thought that it was the increasing material abundance that capitalism brought that created the possibility of socialism and/or communism, alternative modes of production whose nature he elucidated only in very vague terms. In his view, however, this dynamic was not, as some suggested, inscribed in human nature, but was, rather, specific to the capitalist mode of production. Marx also, of course, thought that there was a dark side to this mode of production that orthodox accounts downplayed or denied. Capitalist production relations entailed and generated the ruthless exploitation of labour and were characterised by the relentless commodification of resources, goods and services, alienation, destructive inter-capitalist rivalry, recurrent crises and environmental degradation.[54] There would come a point, he believed, where capitalist property relations would begin to stand in the way of rather than further human progress, which for Marx encompassed non-material as well as material development.[55]

It is also often forgotten that Marx's concept of the 'capitalist mode of production' is, like the concept of capitalism, an abstraction, which, although derived from a study of empirical reality, abstracts from that reality in order to facilitate our understanding of it.[56] In *Capital*, Marx describes the operation of a theoretically pure, ideally typical capitalist mode of production rather than any particular empirical example of it. His is not an historical analysis, even though he utilises numerous historical examples to illustrate and validate his theoretical construct. As Joseph Fracchia observes, in developing his conceptual representation of the essential structure of the capitalist mode of production, Marx abstracts from national variations in the evolution of capitalism, even though most of his examples are drawn from England as the case closest to 'pure' capitalism; abstracts from real human beings, who are represented instead as the personifications of abstract economic categories, the embodiments of particular class interests and relations; and abstracts from the complexities of concrete class relations, except 'those essential to the capitalist mode of production: the bourgeoisie and the proletariat'.[57] As this suggests, Marx also abstracts from different institutional arrangements and

---

[54] See for example, Kohei Saito, 'Karl Marx's Ecosocialism: capital, nature, and the unfinished critique of political economy', *Monthly Review Press* (2017), https://monthlyreview.org/product/karl_marxs_ecosocialism/. Marx wrote about soil degradation in the 1860s.

[55] David McLellan notes the non-material dimensions of Marx's conception of progress in an unpublished article, 'Marx's views on Asiatic societies' (copy available from author).

[56] Matthew Dimick suggests the CLS rejection of capitalism looks like a simple result of 'conflating levels of abstraction': Dimick, 'Is Capitalism a "Thing"?'.

[57] 'I paint the capitalist and landlord in no sense *couleur de rose*. But here individuals are dealt with only in so far as they are the personifications of economic categories, embodiments of particular class-relations and class interests': quoted in Joseph Fracchia, 'Marx's *Aufhebung* of Philosophy and the Foundations of a Materialist Science of History', 30 *History and Theory*, pp. 153–79 (1991), p. 176.

from the real-world complexities of property, property rights and property relations, depicting instead a world comprised of one class with more or less absolute property rights in the means of production and another class with none. For Marx, theoretical abstraction of this sort was necessary to gain a proper grasp of the real, actual societies where capitalist property relations were dominant. As he readily recognised, however, developing a fuller understanding of the history of capitalist societies – of actual social formations – requires empirical analyses of contingencies that do not always correspond to the conceptual model.[58]

Indeed, for Marx, the operation in the real world of a determinative logic derived from relations of production did not 'prevent the same economic base – due to innumerable different empirical circumstances, natural environment, racial relations, external historical influences, etc. – from the standpoint of its main conditions from showing infinite variations and gradations in appearance, which can be ascertained only by analysis of the empirically given circumstances'.[59] Thompson also emphasised this, arguing that it was not possible to guess the 'range and diversity' of particular social forms such as feudalism, capitalism and socialism, 'because, rich as history is, it can never exhaust possibility'. Thompson stressed, however, that,

> while the number of variants may be infinite, it is infinite only within the categories of social 'species'. [Just as there may be] any number of permutations of breeds of dogs, and of mongrel cross-breeds, all dogs are doggy (they smell, bark, fawn over humans, etc.), so all capitalisms remain capitalist (foster acquisitive values, must by their nature leech the proletariat, etc.).[60]

David Harvey makes a similar point. Within capitalist modes of production, 'all manner of contingent and accidental structures of distribution and exchange and a grand diversity of consumption-regimes are possible in principle, *provided that they do not unduly restrict or destroy the capacity to produce surplus-value on an ever-expanding scale*'. Thus, capitalist social formations can be characterised by relatively egalitarian social democratic structures of distribution (of the sort traditionally associated with Scandinavia and Germany) as well as by highly unequal, authoritarian, neoliberal regimes

---

[58] See Fracchia, 'Marx's *Aufhebung*', p. 172.
[59] Marx, *Capital*, volume 3, pp. 791–2. In this sense, as Matthew Dimick points out, responding to claims that 'there is no such thing as capitalism', it is Marx who is 'the theorist of contingency', not critics like Samuel Moyn who, in wishing to stress legal contingency, end up embracing a general idea of 'the economy' that denies the specificity of capitalism: Dimick, 'Is Capitalism a "Thing"?'.
[60] Thompson, 'Peculiarities of the English', pp. 81–2.

(like Chile under Pinochet). There is, as Harvey says, 'no unique pattern of distribution, system of exchange or specific regime of consumption that can be derived from the general laws for the production of surplus-value. But – and this is a big "but" – *the possibilities are not infinite*'.[61]

Just as the ways the same basic determinative logic derived from capitalist property relations manifests itself differently in different places, it also manifests itself differently over time. As we have seen, for example, some argue that in recent decades the ways in which capital secures its pecuniary returns have undergone quite significant change. Making money directly from productive activity still remains vitally important, but, possessed of mountains of cash looking for profitable investment outlets and faced by industrial over-capacity, capital has been driven by its own logic away from securing pecuniary returns from further investment in industrial production (value creation) towards securing returns from financial engineering, IP monopolies, debt and other forms of rent (value extraction and predation). With this 'decisive strategic shift' towards financialisation and rentierism, Lazzarato suggests, the true nature of capital – in essence, money invested to yield a financial return – has become clearer, hence his claim, noted earlier, that 'the concept of capital becomes a reality not with industrial capital but with finance capital'. The concept of capital, he argues, needs to be detached from concrete productive resources and, indeed, from any *direct* connection to production, industrial or otherwise.[62]

Even if one endorses this view, however, it is important to remember that it does not mean that the financial returns from IPRs, rents, debt and the like are not, ultimately, derived from productive activity of some sort – from labour and the efforts of others. What we have seen in recent decades is that the mechanisms of appropriation, the modes whereby capital secures financial returns and part of the efforts of others, have become even more varied and complex and come to require ever more state involvement and support. The power and rights of labour have been diminished to facilitate profit-making, huge bailouts have been organised, new opportunities created for securing financial returns through the constitution of new private property rights, and new protections for property-as-capital put in place. More recently, states have begun to create new opportunities for profitable

---

[61] David Harvey, 'History Versus Theory: a commentary on Marx's method in *Capital*', 20 *Historical Materialism*, pp. 3–38 (2012), p. 16.

[62] Lazzarato, *Governing by Debt*, pp. 29–30, 141. Lazzarato suggests that the creditor–debtor relation has become more important than the capital–labour relation, and that this has marginalised the working class: p. 12. Lazzarato's view resembles that of Levy who argues that Veblen 'was correct to insist that money – capital's first form – remains its primary form. The only kind of capital is "pecuniary capital … and that "the substantial core of all capital is immaterial wealth"': Levy, 'Capital as Process', pp. 494–5.

investment by constructing new economic 'zones' characterised by tax incentives, deregulation, stark imbalances between the rights of capital and labour, and private law-making by corporations.[63] There are echoes here of the joint stock corporations of the era of the primitive accumulation of capital that have been the subject of much recent academic interest, most notably, perhaps, the East India Company, the archetypal company-state with governing and sovereign powers as well as enterprise functions.[64] Noting the resemblance of some of the new techniques for securing financial returns for capital to those used in the era of primitive accumulation, Harvey has described them as involving 'accumulation by dispossession'.[65] Paradoxically, today's new forms of corporate colonialism and anarcho-capitalism are heavily dependent on and strongly supported by states and the ISDS system.[66] As we have seen, further layers of protection for investments have been provided by safeguarding them from democracy, derisking them in various ways and, in some cases, politically constructing profits through subsidies paid for out of general taxation – money that might otherwise be spent on health, education, welfare and housing. This is Brenner's new 'political capitalism' with its overtones of the 'politically-constituted property' forms characteristic of the pre-capitalist era.

What are the implications of all this for Marx's 'laws of motion'? Marx did, indeed, frequently liken them to the laws of nature, comparing their force to that of gravity, and this, together with his famous deployment of the base-superstructure metaphor in the preface to the *Introduction to a Critique of Political Economy*, and the work of both followers and critics who took this metaphor rather too seriously, has undoubtedly contributed to perceptions of him as a rigid, reductionist economic determinist. But these metaphors fail to capture the principles with which Marx operated in much of his work. In this regard, David Harvey suggests that a better analogy for Marx's laws of motion would be the laws of fluid dynamics, as the latter cannot be applied mechanically to things like weather forecasting or climate change without modification. Like the laws of fluid dynamics, Harvey observes, Marx's laws of motion do not, and do not purport to, explain everything, or indeed predict the economic future with any certainty, but, as he says, 'no-one in the physical sciences would dismiss the[m] … just because they

---

[63] Quinn Slobodian, *Crack Up Capitalism*, London: Allen Lane (2021).
[64] Philip Stern, *The Company State: corporate sovereignty and the early modern foundations of the British Empire in India*, Oxford: Oxford University Press (2011); Philip Stern, *Empire, Incorporated: the corporations that built British colonialism*, Cambridge: Belknap Press (2023).
[65] David Harvey, *The New Imperialism*, Oxford: Oxford University Press (2003), pp. 137–82.
[66] David Adler and José Ahumada, 'Why is Biden Endorsing Corporate Colonialism in Honduras?', *LPE Blog*, 11/12/2023, https://lpeproject.org/blog/why-is-biden-endorsing-corporate-colonialism-in-honduras/.

do not provide exact predictions of tomorrow's weather'.[67] In similar vein, E P Thompson preferred the idea of 'logic of process' to that of 'laws of motion', arguing that it much better captured the idea that in 'historical analysis one may identify recurrent patterns of behaviour and sequences of events which may only be described (in a retrospective rather than in a predictive sense) as being causally related' without suggesting a prophetic and scientific determinism.[68] The idea of logic of process thus came closer to encompassing 'the distinctively human dialectic, by which history appears as neither willed nor as fortuitous; as neither *lawed* (in the sense of being determined by involuntary laws of motion) nor illogical (in the sense that one can observe a *logic* in the social process)'.[69] By replacing the notion of laws of motion with that of logic of process, Thompson argued, it was possible to construct metaphors that included the idea of causal relationships while excluding determinist, predictive connotations.[70] When Thompson sought to reveal the historically determining logic of production relations in his historical work, therefore, he used 'determining' in the sense elaborated by Raymond Williams as 'setting limits to' and 'exerting pressure on'.[71]

The moral logic of capitalism

While Thompson was anxious not to overstate the degree of determining force exercised by capitalist property rights structures, however, he was equally anxious not to understate the reach of their determinative power. He was relentlessly hostile to the theoretical reification of the base-superstructure metaphor, with its separation and elevation of 'the economic'.[72] In his view, it sought to capture the crucial dialectic between social being and social consciousness that lay 'at the heart of any comprehension of the historical

---

[67] Harvey, 'History versus Theory', p. 6.
[68] Thompson, 'Open Letter to Leszek Kolakowski', p. 120.
[69] Thompson, 'Peculiarities of the English', p. 81.
[70] Thompson, 'Open Letter', p. 120.
[71] Raymond Williams, *Marxism and Literature*, Oxford: Oxford University Press (1977), pp. 83–9; Thompson, 'Poverty of Theory', pp. 302, 351.
[72] In this respect, Thompson was in broad agreement with Colliot-Thélène when she wondered 'whether the supposed autonomy of the field of the Economic, that is, the attribution to the sphere of economic relations of an intrinsic legality which isolates it in an abstract way from the other modalities of social relations, in particular, the juridical and political modalities, is not an excessively narrow interpretation of the theses of historical materialism as they are presented in the first part of *The German Ideology* or in the classic formulation in the *Preface to a Contribution to the Critique of Political Economy*': Colliot-Thélène, 'Afterword', p. 428. She goes on to note that, for Marx, the separation of the economic was 'not a general rule, valid for all historical forms of social production, but, on the contrary, a property characteristic of commodity relations of production alone': p. 429.

process within the Marxist tradition', but with its mechanical overtones of construction engineering, it did so inadequately, freezing a fluent social process and offending the very sense of the inter-action of social being and social consciousness.[73] We needed to admit, he argued, that the base-superstructure 'signpost was pointing in the wrong direction, while at the same time accept[ing] the existence of the place towards which it was mispointing'.[74] Thompson preferred a metaphor Marx used in *Grundrisse* when he argued that

> in all forms of society there is one specific kind of production which predominates over the rest, whose relations thus assign rank and influence to the others. It is a general illumination which bathes all the other colours and modifies their particularity. It is a particular ether which defines the specific gravity of every being which has materialised within it.[75]

The 'general illumination' metaphor, he argued, not only better captured the more measured concept of determination elaborated by Williams, but it also highlighted that the determinative effects of capitalist property relations were *ubiquitous*, operating simultaneously in both the economic and non-economic spheres. For Thompson, capitalism possesses both 'an economic *and* a moral logic'; social and cultural phenomena do 'not trail after the economic at some remote remove' but are, 'at their source, immersed in the same nexus of relationship'.[76] These logics, he argued, are 'different expressions of the same kernel of human relationship', finding 'simultaneous expression ... in all systems and areas of social life', in norms and culture, and 'in characteristic values and modes of thought as well as in characteristic patterns of accumulation and exchange'.[77] We therefore needed to 'return to the full sense of a mode of production' and to recognise that a mode of production could not be described in purely 'economic' terms

---

[73] Thompson, 'Peculiarities of the English', p. 79.
[74] Thompson, 'Open Letter to Leszek Kolakowski', p. 120.
[75] Marx, *Grundrisse*, pp. 106–7. Thompson, 'History and Anthropology', pp. 218–19. Thompson offers a slightly different translation.
[76] E P Thompson, 'The Long Revolution – II', 10 *New Left Review*, pp. 34–9 (1961), p. 38; Thompson, 'Peculiarities of the English', p. 84; Thompson, 'History and Anthropology', pp. 218–22.
[77] Thompson, 'The Long Revolution II', p. 38. Thompson, 'History and Anthropology', p. 219. Thus, for Thompson, social transitions involved 'the whole culture': Thompson, 'Time, Work-Discipline and Industrial Capitalism', 38 *Past & Present*, pp. 56–97 (1967), p. 80. And the struggles over property were conflicts over the ideas and values as well as over legal rights.

'leaving aside as secondary (less "real") the norms, the culture, the critical concepts around which this mode of production is organised'.[78] Indeed, it was because the logic of capitalist process finds expression in so many social activities, impacts so much on human subjectivities ('human capital'), and exerts a determining pressure on so many aspects of social development that we were entitled to speak of *capitalism*, or of capitalist societies.[79] Arguably, the multiple dimensions of today's 'polycrisis' reflects the problems besetting capitalism as a social order rather than as a mere type of economy.[80]

From this perspective, it is the ever-present logic of historically specific sets of property relations, and the rules of reproduction with which they confront economic actors, that gives history shape, notwithstanding its specificities and notwithstanding human agency, making it possible to see it as a *structured process* rather than as a rigidly structured whole or as a series of random events. It is a structured process with human agencies that, while open-ended, is subject to determinate pressures. In this way, it is possible to give credence both to the logic of modes of production and to human agency within the conditions set by those logics. In doing this, we have to reject the idea, common under capitalism and central to neoliberal thought, that the 'economic' is, or could be, a somehow autonomous sphere, spatially separate from the political and social spheres.[81] We need, rather, to view the logics of process generated by property rights structures as operative

---

[78] Thompson, 'History and Anthropology', p. 219.

[79] Thompson, 'Poverty of Theory', p. 254. Thompson suggests that when Marx writes of the 'complicated bourgeois system' as a totality in *Grundrisse*, he moves across 'an invisible conceptual line from Capital (an abstraction from political economy, which is his proper concern) to capitalism … that is, the whole society'. This whole society, he adds, 'comprises many activities and relations (of power, of consciousness, sexual, cultural, normative) which are not the concern of political economy, which have been defined out of political economy. Therefore, political economy cannot show capitalism as "capital in the totality of its relations": it has no language or terms to do this. Only a historical materialism which could bring all activities and relations within a coherent view could do this': ibid, p. 254.

[80] The idea of a mode of production in its full sense can also help us grasp the different dimensions to and uses of the term 'neoliberalism', which have led some to reject it as a useful category of analysis. Neoliberalism has been variously deployed to describe a market fundamentalist intellectual project, a set of economic policies, and a range of cultural changes linked to growing commodification. Arguably, these different deployments of the term are best viewed as different aspects of *neoliberal capitalism* in the 'full sense'.

[81] Wood, *Democracy Against Capitalism*, pp. 49–75. The philosopher Tony Smith suggests that Marx was '*the* great critic of conceiving a depoliticised economic realm' (his emphasis). For Marx, the seeming separation of the political and economic spheres is 'an illusion, albeit one necessarily generated by the social relations of capitalist society': *Beyond Liberal Egalitarianism*, Chicago: Haymarket (2017), p. 189.

historical principles visible on a day-to-day basis in social life and in concrete institutions and practices, both within the sphere of production and beyond. The material 'base' of society is embodied not only in economic forms but in legal, political and ideological forms that cannot be relegated to a spatially separate, 'superstructural' sphere.[82] Streeck in many ways echoes this approach when he argues that capitalism 'is much more than a combination of private property rights and free markets, and indeed more than just an economy'. It is, rather, an 'institutionalized social order'.[83]

The moral dimensions of the logic of capitalism are implicit in its supporters' accounts of its economic functioning. Contained within them is an account of the kind of behaviour we should expect from economic actors, accounts that reveal a built-in tendency towards unethical behaviour. While some argue that this tendency is primarily attributable to the logic embedded in capitalism's property structures, for the defenders of capitalism it is rooted in human nature. Human beings are rational egoists who must be expected to strive to improve their position at the expense of others. It follows that, although they are supposed to abide by the rules of the game, rule makers and regulators should expect people to deal with these rules (including such things as labour standards, environmental regulations, tax laws and the like) in an instrumental manner, 'from the perspective of how they may be applied, avoided or circumvented for individual benefit'. As a result, 'rule makers cannot expect rule takers to interpret their rules in ways other than in *studied bad faith*'.[84] Indeed, not only is it perfectly 'natural' for people to seek to bend or avoid rules and to circumvent social obligations if it generates market and/or material advantage, but competition may compel them to do so. As Oliver Williamson explains, what we must expect, given the way capitalist competition operates, is institutionalised opportunism, deviousness and bad faith, what he refers to as 'self-interest seeking guile'[85], entailing 'calculated efforts to mislead, distort, disguise, obfuscate, or otherwise confuse'.[86] The inclination to avoid rules and social obligations is

---

[82] Hence Thompson's observation that in the eighteenth century law steadfastly refused to 'keep politely to a "level" but was at every bloody level': 'Poverty of Theory', p. 288. This conclusion is also to be found to *Whigs and Hunters*, where he wrote that analysis of the eighteenth century 'call[ed] into question the validity of separating off the law as a whole and placing it in some typological superstructure ... [for] law was deeply imbricated within the very basis of productive relations, which would have been inoperable without [it]': Thompson, *Whigs and Hunters*, pp. 260–1.
[83] Streeck, *Re-Forming Capitalism*, p. 3.
[84] Streeck, 'Taking Capitalism Seriously', pp. 143–4.
[85] Oliver Williamson, *Markets and Hierarchies: analysis and antitrust implications*, New York: Free Press (1975), p. 255.
[86] Oliver Williamson, *The Economic Institutions of Capitalism*, New York: Free Press (1985), p. 47.

not, of course, confined to capitalism. The difference is that, under capitalism, the ruthless and inventive pursuit of self-interest is in the spirit of the social order itself; it is 'both institutionally expected and empirically prevailing'.[87]

Focusing on the 'logics of process' generated by capitalism's property rights structures also highlights capitalism's dynamic nature. The property rights and institutional structures of empirically existing capitalism(s) are not static; they are always changing. As a result, so too are the specific logics of process by which empirically existing capitalisms operate. In the postwar period, for example, the operative logic of the system was identifiably 'capitalist', notwithstanding the relative strength of labour and the legal and other concessions it was able to extract (inequality and exploitation did not disappear), but for many years it operated in a constrained manner. Over the last half century, however, developments such as the reconcentration of corporate shareholders in large financial institutions and the liberalisation of finance, together with a series of other institutional changes to legal rights structures – some major, some minor – have contributed to a major shift in the balance of power between capital and labour and to changes in the system's dynamics. The logic of capitalism has come to operate in a much less restrained manner: a much 'purer' capitalist logic has emerged. Capitalism has, as Streeck says, become more capitalist; it has 're-formed', returning to its 'normal self'.[88] Moreover, as a result of privatisations and PPPs, this logic has extended its reach into ever more productive spheres and been intensified by the liberalisation of finance, which has made the political regulation and containment of capital so much harder. It has also spread its tentacles into more and more non-economic spheres. The idea that everything is 'capital' or is capable of being capital is a reflection of this, marking the spread and deepening of capitalist social relations and of the language of investment and capitalisation. The extension of this language to ourselves is a measure of the spread and depth of capitalism not only in the economic but also in the cultural sphere.

The intensification of capitalism's economic logic has been accompanied by an intensification of its moral logic. Outdoing and eliminating your rivals by fair or not-too-foul means has always been seen as legitimate. In recent decades, however, entrepreneurially and inventively twisting, avoiding or even breaking rules to one's advantage (preferably without getting caught) has come to be seen, often openly and publicly, not as something to be frowned upon or condemned, but as something to be admired in the unending drive to make ever more money. This was exemplified in one of the 2016 US presidential debates by Donald Trump's response to Hillary Clinton's

---

[87] Streeck, 'Taking Capitalism Seriously', p. 144.
[88] Streeck, 'Taking Capitalism Seriously', pp. 142-44.

claim that he had not paid federal income taxes for a number of years: 'That makes me smart'.[89] It has become part of the system's ethos. The operation of contemporary capitalism encourages what the conservative German economist Götz Briefs has called 'marginal ethics' (*grenzmoral*). These are

> the ethics of those least restrained in the competitive struggle by moral inhibitions, that is of those who because of their minimal ethics have under otherwise equal conditions the best chances of success and who on this account force competing groups, at the penalty of elimination from competition, gradually to adapt in their trading to the respectively lowest level of social ethics (i.e. to the 'marginal ethics').[90]

Indeed, these marginal ethics become so culturally entrenched that people often operate far more unethically than competitive survival and success requires.[91] As Streeck observes, 'the normalized actor under capitalism is someone who does not relent in his [or her] effort to get richer regardless of what he has already achieved; for him "the sky is the limit", and there is no pre-established point where he has "had enough" or is institutionally expected to have enough'.[92]

The problem is that this sort of behaviour risks undermining the very system of which it is part. To function smoothly, capitalism needs some degree of mutual trust, reciprocity, solidarity and goodwill; it needs to be thought, at least to a degree, to be 'just'; and, perhaps, needs at least some agreement on some matters about what constitutes truth. But these are all being eroded. Moreover, as it overdoses on itself, capitalism is also putting the very survival of the planet at risk. Its logic might, theoretically at least, be compatible with gender and racial equality, but it increasingly seems to be fundamentally incompatible with environmental preservation. In principle, capital is indifferent to the social identities of the people from whom it profits: the idea of the formally free and equal individual does not presuppose differences in legal or political status. Indeed, there has been a tendency within many capitalisms for such differences to be eroded. This is not to say, of course, that capital does not make use of existing social hierarchies and oppressions. On the contrary, in practice, it ruthlessly and opportunistically exploits gender and race divisions wherever it can. Environmental preservation, however, is a different

---

[89] Luke Harding, 'As Donald Trump made clear, smart businesses know only idiots pay taxes', *The Guardian*, 16/10/2016.
[90] Quoted in Streeck, 'Taking Capitalism Seriously', p. 145.
[91] The Panama and Paradise papers provide examples of this: many of the people involved are so rich their tax-avoidance schemes seem superfluous.
[92] Streeck, 'Taking Capitalism Seriously', p. 149.

matter. It may be possible to reform the institutional arrangements that make it possible for corporations to externalise costs, and it may be possible for capitalism to accommodate some degree of environmental care, especially where technologies of environmental protection can be profitably developed and marketed. But the system's logic of process, with its competitive drive for constant expansion and accumulation, appears to render capitalism, even at the theoretical level, at odds with environmental protection and the long-term preservation of the essential pre-conditions of life.

The coercive logic of the property system as currently configured means that one simply cannot rely on economic actors to exercise self-restraint in the name of the collective interest. On the contrary, in the current, financially liberalised environment, in which capital has largely freed itself from the restraining hand of the nation state, adhering to ethical norms and taking account of the collective interest when those around you are ignoring them is likely to prove a recipe for failure. It is not merely that the benefits of bending and circumventing rules and avoiding social obligations are often considerable, but that the costs of failing to do so may be even greater. Having moral scruples – or, in the corporate context, seeking to act in a socially and environmentally responsible manner and failing relentlessly to profit maximise – might prove not merely disadvantageous but self-destructive. While, therefore, we must never forget the importance of human agency, we must do so without abandoning the idea of structural determinations. Property rights structures exert a determinative force in the sense that they generate specific logics of economic process, historically specific economic rationalities, which exert pressure on actors and place limits on the strategies available to them. In today's financialised system of corporate governance, for example, it is not enough for the executives of large firms merely to produce at a competitive price and generate profits. They have to generate profits good enough to satisfy institutional investors and financial markets. This confronts them as a pre-requisite of personal survival, an imperative imposed on them behind their backs regardless of their own personal needs or moralities, or whether they are selfish and greedy or altruistic. Even the most upright and socially responsible executive is subject to these pressures: their room for manoeuvre is limited. These pressures are, of course, reinforced by corporate incentive structures. For this reason, the moral philosopher Alasdair MacIntyre argues that some, like those engaged in finance, are, ethically speaking, lost causes. Because of the requirements of their job, he suggests, teaching ethics to traders is as pointless as reading Aristotle to your dog.[93]

---

[93] John Cornwell, 'MacIntyre on Money', *Prospect Magazine*, November 2010. On the ethics of traders, see Gary Stevenson, *The Trading Game*.

As Lazzarato says, 'in capitalism there are no longer "values", there is only "value"'.[94]

The ethics of today's highly financialised capitalism were exemplified by some of the practices preceding the financial crash of 2008, and neatly encapsulated by the case of Fabrice Tourre, one of the relatively small number of individuals held accountable for wrongdoing in its aftermath. Tourre, a Goldman Sachs trader, was the only individual charged in the SEC's fraud case against the firm. He created, on Goldman's behalf, a synthetic collaterialised debt obligation (CDO), a vehicle holding derivatives that enabled investors to make leveraged bets on the loans the derivatives were tied to. It was filled with toxic sub-prime mortgages. Goldman did not tell investors in the CDO that a Goldman Sachs client, hedge fund manager John Paulsen, had helped to select the sub-prime mortgages, nor that he was betting against the loans. The CDO ended up making about $1 billion for Paulson, millions of dollars in fees for Goldman, and, according to the SEC, helped Tourre earn a bonus that boosted his salary to $1.7 million in 2007. A court later held that Tourre sold the CDOs to investors despite knowing they were doomed to fail. In private emails to his girlfriend, he remarked that 'the whole building is about to collapse anytime now ... Only potential survivor, the fabulous Fab[rice Tourre] ... standing in the middle of all these complex, highly leveraged, exotic trades he created without understanding all the implications of these monstrousities [sic]!!'. He knew the 'poor little subprime borrowers [wouldn't] last long' but nevertheless boasted of selling them 'to widows and orphans'. He did not 'fee[l] too guilty about this', however, because, after all, 'the real purpose of [the] job is to make capital markets more efficient and ultimately provide the U.S. consumer with more efficient ways to leverage and finance himself, so there is a humble, noble and ethical reason for my job ... amazing how good I am in convincing myself!!!' In an earlier email sent in March 2007, he referred to the financial products he worked on as 'pure intellectual masturbation, the type of thing which you invent telling yourself: "Well, what if we created a "thing", which has no purpose, which is absolutely conceptual and highly theoretical and which nobody knows how to price?"' Tourre was eventually fined over $800k for defrauding investors in a sub-prime mortgage product. The judge commented that he showed 'no remorse or contrition'.[95]

---

[94] Lazzarato, *Governing by Debt*, p. 143.
[95] See Cedric Durand, *Fictitious Capital*, London: Verso (2017), p. 12; Jennifer Hughes, 'How fabulous Fab and 2008 still haunt markets', *Financial Times*, 7/4/2023; 'Goldman Sachs trader found guilty of fraud', *The Guardian*, 1/8/2013: Tourre is currently assistant professor of economics and finance at Baruch College, City University of New York.

Changing the logic: gradual transformative change?

It is not the purpose of this book to provide a blueprint for an alternative set of property institutions, let alone a ready-made utopia. Truly radical change is likely to generate social practices and arrangements that are so different from our own that they are not only hard to imagine but incapable of being captured by existing conceptual categories.[96] My analysis does, however, have implications for how we think about change and for how we assess the potential effectiveness and impact of different sorts of reforms. To conclude the book, therefore, I want briefly to explore some of these implications, albeit in a suggestive rather than systematic manner, with a view to sketching in general terms what seems to me to be the desired trajectory for change.

One of the clear implications is that better 'regulation', coupled with a few, relatively modest institutional reforms and improvements, is unlikely to cut much mustard. Much more radical reform is needed. Many have expressed grave doubts about the likelihood of such reform, no matter how bad things get. Streeck, for example, argues that 'the stability of capitalism as a socio-economic system depends on its *Eigendynamic* being contained by countervailing forces' but that in recent decades capital has liberated itself from these forces, so there is now little left to temper its excesses and secure its long-term survival. He sees little likelihood of economic recovery in the developed world, expects social divisions to widen and fears for the future of democracy, but sees little prospect of meaningful change in the absence of agents to realise it. 'Is there anything on the horizon', he asked, that could 'break the trend of the past three decades toward an ever more unstable, unpredictable, uncontrollable – in other words, ever more capitalist – global capitalism, with an ever more unequal distribution ... of wealth and risks and opportunities and life chances? I see nothing'.[97] Although he recognises that capitalism has shown itself to be incredibly resilient and is mindful of the numerous premature announcements of its death, Streeck believes that 'this time is different'. With even its master technicians not having a clue what to do, capitalism is 'collapsing by itself' and we have, therefore, to start thinking of it 'as a historical phenomenon ... that has a beginning, but also an end'[98] and to shed the prejudice that

---

[96] See Ireland and Meng, 'Post-Capitalist Property', pp. 391–3. 'Since we can speak of what transcends the present only in the language of the present, we risk cancelling out our imaginings in the very act of articulating them': Terry Eagleton, 'Utopia and its Opposites', *Socialist Register*, 2000, p. 31.
[97] Streeck, *The Current Moment*.
[98] Streeck, 'How Will Capitalism End?', 87 *New Left Review*, pp. 35–64 (May–June 2014), pp. 45–6. It is, Streeck writes, 'a Marxist – or better: modernist – prejudice that capitalism as a historical epoch will end only when a new, better society is in sight, and a revolutionary

capitalism as a historical epoch will end only when a new, better society is in sight. We need to learn to 'think about capitalism coming to an end without assuming responsibility for answering the question of what one proposes to put in its place'. It is not the job of social scientists 'to make people feel good ... [but] to speak the truth'.[99]

Others are also pessimistic about the prospects for radical change, though less gloomy than Streeck. David Harvey argues that capitalism's survival will

> require the mass of the people to give generously of the fruits of their labour to those in power, to surrender many of their rights and their hard won asset values (in everything from houses to pension rights) and to suffer environmental degradations galore, to say nothing of serial reductions in their living standards which will mean starvation for many of those already struggling to survive at rock bottom.

More than a little 'political repression, police violence and militarised state control' is likely to be required 'to stifle the ensuing unrest'. This leads him to wonder whether 'where we are at now' is 'the beginning of a prolonged shake-out in which the question of grand and far-reaching alternatives will gradually bubble up to the surface in one part of the world or another'. The 'longer the uncertainty and misery are prolonged', he suggests, the more the legitimacy of the existing state of affairs is likely to be questioned and 'the more the demand to build something radically different will escalate'.[100]

It would be easy to conclude from this that that nothing less than revolutionary upheaval, in which one set of property institutions is replaced, more or less *en bloc*, by another, will suffice. This is reflected in a tendency (not least among those seeking to defend the property status quo) to depict the choice as a simple one between private ownership of the means of production (and markets) and public or state ownership (and central planning).[101] Now,

---

subject ready to implement it for the advancement of mankind. This presupposes a degree of political control over our common fate of which we cannot even dream after the destruction of collective agency': ibid, p. 46.

[99] Streeck, 'How Will Capitalism End?', p. 46; Streeck, 'Politics in the Interregnum: Q&A with Wolfgang Streeck', *ROAR Magazine*, 23/12/2015, https://roarmag.org/essays/wolfgang-streeck-capitalism-democracy-interview/.

[100] David Harvey, *The Enigma of Capital*, London: Profile Books (2010), pp. 216, 225.

[101] Although it is often attributed to him, Marx seems on at least one occasion to have firmly rejected the idea of replacing capitalist private property in the means of production by state-owned property, arguing that 'crude communism' of this sort merely turned the 'community' into a 'universal capitalist': Karl Marx, *Economic and Philosophical Manuscripts*, London: Lawrence & Wishart (ed Dirk Struik, 1970 [1844]), p. 135. He argued instead for the simultaneous establishment of 'socialised property' and 'individual property': see Ireland and Meng, 'Post-Capitalist Property'.

it might, indeed, turn out to be the case, as Lazzarato suggests, that 'reform has become impossible' and that only revolution will suffice.[102] We need to remember, however, firstly, that the range of institutional possibility is much wider than the simple private versus state ownership dichotomy suggests[103]; and, secondly, that, historically, social transformations have often been the result not of compacted revolutionary moments but of multiple micro-changes over an extended period of time. They have been processes rather than events. In this context, we also need to remind ourselves that the logics of the process of empirically existing capitalisms are not constant and unchanging, but constantly changing. As we have seen, in the last half century or so a wide range of legal and other changes have seen the logic of contemporary capitalism modified, intensified and extended – to the benefit of owners of property-as-capital and to the detriment of the great majority. Can this logic be gradually and incrementally changed once more or even transformed and/or replaced?

The bundle of rights and social relational conceptions of property arguably show how this might be possible. By highlighting the socially constructed and malleable nature of property rights and the role played by law in constituting them, they highlight law's role in creating the logic that drives contemporary capitalism and its potential role in changing this logic.[104] This was one of the key insights animating the CLS movement of the 1980s and 90s and is one of the key insights animating both the LPE and the 'new' legal institutionalist movements of today.[105] It was also one of the implicit messages of the 'old' institutional economist, lawyer, and early Legal Realist Robert Lee Hale, whose work in the first half of the twentieth century influenced the CLS movement and continues to be influential today. Hale was one of those writing in the early twentieth century who stressed that neither property nor markets are natural phenomena but are, to a significant extent, politically and legally constructed, and that there is, therefore, no such thing as a purely 'economic' rationality or distribution of income and wealth.[106]

---

[102] Lazzarato, *Governing by Debt*, p. 40. Capitalism's post-war reformist period, he suggests, 'represents a very minor parenthesis in the history of capitalism'.

[103] A point repeatedly made by Roberto Unger. See his *The Left Alternative*, London: Verso (2005).

[104] For warnings about overstating the constitutive role of law, see Matthew Dimick, "Without Remainder: law and the constitution of economy and society', *Legal Form Forum*, 11/7/2022, https://legalform.blog/2022/07/11/without-remainder-law-social-constitution-adorno-kant-hale-dimick/.

[105] See, for example, Deakin et al, 'Legal Institutionalism'.

[106] See Hale, 'Coercion and Distribution in a Supposedly Non-Coercive State'; see also Barbara Fried, *The Progressive Assault on Laissez-Faire*, Cambridge: Harvard University Press (2001). Even his intellectual opponents concede that Hale was 'one of the most formidable and persistent foes of laissez faire' and that he has 'long been an intellectual

Hale further argued that markets are realms of coercion as well as of freedom, sites where people exercise power over one another. To reproduce themselves, producers and workers have little choice but to engage in market exchange. In doing this they exercise their freedom, but there are always 'background constraints' on the choices available to them. Some of these background constraints emanate from phenomena such as market conditions and the supply and demand for particular products (like labour), but some of them, Hale argued, emanate from the many legal and other rules that shape market bargaining. The most important of these are the legal rules relating to property, for private property rights give their holders the coercive power to exclude and withhold, enabling them, in effect, to determine whether or not the use of their property by others is lawful and to impose terms on those others as the price of making it so.[107] In the network of coercive pressures and counter pressures that make up markets, Hale wrote, 'each pressure consist[s] in the last analysis either of the power to lock or unlock the bars which the law erects against the non-owners of each piece of property, or else of the power to withhold or not to withhold labour'.[108] Owners of productive resources (machinery, buildings, knowledge) can exclude others from access to them; workers can exclude others from access to their labour power. In market exchanges each side is, therefore, to a degree, constrained and coerced by the other. Coercive power is not one-sided; the power of one party is nearly always countered to some degree by the power of the other. This led Hale to conclude that coercion is *ubiquitous*; that all markets are 'structures of mutual coercion', subtly constituted by 'the particular legal rights with which the law endows [some], and the legal restrictions which it places on others'.[109] The coercive power possessed by the parties may be roughly equal, as is often the case when two commercial parties interact, or it might be highly unequal, as if often the case with capital and labour. The

---

thorn in the side of [its] defenders': Richard Epstein, 'The Assault that Failed: The Progressive Critique of Laissez Faire', 97 *Michigan Law Review*, pp. 1697–721 (1999). To prove just how formidable Hale's intellect was, Epstein offers a lengthy 'critique' that leaves Hale's deconstruction of laissez faire largely untouched.

[107] Hale, 'Coercion and Distribution in a Supposedly Non-Coercive State', pp. 472–3.

[108] Robert Hale, 'Economics and Law', in William Ogburn and Alexander Goldenweiser (eds), *The Social Sciences and their Interrelations*, London: Allen & Unwin, pp. 131–42 (1927), p. 138. On occasions Hale used terms other than 'coercion' to try to convey the same meaning: 'compulsion', 'pressure', 'force', 'influence', 'duress' and sometimes even 'oppression'. His use of the term 'coercion', he said, was not intended to suggest the use of direct physical compulsion or deprivation of all choice, nor to carry the 'stigma of impropriety'.

[109] Robert Hale, 'Bargaining, Duress and Economic Liberty', 43 *Columbia Law Review*, pp. 603–28 (1943), p. 625.

greater the differences in bargaining power, the greater the ability of one party to exercise coercive power over and to exploit the other. As Hale observed, the bargaining power of parties and distributional outcomes are also affected by other bodies of law: from the laws governing the movement (free or otherwise) of capital and labour to those governing the right of workers to organise; from the general rules of contract and tort to the rules governing the individual contract of employment; from the rules governing the economic torts to those relating to welfare rights and the right to strike, secondary picketing, lockouts, minimum wages. In this way, as some CLSers highlighted, Hale demonstrated the role played by law in shaping market processes and distributional outcomes – and in constituting both the general operating logic of the system and the specific ways that logic operates in particular capitalisms. In doing this, he not only enriched our understanding of the role of law in shaping social dynamics and the distribution of income and wealth, but its potential role in effecting changes to those dynamics and distributions.[110]

A Haleian approach to thinking about change was recently adopted by Jean-Philippe Robé in his analysis of the 'World Power System' and the climate crisis. The World Power System, Robé argues, 'is a combination of large- and small-scale powers, of macro- and micro-authorities', which are to be found not only in the economic sphere but also in all kinds of social institutions, from families to schools to armies. In Robé's view, this power system is 'out-of-control'. The question is, how can we get it to evolve and 'find levers to guide this evolution'? Addressing the specific and urgent issue of climate change, he does not dismiss the need for radical changes to the property rights structures surrounding productive activity, but argues that the urgency of the climate crisis means there is insufficient time to 'change everything' and that we have try to work from '*within* the system that is already there'. To do this, we have to focus on the 'detail' of its operation and try to identify micro-changes that will have an immediate impact on the system's dynamics. Against that backdrop, Robé argues that there are certain accounting changes – that, he suggests, could be 'decided overnight by G7' – that would have an immediate impact by altering the way the logic of the system operates in relation to climate change. As things stand, Robé argues, certain natural resources can be consumed by business enterprises without cost and without financial consequences, for the accounting rules currently address only the preservation of financial capital at the expense of the preservation of natural environmental 'capital', such as the ability of the environment to absorb CO^2. Robé therefore advocates changes to the rules on accounting that would force firms to internalise the costs associated with

---

[110] Duncan Kennedy led the way here: see 'The Stakes of Law; or Hale and Foucault!

their productive activities by 'enlarg[ing] the notion of capital to include the preservation of our CO^2 budget'. Such full-cost accounting, he argues, would deprioritise, at least to a degree, the preservation of financial property above all else. The underlying idea is to 'use the forces of capitalism in favor of sustainability by changing the computation of profit', so that the level of profit would depend on the preservation of CO^2.[111]

Of course, identifying pathways to change is one thing, bringing them about is quite another. Even the more modest, within-system changes advocated by Robé – let alone the more radical, system-transformative changes that are, in my view, required – are likely to meet with fierce opposition from the wealthy and the corporations who benefit handsomely from the property status quo and from the changes made to it over the last half century. The latter are likely to be supported by many working in the mainstream media outlets and think-tanks that these people increasingly own, control and/or finance and that do so much to shape public opinion and public policy, and by their well-paid 'agents of wealth protection'. And there will always, of course, be academic voices available to defend the status quo and to oppose meaningful change. In similar vein, while the idea of introducing a positive social obligation norm into property law, particularly in relation to important productive resources, has much to commend it, it too would not only be likely to encounter serious opposition were it to become a real possibility but also struggle to have much effect on a productive sphere dominated by ruthless, profit-seeking multi-national enterprises and financial institutions. The economic pressures, incentive structures and moral logic of the property system of contemporary capitalism would in most cases almost certainly overwhelm any such norms. For measures of this sort to have a real impact, their introduction would have to be preceded or accompanied by a range of reforms to existing property rights structures that alter or diminish the force and scope of the pressures currently faced by those managing key productive resources.

Realising transformative change will, therefore, be a difficult, complex and multi-dimensional task. As David Harvey says, we need to develop 'a sophisticated understanding of how social change occurs'. To this end, Harvey has proposed a 'co-evolutionary' theory of (and approach to) change that identifies seven 'activity spheres', all of which, he says, have to be acted in and upon by those seeking social transformation. Although Harvey does not wish to give priority to any of these spheres, suggesting that transformative change could start in any of them, it is significant that he argues that a 'whole new conception of property' is a pre-requisite of radical change and that

---

[111] Jean-Philippe Robé, 'Property, Power and Politics Reviewed – A Reply to Critics', 3 *Journal of Political Economy*, pp. 592–602 (2023).

existing property forms have to be challenged head on if existing class power is effectively to be challenged.[112]

Thinking in terms of system logics can help us to identify the kinds of changes to property rights, particularly in productive resources, that might set us on the right path. Radical reform does not mean abolishing private property in personal possessions or striving for an economic system without markets or any private ownership of productive resources.[113] What it does mean, in general terms, is recognising the *social* nature of production in today's globalised capitalism and finding ways to 'socialise' key productive activities. It means making production less subject to the power of capital, reducing the scope for profiting from the efforts of others, loosening and constraining the imperatives imposed by the market, and widening the scope for self-mastery and individual and collective agency by fostering the development of more inclusive, participatory and co-operative productive enterprises and decision-making processes. It means, in other words, striving to enhance individual freedom and retaining what Marx called 'the positive essence of private property',[114] while at the same creating more space for the collective pursuit of solutions to societal issues and problems and more space for the realisation of the goals and values identified by progressive property theorists – community, solidarity, human flourishing, equality, environmental stewardship, civic responsibility. It means trying to get the out-of-control 'World Power System' back under some degree of control and creating a world in which social relations are more transparent.

There are many different ways that the abstract idea of 'socialisation' could be given definite form, many different measures, of varying degrees of radicalism, that could contribute to its realisation. In the UK, for example, it is not difficult to make a strong case for the deprivatisation of key utilities, for it is very hard credibly to claim that the privatisation of areas such as rail and water has generated greater 'efficiency' and better service provision, let alone the kind of investments needed to upgrade, modernise and 'green' these sectors. Privatisation has, rather, led to ruthless profit extraction (usually underwritten by state subsidies), often declining services, frequent company

---

[112] Harvey, *The Enigma of Capital*, pp. 228, 233.
[113] Nor is it to say that markets could not or should not be used to exert some pressure on producers to operate with minimum levels of productive efficiency. In this context, it is worth considering the distinction drawn by Wood between the market as opportunity and the market as imperative: *The Origin of Capitalism*.
[114] Marx firmly rejected the 'abstract negation' of private property, arguing that this would entail the negation of the 'entire world of culture and civilisation [and] regression to the unnatural simplicity of the poor and undemanding man who has not only failed to go beyond private property, but has not yet even reached it': Marx, *Economic and Philosophical Manuscripts*, pp. 133–5.

collapses and under-investment. Britain's infrastructure is slowly crumbling. The privatisation of municipal service provision and part privatisation of healthcare could also be reversed to remove them from realms where the logic of financial profit is dominant.

The operation of the financialised logic of contemporary capitalism needs, however, to be softened or, better still, more fundamentally modified beyond the sphere of public utilities and services. The process of change needs to encompass the large enterprises that now dominate production globally. These firms also need to be 'socialised' or part socialised. When key productive resources are privately owned, a wedge is placed between production and the satisfaction of needs (individual and social), for the latter is mediated by the drive to generate a financial return for the passive owners of property-as-capital. As things stand, privately owned productive resources can only be mobilised if their owners believe there is a reasonable prospect of a satisfactory financial return, as highlighted by the rise of states for whom industrial policy increasingly centres on derisking private investments. When ownership is highly financialised, as it is today, the wedge is even bigger, something likely to become a growing problem as we try to deal with the climate crisis.

There are many positive within-system reforms that could be introduced. Bans could be placed on share buy-backs; corporate taxation could be reformed; measures could be taken to deal with corporate tax avoidance (by, among other things, developing a legal concept of 'the enterprise' that brings law in closer touch with empirical reality); executive compensation could be much more tightly regulated (controls on share-price-related compensation, prohibitions on 'golden parachutes' and so on). Employee share ownership plans (ESOPs) or 'inclusive ownership funds' could be introduced.[115] Shareholder voting rights could be differentiated and made subject to minimum holding period requirements.[116] Corporate accounting could be reformed to encompass externalities along the lines suggested by Robé.

More radically, the line of thinking about the fundamentally passive, rentier nature of corporate shareholding, which began with Adam Smith and can be traced through Marx, Veblen, Tawney, Keynes and many others,

---

[115] As proposed by the Labour Party in 2019, these would have required 10 per cent of the shares in all UK companies with more than 250 employees to be owned by inclusive ownership funds.

[116] On differentiated shareholder voting rights, see Colin Mayer, *Firm Commitment*, Oxford: Oxford University Press (2013); Lynne Dallas and Jordan Barry, 'Long-Term Shareholders and Time-Phased Voting', 40 *Delaware Journal of Corporate Law*, pp. 541–646 (2016).

could be resuscitated;[117] corporate shareholders could be recategorised as creditors rather than 'owners' and public corporations reconceptualised, as Berle and Means suggested, as social or quasi-social institutions. This would clear the way for a reallocation of corporate control and revenue rights and for the development of new corporate rights structures and new forms of multi-stakeholder governance.[118] Codetermination systems could be developed; the fiduciary duties of managers could be amended. A long list of possible reforms could be drawn up. Some would be more impactful than others, but they could all contribute in some way to changing the logic by which productive enterprises operate by moving us away from the ideology of shareholder primacy and the idea of corporations as purely private enterprises. Experimentation will be crucial. There are many public and quasi-public, more stakeholder-oriented forms of ownership and governance that could be tried. Moreover, it is not as though opportunities to socialise or part socialise some of these industries do not keep presenting themselves and will not continue to do so in the future given the reliance of so many large companies on public support and subsidies and the frequency with which financial crises are occurring, companies collapsing and bailouts having to be administered. A major opportunity to socialise key areas of finance presented itself after the 2008 crash, for example, but was spurned. Existing (private) property rights structures were maintained at huge public cost.

At the same time, the experimental development of alternative, bottom-up, more inclusive, democratic and participatory organisational forms less subject to a profit-oriented logic (or not subject to it at all) could be encouraged. While remaining mindful of capitalism's remarkable capacity to drive out or to impose its logic on other social forms, we should be fostering social enterprises, municipal and community-led ownership forms aimed at community wealth-building, co-operatives of various types (consumer, worker, housing, producer, marketing), benefit corporations (B corps) and so on.[119] In other contexts, as Elinor Ostrom has shown, people in small communities have successfully managed and shared natural resources like fishing waters, forests and pastures, developing rules for how they should be cared for and used in ways that are both economically and environmentally

---

[117] See Tawney, *The Acquisitive Society*; Laski, *A Grammar of Politics*, Goyter, *The Responsible Company*.

[118] See Lorraine Talbot, *Progressive Corporate Governance for the 21st Century*, London: Routledge (2013); Lenore Palladino, 'Economic Policies for Innovative Enterprises: implementing multi-stakeholder corporate governance' 54 *Review of Radical Political Economics*, pp. 5–25 (2021).

[119] See Nina Boeger and Charlotte Villiers (eds), *Shaping the Corporate Landscape: towards corporate reform and enterprise diversity*, London: Bloomsbury (2018).

sustainable.[120] It is also important to remember that there is no reason why the bundles of rights that make up 'ownership' of particular resources could not be spread between individuals and collective entities, as in the Chinese household responsibility system (HRS), the peasant-led, bottom-up development that did so much to increase agricultural productivity and to lay the foundations for China's economic rise. By dividing the rights in the ownership bundle (Honoré's incidents of ownership) and allocating them variously and with restrictions to individual households and collective bodies, the HRS provided individual farmers with incentives to increase productivity within a broad framework of collective control. The HRS shows how thinking in terms of 'property' and 'ownership' and 'sole and despotic dominion' by individual persons (private or public) can narrow perceptions of the range of institutional possibility by unhelpfully encouraging dichotomised thinking in which individually/privately-owned property is juxtaposed with communally/publicly/state-owned property and free markets with state planning. The range of possibility is much wider and more varied than many appreciate. Freed, even if only in part, from the seeming inexorable force of 'the market' and the imperatives of capitalist accumulation, the scope for people to make their own history could be greatly expanded.[121] We also clearly need to tackle the increasingly unequal distribution of property and wealth (and, therefore, of power), not just for its own sake but to facilitate reform. Wealth taxes of the sort recommended by Piketty, difficult though they would be to achieve, would be welcome, both for reducing inequality and for curbing the power of money over public opinion, politics and policy-making.[122]

While effecting radical change will not, of course, be easy, there is no doubt that in the developed world concern about and dissatisfaction with the system is growing, even among its supporters.[123] At the moment, however, reflecting perhaps the multi-pronged nature of the crisis, the oppositional forces are fragmented, tending to focus on specific issues like climate change and the environment, or gender and racial equality, or economic stagnation and the cost of living, or housing, pensions, inter-generational justice and the like. This fragmentation has damaged our sense of solidarity and

---

[120] Ostrom, *Governing the Commons*. More concretely, we clearly need to tackle the increasingly unequal distribution of property and wealth (and, therefore, of power) not just for its own sake but to facilitate reform. Wealth taxes of the sort recommended by Piketty, difficult though they would be to achieve, would be welcome, both for reducing inequality and for curbing the power of money over public opinion, politics and policy making.

[121] Ireland and Meng, 'Post-Capitalist Property'; Unger, *The Left Alternative*.

[122] See Jane Mayer, *Dark Money*, New York: Doubleday (2016).

[123] See for example, Martin Wolf, *The Crisis of Democratic Capitalism*, London: Allen Lane (2023). Wolf is chief economics commentator of the *Financial Times*.

collective agency. Indeed, some are actively fomenting division, deflecting and distracting, scapegoating, depicting the poly-crisis as a product of 'rampant' uncontrolled immigration, or welfare scroungers, or 'wokism' leading to cultural disintegration, or to overspending and market-interfering governments. Only very occasionally is the finger pointed at the socio-economic system, its property rights structures and class relations, or at rapacious corporations and financiers and the uber-wealthy. Both elite and popular understandings of the causes of our woes tend to downplay or deny altogether the problems arising out of capitalism itself. Politicians and policy makers are eschewing serious consideration of how contemporary capitalism might radically be reformed, focusing instead on keeping the system going by helping property-as-capital to find new profitable outlets for investment and identifying ways in which people might be made to adapt to it.

It is because of the demonstrable, multiple failures of contemporary financialised capitalism that we need to challenge the property status quo and the increasingly socially and environmentally destructive logic of process it generates. It is because of this that the way in which we conceptualise property – property 'framing' – is important. We need to think about property, and particularly property-as-capital, less in terms of simple (often reified) 'things' and thing-ownership and more in terms of rights bundles and social relations. Only then will we develop a better understanding of how our property system works in empirical reality, and of the links between the riches of the wealthy and the efforts, labour and lack of wealth of the great majority. We need, in other words, to stop 'seeing through' property as thing-ownership in the sense of using it as the only eyes through which we see the world, and to start 'seeing through' it in the sense of penetrating it and seeing what lies behind it.

References

Adams H C, *Public Debts: a study in the science of finance*, New York: Appleton (1887).
Adkins L, Cooper M, and Konings M, 'Class in the 21st Century: asset inflation and the new logic of inequality', 53 *Environment and Planning A: Economy and Space*, pp. 548–572 (2021).
Adkins L, 'How Wealth Inequalities are Made: an interview with Céline Bessière and Sibylle Gollac', 38 *Australian Feminist Studies*, pp.1–16 (2023).
Adler D and Ahumada J, 'Why is Biden Endorsing Corporate Colonialism in Honduras?', LPE Blog, 11/12/23.
Albert M, 'The *Howey* test turns 64', 2 *William & Mary Business Law Review*, pp. 1–50 (2011).
Alchian A and Demsetz H, 'Production, Information Costs and Economic Organization', 62 *American Economic Review*, pp. 777–795 (1972).
Alexander G, *Commodity and Propriety: competing visions of property in American legal thought*, Chicago: Chicago University Press (1997).
Alexander G, 'Property as a Fundamental Constitutional Right? The German Example', 88 *Cornell Law Review*, pp. 733–778 (2003).
Alexander G, 'The Social-Obligation Norm in American Property', 94 *Cornell Law Review*, pp. 745–819 (2009).
Alexander G, Peñalver E, Singer J W and Underkuffler L, 'A Statement of Progressive Property', *Cornell Law Faculty Publications*, Paper 11 (2009).
Alschuler A, 'Rediscovering Blackstone', 145 *University of Pennsylvania Law Review*, pp. 1–55 (1996).
Alvaredo F, Atkinson A B, and Morelli S, 'The Challenge of measuring UK wealth inequality in the 2000s', *LSE International Inequalities Institute*, Working Paper 4 (December 2015).
Alvaredo F, Garbini B, and Piketty T, 'On the Share of Inheritance in Aggregate Wealth', 84 *Economica*, pp. 239–260 (2017).
Anderson E, *Private Government: how employers rule our lives (and why we don't talk about it)*, Princeton: Princeton University Press (2017).
Angus I, 'The Meaning of So-called Primitive Accumulation', 74 *Monthly Review*, (April 2023).

Appadurai A, 'Afterword: the dreamwork of capitalism', 35 *Comparative Studies of South Asia, Africa and the Middle East*, pp. 481–85 (2015).

Applebaum E and Batt R, *Private Equity at Work*, New York: Russell Sage (2014).

Arbogast T, 'Who are These Bond Vigilantes Anyway? The Political Economy of Sovereign Debt Ownership in the Eurozone', *MpIfG Discussion Paper 20/2* (2020).

Aristotle, *Politics*, Oxford: Oxford University Press (revised ed. 2009).

Aristotle, *Nicomachean Ethics*, Oxford: Oxford University Press (revised ed. 2009).

Atiyah P S A, *The Rise & Fall of Freedom of Contract*, Oxford: Oxford University Press (1979).

Atkinson A B, 'Wealth and Inheritance in Britain from 1896 to the Present', 16 *Journal of Economic Inequality*, pp. 137–169 (2018).

Austin J, *Lectures on Jurisprudence*, volume 2, London: John Murray (4th ed., ed Robert Campbell, 1873).

Aylmer G E, 'The Meaning and Definition of "Property" in Seventeenth-Century England', 86 *Past and Present*, pp. 87–97 (1980).

Babie P A, 'A Great Exploitation: the true legacy of property – a review essay', 31 *International Journal of the Semiotics of Law*, pp. 977–993 (2018).

Backus M et al, 'Common Ownership in America, 1980–2017', 13 *American Economic Journal: Microeconomics*, pp. 273–308 (2021).

Baines J and Hager S, 'From Passive Owners to Planet Savers? Asset Managers, Carbon Majors and the Limits of Sustainable Finance', 27 *Competition and Change*, pp. 449–471 (2023).

Baker J H, *An Introduction to English Legal History*, Oxford: Oxford University Press (5th ed., 2019).

Banaji J, *Theory as History: essays on modes of production and exploitation*, Leiden: Brill (2010).

Banaji J, *A Brief History of Commercial Capitalism*, Haymarket: Chicago (2019).

Banner S, *American Property*, Cambridge: Harvard University Press (2011).

Barker T, 'Some Questions about Political Capitalism', 140/41 *New Left Review*, pp. 35–51 (March–June 2023).

Baron J, 'The Contested Commitments of Property', 61 *Hastings Law Journal*, pp. 917–967 (2010).

Becker L, 'Too Much Property', 21 *Philosophy & Public Affairs*, pp. 196–206 (1992).

Beckert J, *Imagined Futures: fictional expectations and capitalist dynamics*, Cambridge: Harvard University Press (2016).

Bentham J, *An Introduction to the Principles of Morals and Legislation*, Oxford: Clarendon Press (1876 [1780], from the revised ed. 1823).

Bentham J, 'Defence of Usury', in *The Works of Jeremy Bentham*, volume 3, New York: Russell & Russell (1962 [1787]).

Berle A and Means G, *The Modern Corporation and Private Property*, New York: Macmillan (1932) / New York: Harcourt Brace (revised ed. 1967).

Berle A, 'Corporate Devices for Diluting Stock Participations', 31 *Columbia Law Review*, pp. 1239–1265 (1931).

Berle A, 'For Whom Corporate Managers *are* Trustees', 45 *Harvard Law Review*, pp. 1365–1372 (1932).

Berle A, 'Modern Functions of the Corporate System', 62 *Columbia Law Review*, pp. 433–449 (1962).

Bessière C and Gollac S, *The Gender of Capital: how families perpetuate wealth inequality*, Cambridge: Harvard University Press (2023).

Bhandar B, *Colonial Lives of Property: law, land and racial regimes of ownership*, Durham, North Carolina: Duke University Press (2018).

Black S et al, 'Poor Little Rich Kids? The role of nature versus nurture in wealth and other economic outcomes and behaviors', *NBER Working Paper No 21409* (2015, revised 2019).

BlackRock, *2022 Voting Spotlight*, BlackRock Investment Stewardship (2022), blackrock.com/stewardship

Blackstone W, *Commentaries on the Laws of England, Books I-IV*, Oxford: Oxford University Press, (general ed Wilfred Prest, 2016 [1765–69]).

Blaufarb R, *The Great Demarcation: the French revolution and the invention of modern property*, Oxford: Oxford University Press (2016).

Bloch M, *Feudal Society*, London: Routledge (2014 [1940])

Bodenheimer E, 'Modern Analytical Jurisprudence and the Limits of its Usefulness', 104 *University of Pennsylvania Law Review*, pp. 1080–1086 (1956).

Boeger N and Villiers C (eds), *Shaping the Corporate Landscape: towards corporate reform and enterprise diversity*, London: Bloomsbury (2018).

Bonetti A, 'Housing as an Asset Class, Italian Edition', *Italics*, 24/9/21.

Bouckaert B, 'What is Property?', 13 *Harvard Journal of Law and Public Policy*, pp. 475–816 (1990).

Bourdieu P, *Outline of a Theory of Practice*, Cambridge: Cambridge University Press (1977)

Boyle J, 'Enclosing the Genome: what the squabbles over genetic patents could teach us', in H Tavani (ed.), *Ethics, Computing and Genomics*, Sudbury: Jones & Bartlett, pp. 255–278 (2005).

Bracha O, *Owning Ideas: a history of Anglo-American intellectual property*, JD Thesis, Harvard Law School (2005).

Brandeis L, 'Business - a profession', *System* (October 1912), later republished in L Brandeis, *Business - a profession*, Boston: Small Maynard (1914).

Braudel F, *The Wheels of Commerce*, London: Collins (1983 [1979]).

Braun B, 'Asset Manager Capitalism as a Corporate Governance Regime', in J Hacker et al (eds), *The American Political Economy*, New York: Cambridge University Press, pp. 270–294 (2021).

Braun B, 'Exit, Control and Politics: structural power and corporate governance under asset manager capitalism', 50 *Politics and Society*, pp. 630–654 (2022).

Brenner R, 'The Origins of Capitalist Development: a critique of Neo-Smithian Marxism', 104 *New Left Review*, pp. 25–92 (July–August 1977).

Brenner R, 'Agrarian Class Structure and Economic Development in Pre-Industrial Europe', 70 *Past and Present*, pp. 30–75 (1977), reprinted in T H Aston and C H E Philip (eds), *The Brenner Debate*, Cambridge: Cambridge University Press, pp. 10–63 (1985).

Brenner R, 'The Agrarian Roots of Modern Capitalism', 97 *Past and Present*, pp. 16–113 (1982), reprinted in T H Aston and C H E Philip (eds), *The Brenner Debate*, Cambridge: Cambridge University Press, pp. 213–327 (1985).

Brenner R, 'Ellen Meiksins Wood (1942-2016)', https://solidarity-us.org/atc/181/p4598/.

Brenner R, 'Escalating Plunder', 123 *New Left Review*, pp. 5–27 (May–June 2020).

Brenner R, 'From Capitalism to Feudalism? Predation, decline and the transformation of US politics', lecture delivered at University of Massachusetts, 27/4/21, https://www.youtube.com/watch?v=XZJ-Bz4U4As

Brick H, *Transcending Capitalism*, Ithaca: Cornell University Press (2006).

Bricker J et al, 'Changes in US Family Finances from 2010 to 2013: evidence from the survey of consumer finances', 100 *Federal Reserve Bulletin* (September 2014).

Burgin A, *The Great Persuasion*, Cambridge: Harvard University Press (2012).

Burrough B and Helyar J, *Barbarians at the Gate*, New York: Harper & Row (1989).

Cabrelli D, 'Addressing the Falling Labour share in the UK and beyond', 27 *Edinburgh Law Review*, pp. 1–33 (2023).

Campbell D, 'The Role of Monitoring and Morality in Company Law', 7 *Australian Journal of Corporate Law*, pp. 343–365 (1997).

Cannan E, 'Early History of the Term Capital', 35 *Quarterly Journal of Economics*, pp. 469–481 (1921).

Canterbery E R, *Wall Street Capitalism: the theory of the bondholding class*, Singapore: World Scientific Publishing (2000).

Caves R, 'Mergers, Takeovers, and Economic Efficiency: foresight vs hindsight', 7 *International Journal of Industrial Organisation*, pp. 151–174 (1989).

Chadwick A, 'Capital without Capitalism? Or capitalism without determinism?', 30 *Social and Legal Studies*, pp. 302–311 (2021).

Chang H-J, *Kicking Away the Ladder*, London: Anthem (2003).

Chang H-J, *Bad Samaritans*, New York: Random House (2007).

Chayes A, 'The Modern Corporation and the Rule of Law', in Edward Mason (ed.), *The Corporation in Modern Society*, Cambridge: Harvard University Press (1959), reprinted New York: Atheneum, pp. 25–45 (1966).

Cheffins B, *Company Law: theory, structure and operation*, Oxford: Clarendon Press (1997).
Chiapello E, 'Accounting and the birth of the notion of capitalism', 18 *Critical Perspectives on Accounting*, pp. 263–296 (2007).
Christodoulidis E and Goldoni M, 'Marxism and the political economy of law', in E Christodoulidis, R Dukes and M Goldoni (eds), *Research Handbook on Critical Legal Theory*, Cheltenham: Edward Elgar, pp. 95–113 (2019).
Christophers B, *The New Enclosure: the appropriation of public land in neoliberal Britain*, London: Verso (2018).
Christophers B, *Rentier Capitalism*, London: Verso (2020).
Claassen R and Katz L, 'Property: authority without office?', 3 *Journal of Law and Political Economy*, pp. 570–575 (2023).
Coase R, 'The Nature of the Firm', 4 *Economica*, pp. 386–405 (1937).
Code civil des Français, Paris: Imprimerie de la République (1804).
Cohen M, 'Property and Sovereignty', 13 *Cornell Law Quarterly*, pp. 8–30 (1927).
Colliot-Thélène C, 'Afterword' to I I Rubin, *A History of Economic Thought*, London: Ink Links, pp. 385–429 (1979).
Commons J R, *The Distribution of Wealth*, London: Macmillan (1893).
Conaghan J, 'The Essence of Rape', 39 *Oxford Journal of Legal Studies*, pp. 151–82 (2019).
Corbin A, 'Taxation of Seats on the Stock Exchange', 31 *Yale Law Journal*, pp. 429–431 (1922).
Cornwell J, 'MacIntyre on Money', *Prospect Magazine*, November 2010.
Credit Suisse Research Institute, *Global Wealth Report 2021*, www.credit-suisse.com/about-us/en/reports-research/global-wealth-report.html
Centre for Research on Socio-Cultural Change (CRESC), *The Great Train Robbery: rail privatisation and after*, Manchester: CRESC (2013).
Crosland A, 'The Transition from Capitalism', in D Reisman (ed.), *Democratic Socialism in Britain*, volume 9, London: Routledge, pp. 33–68 (1951).
Crosland A, *The Future of Socialism*, London: Jonathan Cape (1956).
Dagan H, 'The Craft of Property', 91 *California Law Review*, pp. 1517–1571 (2003).
Dagan H, 'Autonomy and Property', in H Dagan and B Zipursky (eds), *Research Handbook on Private Law Theory*, Cheltenham: Edward Elgar, pp. 185–202 (2020).
Dagan H, *A Liberal Theory of Property*, Cambridge: Cambridge University Press (2021).
Dallas L, and Barry J, 'Long-term shareholders and time-phased voting', 40 *Delaware Journal of Corporate Law*, pp. 541–646 (2016).
Daugareilh I et al, 'The Platform Economy and Social Law: key issues in comparative perspective', *ETUI Research Paper – Working Paper 2019.10* (2019).
Daunton M, 'Open Fields and Enclosure: the demise of commonality', in M Daunton, *Progress and Poverty: an economic and social history of Britain, 1700-1850*, Oxford: Oxford University Press (1995).

Davies J H, 'Keynes on the Socialization of Investment', 19 *International Journal of Social Economics*, pp. 150–163 (1992).
Davies M, 'Review of J E Penner, *The Idea of Property in Law*', 7 *Social and Legal Studies*, pp. 577–580 (1998).
Davies M, *Property*, London: Routledge-Cavendish (2007).
Deakin S, 'The Coming Transformation of Shareholder Value', 13 *Corporate Governance; An International Review*, pp. 11–18 (2005).
Deakin S, Gindis D, Hodgson G, Kainan H and Pistor K, 'Legal Institutionalism: capitalism and the constitutive role of law', 45 *Journal of Comparative Economics*, pp. 188–200 (2017).
Deazley R, 'The Myth of Copyright at Common Law', 62 *Cambridge Law Journal*, pp. 106–133 (2003).
Deazley R, 'Commentary on *Hinton v Donaldson*' and 'Commentary on *Donaldson v Becket*' in L Bently and M Kretschmer (eds), *Primary Sources on Copyright, 1450-1900*, http://www.copyrighthistory.org
de Soto H, *The Mystery of Capital*, London: Black Swan (2001).
Dickerson A P et al, 'Short Termism and Underinvestment in Financial Systems', 58 *Manchester School*, pp. 351–367 (1995).
Dickerson A P et al, 'The Impact of Acquisitions on Company Performance', 49 *Oxford Economic Papers* 344 (1997).
Dickerson A P et al, 'Takeover Risk and Dividend Strategy: a study of UK firms', 46 *Journal of Industrial Economics*, pp. 281–300 (1998).
Dickinson H T, 'Review Article: comments on William Blackstone's *Commentaries on the Laws of England*', 104 *History*, pp. 710–728 (2019).
Dickson, P G M, *The Financial Revolution in England*, London: Macmillan (1967).
Dimick M, 'Without Remainder: law and the constitution of economy and society', *Legal Form Forum*, 11/7/2022.
Dimick M, 'Is Capitalism a Thing?', LPE Blog, 23/10/23.
Dimoulis D, and Milios J, 'Commodity Fetishism vs Capital Fetishism', 12 *Historical Materialism*, pp. 3–42 (2004).
Di Muzio T, 'Towards a Genealogy of the New Constitutionalism', in S Gill and A C Cutler (eds), *New Constitutionalism and World Order*, Cambridge: Cambridge University Press, pp. 81–94 (2014).
di Robilant A, 'Property: a bundle of sticks or a tree?', 66 *Vanderbilt Law Review*, pp. 869–932 (2013).
di Robilant A and Syed T, 'Property's Building Blocks: Hohfeld in Europe and beyond', in S Balganesh, T Sichelman and H Smith (eds), *Wesley Hohfeld a Century Later*, Cambridge: Cambridge University Press, pp. 223–257 (2022).
Dodd E M, 'For Whom are Corporate Managers Trustees?', 45 *Harvard Law Review*, pp. 1145–1163 (1932).

Dodd E M, 'Is the Effective Enforcement of the Fiduciary Duties of Corporate Managers Practicable?', 2 *University of Chicago Law Review*, pp. 194–207 (1935).

Domhoff G W, 'Wealth, Income and Power', whorulesamerica.ucsc.edu/power/wealth.html

Douglas S and McFarlane B, 'Defining Property Rights', in J E Penner and H Smith (eds), *Philosophical Foundations of Property Law*, Oxford: Oxford University Press, pp. 219–243 (2013).

Douglas W O, 'Protecting the Investor', 23 *The Yale Review*, pp. 522–533 (1934).

Douglas W O, *Democracy and Finance*, New Haven: Yale University Press (1940).

Duménil G and Lévy D 'Costs and Benefits of Neoliberalism: a class analysis', in G Epstein (ed.), *Financialization and The World Economy*, Cheltenham: Edward Elgar, pp. 17–45 (2005).

Durand C, *Fictitious Capital*, London: Verso (2017).

Durand C, *Techno-féodalisme*, Paris: Zones (2020).

Durbin E, *The Politics of Democratic Socialism*, London: Routledge (1940).

Eagleton T, 'Utopia and its Opposites', *Socialist Register*, pp. 31–40 (2000).

Easterbook F and Fischel D, 'The Proper Role of a Target's Management in Responding to a Tender Offer', 94 *Harvard Law Review*, pp. 1161–1204 (1981).

Easterbrook F and Fischel D, 'Voting in Corporate Law' (1983) 26 *Journal of Law and Economics*, pp. 395–427 (1983).

Easterbrook F and Fischel D, *The Economic Structure of Corporate Law*, Cambridge: Harvard University Press (1991).

Egan M, 'US billionaires have become $565 richer during the pandemic', CNN *Business*, 4/6/2020.

Egan M, 'US Billionaires have grown $1.1 trillion richer during the pandemic', CNN *Business*, 26/1/2021.

Ellickson R, 'Two Cheers for the Bundle-of-Sticks Metaphor, Three Cheers for Merrill and Smith', 8 *Econ Journal Watch*, pp. 215–222 (2011).

Epstein G (ed.), *Financialization and The World Economy*, Cheltenham: Edward Elgar (2005).

Epstein G, 'Introduction', in G Epstein (ed.), *Financialization and The World Economy*, Cheltenham: Edward Elgar, pp. 3–16 (2005).

Epstein G and Jayadev A, 'The Rise of Rentier Incomes in OECD Countries', in G Epstein (ed.), *Financialization and The World Economy*, Cheltenham: Edward Elgar, pp. 46–76 (2005).

Epstein R, *Takings: private property and the power of eminent domain*, Cambridge: Harvard University Press (1985).

Epstein R, 'The Assault that Failed: the progressive critique of laissez faire' 97 *Michigan Law Review*, pp. 1697–1721 (1999).

Epstein R, 'Bundle-of-Rights Theory as a Bulwark Against Statist Conceptions of Private Property', 8 *Econ Journal Watch*, pp. 223–235 (2011).

Ely R T, 'Political Economy' in Richard T Ely (ed.), *Political Economy, Political Science and Sociology*, Chicago: University Association, pp. 3–39 (1899).

Erturk I et al, 'General Introduction' in I Erturk et al (eds), *Financialization at Work*, London: Routledge, pp. 1–43 (2008).

Fama E, 'Agency Problems and the Theory of the Firm', 88 *Journal of Political Economy*, pp. 288–307 (1980).

Fancy T, 'ESG and sustainability investing are deadly distractions in the climate crisis', *Climate and Capital Media*, 20/8/21

Fancy T, *The Secret Diary of a Sustainable Investor*, August 2021, https://medium.com/@sosofancy/the-secret-diary-of-a-sustainable-investor-part-1-70b6987fa139

Fetter F, 'Clark's Reformulation of the Capital Concept', in F Fetter (ed.), *Capital, Interest and Rent*, Kansas City: Sheed Andrews & McMeel, pp. 119–142 (1977 [1927]).

Fetter F, 'Capital', in E Seligman and A Johnson (eds), *Encyclopaedia of the Social Sciences,* volume 3, New York: Macmillan, pp. 187–190 (1930).

Fetter F, 'Reformulation of the Concepts of Capital and income in Economics and Accounting', 12 *The Accounting Review,* pp. 3–12 (1937).

Fichtner J, 'The Rise of Institutional Investors', in Mader et al (eds), *Routledge International Handbook of Financialization*, London: Routledge, pp. 265–275 (2020).

Fichtner J et al, 'The New Permanent Universal Owners', 49 *Economy & Society*, pp. 493–515 (2020).

Fischel D, 'The Corporate Governance Movement', 35 *Vanderbilt Law Review*, pp. 1259–1292 (1982).

Flannigan R, 'Shareholder Fiduciary Accountability', *Journal of Business Law*, pp. 1–30 (2014).

Folkman P et al, 'Working for Themselves? Capital market intermediaries and present day capitalism', 49 *Business History*, pp. 552–572 (2007).

Fox A, *Beyond Contract*, London: Faber & Faber (1974).

Fracchia J, 'Marx's *Aufhebung* of Philosophy and the Foundations of a Materialist Science of History', 30 *History and Theory*, pp.153–179 (1991).

Frank J, 'Book Review of Berle & Means, *The Modern Corporation and Private Property*', 43 *Yale Law Journal*, pp. 989–1000 (1933).

Franks J and Mayer C, 'Hostile Takeovers and the Correction of Managerial Failure', 40 *Journal of Financial Economics*, pp. 163–181 (1996).

Frémeaux N and Leturcq M, 'Inequalities and the Individualization of Wealth', 184 *Journal of Public Economics*, pp. 1–18 (2020).

Freyfolge E, 'Private Ownership and Human Flourishing: an exploratory overview', 24 *Stellenbosch Law Review*, pp. 430–454 (2013).

Fried B, *The Progressive Assault on laissez-Faire: Robert Lee Hale and the first law and economics movement*, Cambridge: Harvard University Press (1998).

Froud J et al, *Financialization and Strategy: narrative and numbers*, London: Routledge (2006).

Fukuyama F, *The End of History and the Last Man*, New York: Free Press (1992).

Gabor D, 'The Wall Street Consensus', 52 *Development and Change*, pp. 429–459 (2021).

Gabor D and Kohl S, *My Home is an Asset Class*, Greens/EFA (January 2022), https://www.greens-efa.eu/en/article/document/my-home-is-an-asset-class

Gabor D, 'This economic chaos is a form of class war on the British public', *The Guardian*, 6/10/22.

George J, *A View of the Existing Law Affecting Unincorporated Joint Stock Companies*, London: McDowall (1825).

Gill S, 'Globalisation, Market Civilisation and Disciplinary Neoliberalism', 23 *Millennium: Journal of International Studies*, pp. 399–423 (1995).

Gill S, 'New Constitutionalism, Democratisation and Global Political Economy', 10 *Pacifica Review*, pp. 23–38 (1998).

Gill S and Cutler A C, 'General Introduction' to S Gill and A C Cutler (eds), *New Constitutionalism and World Order*, Cambridge: Cambridge University Press, pp. 1–19 (2014).

Golland A et al, 'Proxy Voting for the Earth System: institutional shareholder governance of global tipping elements' (2022), https://ssrn.com/abstract=4067103 or http://dx.doi.org/10.2139/ssrn.4067103

Gordon J N, 'The Rise of Independent Directors in the United States, 1950-2005', 59 *Stanford Law Review*, pp. 1465–1568 (2007).

Gordon R W, 'Paradoxical Property', in John Brewer and Susan Staves (eds), *Early Modern Conceptions of Property*, London: Routledge, pp. 95–110 (1996).

Gower L C B, 'Corporate Control: the battle for the Berkeley', 68 *Harvard Law Review*, pp. 1176–1193 (1955).

Gower L C B, 'Review of F Emerson & F Latcham, *Shareholder Democracy*', 68 *Harvard Law Review*, pp. 922–928 (1955).

Gower L C B, *Principles of Modern Company Law*, London: Stevens/Sweet and Maxwell (3rd ed., 1969; 4th ed., 1979; 6th ed., 1997).

Goyder G, *The Responsible Company*, Oxford: Blackwell (1961).

Graham N, *Lawscape: property, environment, law*, Abingdon: Routledge-Glasshouse (2011).

Graham N, 'Dephysicalised Property and Shadow Lands', in R Bartel and J Carter (eds), *Handbook on Space, Place and Law*, Cheltenham: Edward Elgar, pp. 281–291 (2021).

Gray K, 'Property in Thin Air', 50 *Cambridge Law Journal*, pp. 252–307 (1991).

Getzler J, 'Theories of Property and Economic development', 26 *Journal of Interdisciplinary History*, pp. 639–669 (1996).

Graziadei M, 'The Structure of Property Ownership and the Common Law/Civil Law Divide', in M Graziadei and L Smith (eds), *Comparative Property Law*, Edward Elgar: Cheltenham, pp. 71–99 (2017).

Greer A, *Property and Dispossession*, Cambridge: Cambridge University Press (2018).

Grewal D S, 'The Laws of Capitalism', Book Review of Thomas Piketty, *Capital in the Twenty First Century*, 128 *Harvard Law Review*, pp. 626–667 (2014).

Grewal D S and Britton-Purdy J, 'Liberalism, Property and the Means of Production', LPE Blog, 25/1/2021

Grey T C, 'The Disintegration of Property', 22 *Nomos*, pp. 69–85 (1980).

Gutiérrez G and Philippon T, 'Investmentless Growth', *Brookings Papers on Economic Activity* (Fall, 2017).

Hager S B, *Public Debt, Ownership and Power*, PhD, Toronto: York University (2013).

Hager S B, 'What Happened to the Bondholding Class? Public debt, power and the top one per cent', 19 *New Political Economy*, pp. 155–182 (2014).

Hager S B, 'Corporate Ownership of the Public Debt: mapping the new aristocracy of finance', 13 *Socio-Economic Review*, pp. 505–523 (2015).

Hager S B, 'Public Debt as Corporate Power', *Working Papers on Capital as Power* (2015).

Hager S B, *Public Debt, Inequality and Power*, Oakland: University of California Press (2016).

Hager S B, 'The Rise of the American Bondholding Class', *Roar Magazine* (2016), https://roarmag.org/magazine/sandy-hager-public-debt-bond holding-class/

Hale R L, 'Law-Making by Unofficial Minorities', 20 *Columbia Law Review*, pp. 451–456 (1920).

Hale R L, 'Coercion and Distribution in a Supposedly Non-Coercive State', 38 *Political Science Quarterly*, pp. 470–94 (1923).

Hale R L, 'Economics and Law', in W Ogburn and A Goldenweiser (eds), *The Social Sciences and their Interrelations*, London: Allen & Unwin, pp. 131–142 (1927).

Hale R L, 'Bargaining, Duress and Economic Liberty', 43 *Columbia Law Review*, pp. 603–628 (1943).

Hallowell A I, 'The Nature and Function of Property as a Social Institution', 1 *Journal of Legal and Political Sociology*, pp. 115–39 (1943).

Hann C M, 'Introduction: the embeddedness of property', in C M Hann (ed.), *Property Relations: renewing the anthropological tradition*, Cambridge: Cambridge University Press, pp. 1–40 (1988).

Hann C M, 'The Tragedy of the Privates? Post-socialist property relations in anthropological perspective', *Max Planck Institute for Social Anthropology Working Papers*, No 2 (2000).

Hann C M, 'The State of the Art: a new double movement? Anthropological perspectives on property in the age of neoliberalism', 5 *Socio-Economic Review*, pp. 287–318 (2007).

Hansmann H and Kraakman R, 'The Essential Role of Organizational Law', 110 *Yale Law Journal*, pp. 387–440 (2000).

Hansmann H, Kraakman R and Squire R, 'Law and the Rise of the Firm', 119 *Harvard Law Review*, pp. 1333–1403 (1996).

Hansmann H and Kraakman R, 'The End of History for Corporate Law', 89 *Georgetown Law Journal*, pp. 439–468 (2001).

Harding L, 'As Donald Trump made clear, smart businesses know only idiots pay taxes', *The Guardian*, 16/10/2016.

Harris J W, *Property and Justice*, Oxford: Clarendon Press (1996).

Harris J W, 'Reason or Mumbo Jumbo: the common law's approach to property', 117 *Proceedings of the British Academy*, pp. 445–475 (2002).

Harris J W, 'The Elusiveness of Property', 48 *Scandinavian Studies of Law*, pp. 123–131 (2005).

Hart H L A, 'Definition and Theory in Jurisprudence' in Hart, *Essays in Jurisprudence and Philosophy*, Oxford: Clarendon Press, pp. 21–48 (1983 [1953]).

Hart H L A, *The Concept of Law*, Oxford: Oxford University Press (1961).

Hart H L A and Honore A M, *Causation in Law*, Oxford: Oxford University Press (1959).

Harris R, *Industrializing English Law*, Cambridge: Cambridge University Press (2000).

Harvey D, *The New Imperialism*, Oxford: Oxford University Press (2003).

Harvey D, *A Brief History of Neoliberalism*, Oxford: Oxford University Press (2005).

Harvey D, *The Enigma of Capital*, London: Profile Books (2010).

Harvey D, 'History versus Theory: a commentary on Marx's method in *Capital*', 20 *Historical Materialism*, pp. 3–38 (2012).

Hawley J and Williams A, 'The Emergence of Universal Owners', 43 *Challenge*, pp. 43–61 (July-August 2000).

Heller M, 'The Boundaries of Property', 108 *Yale Law Journal*, pp. 1163–1223 (1999).

Henwood D, *Wall Street*, London: Verso (1997).

Herman S, 'The Uses and Abuses of Roman Law Texts', 29 *American Journal of Comparative Law*, pp. 671–690 (1981).

Hilferding R, *Finance Capital*, London: Routledge & Kegan Paul (1981 [1910]).

Hirschl R, 'The Political Origins of the New Constitutionalism', 11 *Indiana Journal of Global Legal Studies*, pp. 71–108 (2004).

Hirschl R, *Towards Juristocracy: the origins and consequences of the new constitutionalism*, Boston: Harvard University Press (2004).

Hodgson G and Callinicos A, 'Institutionalism versus Marxism: perspectives for social science – a debate between Geoffrey Hodgson and Alex Callinicos', University of Hertfordshire Working Papers (2001).

Hodgson G, 'Frank A Fetter (1863-1949): Capital (1930)', 4 *Journal of Institutional Economics*, pp. 127–137 (2008).

Hodgson G, *Conceptualising Capitalism*, Chicago: University of Chicago Press (2015).

Hodgson G, 'Conceptualising Capitalism: a summary', 20 *Competition and Change*, pp. 37–52 (2016).

Hohfeld W, 'Some Fundamental Legal Conceptions as Applied in Judicial Reasoning', 23 *Yale Law Journal*, pp. 16–59 (1913).

Hohfeld W, 'Fundamental Judicial Conceptions as Applied in Judicial Reasoning', 26 *Yale Law Journal*, pp. 710–770 (1917).

Honoré A M, 'Ownership', in A G Guest (ed.), *Oxford Essays in Jurisprudence*, Oxford: Oxford University Press, pp. 107–147 (1961).

Honoré A M, 'Property and Ownership: marginal comments', in T Endicott et al (eds), *Properties of Law: essays in honour of Jim Harris*, Oxford: Oxford University Press, pp. 129–137 (2006).

Holdsworth W S, 'The History of the Treatment of *Choses* in Action by the Common Law', 33 *Harvard Law Review*, pp. 997–1030 (1920).

Holdsworth W S, *A History of English Law*, London: Methuen (1922-38)

Hoppit J, 'Attitudes to Credit in Britain, 1680-1790', 33 *Historical Journal*, pp. 305–322 (1990).

Hunter R, 'Critical Legal Studies and Marx's Critique: a reappraisal', 31 *Yale Journal of Law & the Humanities*, pp. 389–412 (2021).

Hutchinson A, 'Razzle Dazzle', 1 *Jurispridence*, pp. 39–61 (2010).

ILO and OECD, *The Labour Share in G20 Economies*, G20 Employment Working Group (2015), https://www.oecd.org/g20/topics/employment-and-social-policy/The-Labour-Share-in-G20-Economies.pdf

Ireland P, 'The Rise of the Limited Liability Company', 12 *International Journal of the Sociology of Law*, pp. 239–60 (1984).

Ireland P, 'Capitalism without the Capitalist: the joint stock company share and the emergence of the modern doctrine of separate corporate personality', 17 *Journal of Legal History*, pp. 41–73 (1996).

Ireland P, 'History, Critical Legal Studies and the Mysterious Disappearance of Capitalism', 65 *Modern Law Review*, pp. 120–140 (2002).

Ireland P, 'Property and Contract in Contemporary Corporate Theory', 23 *Legal Studies*, pp. 453–509 (2003).

Ireland P, 'Limited Liability, Shareholder Rights, and the Problem of Corporate Irresponsibility', 34 *Cambridge Journal of Economics*, pp. 837–856 (2010).

Ireland P, 'Law and the Neoliberal Vision: financial property, pension privatization and the ownership society', 62 *Northern Ireland Legal Quarterly*, pp. 1–32 (2011).

Ireland P, 'The Corporation and the New Aristocracy of Finance', in J-P Robe, A Lyon-Caen and S Vernac (eds), *Multinationals and the Constitutionalization of the World-Power System*, London: Routledge, pp. 53–105 (2016).

Ireland P, 'Corporate Schizophrenia: the institutional origins of corporate social irresponsibility', in N Boeger and C Villiers (eds), *Shaping the Corporate Landscape: towards corporate reform and enterprise diversity*, Oxford: Hart, pp. 13–39 (2017).

Ireland P, 'Making Sense of Contemporary Capitalism using Company Law', 33 *Australian Journal of Corporate Law*, pp. 379–401 (2018).

Ireland P and Meng G, 'Post-Capitalist Property', 46 *Economy and Society*, pp. 369–397 (2017).

Jensen M, 'Eclipse of the Public Corporation', 89 *Harvard Business Review*, pp. 61–75 (September–October 1989).

Jensen M and Meckling W, 'Theory of the Firm: managerial behaviour, agency costs and ownership structure', 3 *Journal of Financial Economics*, pp. 305–360 (1976).

Jensen M and Ruback R, 'Market for Corporate Control: the scientific evidence', 11 *Journal of Financial Economics*, pp. 5–50 (1983).

Jessop B, 'Knowledge as a Fictitious Commodity: insights and limits of a Polanyian perspective', in A Buğra and K Ağartan (eds), *Reading Karl Polanyi for the Twenty-First Century: market economy as a political project*, London: Palgrave Macmillan, pp. 115–134 (2007).

Johnston N, 'The History of the Parliamentary Franchise', *House of Commons Library*, Research Paper 13/14 (2013).

Katz L, 'Exclusion and Exclusivity in Property Law', 58 *University of Toronto Law Journal*, pp. 275–315 (2008).

Kay J, 'Forty Years of taxing on UK runways', *Financial Times* 4/1/11.

Kay Review of UK Equity Markets and Long Term Decision Making (Final Report, July 2012).

Kennedy D, 'The Structure of Blackstone's Commentaries', 28 *Buffalo Law Review*, pp. 209–382 (1979).

Kennedy D, 'The Role of Law in Economic Thought: essays on the fetishism of commodities', 34 *American University Law Review*, pp. 939–1001 (1985).

Kennedy D, 'The Stakes of Law; or Hale and Foucault!', 4 *Legal Studies Forum*, pp. 327–366 (1991).

Kennedy D, *A Critique of Adjudication*, Cambridge: Harvard University Press (1997).

Kennedy M, *Interest and Inflation Free Money*, British Columbia: New Society Publishers (revised ed. 1995 [1987]).

Kershaw D, *Principles of Takeover Regulation*, Oxford: Oxford University Press (2016).

Keynes J M, *The End of Laissez-Faire*, Amherst: Prometheus Books (2004 [1926]).

Keynes J M, *The General Theory of Employment, Interest and Money* (1936), reprinted in E Johnson and D Moggridge (eds), *The Collected Writings of John Maynard Keynes*, volume 7, London: Macmillan (1973[1936]).

Khurana R, *From Higher Aims to Hired Hands*, Princeton: Princeton University Press (2007).

Kim J, 'Propertization: the process by which financial corporate power has risen and collapsed', 1 *Review of Capital as Power*, pp. 58–82 (2018).

King B E, 'The Basic Concept of Professor Hart's Jurisprudence', 21 *Cambridge Law Journal*, pp. 270–303 (1963).

Klein D and Robinson J, 'Property: a bundle of rights? Prologue to the property symposium', 8 *Econ Journal Watch*, pp. 193–204 (2011).

Koffler J S, 'Capital in Hell: Dante's lessons on usury', 32 *Rutgers Law Review*, pp. 609–660 (1979).

Kotz D M, *Bank Control of Large Corporations in the United States*, Berkeley and Los Angeles: University of California Press (1978).

Kraakman R et al (eds), *The Anatomy of Corporate Law: a comparative and functional approach*, Oxford: Oxford University Press (2004).

Krätke M R, 'The Political Economy of (Public and Private) Debt', Workshop on Debt, University of Lancaster, https://www.academia.edu/5550526/Political_economy_of_public_debt

Kukk M et al, 'The Gender Wealth Gap in Europe', 69 *Review of Income and Wealth*, pp. 289–317 (2023).

Lacey N, 'Analytical Jurisprudence versus descriptive sociology revisited' (2006), 84 *Texas Law Review*, pp. 945–982 (2006).

Lacey N, 'Jurisprudence, History, and the Institutional Quality of Law', 101 *Virginia Law Review*, pp. 919–45 (2015).

Lametti D, 'The Concept of Property: relations through objects of social wealth', 53 *University of Toronto Law Journal*, pp. 325–378 (2003).

Landes E and Posner R, 'The Economics of the Baby Shortage', 7 *Journal of Legal Studies*, pp. 323–348 (1976).

Laski H, *A Grammar of Politics*, London: Allen & Unwin (1925).

Lawson F H and Rudden B, *Law of Property*, Oxford: Oxford University Press (3rd ed., 2002).

Lazonick W, 'Controlling the Market for Corporate Control: the historical significance of managerial capitalism', 1 *Industrial & Corporate Change*, pp. 445–488 (1992).

Lazonick W and O'Sullivan M, 'Maximizing Shareholder Value: a new ideology for corporate governance', 29 *Economy and Society*, pp. 13–35 (2000).

Lazzarato M, *Governing by Debt*, Cambridge: MIT Press (2015).

Leacock E, 'The Montagnais-Naskapi of the Labrador Peninsula', in R Bruce Morrison and C Roderick Wilson (eds), *Native Peoples: the Canadian experience*, Toronto: McClelland & Stewart, pp. 140–171 (1986).

Lehavi A, *The Construction of Property*, Cambridge: Cambridge University Press (2013).

Levy J, 'Capital as Process and the History of Capitalism', 91 *Business History Review*, pp. 483–510 (2017).

Lippman W, *Drift and Mastery*, Madison: University of Wisconsin Press (1985 [1914]).

Lobban M, 'Legal Theory and Legal History: prospects for a dialogue', in M Del Mar and M Lobban (eds), *Law in Theory and History: new essays on a neglected dialogue*, London: Bloomsbury, pp. 3–21 (2014).

Locke J, *Two Treatises of Government*, Cambridge: Cambridge University Press (1963, ed P Laslett).

Lojkine U, 'Critical Political Economy beyond the Production/Circulation Dichotomy', LPE Blog, 17/5/2021.

Lowie R, *Primitive Society*, New York: Boni & Liveright (1920).

Lowie R, 'Incorporeal Property in Primitive Society', 37 *Yale Law Journal*, pp. 551–563 (1928).

Macfarlane A, *The Origins of English Individualism*, Oxford: Blackwell (1978).

Maddison J, 'Property', *National Gazette*, (March 29, 1792), reprinted in Marvin Meyers (ed.), *The Mind of the Founder*, Indianapolis: Bobbs Merrill (1973).

MacLeod H D, *Principles of Economical Philosophy*, London: Longmans, Green Reader & Dyer (2nd ed., 1872).

Macleod H D, *The Theory of Credit*, London: Longmans, Green & Co (1889).

MacPherson C B, *The Political Theory of Possessive Individualism*, Oxford: Oxford University Press (1962).

Maine H, *Ancient Law*, London: Dent (1917 [1861]).

Malcolmson R, *Life and Labour in England, 1700-80*, London: Hutchinson (1981).

Manne H, 'Book Review of Richard Eells, *Corporation Giving in a Free Society*', 24 *University of Chicago Law Review*, pp. 194–202 (1956).

Manne H, 'The "Higher Criticism" of the Modern Corporation', 62 *Columbia Law Review*, pp. 399–432 (1962).
Manne H, 'Mergers and the Market for Corporate Control', 73 *Journal of Political Economy*, pp. 110–120 (1965).
Manne H, *Insider Trading and the Stock Market*, New York: Free Press (1966).
Manne H, 'Our Two Corporation Systems: law and economics', 53 *Virginia Law Review*, pp. 259–284 (1967).
Manne H (ed.), *Economic Policy and the Regulation of Corporate Securities: a symposium*, Washington DC: American Enterprise Institute for Public Policy Research (1969).
Manning B, 'Review of J.A. Livingston, *The American Stockholder*', 67 *Yale Law Journal*, pp. 1477–1496 (1958).
Manning S, 'Britain's colonial shame', *Independent*, 24/2/13.
Mark G, 'The Personification of the Business Corporation in American Law', 54 *University of Chicago Law Review*, pp. 1441–1483 (1987).
Marx K, *Economic and Philosophical Manuscripts*, London: Lawrence & Wishart (ed Dirk Struik) 1970 [1844]).
Marx K, *The Poverty of Philosophy*, Moscow: Progress (1955 [1847])
Marx K, *Wage Labour and Capital*, Moscow: Progress (1974 [1847]).
Marx K, *Grundrisse*, (Penguin ed. 1973 [1857–8], with a foreword by Martin Nicholas).
Marx K, *Capital*, volume 1, London: Lawrence and Wishart (1954 [1867]).
Marx K, *Capital*, volume 2, London: Lawrence and Wishart (1956 [1885]).
Marx K, *Capital*, volume 3, London: Lawrence and Wishart (1959 [1894]).
Mason E, 'Introduction', in E Mason (ed.), *The Corporation in Modern Society*, Cambridge: Harvard University Press (1959), reprinted New York: Atheneum, pp. 1–24 (1966).
Mayer C, *Firm Commitment*, Oxford: Oxford University Press (2013).
Mayer J, *Dark Money*, New York: Doubleday (2016).
Mazzucato M, *The Entrepreneurial State*, New York: Anthem (2013).
Mazzucato M, 'Preventing Digital Feudalism', *Project Syndicate*, 2/10/19, https://www.project-syndicate.org/commentary/platform-economy-digital-feudalism.
Meriküll J et al, 'What Explains the Gender Gap in Wealth?', 19 *Review of Economics of the Household*, pp. 501–547 (2021).
Merrill T, 'Property and the Right to Exclude', 77 *Nebraska Law Review*, pp. 730–755 (1998).
Merrill T, 'The Property Prism', 8 *Econ Watch Journal*, pp. 247–254 (2011).
Merrill T, 'The Property Strategy', 160 *University of Pennsylvania Law Review*, pp. 2061–2095 (2012).
Merrill T, 'Possession as a Natural Right', 9 *New York University Journal of Law & Liberty*, pp. 345–374 (2015).

Merrill T and Smith H, 'Optimal Standardization in the Law of Property', 110 *Yale Law Journal*, pp. 1–70 (2000).

Merrill T and Smith H, 'What Happened to Property in Law and Economics?', 111 *Yale Law Journal*, pp. 357–398 (2001).

Merrill T and Smith H, *Property: principles and policies*, Foundation Press (2007).

Merrill T and Smith H, 'The Morality of Property', 48 *William and Mary Law Review*, pp. 1849–1895 (2007).

Merrill T and Smith H, 'Making Coasean Property More Coasean', 54 *Journal of Law and Economics*, pp. S77–S104, (2011).

Metcalf H (ed.), *Business Management as a Profession*, Chicago: AW Shaw & Co (1927).

Mian A et al, 'The Saving Glut of the Rich', *Princeton Economics*, Working Paper 2 (2021), https://scholar.harvard.edu/files/straub/files/mss_richsavingglut.pdf

Miles K, *The Origins of International Investment Law*, Cambridge: Cambridge University Press (2013).

Mincke W, 'Property: assets or power? Objects or relations as substrata of property rights', in J W Harris (ed.), *Property Problems from Genes to pension Funds*, pp. 77–88 (1997).

Miola I and Picciotto S, 'On the Sociology of Law in Economic Relations', 31 *Social & Legal Studies*, pp. 139–161 (2022).

Mitchell T, *Rule of Experts: Egypt, techno-politics, modernity*, Berkeley: University of California Press (2002).

Morgan L H, *Houses and House-life of the American Aborigines*, Washington DC: Government Print Office (1881).

Morozov E, 'Critique of Techno-Feudal Reason', 133/34 *New Left Review*, pp. 133–4 (January–April 2022).

Moyn S, 'Thomas Piketty and The Future of Legal Scholarship', 128 *Harvard Law Review*, pp. 49–55 (2014).

Moyn S, 'Reconstructing Critical Legal Studies', Yale Law School, Public Law Research Paper (4 August 2023).

Muldrew C, 'Interpreting the Market: the ethics of credit and community relations in early modern England', 18 *Social History*, pp. 163–183 (1993).

Muldrew C, *The Economy of Obligation*, London: Macmillan (1998).

Munzer S, *A Theory of Property*, Cambridge: Cambridge University Press (1990).

Munzer S, 'A Bundle Theorist Holds on to his Collection of Sticks', 8 *Econ Watch Journal*, pp. 265–273 (2011).

Munzer S, 'Property and Disagreement' in J E Penner and H Smith (eds), *Philosophical Foundations of Property Law*, Oxford: Oxford University Press, pp. 289–319 (2013).

Nace T, *Gangs of America*, San Francisco: Berrett-Koehler (2003).

Nadasdy P, '"Property" and Aboriginal Land Claims in the Canadian subarctic: some theoretical considerations', 104(1) *American Anthropologist*, pp. 247–261 (2002).

Nash J, 'Packaging Property: the effect of paradigmatic framing of property rights', 83 *Tulane Law Review*, pp. 691–734 (2009).

Nash J and Stern S, 'Property Frames', 87 *Washington University Law Review*, pp. 449–504 (2010).

Nedelsky J, *Property and the Limits of American Constitutionalism*, Chicago: University of Chicago Press (1990).

Nitzan J and Bichler S, *Capital as Power*, New York: Routledge (2009).

North D and Thomas R, *The Rise of the Western World*, Cambridge: Cambridge University Press (1973).

Noyes C R, *The Institution of Property*, New York: Longmans (1936).

O'Connor M, 'Restructuring the Corporation's Nexus of Contracts: recognizing a fiduciary duty to displaced workers', 69 *North Carolina Law Review*, pp. 1189–1260 (1991).

OECD, *In It Together: why less inequality benefits all*, Paris: OECD Publishing (2015).

OECD, *Blended Finance Guidance*, 29/9/2020, https://www.oecd.org/dac/financing-sustainable-development/blended-finance-principles/

O'Hara P A, 'Thorstein Veblen's Theory of Collective Social Wealth', 7 *History of Economic ideas*, pp. 153–79 (1999).

Ostrom E, *Governing the Commons*, Cambridge: Cambridge University Press (1990).

Pagano U, 'The Crisis of Intellectual Monopoly Capitalism', 38 *Cambridge Journal of Economics*, pp. 1409–1429 (2014).

Palladino L, 'Economic Policies for Innovative Enterprises: implementing multi-stakeholder corporate governance', 54 *Review of Radical Political Economics*, pp. 5–25 (2021).

Parkinson J, *Corporate Power and Responsibility*, Oxford: Clarendon Press (1993).

Parsons T, 'Capitalism in Recent German literature: Sombart and Weber', 36 *Journal of Political Economy*, pp. 641–661 (1928).

Pazzanese C, 'How Political Ideas Keep Economic Inequality Going', interview with Thomas Piketty, *Harvard Gazette*, 3/3/20.

Penner J E, *The Idea of Property in Law*, Oxford: Oxford University Press (1997).

Penner J E, 'Misled by "Property"', 18 *Canadian Journal of Law and Jurisprudence*, pp. 75–94 (2005).

Penner J E, 'Potentiality, Actuality and Stick Theory', 8 *Econ Journal Watch*, pp. 274–278 (2011).

Penner J E, 'Property' in A S Gold et al (eds), *The Oxford Handbook of the New Private Law*, Oxford: Oxford University Press, pp. 277–292 (2020).

Penner J E, *Property Rights: a re-examination*, Oxford: Oxford University Press (2020).

Pennington R, 'Terminal Compensation for Employees of Companies in Liquidation', 25 *Modern Law Review*, pp. 715–719 (1962).

Pennington R, 'Can Shares in Companies be Defined?', 10 *Company Lawyer*, pp. 144–152 (1989).

Pennington R, *Company Law*, London: Butterworths (6th ed., 1990).

Philbrick F, 'Changing Conceptions of Property in Law', 86 *University of Pennsylvania Law Review*, pp. 691–732 (1938).

Picciotto S, 'Regulation: managing the antinomies of economic vice and virtue', 26 *Social & Legal Studies*, pp. 676–699 (2017).

Piketty T, *Capital in Twenty-First Century*, Cambridge: Belknap Press (2014).

Piketty T, *Capital and Ideology*, Cambridge: Belknap Press (2019).

Pistor K, *The Code of Capital*, Princeton: Princeton University Press (2019).

Piterberg G and Veracini L, 'Wakefield, Marx and the World Turned Inside Out', 10 *Journal of Global History*, pp. 457–478 (2015).

Pocock J G A, *Virtue, Commerce and History*, Cambridge: Cambridge University Press (1985).

Polanyi K, *The Great Transformation*, Boston: Beacon Press (2002 [1944]),

Pollock F, 'What is a Thing?', 10 *Law Quarterly Review*, pp. 318–322 (1894).

Pollock F and Maitland F W, *The History of English Law Before the Time of Edward I*, Indianapolis: Liberty Fund (2010), taken from 2nd ed., Cambridge University Press (1898), volume 2.

Posner R, 'The Regulation of the Market in Adoptions', 67 *Boston University Law Review*, pp. 59–72 (1987).

Pottage A, 'Instituting Property', 18 *Oxford Journal of Legal Studies*, pp. 331–344 (1998).

Praduroux S, 'Objects of property rights: old and new', in M Graziadei and L Smith, *Comparative Property Law*, Edward Elgar: Cheltenham, pp. 51–70 (2017).

Pretto-Sakmann A, *Boundaries of Personal Property: shares and sub-shares*, Oxford: Hart (2005).

Pryor F, *Capitalism Reassessed*, Appendix 2 'Etymology of Capitalism', Cambridge: Cambridge University Press (2006), https://www.swarthmore.edu/SocSci/Economics/fpryor1/Appendices.pdf

Quinault R, 'Gladstone and Slavery', 52 *Historical Journal*, pp. 363–383 (2009).

Radin M, 'The Liberal Conception of Property', 88 *Columbia Law Review*, pp. 1667–1696 (1988).

Radin M, *Reinterpreting Property*, Chicago: University of Chicago Press (1993).

Rahmatian A, 'The Property Theory of Lord Kames', 2 *International Journal of Law in Context*, pp. 177–203 (2006),

Rainer F, 'Word Formation and Word History: the case of CAPITALIST and CAPITALISM', in Olivier Bonami et al (eds), *The Lexeme in Descriptive and Theoretical Morphology*, Berlin: Language Science Press, pp. 43–65 (2018).

Ramirez M, 'Credit, Indebtedness and Speculation in Marx's Political Economy', 8 *Economic Thought*, pp. 46–62 (2019).

Rasulov A, 'CLS and Marxism: a history of an affair', 5 *Transnational Legal Theory*, pp. 622–639 (2014).

Ravenscraft D and Scherer F M, 'The Profitability of Mergers', 7 *International Journal of Industrial Organisation*, pp. 101–116 (1989).

Rawls J, *Theory of Justice*, Cambridge: Harvard University Press (revised ed. 1999 [1971]).

Raz J, *The Concept of a Legal System*, Oxford: Oxford University Press (1980).

Raz J, *Between Authority and Interpretation*, Oxford: Oxford University Press (2009).

Reeve A, 'The Meaning and Definition of Property in Seventeenth-Century England', 89 *Past and Present*, pp. 139–142 (1980).

Reich C, 'The New Property', 73 *Yale Law Journal*, pp. 733–787 (1964).

Reich C, 'The New Property after 25 Years', 24 *University of San Francisco Law Review*, pp. 223–272 (1989–90).

Reynolds S, 'Tenure and Property in Medieval England', 88 *Historical Research*, pp. 563–576 (2015).

Rikap C, *Capitalism, Power and Innovation*, London: Routledge (2021).

Riley D and Brenner R, 'Seven Theses on American Politics', 138 *New Left Review*, pp. 5–27 (November–December, 2022).

Robé J-P, *Property, Power and Politics*, Bristol: Bristol University Press (2020).

Robé J-P, 'Taming Property', 4(1) *RED*, pp.162–69 (2022).

Robé J-P, 'Property, Power and Politics Reviewed - A Reply to Critics', 3 *Journal of Political Economy*, pp. 592–602 (2023).

Roberts M, 'Covid and Fictitious Capital' (January 2021), https://thenextrecession.wordpress.com/2021/01/25/covid-and-fictitious-capital/

Roos J, 'From the Demise of Social Democracy to the End of Capitalism: the intellectual trajectory of Wolfgang Streeck', 27 *Historical Materialism*, pp. 248–288 (2019).

Roos J, *Why Not Default? The political economy of sovereign debt*, Princeton: Princeton University Press (2019).

Rose C, 'Property as the Keystone Rights?', 71 *Notre Dame Law Review*, pp. 329–369 (1996).

Rose C, 'Canons of Property Talk, or, Blackstone's Anxiety', 108 *Yale Law Journal*, pp. 601–632 (1998).

Rose C, 'Ostrom and the Lawyers', 5 *International Journal of the Commons*, pp. 28–49 (2011).

Rosser E, 'The Ambition and Transformative Potential of Progressive Property', 101 *California Law Review*, pp. 107–171 (2013).

Rosser E, 'Destabilizing Property', 48 *Connecticut Law Review*, pp. 397–472 (2015).

Rossi E, 'Reconsidering the Dual Nature of Property Rights: personal property and capital in the law and economics of property rights' (2020), https://papers.ssrn.com/sol3/papers.cfm?abstract_id=3659193

Rotherham C, 'Review of James Penner, *The Idea of Property in Law*', 61 *Modern Law Review*, pp. 119–121 (1998).

Rouhani O et al, 'Revenue-Risk-Sharing Approaches for PPP Provision of Highway Facilities', 6 *Case Studies on Transport Policy*, pp. 439–448 (2018).

Rubin, I I, *A History of Economic Thought*, London: Ink Links (1979).

Rudden B, 'Things as Thing and Things as Wealth', 14 *Oxford Journal of Legal Studies*, pp. 81–97 (1994).

Ryan A, *Property and Political Theory*, Oxford: Basil Blackwell (1984).

Saez E and Zucman G, 'Wealth Inequality in the United States since 1913: evidence from capitalized income data', 131 *Quarterly Journal of Economics*, pp. 519–578 (2016).

Saito K, *Karl Marx's Ecosocialism*, New York: Monthly Review Press (2017).

Sylla N S and Gabor D, 'Planting Budgetary Time-Bombs in Africa', *Groupe d'études géopolitiques*, 23/12/2020.

Sarooshi D, *International Organizations and their Exercise of Sovereign Powers*, Oxford: Oxford University Press (2005).

Sayer D, *Method*, Hassocks, Sussex: Harvester Press (1979).

Sayer D, *The Violence of Abstraction*, Oxford: Basil Blackwell (1989).

Schneiderman D, 'Constitutional Approaches to Privatization: an inquiry into the magnitude of neo-liberal constitutionalism', 63 *Law and Contemporary Problems*, pp. 83–109 (2000).

Schneiderman D, 'Investment Rules and the New Constitutionalism', 25 *Law & Social Inquiry*, pp. 757–787 (2000).

Schneiderman D, 'Investment Rules and the Rule of Law', 8 *Constellations*, pp. 521–537 (2001).

Schneiderman D, *Constitutionalizing Economic Globalization*, Cambridge: Cambridge University Press (2008).

Schneiderman D, 'How to Govern Differently: neo-liberalism, new constitutionalism and international investment law', in S Gill and A C Cutler (eds), *New Constitutionalism and World Order*, Cambridge: Cambridge University Press, pp. 165–78 (2014).

Schorr D, 'How Blackstone became a Blackstonian', 10(1) *Theoretical Inquiries in Law*, pp. 103–126 (2009).

Schroeder J, 'Chix, Nix, Bundle-O-Stix: a feminist critique of the disaggregation of property', 93 *Michigan Law Review*, pp. 239–319 (1993).

Schumpeter J, *History of Economic Analysis*, Oxford: Oxford University Press (1954).

Scott C, 'Hunting Territories, Hunting Bosses and Communal Production among Coastal James Bay Cree', 28 *Anthropologica*, pp. 163–173 (1986).

Scott K, 'Agency Costs and Corporate Governance' in P Newman (ed.), *New Palgrave Dictionary of Economics and the Law*, London: Macmillan, pp. 26–30 (1998).

Sée H, *Modern Capitalism: its origin and evolution*, translated by Vanderblue and Dorio (2004 [1928]).

Seipp D, 'The Concept of Property in the Early Common Law', 12 *Law and History Review*, pp. 29–91 (1994).

Shleifer A and Summers L, 'Breach of Trust in Hostile takeovers', in A J Auerbach (ed.), *Corporate takeovers: causes and consequences*, Chicago: University of Chicago Press, pp. 33–56 (1998).

Singer J W, 'Property and Social Relations: from title to entitlement', in G E van Maanan and A J van der Walt (eds), *Property Law on the Threshold of the 21st Century*, Antwerp: Maklu, pp. 69–90 (1996).

Singer J W, 'Democratic Estates: property law in a free and democratic society', 94 *Cornell Law Review*, pp. 1009–1062 (2009).

Sklair J and Gilbert P, 'Giving as "De-Risking": philanthropy, impact investment and the pandemic response', 4 *Public Anthropologist*, pp. 51–77 (2022).

Slobodian Q, *The Globalists*, Cambridge: Harvard University Press (2018).

Slobodian Q, *Crack Up Capitalism*, London: Allen Lane (2021).

Smith A, *Lectures on Jurisprudence*, Oxford: Oxford University Press, (1978 [1762–3]).

Smith A, *The Wealth of Nations*, Indianapolis: Liberty Classics (eds R H Campbell et al, 1981 [1776]).

Smith H, 'Exclusion versus Governance: two strategies for delineating property rights', 31 *Journal of Legal Studies*, pp. S483–S487 (2002).

Smith H, 'Exclusion and Property Rules in the Law of Nuisance', 90 *Virginia Law Review*, pp. 965-1049 (2004).

Smith H, 'Property and Property Rules', 79 *New York University Law Review*, pp. 1719–1798 (2004).

Smith H, 'Intellectual Property as Property', 116 *Yale Law Journal*, pp. 1742–1822 (2007).

Smith H, 'Property is not just a bundle of rights', 8 *Econ Journal Watch*, pp. 279–291 (2011).

Smith H, 'On the Economy of Concepts in Property', 16 *University of Pennsylvania Law Review*, pp. 2097–2018 (2012).

Smith H, 'Property as the Law of Things', 125 *Harvard Law Review*, pp. 1691–1726 (2012).

Smith H, 'Semicommons in Fluid Resources', 20 *Marquette Intellectual Property Law Review*, pp. 195–212 (2016).

Smith M et al, 'Capitalists in the Twenty-First Century', *NBER Working Paper 25442* (June 2019).

Smith T, *Beyond Liberal Egalitarianism*, Chicago: Haymarket (2017).

Soederberg S, *The Politics of the New International Financial Architecture*, London: Zed (2004).

Sokol, Mary, 'Bentham and Blackstone on Incorporeal Heriditaments', 15 *Journal of Legal History*, pp. 287–305 (1994).

Sornarajah M, *Resistance and Change in the International Law on Foreign Investment*, Cambridge: Cambridge University Press (2015).

Stedman Jones D, *Masters of the Universe: Hayek, Friedman and the birth of neoliberal politics*, Princeton: Princeton University Press (2012).

Stern P, *The Company State: corporate sovereignty and the early modern foundations of the British Empire in India*, Oxford: Oxford University Press (2011).

Stern P, *Empire, Incorporated: the corporations that built British colonialism*, Cambridge: Belknap Press (2023).

Stout L, 'Uncertainty, Dangerous Optimism and Speculations', 97 *Cornell Law Review*, pp. 1177–1212 (2012).

Stevenson G, *The Trading Game: a confession*, London: Allen Lane (2024)

Strahilevitz L, 'Information Asymnmetries and the Right to Exclude', 104 *Michigan Law Review*, pp. 1835–1897 (2006).

Strathern M, *Substance and Effect: anthropological essays on persons and things*, London: Athlone (1999).

Streeck W, 'Institutions in History: bringing capitalism back in', *MPIfG Discussion Paper 09/8*, Cologne: Max-Planck-Institut (2009).

Streeck W, *Re-Forming Capitalism*, Oxford: Oxford University Press (2009).

Streeck W, 'E Pluribus Unum? Varieties and commonalities of capitalism', *MPIfG Discussion Paper 10/12*, Cologne: Max-Planck-Institut (2010).

Streeck W, 'Taking Capitalism Seriously: towards an institutionalist approach to contemporary political economy', 9 *Socio-Economic Review*, pp. 137–167 (2011).

Streeck W, 'Interview', *The Current Moment*, 3/1/2012.

Streeck W, 'On Re-Forming Capitalism', *The Montreal Review*, March 2012.

Streeck W, 'How will Capitalism end?', 87 *New Left Review*, pp. 35–64 (May–June 2014).

Streeck W, *Buying Time*, London: Verso (2014).

Streeck W, 'Politics in the Interregnum: Q&A with Wolfgang Streeck', *ROAR Magazine*, 23/12/15.

Streeck W, 'Social Democracy's Last Rounds', *Jacobin*, 25/2/16.

Supiot A, *Homo Juridicus: on the anthropological function of law*, London: Verso (2005).

Sutherland K, 'Marx in Jargon', http://worldpicturejournal.com/article/marx-in-jargon/

Sweet G, 'Impediments to the Transfer of Land', *Papers Read Before the Juridical Society, 1858–74*, London: Stevens (1873).

Syed T, 'Did CLS have (much of) any Theory?', LPE Blog, 10/10/23.

Talbot L, *Progressive Corporate Governance for the 21st Century*, London: Routledge (2013).

Tamanaha B, *A Realistic Theory of Law*, Cambridge: Cambridge University Press (2017).

Tawney R H, *The Acquisitive Society*, London: G Bell (1921).

Tett G, 'Elite's grip on US bonds lays bare fiscal divide', *Financial Times*, 15/11/13.

Tooze A, 'Review of Streeck's *Buying Time*', *London Review of Books*, 5/1/17.

Tooze A, 'Neoliberalism's World Order', Review of Quinn Slobodian's *The Globalists*, *Dissent Magazine* (Summer 2018).

Tooze A, 'Welcome to the World of the Polycrisis', *Financial Times*, 28/10/22.

Thompson E P, 'The Long Revolution – II', 10 *New Left Review*, pp. 34–39 (1961).

Thompson E P, 'Time, Work-Discipline and Industrial Capitalism', 38 *Past & Present*, pp. 56–97 (1967).

Thompson E P, *Whigs and Hunters*, London: Allen Lane (1975).

Thompson E P, 'Interview', 3 *Radical History Review*, pp. 4–25 (1976).

Thompson E P, 'Caudwell', *Socialist Register*, pp. 228–276 (1977).

Thompson E P, 'The Peculiarities of the English', in *The Poverty of Theory and Other Essays*, London: Merlin Press (1979 [1978]).

Thompson E P, 'The Poverty of Theory', in E P Thompson, *The Poverty of Theory and Other Essays*, London: Merlin Press (1979 [1978]).

Thompson E P, 'Open Letter to Leszek Kolakowski', in E P Thompson, *The Poverty of Theory and Other Essays*, London: Merlin Press (1979 [1978]).

Thompson E P, 'The Moral Economy of the English Crowd in the 18th Century', in E P Thompson, *Customs in Common*, London: Merlin Press (1991 [1971]).

Thompson E P, 'History and Anthropology', in E P Thompson, *Making History: writings on history and culture*, New York: New Press, pp. 199–225 (1995).

Thomson A, 'Law and the Social Sciences: the demise of legal autonomy', paper delivered at Critical Legal Studies Conference, University of Kent (1981).

Thomson A, 'The Law of Contract', in I Grigg-Spall and P Ireland (eds), *The Critical Lawyers Handbook*, London: Pluto, pp. 69–76 (1992).

Travis H, 'Pirates of the Information Infrastructure: Blackstonian copyright and the First Amendment', 15 *Berkeley Technology Law Journal*, pp. 777–864 (2000).

Troy L et al, 'Pathways to Home Ownership in an Age of Uncertainty', *Australian Housing and Urban Research Institute* (2023).

Turner B, 'The Anthropology of Property' in M Graziadei and L Smith, *Comparative Property Law*, Edward Elgar: Cheltenham, pp. 26–48, (2017)

Tylor E, *Anthropology*, London: Macmillan (1881).

Underkuffler L, 'Property: A Special Right', 71 *Notre Dame Law Review*, pp. 1033–1058 (1996).

Unger R, *The Left Alternative*, London: Verso (2nd ed., 2009).

Vandevelde K, 'The New Property of the Nineteenth Century: the development of the modern concept of property', 29 *Buffalo Law Review*, pp. 325–367 (1980).

Van Harten G, 'Investment Rules and the Denial of Change', 60 *University of Toronto Law Journal*, pp. 893–904 (2010).

Van Harten G, *The Trouble with Foreign Investor Protection*, Oxford: Oxford University Press (2020).

Varoufakis Y, *Technofeudalism; What Killed Capitalism*, London: Bodley Head (2022).

Veblen T, *The Theory of the Leisure Class*, New York: Macmillan (1899).

Veblen T, *The Theory of Business Enterprise*, New York: Scribner (1904).

Veblen T, 'Fisher's Income and Capital', 23 *Political Science Quarterly*, pp. 112–128 (1908).

Veblen T, 'On the Nature of Capital (I)', 22 *Quarterly Journal of Economics*, pp. 517–542 (1908).

Veblen T, 'On the Nature of Capital (II): investment and intangible assets and the pecuniary magnate', 23 *Quarterly Journal of Economics*, pp. 104–136 (1908).

Veblen T, *The Instinct of Workmanship and the State of the Industrial Arts*, New York: Macmillan (1914).

Veblen T, *The Vested Interests and the Common Man*, New York: Huebsch (1919).

Veblen T, *Absentee Ownership*, New York: Huebsch (1923).

von Benda-Beckmann F, von Benda-Beckmann K and Wiber M, 'The Properties of Property', in von Benda-Beckmann et al (eds), *Changing Properties of Property*, New York: Bergahn Books, pp. 1–39 (2006).

Wakefield E G, 'England and America' in M F Lloyd Pritchard (ed.), *Collected Works*, Glasgow: Collins, pp. 313–718 (1968 [1833]).

Waldron J, *The Right to Private Property*, Oxford: Clarendon Press (1988).

Waldron J, 'Property and Ownership', in *Stanford Encyclopedia of Philosophy*, https://plato.stanford.edu/entries/property/

Weber M, *Economy and Society*, reprinted in W Runciman (ed.), *Max Weber: selections in translation*, Cambridge: Cambridge University Press (1978).
Wedderburn K W, *Company Law Reform*, Fabian Tract 363, The Fabian Society (1965).
Weeks J, *Capital and Exploitation*, Princeton: Princeton University Press (1981).
White L, *The Evolution of Culture*, New York: McGraw Hill (1959).
Wighton D, 'Mandelson plans a microchip off the old block', *Financial Times*, 23/10/98.
Williams R, *Marxism and Literature*, Oxford: Oxford University Press (1977).
Williamson O, 'Corporate Control and the Theory of the Firm', in H Manne (ed.) *Economic Policy and the Regulation of Corporate Securities: a symposium*, Washington DC: American Enterprise Institute for Public Policy Research, pp. 281–336 (1969).
Williamson O, *Markets and Hierarchies: analysis and antitrust implications*, New York: Free Press (1975).
Williamson O, *The Economic Institutions of Capitalism*, New York: Free Press (1985).
Winters J A, 'Wealth Defense and the Complicity of Liberal Democracy', LVIII *Nomos*, pp. 158–225 (2017).
Wood E M, 'Marxism and the Course of History', 147 *New Left Review*, pp. 95–108, (September–October 1984).
Wood E M, 'The Separation of the Economic and Political in Capitalism', 127 *New Left Review*, pp. 66–95 (May–June 1981).
Wood E M, *The Pristine Culture of Capitalism*, London: Verso (1991).
Wood E M, *Democracy Against Capitalism*, Cambridge: Cambridge University Press (1995).
Wood E M and Wood N, *A Trumpet of Sedition*, London: Pluto (1997).
Wood E M, *The Origin of Capitalism: a longer view*, London: Verso (1999).
Wood E M, *The Ellen Meiksins Wood Reader*, London: Brill (ed Larry Patriquin, 2012).
Wood F S, 'The Status of Management Stockholders', 38 *Yale Law Journal*, pp. 57–76 (1928).
Wolf M, *The Crisis of Democratic Capitalism*, London: Allen Lane (2023).
Wolff E N, 'The Asset Price Meltdown and the Wealth of the Middle Class', *NBER, The Digest, No 4*, (April 2013).
Wolfe A, 'The Modern Corporation: private agent or public actor', 50 *Washington & Lee Law Review*, pp. 1673-1696 (1993).
Worthington S, *Equity*, Oxford: Oxford University Press, (2nd ed., 2006).
Worthington S, 'The Disappearing Divide between Property and Obligation' (2007) 42 *Texas International Law Journal*, pp. 917–940 (2007).

World Inequality Lab, *World Inequality Report 2022* (WIR), co-ordinated by L Chancel, T Piketty, E Saez and G Zucman, https://wir2022.wid.world/www-site/uploads/2021/12/WorldInequalityReport2022_Full_Report.pdf

Wyman K, 'The New Essentialism in Property', 9 *Journal of Legal Analysis*, pp. 183–246 (2017).

Wyman K, 'Property as Intangible Property', in P Miller and J Oberdiek (eds), *Oxford Studies in Private Law Theory*, volume 1, Oxford: Oxford University Press, pp. 81–106 (2020).

Zucman G, 'Global Wealth Inequality', 11 *Annual Review of Economics*, pp. 109–138, (2019).

Index

References to notes show both the page number and the note number (191n22)

A

'absentee ownership' 72, 135
abstraction 8, 9, 121, 123–5, 192, 193
  dangers of 109–19
  and Marx 239–40
  see also thing-ownership conception of property
'accumulation by dispossession' 191n22, 242
acquisitions 147–8
actions of ejectment (land) 28
actions of trover (personal possessions) 28
Adkins, Lisa 87n69
adoption market 84n58
affirmative asset partitioning 150
Africa 212
agency theories of the corporation *see* contractual theories of the corporation
'agents of wealth defence' 102–3, 205, 256
agriculture 38
  'agricultural revolution', seventeenth century 43
  HRS (Household Responsibility System), China 173, 260
Alchain, Armen 142, 145–6
Alexander, Gregory 46n29, 53, 106, 168n118, 179n177
alienability 176, 177
American Law Institute, First Restatement of Property (1936) 34
American Law Institute, Fourth Restatement of Property Law 167, 169, 171
American Revolution 76
analytical jurisprudence analysis 2, 3n7, 4, 8, 189, 192n27
  abstraction 109–19
  dominium in Roman law 119–21
  idea of property in law 121–32
  new essentialism 105–7, 121
  ubiquity of property institutions 107–9
Anderson, Elizabeth 34n120, 41n9, 75, 76, 129, 228n17

Anglo-Saxon concepts of property 25
anthropology 4, 107–8, 118, 173, 186n4
  concepts of property in 23, 24, 27
  property institutions 51–3
Appadurai, Arjun 103
Arbogast, Tobias 86, 98–9
asset management firms 9, 160–2, 164, 210
asset-stripping 165
Association for Molecular Pathology v Myriad Genetics Inc., 569 US 576 81
Atkinson, Anthony 87
austerity 10, 201
Austin, John 29, 30
Austrian School 63
authors, rights of *see* copyrights; literary property
autonomy 14n12, 76
  private property, individual autonomy and identity 47–9, 50, 53
Aylmer, G E 24, 28

B

B corps (benefit corporations) 259
babies, for adoption 84n58
'baby boomer' generation 95
bad faith 246–7
bailouts 10, 190, 201–2, 241, 259
Baines, John 162, 163, 164
Baker, J H 25, 26
Bank of England 20n38
'Bank of Mum and Dad' 95
banks 10, 104, 190, 201
Banner, Stuart 17n26
Baron, Jane 167n116, 174
'barren path' 131
Beckert, Jens 103
Bentham, Jeremy 30n98, 37, 228
Berle, Adolf 9, 136n9, 137, 138n12, 142, 144, 145, 146, 147, 177n171, 259
Bezos, Jeff 1–2
'Big Three' asset management firms 160, 162, 163, 164

289

bills
  as choses in action 21, 22
bills of exchange 64
BITS (bilateral investment treaties) 207
Black Act 1723 42n14
BlackRock 160, 161, 162, 163–4
Blackstone (private equity firm) 79
Blackstone, William 5, 6, 14, 17, 18, 19, 21, 22, 23, 29, 31, 39, 45, 47, 54–5, 56–7, 84, 169, 180n182, 185, 191–2, 223
  'sole and despotic dominion' definition of property 5, 7, 13, 15, 16, 26, 30, 43, 44, 89, 172, 180n182, 186–7, 191, 226, 260
  'total exclusion' 5, 13, 26, 44
  see also thing-ownership conception of property
Blanc, Louis 61
Blaufarb, Rafe 24, 26, 46, 47
'blended finance' 212
Bloch, Marc 25
Bodenheimer, Edgar 131n117
bonds 8, 16
  bondholder rights 210
  'bondholding class' 96, 98
Bouckaert, Boudewijn 181n186
Bourdieu, Pierre 225–6
Boyle, James 83n55
'BPrN the Basic Property Norm - the Property Exclusionary Norm for Tangible Property' 125
Brandeis, Louis 136
Braudel, Fernand 59, 61
Braun, Benjamin 161n94
Brenner, Robert 11, 82, 187, 188, 189, 190–1, 201–2, 237–8, 242
Bretton Woods system 101, 139, 141, 157, 204
Brick, Howard 60
Brief, Götz 11–12, 248
bundle of rights conception of property 5, 6, 10–11, 23, 29, 30–5, 37, 38, 76, 105, 121, 122, 171, 179, 182–3, 224, 225, 227, 229, 232, 253, 260
  hostility to 167–9
business debt 86
  see also debt
buy-to-let housing, UK 79

C

Campbell, David 149, 155–6
capital 74, 83
  development of terminology and concept 58–9
  difference from wealth 63–4
  distribution of 8, 87–93
  'fictitious capital' 65–6, 104
  historicising private property and capital 186–94
  industrial capital 62, 63
  and investment 59, 63–4, 71–5
  merchant capital 62, 63
  money-lending/interest-bearing 62, 63, 74
  nature of 7–8
  need for wage labour 73–4
  primitive (original) accumulation of 42, 188, 191, 196, 242
  see also property-as-capital
capitalism 3, 9, 11, 37, 43, 54, 112, 118
  bringing capitalism back in 232–4
  corporate capitalism 51, 76
  development of terminology and concept 60–2
  emergence of 28
  end of 251–2
  as the 'end of history' 55
  ethics and contemporary capitalism 12
  feudal characteristics of 82
  logic of process of 11, 234–43, 245, 247, 249
  moral logic of 243–50
  'new political capitalism' 242
  political capitalism 190–1
  rise of 22, 117
  socially democratic form of 11
  universalisation of 185–6
capitalist
  development of terminology and concept 59–60
CDOs (collateralised debt obligations) 250
central banks 43
Chadwick, Anna 180n180, 231
Chang, Ha-Joon 84
change, transformative 251–61
Chayes, Abran 139
cheques 21, 64
children, status of 45n23
China 90, 91, 173
  HRS (Household Responsibility System) 173, 260
choses in action 20, 21–2, 44, 64, 65, 125
choses in possession 20
Christophers, Brett 80, 82
circuits of capital 62–3
circulation, sphere of 63, 228
civic humanism 57
civic republicanism 46n29
civil government 197
classes, relations between 11, 47, 223
climate change 159–60, 162, 163, 232, 248–9, 255–6
Clinton, Hillary 247–8
CLS (Critical Legal Studies) 168, 169, 195, 234–5, 234n39, 253, 255
CO_2 budgets 256
Coase, Ronald 145
coding, legal 180, 202n70, 230–1
coercion, and markets 254–5
'co-evolutionary' theory of change 256–7
cognitive framing 224–5, 261

INDEX

Cohen, Morris 34, 48, 77, 79, 100, 181
Coke, Sir Edward 28n88
collaterialised debt obligations (CDOs) 250
Colliot-Théléne, Catherine 235n32, 243n72
colonialism 78, 195–6, 206
'commercialisation model' of economic history 186
commodity production 43
common resources
  community-based management of 259–60
  intangible commons, new enclosures 83–5
  'tragedy of the commons' 85n61
Commons, John 32
communal ownership 118
communism 6, 7n18, 118
'communist dictatorships', American workplaces as 75
Companies Acts (1844–62) 199
consumer debt 86
  see also debt
contractual theories of the corporation 142, 149–56, 157, 158, 171, 177–8
co-operatives 259
Copyright Act 1842 17n25
Copyright Act (Statute of Anne) 1710 17–18, 19
copyrights 16, 17–20, 21, 29, 31, 170
Corbin, Arthur 33
corporate control, market for 142–9
corporate debt 86
  see also debt
corporate governance 9, 138, 157–66, 172
corporate managers 136
corporate personality 68
corporate scandals 159
corporate social responsibility 160, 162
corporations 9, 75, 132, 242
  Anglo-American model of 153, 166, 176–7
  contractual theories of 142, 149–56, 157, 158, 171, 177–8
  exclusion/exclusivity in corporate control 9, 69, 135–6, 149, 150, 152, 154
  modern corporations and threats to shareholder rights 133–9
  as separate entities 134
  and social democracy 139–42
  as social or quasi-social institutions 137–8, 142, 259
  socialisation of 258
  'zombie corporations' 201n69
  see also multinational corporations
cost control 42–3
COVID-19 pandemic 1, 86, 88, 91, 101, 184, 201–2, 214, 215
Cowell, John 24, 28
credit 20, 21, 187
  changing patterns of 43–4
credit card debt 86
  see also debt

Credit Suiss Global Wealth Report 91
Cree community 116
Critical Legal Studies (CLS) 168, 169, 195, 234–5, 234n39, 253, 255
Crosland, Anthony 141–2
'cultural capital' 58
currency deriskiing 213
  see also derisking

D

Dagan, Hanoch 35, 49, 50
data, private ownership and control of 80–1
Daunton, Martin 42n13
Davies, Margaret 47, 49, 192
debt 31, 125
  debt bondage 85
  profiting from 85–7
  rights arising from 20–1
  as a saleable commodity 22n25
  securitisation 86–7
'debt state' 101–2, 204
decolonisation 206
'delegated private government', private property as 48
demand derisking 212
  see also derisking
democracy 10, 233
  and the 'new constitutionalism' 205–10, 242
Demsetz, Harold 142, 145
deprivatisation 257–8
  see also nationalisation
deregulation 54, 219
derisking 10, 219, 242
  of housing as an asset class 79, 214–15
  of new property 211–17
derivatives 66, 104, 250
di Robilant, Anna 29, 34, 119, 120–1
digital industries 81, 82, 219
directors, of corporations 138, 140, 146
'discrete-asset' framing 225
distributive justice 127–8
  see also wealth inequalities
Dodd, E. Merrick 138
Domhoff, G William 92n93
dominium in Roman law 119–21, 193
Donaldson v Becket (1774) 1 English Reports 837; 98 English Reports 257 19
Douglas, William O. 138
Drucker, Peter 139
dual nature of property 7, 50, 51, 62–6
  capital, capitalist and capitalism 57–62
  institutionalising modern property 39–47
  joint stock company shares 66–70
  personal possessions *versus* productive resources 48–57
  private property, individual autonomy and identity 47–9, 50, 53
  see also property-as-capital
Durand, Cedric 82

291

Durbin, Evan 141
Duvergier v Fellows (1828) 5 Bing 24 67
Dyson, Sir James 2

E

East India Company 242
Easterbrook, Frank 142, 147, 152–3, 154–5, 156
Ebrahimi v Westbourne Galleries [1973] AC 360 68n135
ECHR (European Convention on Human Rights) 36, 182
economic development 54, 84
economic, the, separation from the political 189–90, 192
ECtHR (European Court of Human Rights) 36, 182, 210
efficiency 153–4, 176
egalitarian social movements 76
ejectment, actions of (land) 28
electricity utilities, privatisation of, UK 80
Ely, Richard 32
Emergency Economic Stabilization Act 2008 201
employee share ownership plans (ESOPs) 258
enclosure 28, 41–2, 44, 55–6, 77, 80, 181, 199
  new enclosures 83–5
'end of history' thesis 55, 185
energy crisis 86
energy market, UK 215
Engels, F 61, 118n53
Enlightenment, the 54, 76, 186
  see also Scottish Enlightenment
environmental issues 131, 159–60, 232, 248–9
Epstein, Richard 168, 182–3
ESG (environment, social and governance) issues 160, 161, 162, 163
ESOPs (employee share ownership plans) 258
'essence' of property 2, 105–6, 107, 110, 121, 122, 194, 224
ethics 12, 249–50
  'marginal ethics' *(grenzmoral)* 11–12, 248
Europe
  gender wealth gap 94
  housing, as an asset class 79
  inheritance, and wealth inequality 96
  public debt ownership 98–9
  wealth inequality 90
European Central Bank 208, 210
European Convention on Human Rights (ECHR) 36, 182
European Court of Human Rights (ECtHR) 36, 182, 210
European Court of Justice 208, 210
European Union 208
exchange, sphere of 228
exchange value 18, 19

exclusion/exclusivity 6, 106, 115, 121, 122, 124, 125, 126, 129, 130, 132, 166, 169
  'exclusivity axiom' 7, 48
  information cost theories of property 171–5, 175–6, 181
  land ownership 39, 47, 78, 112, 170
  private property 5, 34n21, 42, 48, 167, 173
  shareholders and corporate control 9, 69, 135–6, 149, 150, 152, 154
  'total exclusion' (Blackstone) 5, 13, 26, 44
expropriation 207

F

Fabians, the 61n102
Fama, Eugene 152
'family resemblance' 36, 105, 110n24
Fancy, Tariq 163
Federal Reserve 201–2
feminism 49, 229
Ferguson, Adam 117
fetishism 74
Fetter, Frank 63, 64, 65
feudalism 187, 193
  concepts of property in 25
  feudal characteristics of contemporary capitalism 82
'fictitious capital' 65–6, 104
'fictitious commodity'
  knowledge as 112n37
  land as 42
Fielding, Henry 40
financial crash, 1929–30 220–1
financial crash, 2008 86, 101, 159, 184, 201, 250, 259
financial derisking 212
  see also derisking
financial institutions 157, 158
financial instruments 21–2, 64, 66, 104
financial liberalisation 11, 157, 164, 247, 249
financial property 9–10, 200
  future-dependence of 202–3
  new financial aristocracy 202–5
  and wealth inequality 92–3
'financial revolution' 22
  in government funding 20
financialisation 104, 241
financialised corporate governance 157–66
Fink, Larry 161, 162, 163, 164
First World War 220
Fischel, Daniel 142, 147, 150n62, 153, 154–5, 156
Forbes World's Billionaires List 1
formalism 171, 174
Fracchia, Joseph 239
framing 224–5, 261
France 39, 46, 101
  'Great Demarcation' 46–7
  historic concepts of property in 24, 25, 26
  influence of Roman law 120

Old Regime property law 24
wealth inequality 90, 95
franchise, restriction of 203
Franks, Julian 148
free enterprise 62n103
free market 54
 free market economy 218
 free market exchange 46
 free market society 76, 129
 ideologies of 37
free trade agreements 207
French Civil Code of 1804, Article 544 13, 47, 120
French Revolution 76
Fukuyama, Francis 55, 185
full liberal ownership 13, 43, 111, 226
'full-blooded ownership' 111–12, 114, 117
functionalism 171, 174
future, the, speculators on 103–4

G

G7 255
G20 216
Gabor, Daniela 211, 212, 215, 216, 217
Galbraith, J K 147
Gaudemet, Jean 119–20
gender
 gendered division of labour 94
 private property 49
 property ownership 78
 reproductive labour 229
 suffrage, nineteenth century 40–1
 wealth inequalities 93–5
gene sequences, intellectual property rights (IPRs) 81
'general citizenry' (*Staatsvolke*) 101, 102, 204
'general illumination' metaphor 244
genetically modified organisms, intellectual property rights (IPRs) 81
Germany 101, 233
 Grundgesetz (Constitution) 36, 53
 influence of Roman law 120
 property law 23, 35–6, 53, 179n177
Getzler, Joshua 55, 56
Gill, Stephen 205
Gladstone, William, slavery and family wealth 196, 197
Global Gender Wealth Equity Report 93–4
globalisation 204n77, 217, 218
Goldman Sachs 250
Golland, Ami 162–3
Gordon, Jeffrey 141n23
Gordon, Robert 14, 15, 22, 103–4
government funding, 'financial revolution' in 20
government stock 21, 64
Gower, L C B 68, 69, 140
Gray, Kevin 37, 48, 84, 121–2, 179
Graziadei, Michele 120

'Great Demarcation', France 46–7
Great Reform Act 1932 203n73
Greece 210
green transition 216
Greer, Allan 26, 116n49, 186n4, 230
grenzmoral ('marginal ethics') 11–12, 248
Grey, Thomas C 13, 37, 47n35, 184
Grundgesetz (Constitution), Germany 36, 53

H

Hager, Sandy 96–7, 162–164
Hale, Robert Lee 34, 48, 253–5
Hallowell, Irving 108, 192
Hann, Chris 27, 28, 51n55
Hansmann, Henry 150n60, 153, 185
Harris, James W 29, 37n133, 50, 51, 107–8, 110–12, 113–14, 115, 116–17, 189
Hart, H L A 124, 131n117, 132, 222
Harvey, David 191n22, 240–1, 242–3, 252, 256–7
Hawley, James 161n92
Hayek, F 209, 224
hedge funds 158, 210
Hegel, G W F 48
Herman, Shael 120
'hermit's property right' 173
high net-worth individuals 87
Hinduja brothers 2
Hinton v Donaldson (1773) 5 Brn 508 19
Hirschl, Ran 210
history 4
 concepts of property in 23–6
 property as a historical category 222–4
 staged (stadial) versions of 3n8, 54, 117, 185, 235
 and theory 222–3
Hodgson, Geoffrey 58, 83
Hohfeld, Wesley Newcombe 5, 6, 11, 32–3, 35, 124, 227, 229
'Hohfeld-Honoré synthesis' 125
Holdsworth, W F 21, 28, 112
Honoré, Tony 6, 35, 105, 111, 173
household debt 86
 ownership of 99–100
housing 87n69, 91–2
 buy-to-let housing, UK 79
 home ownership, gender wealth gap in 94
 institutional investment in 79, 214–15
 intergenerational inequalities 95–6
 investment/s 79
 property wealth 87, 91
Howey (*Securities and Exchange Commission v W J Howey Co.* 328 US 293 [1946]) 8, 11, 71–2, 75, 200, 229
HRS (Household Responsibility System), China 173, 260
'human capital' 58, 245
Hume, David 54, 117, 185
Hutchinson, Allan 123

I

identity, private property and individual autonomy 47–9, 50, 53
imperialism 206
  see also colonialism
'improvement', political economy of 56, 57, 78, 181
'inclusive ownership funds' 258
income inequalities 87–8, 147
  decline in 141
incorporeal hereditaments 16
incorporeal property rights 19, 31
indentured servitude 85
'indeterminacy' thesis 234
index funds 160, 162
indigenous societies 23, 78, 130
  defence of territorial claims in Western courts 115–16
industrial capital 62, 63, 83
inequality 11
  intergenerational inequalities 95–6
  see also income inequalities; wealth inequalities
information cost theories of property 9, 133, 166–78
'infrastructure rentierism' 80
inheritance, and wealth inequality 88, 96
innovation, and intellectual property rights (IPRs) 84–5
institutional investment 79, 97n116, 98, 142–3, 157, 160, 211, 212, 214, 215, 216–17, 249
intangible commons, new enclosures 83–5
intangible property 5, 8, 9, 16–17, 29, 34, 35, 36, 37, 65–6, 125–7, 170–1, 176, 181, 198, 217, 227
intellectual property (IP) 6, 8, 79, 81, 170, 172, 182, 200, 231
intellectual property rights (IPRs) 56, 57, 79, 84–5, 126–7, 200, 207, 220, 227, 241
interest, payment of 85–6
intergenerational inequalities 95–6
'internal' aspects of law 124
international investment law 206
  investment arbitration tribunals 207, 208
  ISDS (investor-state-dispute-settlement) treaties 206, 207, 208–9, 242
International Monetary Fund 54, 84, 186n4, 208, 211
investment climate 78, 157, 204, 206, 219
investment/s 4, 8, 10, 11, 229
  and capital 59
  of former slave owners' compensation 188n10
  Howey test for 71–2
  institutional investment 79, 97n116, 98, 142–3, 157, 160, 211, 212, 214, 215, 216–17, 249
  investment arbitration tribunals 207, 208

prioritising investor interest 199–202
residential housing 79
speculators 103–4
invisible hand of the market 46, 192
IP (intellectual property) 6, 8, 79, 81, 170, 172, 182, 200, 231
IPRs (intellectual property rights) 56, 57, 79, 84–5, 126–7, 200, 207, 220, 227, 241
ISDS (investor-state-dispute-settlement) treaties 206, 207, 208–9, 242
Italy 214

J

Japan 101
Jensen, Michael 142, 145, 147n47, 150
Jessop, Bob 112n37
joint stock company shares 8, 16, 21, 31, 64, 126, 198–9
  reconceptualisation of 66–70
  see also shareholders
joint stock corporations see corporations
'juristocracy' 210

K

Kant, I 48
Katz, Larissa 122, 174
Katz, Wilbur 145, 146
Kay, John 148
Kay Review of UK Equity Markers and Long Term Decision Making 148
Kennedy, Duncan 44, 234–5
Kennedy, Margrit 99n121
Kerry, John 216n125
Kershaw, David 148
Keynes, John Maynard 8, 9, 82, 137, 138–9, 141, 258
Kim, Jim Yong 216
Kluane First Nation 116n47
knowledge
  as a 'fictitious commodity' 112n37
  private ownership and control of 80–1, 85–6
  see also intellectual property (IP); patents
Kraakman, Reinier 150n60, 153, 185
Kukk, Merike 94

L

labour
  capital's need for wage labour 73–4
  declining labour share of GDP 165
  declining power of 219, 220, 241
  position of workers in corporations 140, 149, 159
  reclassification of workers as independent service providers 219
  reproductive labour 229
  separation from means of subsistence 42, 55–6, 77, 79, 187–8, 191, 237
  as source of national wealth 40
  use rights over land 15, 28, 39, 42, 44, 47, 78

INDEX

labour theory of value 40, 73n14
Lacey, Nicola 4, 107n10, 126, 131, 193, 194
Lametti, David 108–9, 113–14
land 15, 24, 44, 51n55, 87, 170
  actions of ejectment 28
  common ownership 15, 39, 42, 52, 78
  enclosure 28, 41–2, 44, 55–6, 77, 80, 83–5, 181, 199
  environmental issues 131
  exclusion/exclusivity 39, 47, 78, 112, 170
  as a 'fictitious commodity' 42
  'land grabs' 80
  ownership 28, 31, 44, 45–6
  and power 40
  privatisation of public land, UK 80
  social relations 39–41
  'trespass to land' 170
  use rights 15, 28, 39, 42, 44, 47, 78
Landes, Elizabeth 84n58
Laski, Harold 135, 136
law
  concept of 122–3
  constitutive role of 195
  dominium, in Roman law 119–21
  idea of property in 121–32
  'internal' aspects of 124
  nature of 122, 123
Law and Political Economy (LPE) movement 235, 253
law of contract 129
law of value 73n14
law-and-economics approach 2, 4, 8, 9, 54, 84n58, 106
  contractual theories of the corporation 149–55
  fictional corporations, rematerialisation of 155–6
  financialised corporate governance 157–66
  information cost theories of property 9, 133, 166–78
  market for corporate control 142–9
  modern corporations and threats to shareholder rights 133–9
  social democracy and the socialised corporation 139–42
  'special' nature of property rights 179–84
laws of motion 11, 235, 237, 242–3
Lawson, F H 104
lawyers
  and 'new constitutionalism' 205–6
  role of in creation and protection of property-as-capital 198–9, 219
Lazzarato, Maurizio 83, 241, 250, 253
Leacock, Eleanor 116
Legacies of British Slave-Ownership, UCL 196, 197
legal coding 180, 202n70, 230–1
legal institutionalist movements 195, 253
legal positivism 192n27

Legal Realists 32, 33, 34, 168, 169, 253
legal, the 189n14
  separation from the political 189–90, 192
'leisure class' 72
Les Trente Glorieuses 140
Levellers, the 76, 78n32
Levy, Jonathan 63, 65, 87, 200, 202, 230
liberalisation 157, 164, 247
liberalism
  liberal arguments for private property 49
  liberal rights tradition 49
Licensing Act 1662 17
limited liability 67, 68, 134, 138, 150, 156, 171, 199
Lippman, Walter 135
literary property 17, 29, 31
  see also copyrights
Lobban, Michael 110, 194
Locke, John 30n99, 57–8, 78, 84, 181
logic of process 11, 234–43, 245, 247, 249
Lowie, Robert 52, 118n53
LPE (Law and Political Economy) movement 235, 253

M

MacFarlane, Alan 118n53
MacIntyre, Alasdair 249
MacLeod, Henry Dunning 22n25, 31–2
Maddison, James 30n99
Maine, Henry 31n104, 52
Maitland, Frederic William 16, 17, 25–6, 193
Manne, Henry 142–5, 151, 157
Manning, Bayless 139, 145, 146
'marginal ethics' (*grenzmoral*) 11–12, 248
market, for corporate control 142–9
market value 18
marketisation 164
market/s 44, 218–19
  and coercion 254–5
  historical development of 114–15, 187
  invisible hand of the market 46, 192
  as 'moral economy' 41, 44, 114
  sixteenth to eighteenth centuries 41, 42–3
Marktvolk ('people of the market') 101, 102, 204, 205
Marx, Karl/Marxism 3n8, 8, 10n137, 11, 33, 42, 48, 54, 55n65, 61, 62, 65–6, 72, 73, 82, 103, 104, 109, 117n52, 118n53, 134, 187, 188, 191, 194n33, 195, 196, 202, 223, 228, 234n39, 235–6, 237, 239–40, 242–3, 244, 252n101, 257
Mason, Edward 139
master-servant relationships 45, 78, 188n11
Mayer, Colin 148
Means, Gardiner 9, 137, 142, 144, 145, 146, 177n171, 259
Meckling, William 142, 145, 147n47, 150
merchant capital 62, 63
mergers 147–8

295

Meriküll, Jaanika 94
Merrill, Thomas 8, 9, 109, 133, 166–78
Mian, Atif 99
middle-classes, residential property wealth 87, 91
Miles, Kate 206
Mill, John Stuart 61
Millar v Taylor (1769) 98 English Reports 201 18–19
Minke, Wolfgang 181n186
Mitchell, Timothy 130
mixed economy 118
'modern slavery' 85
'moneyed'/'monied' men 59
moral arguments for private property 48–9
'moral economy', markets as 41, 44, 114
moral logic of capitalism 243–50
Morgan, Lewis Henry 52, 53n58, 118, 185
mortgage debt 86
Moyn, Samuel 203n76, 235, 236n45
Muldrew, Craig 20, 41, 43n19, 114, 187, 222
multinational corporations 51, 75, 77, 81, 133, 157, 199, 218, 226
  see also corporations

N

Nadasdy, Paul 108, 116n47
NAFTA (North America Free Trade Agreement) 207, 208n94
Nash, Jonathan 225
National Recovery and Resilience Plan, Italy 214
National Westminster Bank v Ainsworth [1965] AC 1175 36n130
nationalisation 141
  see also deprivatisation
natural rights 48, 56, 57, 169
nature, and intellectual property rights (IPRs) 81
negotiable instruments 16
neo-classical economics 54
neoliberalism 6, 11, 37, 181–2, 200–1, 204, 205, 207–8, 209–10, 224, 245n80
  ideology and practice 217–21
Network Rail 214
'new aristocracy of finance' 102
'new constitutionalism' 10, 183, 205–10
new enclosures 83–5
new essentialist theories of property 4, 6–7, 8–9, 105–7, 121, 133, 169, 170, 179–80
New Labour, privatisation policies 80
'new political capitalism' 242
New Private Law 106
'new property' 84
non-discrimination principle 207n91
non-owning classes 77–8
North America Free Trade Agreement (NAFTA) 207, 208n94

North, Douglass 186n4
notes 21, 22, 64
Nourse, Timothy 40
numerus clauses principle 167, 172

O

objects of property 17–23
obligation, and property 36–7
OECD 166, 211
Office for National Statistics (ONS) Wealth and Assets Survey 95
offshore wealth 90
O'Neill v Phillips [1999] UKHL 24, 68n135
original (primitive) accumulation of capital 42, 188, 191, 196, 242
Ostrom, Elinor 85n61, 173, 259–60
'Overton window' 203
owed, being 36
own, historical terminology of 24–5, 26
owners
  anthropological concepts of 27
  historical terminology of 24–5, 26
  'permanent' 161
  state constraints on rights of 5
  'universal' 161
ownership 3, 5, 8, 13, 28, 36, 105, 112, 193
  anthropological concepts of 27
  conceptual limitations of 23–7
  full liberal ownership 13, 43, 111, 226
  'full-blooded ownership' 111–12, 114, 117
  historical terminology of 25, 26
  Honoré's analysis of 6
  'red-blooded' ownership 13
ownership spectrum 111, 114

P

Panama Papers 90
paper money 20n38, 43
Parkinson, John 154
parochial concept of law 122–3
patents 21, 31, 85, 170
  human genes 81
Paulsen, John 250
pay-day loans 86
pay-outs 165
Peel, Thomas 73–4
Peñalver, Eduardo 106
Penner, James 8, 21, 68n135, 121–2, 123–8, 129–31, 132, 133, 167, 177, 180
Pennington, Robert 69–70, 140n21
pension funds 96, 98
peonage 85
'people of the market' *(Marktvolk)* 101, 102, 204, 205
'permanent' owners 161
personal property/possessions 1, 7, 8, 10, 15, 88, 181
  actions of trover 28
  versus productive resources 49–57

INDEX

personal rights 36
'personality-poor' phenomena 21, 126, 128
'personality-rich' phenomena 21, 22, 126, 128, 230
personhood, and private property 49, 50
PFI (private finance initiative) 80
pharmaceutical industry, intellectual property rights (IPRs) 79, 81, 85
Philbrick, Francis 23
Picciotto, Sol 219
Piketty, Thomas 87, 88, 89, 91–2, 141, 182, 196, 260
Pistor, Katharina 11, 180n180, 198, 199, 202n70, 212, 230–2
platform companies 219
Pocock, J G A 46n29
Polanyi, Karl 41, 42, 43, 112, 187, 236
'political capital' 58
political capitalism 190–1
political, the
  influence of the new financial aristocracy 204–5, 209–10
  separation from the economic and the legal 189–90, 192
Pollock, Sir Frederick 16, 17, 25–6, 29, 193
'polycrisis' 3, 261
Portalis, Jean-Etienne-Marie 120
Posner, Richard 84n58
possession 24, 25–6
'post-capitalist' society 141
post-truth world 11–12
poverty 40
power 129, 132
PPPS (public-private partnerships) 80, 212–17, 247
primitive (original) accumulation of capital 42, 188, 191, 196, 242
primitive societies, property institutions 52–3
private equity firms 158
private finance initiative (PFI) 80
'private government', property as 34–5
private pensions 87, 159
private property 3, 5, 13–14, 45, 118
  as 'delegated private government' 48
  exclusion/exclusivity 5, 34n21, 42, 48, 167, 173
  'full-blooded ownership' 111–12, 114, 117
  historicising private property and capital 186–94
  individual autonomy and identity 47–9, 50, 53
  liberal arguments for 49
  moral arguments for 48–9
  protection from democracy 203
  'special' nature of property rights 179–84
  transformative changes 257–8
  see also information cost theories of property; property-as-capital
private rented housing
  UK 79

privatisation 6, 7n18, 11, 38, 164, 201, 219–20, 247
  deprivatisation 257–8
  of productive resources 54
  rail industry, UK 213–14
  reprivatisation 154
  UK 80
production, sphere of 63
production systems
  historical stages of 3n8
productive activity 4
productive resources 112, 181, 184, 188, 226, 255
  community-based management of 173, 259–60
  concentration of ownership of 77–8
  and power 75–7
  privatisation of 54
  profiting from ownership of 75–9
productive resources, property in 4, 7, 8, 28, 35, 44, 57–8
  versus personal possessions 49–57
  see also means of production
Progressivism 32
property 1, 5, 7, 34–5, 45–6, 47–8, 111
  alternative meaning of as attribute, character or quality 24, 24n64
  anthropological concepts of 23, 24, 27
  Blackstone's definition 5
  conceptual limitations of 23–7
  as a 'conceptual mirage' 35–8
  Cowell's definition 16–7, 24
  derisking of new property 211–17
  'essence' of 2, 105–6, 107, 110, 121, 122, 194, 224
  etymology of 24, 25
  framing of 261
  as a historical category 222–4
  historical concepts and terminology of 23–6, 29
  idea of in law 121–32
  objects of 17–23
  and obligation 36–7
  revolution in 38–47
  see also intangible property; ownership; private property; property institutions; property rights; property-as-capital; tangible property
property institutions 2–3, 4, 8, 111, 117, 193–4
  anthropology 51–3
  contexts of 115
  ubiquity of 107–9
property rights 4, 106
  'special' nature of 179–84, 225
  transformative changes 257–8
property status quo 9, 106, 121, 133, 141, 142, 149, 158, 162, 166, 174, 178, 183, 184, 203, 252, 256, 261

property-as-capital 4, 7, 8, 10, 11, 59, 62–6, 73, 74, 183, 226, 229, 231
  creation of 194–9
  derisking new property 211–17
  historicising private property and capital 186–94
  neoliberal ideology and practice 217–21
  'new constitutionalism', and democracy 10, 183, 205–10
  new financial aristocracy 202–5
  prioritising investor interest 199–202
  safeguarding of 185–221
  universalising capitalism 185–6
  and wealth distribution 87
property-as-wealth 63
'property-for-personhood' 50
proprete (propertie) 24
proprietas 24
proprietatum (proprietas) 24
propriété 25
proprietors, anthropological concepts of 27
Proudhon, Pierre-Joseph 37, 61, 72–3
public debt 86
  ownership of 96–9
public expenditure cuts 201
public sector companies, privatisation of, UK 80
public services, private financing of 211–17
public utilities, privatisation of, UK 80
public-private partnerships (PPPS) 80, 212–17, 247

Q

quasi-indexer institutional ownership 165

R

race/ethnicity 78, 95
Radin, Margaret Jane 49–50
railways 67
  deprivatisation of 257–8
  privatisation of, UK 80, 213–14
  railway shares, purchase of with former slave owners' compensation 188n10, 197
Rainer, Franz 59n83, 60–1
Rawls, John 50
Raz, Joseph 113, 122–3, 124, 128, 129, 131
'red-blooded' ownership 13
Reform Act 1832 41n7
reform, and transformative change 251–61
regulation 219
regulatory derisking 212
  see also derisking
'regulatory states' 54
'regulatory takings' 183
Reich, Charles 84, 182
reification 15, 23, 31n101, 33n112, 44, 86, 128, 198, 227, 230, 243, 261
'rentier capitalism' 82
'rentierism', rise of 80–3

rentiers 59, 60, 134, 139, 151, 241
  defence of 142–9
reprivatisation 154
reproductive labour 229
residential housing *see* housing
revolutionary change 252–3
Ricardo, David 40, 60, 73n14
rights *in personam* 20, 32–3, 68, 69, 125, 126, 128, 230
rights *in rem* 20, 32–3, 34, 68, 69, 125, 172, 173, 177
Robé, Jean-Philippe 46, 51, 75–6, 77, 133, 226, 255–6
Roman law
  concepts of property in 25
  dominium in 119–21
Rõõm, Tairi 94
Roos, Jerome 98
Rose, Carol 7
Rosser, Ezra 178
Rossi, Enrico 50
Rotherham, Craig 127, 128, 129
Rudden, Bernard 4, 8, 10, 23, 63–4, 65, 86, 104
'rules of reproduction' 11
Russia 90

S

Saez, Emmanuel 87, 93
saving, obstacles to for young people 95
Sayer, Derek 194–5
Schneiderman, D 208
Schorr, David 15
Scialoja, Vittorio 119
Scottish Enlightenment 3n8, 117
  see also Enlightenment, the
SDGs (Sustainable Development Goals), UN 216
SEC v Bailey, 41 F.Supp. 647 (S.D. Fla 1941) 71n2
Securities Act 1933 71, 138
Securities and Exchange Commission 138, 158
Securities and Exchange Commission v W J Howey Co. 328 US 293 [1946] 8, 11, 71–2, 75, 200, 229
securitisation 86–7
seigneuries, France 46
selfhood, and private property 49
self-interest 43–4, 114, 175, 192, 239
'self-propriety' 78
self-sovereignty 48
'separability thesis' 126, 127
share buy-backs 158–9, 165, 258
shareholders 9, 66–7, 77, 102, 134, 137, 138, 146–7, 199
  as 'absentee owners' 72, 135
  contractual theories of the corporation 149–50, 151–3

creditor-like nature of corporate shareholding 134–6, 139
ESOPs (employee share ownership plans) 258
exclusion/exclusivity 9, 69, 135–6, 149, 150, 152, 154
reform of role of 258–9
shareholder activism 143, 160
shareholder 'exit' 143, 157, 161, 164
shareholder rights
  defence of 142–9
  reform of 258
  threats to 133–9, 141, 142
shareholder value 102, 204
  maximisation of 157–8, 159, 160, 161, 162
see also joint stock company shares
Singer, Joseph 7, 51n53, 106, 179
Singh, David Grewal 201
Slave Compensation Act 1837 196–7
slavery 45, 78, 78n35, 188, 195–6
  compensation of former slave owners 188n10, 196–7
  origin of wealth from 196–7
Slobodian, Quinn 205, 207–8, 209, 218, 220, 223–4
Smith, Adam 7, 40, 41, 43–4, 46, 54, 60, 66, 73n14, 100, 114, 117, 134, 185, 186, 187, 197–8, 222, 258
Smith, Henry 8, 9, 133, 166–78
Smith, Tony 245n81
'social capital' 58
social classes 40
social democracy 6, 146, 233, 240
  and corporations 139–42
social enterprises 259
social movements, egalitarian 76
social relation conception of property 5, 6, 8, 11, 30–5, 37, 183, 224, 227, 229–32, 253
social relations 8, 10, 74, 106
social sciences 4
social security rights 182
socialisation 257–8
socialism 61, 118
'sole and despotic dominion' definition of property (Blackstone) 5, 7, 13, 15, 16, 26, 30, 44, 89, 172, 180n182, 186–7, 191, 226, 260
Sombart, Werner 236
sovereign power 34, 35, 207
Speck, Frank 118n53
speculators/speculation 103–4, 139
Staatsvolke ('general citizenry') 101, 102, 204
stakeholder capitalism 163, 164
State Street 160, 162
'Statement of Progressive Property' 106
states 189–90
  and the international investment regime 205–10

'regulatory states' 54
revenue-raising challenges 211
sovereign power 34, 35, 207
sovereignty within 45–6
Stationer's Company 17
Statute of Anne (Copyright Act) 1710 17–18, 19
Stern, Stephanie 225
'stewardship codes' 160, 162
Strahilevitz, Lior 173
Strathern, Marilyn 27
Straub, Ludwig 99
Streeck, Wolfgang 11, 96n110, 101–2, 204, 232–4, 236–7, 246, 247, 251–2
student accommodation, Italy 214
student loan debt 86
subject-object divide 45
sub-prime mortgages, US 250
see also financial crash, 2008
subsidies, and rail privatisation, UK 213–14
suffrage
  identity requirements for voting 203n73
  nineteenth century 40–1
  universal suffrage 203, 220
  women 41, 203n73
Sufi, Amir 99
Sunday Times Rich List 1–2, 87
surplus value 73, 188
Survey of Consumer Finance 2019, US 95
Sustainable Development Goals (SDGs), UN 216
Swan River Colony, Western Australia 73–4
Sweet, George 31
Swift, Jonathan 64n114
Syed, Talha 29, 119, 120–1

T

takeovers 147–9
tangible property 8, 34, 181, 198
  'BPrN the Basic Property Norm – the Property Exclusionary Norm for Tangible Property' 125
TARP (Troubled Asset Relief Program) 201
Tawney, R H 9, 135–6, 146, 258
tax avoidance/evasion 101, 204, 211, 258
'tax state' 101, 204
technology, and property rights 57–8
Thackeray, William Makepeace 61
Thatcher, Margaret 80, 203n73
theory, and history 222–3
'there is no alternative' concept 55
thing-ownership conception of property 4, 5, 6, 8–9, 10, 13–16, 24, 37–8, 54, 105–7, 112, 121, 122, 179, 183, 184, 192, 224, 225–7, 228, 229, 232, 261
  information cost theories of property 166, 169–71
  rise of 28–30
'things in themselves' 10

Thomas, Robert 186n4
Thompson, E P 11, 41, 194–5, 222–3, 236, 240, 243–5
tobacco companies 208n94
TOCs (train operating companies), UK 213–14
Tonson v Collins (1761) 96 English Reports 180 18, 31
Tooze, Adam 203n76, 224
'total exclusion' (Blackstone) 5, 13, 26, 44
Tourre, Fabrice 250
'traces' 120
trade liberalisation 157
trade unions, declining power of 219, 220
traded options 66
Trade-Related Aspects of Intellectual Property Rights (TRIPS) 207, 215n123
Trade-Related Investment Measures (TRIMs) 207
'tragedy of the commons' 85n61
transport sector
 derisking 212–13, 213–14
'trespass to land' 170
trespassory rules 111
TRIMs (Trade-Related Investment Measures) 207
TRIPS (Trade-Related Aspects of Intellectual Property Rights) 207, 215n123
Troubled Asset Relief Program (TARP) 201
trover, actions of (personal possessions) 28
Trump, Donald 247–8
Tylor, Edward 52

U

UK
 bank bail-outs 201
 declining public wealth 101
 GDP (gross domestic product) decline 89
 pay-outs 165
 private rented housing 79
 privatisation 80, 213–14
 race/ethnicity wealth inequality 95
 wealth inequality 89–90, 94
Ukraine, war in 215
UN
 SDGs (Sustainable Development Goals) 216
 System of National Accounts 88
Underkuffler, Laura 106
'unearned incomes' 72, 135
unfree labour 85
United Housing Foundation Inc v Forman, 421 US 837 (1975) 71
universal nature of law 122, 123
'universal' owners 161
universal suffrage 203, 220
universal truths about property 2, 8, 123, 224
US
 bundle of rights conception of property 32–3
 Constitution 190
 declining public wealth 101
 GDP (gross domestic product) decline 89
 'progressive' property scholars 106
 public debt ownership 96–8
 race/ethnicity wealth inequality 95
 wealth inequality 90, 92, 93
US Constitution 203
US Federal Reserve Survey of Consumer Finances (SCF) 90, 92–3
US Treasury 186n4
US v Leonard (2008) 529 F.3d 83 (2d Cir. 2008) 72n7
use rights over land 15, 28, 39, 42, 44, 47, 78
usury 62, 86

V

Van Harten, Gus 206, 208–9
Vanguard 160, 162
Varoufakis, Yanis 82
Veblen, Thorstein 7, 9, 57–8, 65, 72, 134–5, 136n6, 136n9, 139, 146, 231, 241n62, 258
Vega Asset Management 210
venal offices, France 46
Virgin 214
Von Mises, Ludwig 209, 218n130, 220, 221, 224
Vonovia 79
voting, identity requirements for 203n73
'vulgar economics' 73

W

Wakefield, Edward Gibbon 73–4
Waldron, Jeremy 36, 49, 105, 108
'Wall Street Consensus' 217
'Washington Consensus' 54, 186n4, 217
water utilities 80, 213, 257–8
wealth
 concentration of 3, 8
 difference from capital 63–4
 distribution of 1, 8, 87–93
 origin of in slavery and colonial appropriation 195–6
 and power 9–10
 and property 1, 7
 rising private wealth, declining public wealth 100–3
 wealth/not wealth distinction 1, 7
wealth inequalities 1, 3, 87–8, 147, 209–10
 decline in 141
 gender 93–5
 intergenerational inequalities 95–6
 race/ethnicity 95
 see also distributive justice
wealth taxes 260
Weber, Max 55
welfare rights 182
White, Leslie 52–3, 77–8

INDEX

Williams, Andrew 161n92
Williams, Raymond 243, 244
Williamson, Oliver 246
Winters, Jeffrey 102–3, 205
Wittgenstein, L 36, 105, 110n24
Wolfe, Alan 155n80
Wolff, Edward 92
women
  lack of suffrage rights 41, 203n73
  married women's property 40–1, 45
  reproductive labour of 229
  wealth inequalities 93–5
Wood, Ellen Meiksins 41, 187, 190
Wood, Franklin 134n4
workers *see* labour
World Bank 84, 186n4, 206, 208, 211
World Economic Forum 93–4

World Inequality Report (WIR) 2022 91, 100, 101
World Power System 226, 255, 257
World Trade Organisation 208
Worthington, Sarah 36–7

X

'xenos rights' 209

Y

Yates, Joseph 18, 19
young people, intergenerational inequalities 95–6

Z

'zombie corporations' 201n69
Zucman, Gabriel 87, 90, 93

www.ingramcontent.com/pod-product-compliance
Lightning Source LLC
Chambersburg PA
CBHW051529020426
42333CB00016B/1840